Contemporary Wars and Conflicts over Land and Water in Africa

Contemporary Wars and Conflicts over Land and Water in Africa

Carlson Anyangwe

LEXINGTON BOOKS
Lanham • Boulder • New York • London

Published by Lexington Books
An imprint of The Rowman & Littlefield Publishing Group, Inc.
4501 Forbes Boulevard, Suite 200, Lanham, Maryland 20706
www.rowman.com

86-90 Paul Street, London EC2A 4NE

Copyright © 2022 by The Rowman & Littlefield Publishing Group, Inc.

All rights reserved. No part of this book may be reproduced in any form or by any electronic or mechanical means, including information storage and retrieval systems, without written permission from the publisher, except by a reviewer who may quote passages in a review.

British Library Cataloguing in Publication Information Available

Library of Congress Cataloging-in-Publication Data

Names: Anyangwe, Carlson, author.
Title: Contemporary wars and conflicts over land and water in Africa / Carlson Anyangwe.
Description: Lanham : Lexington Books, [2022] | Includes bibliographical references and index. | Summary: "This book examines land and maritime boundary conflicts, intra and inter-state armed conflicts, transboundary terrorism, and conflict resolution arrangements in Africa. It provides an important contribution to a deeper understanding of conflicts on the continent"—Provided by publisher.
Identifiers: LCCN 2022017578 (print) | LCCN 2022017579 (ebook) | ISBN 9781666910360 (cloth) | ISBN 9781666910384 (paperback) | ISBN 9781666910377 (epub)
Subjects: LCSH: Politics and war—Africa. | Maritime boundaries—Africa. | Terrorism—Africa. | Conflict management—Africa. | Africa—Politics and government—1960- | Africa—Boundaries.
Classification: LCC DT30.5 .A585 2022 (print) | LCC DT30.5 (ebook) | DDC 960.326—dc23/eng/20220411
LC record available at https://lccn.loc.gov/2022017578
LC ebook record available at https://lccn.loc.gov/2022017579

This book is dedicated with love to Javea Alexander Kit, affectionately called 'Ru'.

Contents

List of Acronyms	ix
Preface	xiii
Acknowledgment	xv
Introduction	1
PART ONE: BOUNDARY AND TERRITORIAL CONFLICTS	**23**
1 Claims and Conflicts over Land Territory and Land Boundaries	27
2 Disputes over Maritime Boundary	61
PART TWO: ARMED CONFLICTS WITHIN AND BETWEEN STATES	**103**
3 Sources of Civil Wars: Colonial Hangover	109
4 Sources of Civil Wars: Despotism, Overstay in Power and Historical Discontent	149
5 Noticeable Features of Africa's Civil Wars	169
6 Causes of Interstate Wars in Africa	187
PART THREE: A NEW DIMENSION OF CONFLICTS IN AFRICA: DOMESTIC AND TRANSBORDER TERRORISM	**221**
7 An Overview	225
8 Combating Terrorism through Law	233
9 Punishing Acts of Terrorism	241

PART FOUR: AFRICAN APPROACHES TO CONFLICT RESOLUTION **263**

10 Some Indigenous Mechanisms for Settling Conflicts 265

11 Indigenous System and Transitional Justice: Rwanda's *Gacaca* 285

12 The African Union and Conflict Resolution Arrangements 297

Bibliography 315

Index 329

About the Author 333

Acronyms

AfComHPR	African Commission on Human and Peoples' Rights
AfCtHR	African Court on Human and Peoples' Rights
AFISMA	African-led International Support Mission in Mali
AFRC	Armed Forces Revolutionary Council
AG	Action Group
AIAI	Al Ittihad Al Islamiya
AmConHR	American Convention on Human Rights
AMISOM	African Union Mission to Somalia
AMU	African Maghreb Union
ANC	African National Congress
AQIM	Al Qaeda in the Islamic Maghreb
ASF	African Standby Force
AU	African Union
BIOT	British Indian Ocean Territories
CDF	Civil Defence Forces
CEN-SAD	Community of Sahel-Saharan States
CFA	*Communauté Financière Africaine*
CNDD	*Conseil National pour la Défense de la Démocratie* (National Council for the Defence of Democracy)
COMESA	Common Market for Eastern and Southern Africa
DDR	Disarmament Demobilization and Reintegration
ECCAS	Economic Community of Central African States
ECHR	European Court of Human Rights
ECOMOG	Economic Community Monitoring Group
ECOWAS	Economic Community of West African States
EEZ	Exclusive Economic Zone
EPLF	Eritrean People's Liberation Front

EU	European Union
FDD	*Forces pour la Défense de la Démocratie* (Forces for the Defence of Democracy)
FIS	*Front Islamique du Salut* (Islamic Salvation Front)
FLAM	*Forces de Libération Africaines de Mauritanie* (Liberation Forces of Africans of Mauritania)
FNL	*Forces Nationales de Libération* (National Liberation Forces)
FNL	Front National de Liberation (National Liberation Front)
FNLA	*Frente Nacional de Libertação de Angola* (National Front for the Liberation of Angola)
FNLA	*Front National pour la Libération d'Azawad* (National Front for the Liberation of Azawad)
FRUD	*Front pour la Restoration de l'Unité et de la Démocratie* (Front for the Restoration of Unity and Democracy)
IACHR	Inter-American Commission on Human Rights
ICC	International Criminal Court
ICJ	International Court of Justice
ICTR	International Criminal Court for Rwanda
ICU	Islamic Courts Union
IFP	Inkatha Freedom Party
IGAD	Intergovernmental Authority on Development
ISIL	Islamic State of Iraq and the Levant
ISIS	Islamic State in Iraq and Syria
ISWAP	Islamic State West Africa Province
ITLOS	International Tribunal for the Law of the Sea
JEM	Justice and Equality Movement
JVC	Joint Verification Commission
LRA	Lord's Resistance Army
LTRC	Liberian Truth and Reconciliation Commission
LURD	Liberians United for Reconciliation and Democracy
MDL	Movement for Democracy in Liberia
MFDC	*Mouvement des Forces Démocratiques de Casamance* (Movement of Casamance Democratic Forces)
MNJTF	Multinational Joint Task Force
MNLA	*Mouvement National pour la Libération d'Azawad* (National Movement for the Liberation of Azawad)
MOU	Memorandum of Understanding
MPLA	*Movimento Popular de Libertação de Angola* (Popular Movement for the Liberation of Angola)
NATO	North Atlantic Treaty Organization

NCNC	National Council of Nigeria and the Cameroons
NPC	Northern People's Congress
NPFL	National Patriotic Front of Liberia
OAU	Organization of African Unity
OHCHR	Office of the High Commissioner for Human Rights
OIF	*Organisation Internationale de la Francophonie* (International Francophonie Organization)
OLF	Oromo Liberation Front
ONUMOZ	United Nations Peacekeeping Force in Mozambique
PLO	Palestine Liberation Organization
POLISARIO	*Frente Popular de Liberación de Saguia el Hamra y Rio de Oro* (Popular Front for the Liberation of Saguia el-Hamra and Rio de Oro)
PRDF	Ethiopian People's Revolutionary Democratic Front
PSC	Peace and Security Council
RDR	*Rassemblement des Républicains* (Rally of Republicans)
RDR	*Rassemblement Démocratique pour le Rwanda* (Democratic Rally for Rwanda)
RENAMO	*Resistência Nacional Moçambicana* (Mozambican National Resistance)
RPF	Rwandan Patriotic Front
RPP	*Rassemblement du Peuple pour le Progrès* (People's Rally for Progress)
RUF	Revolutionary United Front
SADR	Saharawi Arab Democratic Republic
SNM	Somali National Movement
SPLA	Sudanese People's Liberation Army
SPLA/M	Sudan People's Liberation Army/Movement
SSDF	Somali Salvation Democratic Front
SWAPO	South West Africa People's Organization
TFG	Transitional Federal Government
TPDF	Tanzania People's Defence Force
TPLF	Tigrayan People's Liberation Front
UK	United Kingdom
ULIMO	United Liberation Movements of Liberia
UN	United Nations
UNAMSIL	United Nations Mission in Sierra Leone
UNAVEM	United Nations Angola Verification Mission
UNCLOS	United Nations Convention on the Law of the Sea
UNEF	United Nations Emergency Force
UNESCO	United Nations Educational, Scientific and Cultural Organization

UNGA	United Nations General Assembly
UNHCR	United Nations High Commissioner for Refugees
UNICEF	United Nations International Children's Emergency Fund
UNITA	*União Nacional para a Indepêndecia Total de Angola* (National Union for the Total Independence of Angola)
UNITAF	United Task Force
UNLA	Uganda National Liberation Army
UNLF	Uganda National Liberation Front
UNODOC	United Nations Office on Drugs and Crimes
UNOMIL	United Nations Observer Mission in Liberia
UNOSOM	United Nations Operations in Somalia
UNOVER	United Nations Observer Mission to Verify the Referendum in Eritrea
UNSC	United Nations Security Council
UNTAG	United Nations Transitional Assistance Group
UPC	*Union des Populations du Cameroun* (Cameroun People's Union)
US	United States
USC	United Somali Congress
VCLT	Vienna Convention on the Law of Treaties
ZANLA	Zimbabwe African National Liberation Army
ZANU	Zimbabwe African National Union
ZANU-PF	Zimbabwe African National Union – Patriotic Front
ZAPU	Zimbabwe African People's Union
ZIPRA	Zimbabwe People's Revolutionary Army
ZOPAC	*Zones de Pacification* (Pacification Zones)

Preface

My interest in African conflicts was kindled by the most recent but neglected armed conflict in the continent, the ongoing David and Goliath decolonization struggle in the easternmost end of the Gulf of Guinea between small English-speaking Ambazonia, heroically fighting for freedom from colonial annexation and oppression, and the adjacent bigger French-speaking *République du Cameroun*, the colonial occupier-oppressor. It is a war strikingly the same as the decolonization struggles in Africa from the 1960s to the 1980s.

There is a wealth of case or area studies on conflicts in Africa. But in this book, I adopt a holistic approach, presenting the continent's conflicts as comprehensively but succinctly as I can and in a manner that is easy to read, follow and understand. There is nothing fatalistic about these conflicts. Africa's endemic and recurrent conflicts, endless communal self-destruction and characteristic cheapening of African lives are preventable, if only good leadership can find fertile ground in the continent.

Acknowledgment

I would like to acknowledge my gratefulness to the sources I have drawn from and dutifully acknowledged in the text. I would also like to thank Lexington Books as well as Shelby Russel, Sydney Wedbush, and Monica Sukumar for their highly professional service and support. Finally, I thank my family for its silent encouragement and understandable endurance of endless hours of my disconnect resulting from 'capture' by my computer.

Introduction

This book is a terse presentation of conflicts in 'postcolonial' Africa (i.e. conflicts since the end of white rule) and examines approaches to conflict resolution in the continent. It deals with land and maritime conflicts, intra- and interstate conflicts, the new dimension of conflicts in Africa represented by domestic and transboundary terrorism, and African traditional and modern approaches to conflict resolution. This general introduction does two things. First, it indicates the meaning of some key terms[1] used in the book. Second, it expatiates on conflict theory, Africa's recurrent conflicts and the matter of conflict resolution.

ELUCIDATION OF SOME TERMS

The first term that calls for elucidation is 'boundary'. A boundary is every separation, natural or artificial, which marks the confines or line of division of two contiguous properties. In the law relating to state territory, a boundary is an imaginary line on the surface of the earth, separating the territory of one state from that of another.

> A boundary is not merely a line but a line in a borderland. The borderland may or may not be a barrier. The surveyor may be most interested in the line. To the strategist the barrier, or its absence, is important. For the administrator, the borderland may be the problem, with the line the limit of his authority. (Jones, 1945: 7)

In international law, boundaries are one of the most significant manifestations of state territorial sovereignty. When recognized expressly by treaty, or when generally acknowledged without express declaration, state boundaries constitute part of a state's title to the territory (Shearer, 1994: 172). Resources may straddle land or maritime boundaries. In that case, adjacent states may embrace arrangements for their joint exploitation.

Boundary disputes have occasioned many important international arbitrations and instructive decisions of the International Court of Justice. In 1986, for example, a special Chamber of the Court delivered an instructive judgement in the frontier dispute between Burkina Faso and Mali. The decision is important in two respects. First, the chamber of judges paid due regard to and relied upon the principle of *uti possidetis*, the role of equitable principles, the prior history of the administrative organization as to the relevant area and the extent to which the alleged acquiescence of one party might be taken into account. Second, the judges attached a degree of weight to the materials laid before them by the parties. The materials that the judges treated as sufficient included the legislative and regulatory texts, administrative orders and decrees, cartographic documentation and geographical contour features.

Writers on the subject of boundaries make a firm distinction between 'natural' and 'artificial' boundaries. Natural boundaries consist of rivers, mountains, seashore, forests, lakes and deserts, where these divide the territory of two or more states. Used in a political sense, however, the term 'natural boundary' has a far wider significance. It denotes the line defined by nature (geography) up to which a state considers its territory should be extended or delimited at the expense of, or as protection against, other states. Artificial boundaries consist either of signs purposely erected to indicate the course of the imaginary boundary line or parallels of longitude or latitude.

Land boundaries and maritime boundaries are two distinct areas of the law, to which different factors and considerations apply. The solutions in one case are not transposable to the other. Maritime boundary includes boundaries that are recognized by the UN Convention on the Law of the Sea, for example, boundaries of territorial waters, contiguous zones and exclusive economic zones. Maritime boundary does not include lake or river boundaries. A potential maritime boundary is one which lacks a treaty or other agreement defining the exact location of the maritime boundary. Maritime zones are areas of ocean or sea which are or will be subject to national or international authority. The zones are delimited as parts of the seabed, water column and sea surface, the subdivision being on the grounds of political jurisdiction relating to the use and ownership of marine resources.

The term 'maritime boundary dispute' refers to a dispute relating to the demarcation of the different maritime zones between or among states. Sometimes, maritime boundary disputes could be intense and protracted. States need well delimited maritime boundaries because they would want to explore and exploit for minerals and food the areas that international law determines as falling within their sovereignty or under their jurisdiction. A maritime dispute may have the untoward effect of freezing the exploitation of marine resources in the disputed area until the dispute is definitively resolved. It may also affect good neighbourliness, harmony and friendly relations between the states involved. The expeditious settlement of such a dispute is of key importance for the peaceful co-existence of the contending coastal states. Unfortunately, most maritime disputes take time to resolve because of the technicality of the subject and the intensity with which they are fought by the litigants.

The second term that calls for elucidation is 'dispute', and this term needs to be distinguished from 'conflict'. Generally, a dispute is a disagreement or a quarrel on a matter of law or fact. In *Mavrommatis Palestine Concession (Jurisdiction)*,[2] the Permanent Court of International Justice authoritatively stated that a dispute is 'a disagreement over a point of law or fact, a conflict of legal views or of interests between two persons'. The expression 'international disputes' covers not only disputes between states as such. It also covers other cases that have come within the ambit of international regulations. Such cases include certain categories of disputes between states on the one hand and individuals, bodies corporate and non-state entities on the other hand. For example, investment disputes between capital-receiving states and private foreign investors are international disputes. The settlement of those disputes is provided for under the Convention of 18 March 1965, for the Settlement of Investment Disputes between States and Nationals of Other States. That convention applies to legal disputes only.

In the context of peace and security studies, a conflict is a fight or struggle and connotes physical violence. The absence of direct violence is described as 'negative peace' in contradistinction to 'positive peace' which is a kind of peace that exists in the presence of social justice through equal opportunity, a fair distribution of power and resources, equal protection and impartial enforcement of the law. The concept of positive peace is conjured to address the root causes of conflict and structural violence in a preventive way. By structural violence is meant conditions of an indirect and insidious nature typically built into the very system of society and cultural institutions, which do not entail the use of force, but which have comparable effects. Systems based on repression, oppression, exploitation, domination or subjugation are examples of structural violence.

In international law, a distinction has historically been drawn between international and non-international armed conflicts. This difference is founded upon the distinction between interstate relations and intrastate matters. Interstate relations were the proper focus for international law. By contrast, intrastate matters traditionally fell within the domestic jurisdiction of states and were thus, in principle, impervious to international legal regulation. However, this difference has been breaking down in recent decades. In the sphere of humanitarian law, this can be seen in the gradual application of rules of international humanitarian law to internal armed conflicts. In *Tadic* (1994)[3] the Appeals Chamber of the International Tribunal on War Crimes in former Yugoslavia clarified that:

> An armed conflict exists whenever there is a resort to armed force between states or protracted armed violence between government authorities and organised armed groups or between such groups within a state. International humanitarian law applies from the initiation of such armed conflicts and extends beyond the cessation of hostilities until a general conclusion of peace is reached; or, in the case of internal conflicts, a peaceful settlement is reached. Until that moment, international humanitarian law continues to apply in the whole territory of the warring states or, in the case of internal conflicts, the whole territory under the control of a party, whether or not actual combat takes place.

A war or an armed conflict need not be widespread. Military operations may be confined to a specific geographical location or theatre of war. It does not need to be of long duration as was the Reconquista which lasted 781 years or the Anglo-French wars which lasted 748 years or the Roman-Persian wars which lasted 681 years or even World War II which lasted six years. It may last just a few days, as was the Six Days War between Israel and Arab countries. A war also need not be an armed conflict between countries. It may be an armed conflict between belligerents within a state, known as civil war or intrastate war.

The third term to elucidate is 'expansionism'. Expansion is the enlargement of the scale or scope of something. In relation to territory, it means an increase in the amount of a state's territory or area of control. This increase in the territory would often entail an increase in population size since the added territory would often have inhabitants, sedentary or nomadic. The expressions 'territorial aggrandizement' and 'territorial expansionism' tend to be used interchangeably. The two are synonymous since aggrandizement in relation to territory means to enlarge or increase the territorial size of a state, to cause the size of a state to appear greater than is the case.

The fourth term to elucidate is 'frontier'. In international law, the frontier is that portion of the territory of any country which lies close along the borderline of another country. That portion of the territory 'fronts' or faces the borderline of the adjacent country. The term 'border between two countries' means something more than the boundary line itself. It includes a tract or strip of territory, of indefinite extent, contiguous to the line.

The fifth term to elucidate is 'territory'. Territory is a geographical area under the jurisdiction of a politically organized authority or sovereign power. It is the basic characteristic of a state, one of the essential elements of statehood and the element most widely accepted and understood. Territory is a fundamental legal concept in international law and has a central role in the scheme of that law. International law is based on the concept of the state, but without territory a legal person cannot be a state. A state is deemed to exercise exclusive power over its territory. Two basic legal rules have been developed to protect the inviolability of the state: respect for the territorial integrity of states and the norm prohibiting interference in the internal affairs of other states. However, transnational concerns such as human rights and self-determination tend to impinge on the territorial exclusivity of the state.

> In international law a change in ownership of a particular territory involves also a change in sovereignty; it involves a change in the legal authority governing the area. The nationality of the inhabitants is altered, as is the legal system under which they live, work and conduct their relations. (Shaw, 1997: 331)

CONFLICT THEORY

Conflict is a pervasive social phenomenon. It occurs at all levels of life – personal, group, organizational, state or international. It usually includes an ingredient of struggle, strife or collusion, but not mere competition. Social conflicts encompass a broad range of struggles such as class, racial, religious, political and community contestations resulting in riots, rebellions, revolutions, strikes, marches, demonstrations or protest rallies (Oberschall, 1978). The object of a conflict could be scarce resources, power, claim to status (e.g. the status of a free people) or values (e.g. freedom, democracy, human rights, rule of law, authoritarianism). Value conflicts arise over ideological differences or differing standards on the evaluation of ideas or behaviours. The actual or perceived differences in values do not necessarily lead to conflict. It is only when values are imposed on groups, or groups are prevented from upholding their value systems, that conflict arises. Structural conflict is caused by unequal or unfair distributions of power and resources. Every conflict involves organized actors, incompatibility in the actors' objectives and the conscious behaviour to achieve set goals (Wallensteen, 1988). Actors involved in a conflict seek to have the upper hand in it by striving to neutralize, injure or eliminate rivals (Hefny, 1995).

Conflict scholarship assumes that conflict is 'natural' and can be expected as an inevitable part of life (Jackson & Rosberg, 1986; Gluckman, 1963; Rex, 1981; Coser, 1956; Dahrendorf, 1965). It sees conflict as part of life's endless cycle of thesis, antithesis and synthesis, resulting in world progress. According to radical assumptions, every society is eternally in conflict (over needs, interests, wants, expectations and obligations) as an integral part of human interaction and which accounts for social change. Conflict is always present in human reactions and if institutionalized could contribute greatly to human progress and development. However, if improperly articulated and poorly managed, conflict exhibits that barbaric instinct of human nature. The implication of this thesis is that conflict, as a social and political phenomenon, cannot be eliminated, prevented or completely resolved. It is something society has to live with. The only challenge is to manage it in a constructive way that allows for the expression of disagreement and legitimate struggle without violence. Examples of legitimate struggles without violence are non-violent political contests for power, and non-violent protests for social, cultural, economic and political reforms.

In the discipline of sociology, conflict theory posits that society functions in a way that each individual participant and groups within it struggle to maximize their benefits. This inevitably contributes to social change through revolutions and changes in politics. The theory is mostly applied to explain the conflict between social classes such as proletariat versus bourgeoisie and ideologies such as capitalism versus socialism. It attempts to refute functionalism which, under moderate assumptions, is allowed to operate as an equally acceptable theory since it accepts that even negative social institutions play a part in society's self-perpetuation. Functionalism considers that societies and organizations function so that each individual and group performs a specific role like the organs of a body, each of which has a specific function. According to this perspective, conflict in society serves certain functions: it helps establish and maintain group identities and independence; it demonstrates the closeness and importance of relationship and builds new relationships; it creates coalitions; it serves as a safety valve mechanism; it helps parties assess each other's power and can work to redistribute power in a system of conflict; it enhances group cohesion through issue and belief clarification; and it creates or modifies rules, norms, laws and institutions.

The essence of conflict theory is best epitomized by the classic 'pyramidal structure' in which an elite dictates terms to the larger masses. All major institutions, laws and traditions in society are designed to support those in power or the groups that are perceived to be superior in the society. Those in power seek to stay in power and those perceived to be superior seek to maintain their position of superiority. The assumptions of modern conflict theory are built around concepts of competition, structural inequality, revolution and war. Conflict theory postulates that competition rather than consensus is characteristic of human relationships and that competition over scarce resources such as money, leisure, sexual partners and so on is at the heart of all social relationships. The basic contention about structural inequality is that inequalities in power and reward are built into all social structures and that individuals and groups that benefit from any particular structure strive to see it maintained. The idea of revolution, advanced by conflict theorists, is that change occurs as a result of conflict between the competing interests of social classes rather than through adaptation. That change is often abrupt and revolutionary rather than evolutionary. Conflict theorists consider even war as a unifier of the societies involved. They however concede that war may bring an end to whole societies.

AFRICA'S RECURRENT CONFLICTS

Conflicts in pre-colonial Africa were essentially inter-ethnic wars of conquest, domination and extension of influence. These wars became more frequent and more deadly when Arab and European slave traders arrived on the continent and ushered in a period of transcontinental trade in Africans as slaves. The abolition of this cruel trade in human merchandise did not witness an end to conflicts in the continent. The colonial intervention inevitably bore in its train wars of resistance against colonial invasion and occupation. But that resistance was futile. Superior arms ensured victory for the colonialists everywhere. It would take another sixty or seventy years of relative 'peace' before Africa witnessed yet another round of armed conflicts. These were decolonization wars, anti-colonial struggles for national liberation. Between the 1950s and 1980s, nationalist struggles for independence were fought in countries where the colonial power rejected consensual decolonization.

Some decolonization struggles involved non-violent revolution; others involved national liberation wars by pro-independence groups in colonial territories where the colonial power rejected consensual decolonization. The decolonization of Africa took place in the mid-to-late 1950s to 1990. Sudden and radical regime changes took place on the continent as colonial territories made the transition to independent states. The process was often quite disorganized. It was often marred with violence, political turmoil, widespread unrest and organized revolts in both northern and sub-Saharan African countries. Struggles for liberation from colonial oppression and exploitation included the Algerian War of Independence against France; the Angolan, Guinea-Bissau and Mozambican Wars of Independence against Portugal; the Zimbabwe and Namibian liberation struggles; the Congo Crisis in the Belgian Congo; and the Mau Mau Uprising in British Kenya. The forced departure of the colonial powers did not, however, signal an end to armed conflicts in Africa.

Africa continues to be a continent of endless conflicts, most of them 'anarchic, internal, and tragic' (Tatah Mentan, 2004: 123). Achievement of independence has not inoculated African countries against armed violence. The promise of independence has not ushered in an era of peace, security and prosperity. Quite the contrary. Here and there, thinly disguised resource, power, hegemonic and expansionist conflicts erupt. Incumbent rulers, most of them illegitimate, wage war under the smokescreen of preserving 'territorial integrity', promoting 'national unity' or fighting against domestic 'terrorism' or insurgency. These conflicts have quickly quashed hopes for peace, security, development and prosperity in Africa. 'Postcolonial' Africa continues to experience major challenges by way of conflicts over land and water and conflicts in the form of claims to ethnic communities within the territory of an adjacent state. These are in fact natural resource, human resource and territorial aggrandizement conflicts. They are often dressed up as claims to territory and disputes over land and maritime boundary demarcation. Other conflicts, power-related, take the form of interstate wars, civil wars and armed conflict in the context of domestic and transnational terrorism.

Africa has thus been the epicentre of conflicts in the world since the 1950s when struggles against white colonialism began. In the post-white colonial period, at least thirty wars, civil and interstate, were fought in Africa between 1970 and 2000. In 1996 alone, fourteen African countries were in the throes of armed conflicts. Armed conflicts have seriously undermined long-term stability, prosperity and peace in the continent. Some African conflicts stem from 'postcolonial' governance issues while others can be traced to deep historical roots going back to pre-colonial and colonial periods.

Although armed conflicts have not yet been eliminated in the continent, nevertheless, since about 2010 they have diminished, and military coups d'état, which had become 'fashionable' at one time, have been dampened. Still, new types of armed conflicts have emerged in the form of domestic and transborder jihadist terrorism. Access by these groups to sophisticated weapons has added a fillip to their tentacular operations. Some of these weapons come from the Middle East. Others come from Libya, which had many weapons available following the French-led destruction and collapse of that country and the murder of its leader, Muamar Gaddafi. Moreover, the French sell arms to Saudi Arabia which passes some of it to the jihadist groups in Africa. The Boko Haram terrorist group in Nigeria has spread across the border into the Muslim north of Cameroun and Chad and made incursions into the Central African Republic. ISIS-affiliated Al-Qaeda in the Maghreb, known as the Islamic State West Africa Province (ISWAP), has a foothold in Mali, Niger and northern Burkina Faso. Another affiliated group tried but failed to establish a bridgehead in the Cabo Delgado province of Mozambique. A well-known Al-Qaeda-affiliated Islamic group, Al-Shabaab, has dug in its heels in Somalia and occasionally makes deadly incursions into Kenya.

Muslims do not hold a monopoly on anti-secular rebellions, however. In northern Uganda, for example, the LRA, established in 1987 by prophetess Alice Lekwana who was driven into Sudanese exile in 1990, seeks to establish a government in Kampala based on the Ten Commandments. In what was seen as an attempt to discourage Ugandan backing for the South Sudan SPLA/M, the LRA was re-armed by the Khartoum authorities in 1996. Since 1996, several thousand civilians have been killed or wounded and some 61,000 children have been abducted, many of them to serve as child soldiers in LRA units.

A conflict need not be violent and need not involve struggle. Where conflict is violent, the violence could be physical or psychological. In cases of physical violence, persons are hurt somatically to the point of killing. Psychological violence by contrast is psychic and includes techniques that serve to decrease mental potentialities such as lies, brainwashing, indoctrination and threats (Galtung, 1969). Cases of violent armed confrontation or struggle usually involve state and/or non-state actors. Such conflicts may last for days or months or even years. Some of the fighters get killed and others get injured. Africa has experienced, and still experiences, not only domestic or internal conflicts but also non-domestic conflicts. The former embrace two types, urban and rural riots as well as civil wars, including 'secessionist' wars. Urban and rural conflicts tend to get less media and world attention because they are generally localized and do not involve the use of arms. The geographical scope of such conflicts is often limited and casualties and injuries, if any, tend to be very few. Non-domestic conflicts include decolonization conflicts, interstate conflicts, as well as land and maritime boundary conflicts.

African rural conflicts stem from a variety of sources: disputes between agricultural peasant farmers and pastoralist herdsmen over the farm and grazing land, disputes between peasant farmers within the same ethnic group over cultivable land, inter-community disputes over livestock and water sources and, sometimes, inter-ethnic disputes over land boundaries dividing ethnic groups. Rural conflicts sometimes develop into rebellions and armed fighting between the ethnic groups concerned or between ethnic groups and the state when the latter sends in the military to stop the violence or to take side. For example, the Karamjong of Uganda and the Pokot of Kenya are on either side of the Kenya/Uganda border and have often fought over grazing land and cattle since the 1980s. Conflicts among pastoralists or among agriculturalists or between pastoralists and agriculturalists, over fertile and cultivable land, are common in many African countries. Despite being the most widespread of internal conflicts, most of these conflicts are under-reported, unless large-scale killing and injuries take place and the state intervenes militarily. Even then, reports tend to focus on the killings and injuries, ignoring the root causes of the killing.

Some countries have sought to manage these rural conflicts by introducing changes in their land laws and by expropriating large tracts of land for large-scale industrial farming or for ranching. These new developments often run counter to customary law systems of land tenure and result in the rise of rural inequalities between rich and poor/landless farmers, between rich ranchers and poor cattle owners, and even landlessness in some cases and the attendant phenomenon of influx to the cities. These changes have led to the considerable competition for scarce land resources. Environmental degradation in land productivity and scarcity of water has intensified competition for land. Added to this is the intensity and frequency of conflict among cattle grazing people. In countries with serious rebel movements, rebels often raid pastoralists for cattle in order to sell them for arms or food. The pastoralists in their turn acquire arms to defend themselves. Examples of conflicts among pastoralists or between pastoralists and agriculturalists include those among the Somali, the Oromo in Ethiopia, the Karamjong in Uganda, the Pokot in Kenya, the Hausa/Fulani in Nigeria, the Bororo in former British Southern Cameroons (now Ambazonia), the Foulbé in French Cameroun and the Masai in Tanzania and Kenya.

It is a trite observation that the rate of urbanization in Africa is very high. People abandon villages for the towns because there is nothing in the village to look forward to. There is no employment, no electricity, no pipe-borne water, no health facilities and no roads even. African governments concentrate development in the towns to the near exclusion of the villages. The urban population continues to increase, creating frustration and disillusionment which in turn make urban physical violence more common than in the past. Disillusionment and frustration are made worse by the bad performance of African economies and the resultant high level of urban unemployment. The youth make up more than half the population of African countries. Governments spend comparatively far too much money on the military than on education, healthcare, housing and other social services. As a result, the social sector has continued to deteriorate over the years. These conditions are in themselves sufficient to provoke and sustain major and continuous violence in urban areas. They are the same conditions that provoked rebellions and revolutions in eighteenth- and nineteenth-century Europe and in early twentieth-century Asia. It is a miracle that in Africa that level has not yet been reached.

African politicians are concentrated in the cities and major towns because that is where politics are conducted. In particular, the capital city of African states is where power and everything else is concentrated. It is home to various constituencies: the rich and the poor, the usually and understandably militant university students, opposition political parties, local and international media, advocacy NGOs and civil society groups, and diplomatic missions accredited to the state. It is generally in the capital city that differences in wealth are exhibited and contrasted and where the ruling elite display conspicuous consumption, ostentation and extravagant living. Given these conditions and the presence of the most politically conscious and sensitized actors, it is not surprising that politicians mobilize their supporters and organize political activities which often result in conflicts between ethnic supporters of rival camps. Even in the context of voting, ethnicity is the driver of how people vote in Africa. In the cities, physical violence along ethnic lines is more often than not provoked by politics and politicians. One recalls such conflicts as the one between the Luo and the Kikuyu in Nairobi in 2008 and the one between the Ibo and the Hausa/Fulani in some cities in northern Nigeria. It is easy to provoke ethnic violence in African cities because people who move to cities settle in areas inhabited by persons of their own ethnicity. They do so as a precautionary protective measure out of concern for their safety and security. A person feels safer among his kith and kin. These provide the first line of protection before the government intervenes, often late and sometimes not at all.

In any African country, ethnic conflict is likely to erupt in a situation where one cultural group becomes more loyal to itself than to the nation, where those wielding political power favour a particular ethnic group, where an ethnic group monopolizes political power to the detriment of other ethnicities or where different ethnicities refuse to accept each other as citizens belonging to one country. Such a situation is potentially volatile, is easily amenable to political manipulation and portends an ethnic conflict because most countries in Africa are exceptionally diverse in ethnicity and languages. The situation is exacerbated in an environment of gross disregard for minority rights and of failure by the government to promote a multi-ethnic cultural system that harmonizes diversity. Leaders of African dualist or multi-ethnic countries are still unable to create an acceptable genuine and coherent national identity. The increasing salience of popular religious identities, often mixed with competing ethnicities, worsens disorder in most African countries.

There are other manifestations of urban violence such as religious conflict, usually Muslims against Christians, and class conflict pitting urban poor against the urban elite. Other manifestations of urban violence are cases of vandalism consisting of attacks on government properties and installations, these being perceived as symbols of misrule and oppression. Attacks on shops and houses of the middle class and the rich is a way of venting anger on the snobbish and aloof well-to-do elite who are perceived as an exploitative class. The xenophobic anger seen in some countries, expressed through attacks on foreigners and their properties, is simply a case of scapegoating foreigners for internal woes. Urban violence is often triggered by a specific incident or situation and could be leaderless, in which case it is anarchistic or xenophobic. It is usually brief, lasting for just a day or just a few days, but could be intermittent or continuous. Urban violence during the colonial period was directed against the colonizer as a response to deplorable living conditions and the colonial control system. In 'postcolonial' Africa, urban violence has taken the form of reaction to poverty and poor social and economic conditions, lack of or poor service delivery, protest against state violence and struggles between supporters of rival political parties, often ethnically based.

The commonest type of political conflict in Africa consists of rebellions by groups outside the military establishment seeking to overthrow a government. Rebel groups are generally initiated by urban elites dissatisfied with the way the government treats them and their region or ethnic group. These elites mobilize a section of their regional or ethnic supporters. They acquire arms clandestinely. They canvass for and obtain support from a neighbouring country and sometimes from outside powers as well. Grievances against the government prompting an armed uprising may be shared by other ethnic groups, in which case the rebellion becomes more widespread. Rebellions seeking secession are often driven by perceived political, economic and cultural oppression. A coup d'état is a violent and undemocratic change of government by the military. It is one of the most common methods of capturing power in Africa (Anyangwe, 2012; Hutchful & Bathily, 1998).

The cause of many interstate conflicts in Africa is dissatisfaction with the boundary alignment between the states concerned. Many African borders are imprecise. Some are straddled by a large and strategic ethnic group. Some others pass through strategic territory desired by an adjacent state. Again, some other borders traverse areas rich with mineral resources but are found only on one side of the border, thus excluding the other country. These peculiar situations 'on the ground' often lead to border conflicts because they become the bases of a claim by one state to a redefinition of the boundary or to sovereignty over territory which falls on the other side of the border. Such claims are always resisted and so invariably lead to interstate armed conflicts. The first African border war was between Algeria and Morocco from September 1963 to February 1964 when Morocco tried to seize Algeria's Tindouf and Béchar provinces. The Sand War, as the conflict was dubbed, resulted in no territorial changes being made. Following OAU mediation, Morocco abandoned its intentions to control those Algerian provinces. The factors that contributed to the outbreak of this conflict were the absence of a precise demarcation of the border between the two countries, the discovery of important mineral resources in the disputed area and Morocco's 'Greater Morocco' expansionist claim. This armed conflict prompted the OAU to adopt the fundamental principle of intangibility of African borders as obtained on the date of achievement of independence. The latest and longest African border dispute is that between Ethiopia and Eritrea. In-between, there were short border disputes in the continent, mainly in West Africa.

The main causes of African conflicts include political power struggles, flawed democratization, regionalization or ethnicization of political parties, uneven distribution of resources, economic crisis, social decay and ethnic and religious polarization. Civil wars often arise from struggles for power within the state between contending groups. The reason for the frequent struggles for power is that governance in Africa is seldom democratic and inclusive. Those in power tend to overstay their welcome. They are determined to stay in power by all means and for as long as they possibly can. A bad example is Paul Biya's despotic stay in power in Cameroun for forty years already. When constituencies and political formations are unrepresented in government or are excluded from the governance of the country or are silenced, they invariably organize themselves and begin to fight back, not with ballots, since that route is closed, but with bullets. The same happens when the state fails to distribute resources evenly and ensure community participation in the development process. The state's inability to develop rural economy and rural areas causes regional tensions. Decisions about resource distribution are centralized, compounding maladministration because it leads to uneven distribution of resources and uneven infrastructural development. Neglected regions rise against the regime to claim their legitimate share of the proverbial 'national cake'.

This is particularly so where the neglected regions are not represented in the central government and so have no one to speak for them. Regionalization of political parties or the ethnic capture of a broad-based and popular political party may polarize a country. Ethnically based parties or a broad-based party captured by a tribal coterie often do not transcend ethnic divisions. They transfer notions of identity and allegiance away from the interest of the whole country. As a result, any ensuing conflict involving the regional political party at once becomes both regional and ethnical. In the Angolan civil war, for example, the MPLA was perceived as representing the interests of the Mbundu and Mesticos while UNITA was considered the guardian of the Ovimbundu ethnic group. The 1994 violent conflict between the ANC and the IFP in KwaZulu Natal, South Africa, was largely considered as a fight between ethnic Xhosa represented by the ANC and ethnic Zulu represented by the IFP.[4]

A state may make a territorial claim as a strategy to protect the interests of members of its ethnic group living in another country. It may also seek to eliminate members of rival ethnic groups that are supporting subversive members of its ethnic group in another country. Either course of action often engenders cross-border ethnic and religious tensions leading ultimately to an interstate conflict. Religion as a cause of violent conflict in Africa turns around the dichotomy between Christians and Muslims, especially in Nigeria, Somalia, Central African Republic, Ivory Coast, Sudan and to a less extent in Uganda. In Uganda, the Lord's Resistance Army, purveyor of a Fundamentalist strain of the Christian religion, has been fighting the government of that country for decades to overthrow it and institute a religious-based governance. In Nigeria and Somalia, religious conflict has since taken the form of an Islamic crusade by Boko Haram (in Nigeria) and Al-Shabaab (in Somalia) to impose Islamic rule in those countries. While there are cases where religious differences cause conflicts in Africa, it is nevertheless the case that leaders try to exploit religious differences for personal gain. Until recently, there had never been any tension between Christians and Muslims in Ivory Coast or in the Central African Republic. In fact, sectarian violence was unheard of in African countries because these were open and welcoming societies. In most parts of East and West Africa, Christians and Muslims co-exist with no difficulties. But then, in some countries, unscrupulous leaders often try to create sectarian violence as a means of political influence.

External intervention in Africa's armed conflicts has the effect of expanding both the scope and the intensity of the conflicts. It raises the level of violence, death, injury and destruction. Antagonists in countries benefiting from external intervention seek such intervention either to expand their war-fighting capacity or to avoid defeat at the hands of the enemy. Cuba, East European countries, the United States, the Soviet Union and apartheid South Africa all got involved in the Angolan civil war in support of one side or the other. In Sudan, the SPLA of John Garang was supported by Ethiopia, Libya, South Yemen, Uganda and Kenya, while Egypt, Iran and Iraq supported the Khartoum government. Residual problems from the end of white colonization, for the most part resulting from untidy departures by the colonial power, still provoke armed conflicts in the form of national liberation struggles in some parts of Africa as in the case of Ambazonia (formerly the trust territory of the British Southern Cameroons) and Western Sahara.

Explanations offered for Africa's violent conflicts include specific histories and geographical conditions, uneven levels of economic development and specific sub-regional dynamics – a reflection of the continent's diversity and complexity (Adebayo, 1999; Annan, 2004). In the 1960s, newly independent African states inherited arbitrarily drawn colonial boundaries, most of them during the scramble for Africa in 1884/1885. Some borders were not clear. Some others disadvantaged one group of people. Still, some others resulted from vague internal divisions of territories held by the colonial power as a single territory, for example, the territories held by France as one territory known as French West Africa and others known as French Equatorial Africa. The very nature of political power in African states is a key factor of conflict across the continent. Political control becomes excessively important, and the stakes become dangerously high, in an environment where there is insufficient accountability of leaders, lack of transparency in regimes, inadequate checks and balances, non-adherence to the rule of law, absence of peaceful means to change or replace leadership and lack of respect for human rights. Enduring denial of political, civil, economic, social, cultural and other human rights is a root cause of violent conflicts which in turn lead to further gross human rights violations.

In the competition for oil and other precious or strategic resources in Africa, interests external to Africa continue to play a large and sometimes decisive role, both in suppressing conflict and sustaining it. Foreign interventions are not limited, however, to sources beyond Africa. Adjacent states, inevitably affected by conflicts taking place next door, may also have other significant interests, not all of them necessarily benign. For example, neighbouring states intervened directly and indirectly in the civil wars in Liberia and Sierra Leone. While African peacekeeping and mediation efforts have become more prominent in recent years, the role that African governments play in supporting, sometimes even instigating conflicts in adjacent states, must be candidly acknowledged.

Despite the devastation that armed conflicts bring, there are many who profit from chaos and lack of accountability. These may thus have little or no interest in stopping a conflict but much interest in prolonging it. Very high on the list of those who profit from conflicts in Africa are international arms merchants. Also high on the list are the protagonists themselves. In Liberia, for example, the control and exploitation of diamonds, timber and other raw materials was one of the principal objectives of the warring factions. Control over these resources financed the various factions and gave them the means to sustain the conflict. Clearly, many of the protagonists had a strong financial interest in seeing the continuation of the conflict. The same can be said of Angola where protracted difficulties in the peace process owed much to the importance of control over the exploitation of the country's lucrative diamond fields. In Sierra Leone, the chance to plunder natural resources and loot central bank reserves was a key motivation of those who seized power from an elected government in May 1997.

The 'greed and grievance' baseline thesis on the causes of civil wars (Collier & Hoeffler, 2002) draws support from examples like these. According to that theory, the grievance has to do with issues like identity, inequalities, religion and so on and is not a cause of civil wars. Greed, by contrast, is concerned with issues of economic deprivation and is overwhelmingly the cause of civil wars because insurgents join rebellions for the purpose of self-enrichment so as to better their economic lot. Self-enrichment being their objective, rebels first make an informal cost-benefit analysis to determine whether joining a rebellion would procure greater economic rewards than not joining it.

This is an attractive theory. However, its generalizability is open to doubt. The motivation behind many internal conflicts cannot be pinned down to just a single cause. In some cases, greed is merely an effect of civil war, not its cause. In other words, after the onset of civil war greed develops and then feeds on and prolongs the conflict. In fact, greed and grievance are often tied together and interact with one another, greed generating grievance and rebellion, which in turn legitimize further greed (Keen, 2000). In some other cases, internal conflict is motivated and driven by altruism, for example, fighting for decolonization or fighting to end political repression and to institute a free and democratic society. The main criticisms of the greed and grievance theory are the polarity of the theory; the fact that in every internal armed conflict many factors come into play, the motivation incapable of being confined to just one motive such as simply a greed scenario; the narrowly defined quantitative measures and simplified methods of data collection analysis; the omission of factors like governance management mechanisms for natural resources; and the discounting of the influence that charismatic leaders can have on rebel groups motivating them to fight for reasons other than for greed (David Keen, 2000; Roland Bensted, 2011; Adrien Ratsimbaharison, 2011; Bodea & Elbadawi, 2007; Vinci, 2006). There might well be superior explanations of the motivation of armed groups in civil wars, and these are to be found in the 'fungible concept of power and the primary motivation of survival' (Vinci, 2006).

In addition to these identified broader sources of conflicts in Africa, a number of other factors are especially important in particular situations and subregions. In some parts of Africa, they include the competition for scarce land and water resource in densely populated areas. In Rwanda, multiple waves of displacements resulted in situations where several families often claimed the right to the same piece of land. In communities where oil is extracted, such as in Nigeria's Niger Delta, conflicts arise over local complaints that the community does not adequately reap the benefits of such resources or that it suffers excessively from the degradation of the natural environment.

Poverty as a cause of conflict is probably much more complex than one of simple cause and effect. For example, some of Africa's most tragic countries are some of the world's richest in natural resources. Congo-Kinshasa, Sierra Leone and Angola are cases in point. On the other hand, there are very poor countries that are at peace. A good example is Mali before the Azawad rebellion in 2012 and the French resource looting and plundering of the country and alleged complicity with jihadists. Similarly, ethnic divisions in themselves do not cause conflicts. Ethnicity becomes a cause of conflict only when cynical leaders capitalize on ethnic differences or disagreements and exploit them for personal gains. Tanzania during and after President Julius Nyerere experienced no armed conflicts even though the country has many ethnic groups. On the other hand, Somalia is ethnically homogenous but yet has plunged into continuous chaos for decades with apparently no end to the chaos in sight. Lesotho is mono-ethnic but has not escaped the violence trap. Arguably, the Hutu/Tutsi divide and armed violence in Rwanda and also in Burundi does not reflect a permanent situation. Rather, it would seem to represent a divide and conquer strategy by which colonial authorities and 'postcolonial' politicians sought to perpetuate their rule.

Depending on its scale, intensity and duration, an armed conflict causes enormous humanitarian problems, economic dislocation and property and infrastructural destruction. All armed conflicts, whatever their scale or intensity or duration, are therefore extremely costly in terms of human suffering and destruction of property and infrastructure. More importantly, armed conflicts inflict emotional wounds and engender memories of revenge over a long period of time. Conflicts eat up scarce resources. For example, in monetary terms alone, the Mozambican war cost $15 billion (Smock & Hrach, 1993). Furthermore, armed conflicts aggravate poverty. The poor become poorer. Development is arrested. Infrastructure such as schools, roads, hospitals, as well as water and electricity sources are destroyed. Armed conflicts take a heavy toll on the population. Thousands, if not millions, of people are killed, and others forcibly displaced as IDPs and refugees in miserable refugee camps. In the 1980s, Africa lost 3 million people to wars. In 1990, more than 2.5% of all Africans were refugees, and 8.6 million Africans were internally displaced. By 2006, 8.6 million Africans were living as refugees as a result of war. In Sudan alone, more than 800,000 people were displaced while an additional 110,000 were forced out of their homes into neighbouring Chad. In Rwanda, the genocide took over 800,000 lives in just 100 days. In Liberia, more than 250,000 people were killed during the civil war. In Uganda, at least 12,000 people were killed during the civil war. All over Africa, many more people die as a result of the conflict. The death toll during the Congo-Kinshasa civil war stood at about 4 million people.

Additionally, millions of children are abducted and used as soldiers and sex slaves. It is estimated that 25,000 Ugandan children were abducted between 1987 and 2006. Abducted children experience violence as victims and are forced to attack and kill strangers, friends or family members. Girls are subjected to sex slavery and end up being teenage mothers. Armed conflicts have robbed many African children of their childhood. Fleeing refugees and internally displaced persons are attacked. Villages are burnt, livestock stolen and property destroyed. This makes it harder for former residents to return to where they once lived. Famine among the displaced people is a recurring problem. They are unable to grow food or earn money to feed themselves. Malnutrition and starvation become widespread. Places of refuge are crowded, unsanitary and miserable. A current example of this large scale of humanitarian disaster due to massive and widespread killing and destruction is the pathetic situation in the former trust territory of the British Southern Cameroons (Ambazonia) where the people are fighting for survival in an illegal war unleashed on them by Cameroon since 2017. Conservative estimates as at the end of 2021 put the number of persons killed so far at between 30,000 and 40,000, the number of villages and homes burnt to the ground at 400, the number of refugee flows to other countries at 160,000, the number of internally displaced persons at 800,000 and the number of persons needing urgent humanitarian relief at 2 to 4 million.

Armed conflicts also affect global security because they spread. Across Africa, adjacent states get drawn into a domestic conflict. Uganda played a large role in the Congo-Kinshasa and South Sudan conflicts. Zimbabwe got involved in the Mozambique civil war. Zambia played a role in the Rhodesia war of independence. Beyond Africa, the refugee outflow due to conflicts in Africa has become a burden on northern economies, Europe and America.

CONFLICT MITIGATION AND RESOLUTION

Conflicts cannot be completely eradicated. But optimists believe that the adoption of good governance measures will contribute to minimizing the occurrence of civil wars. Suggested measures include democratic principles, internal self-determination, political pluralism, participation of all in governance, legitimate leadership, respect for human rights, employment opportunities for the youths and peacebuilding. Adopting and adhering to democratic principles would be the path to peace and stability. Devolution of power to the periphery is also key to avoiding civil strife. Addressing issues of ethnicity and inequalities is crucial to peace and stability. Participation by all the parties concerned in the peace process is critical in resolving conflicts. There are, however, some challenges to conflict resolution in Africa. One serious constraint is the reluctance of African states to accept mediation. They fear to admit inability to manage their own affairs. Officials from other states are also generally viewed by non-state actors as partial to the status quo, thereby rendering them unattractive as impartial mediators. Another serious challenge is the difficulty in predicting when a conflict is likely to occur. This has implications for conflict management. Another challenge to conflict resolution is that there are no immediate incentives for peace. A state involved in the conflict has nothing immediate to offer as peace dividends to the other party or parties to the conflict. Parties involved in a conflict would be happy to sign a peace deal if there are incentives for signing.

Preventing conflict is essentially a long-term process and needs long-term strategies and policies whose impact will prevent the emergence of conditions which give rise to conflicts. At the national level, it is vital to put in place policies and strategies aimed at minimizing serious conflict in the long run. It is in the interest of each country to develop policies and strategies, together with effective and efficient mechanisms, to deal with the causes of conflict and to manage and resolve them. The task of 'nation building' in Africa's heterogeneous states can only be undertaken by focused legitimate leadership and not by mere sloganeering about 'national unity', 'national sovereignty' and 'territorial integrity'. That leadership must develop a political system whose rules allow open competition for power on a level playing field and which guarantee the possibility of alternate groups achieving power within a reasonable period of time. In that way, every section and part of the country feels involved in the exercise of power and the governance of the country. That gives them a true sense of national belonging and of being part and parcel of the nation. Economic resources and development funds should be evenly distributed between regions and groups in the country without discrimination of any kind. The judicial system needs to be strengthened and vested with capacity and jurisdiction to enable the courts to deal with all types of domestic conflicts and to do so impartially, without fear or favour, and with finality. This requires judicial reforms and an absolute guarantee of judicial independence secured by the recruitment of suitably qualified persons of knowledge and integrity, attractive salaries and security of tenure as a judicial officer. Many conflicts in Africa, especially electoral, constitutional, form of state and other political conflicts degenerate into violent conflicts or civil wars because the courts are fearful of government and fail to resolve them by applying the rules of law impartially.

Early warning mechanisms are widely regarded as serving an important role in conflict prevention. But early warning without early action is of little use. Early action following upon an early warning is crucial in dealing with insipient conflicts, conflicts in gestation. The critical concern today is no longer the lack of early warning of impending crisis, but rather the need to follow up early warning with early and effective action. Whether the response to a conflict or crisis involves diplomatic efforts, a peacekeeping deployment or a humanitarian intervention, the sooner action is taken the more effective it is likely to be. A stitch in time saves nine. When violent conflict erupts, a genuine effort is needed to exhaust political options before such a confrontation intensifies. It is important that before international action is required, the government in situations of potential or actual conflict should genuinely consider the appointment of special mediators or special commissions to look into the sources of the dispute, whether domestic or with another country, to build confidence and recommend practical solutions which must honestly be applied and in good faith. Such efforts might include, among others, the involvement of respected persons from elsewhere in Africa particularly within the AU or from the broader international community.

Conflict resolution requires prior conflict analysis. The elements to be analysed and considered include conflict history, conflict context, the parties directly involved in waging the conflict, additional parties in the conflict and how they got involved, the patent and latent issues to the conflict, the power that one party probably has over the other and the source of that power, the stages of the conflict and the alternatives and options for a settlement (Wehr, 2018; Moore, 2014). Enduring denial of political, civil, economic, social, cultural and other human rights is a root cause of violent conflicts, which in turn leads to further gross human rights violations.

Peace-making is understood as actions taken to get parties to a conflict to reach an agreement and so resolve the conflict through peaceful means, that is to say, pacific settlement of disputes as envisaged in Chapter VI of the UN Charter. One action for making peace that is often resorted to is diplomacy. Diplomatic efforts are usually the most cost-effective and the most quickly deployed in resolving a conflict. Negotiation, mediation, good offices, fact-finding missions and judicial resolution may all be resorted to in addressing conflicts. The objective of resolving conflict often includes facilitating peace dialogue, defusing tensions, promoting national reconciliation, advancing respect for human rights and institutionalizing peace. Where a peace process is needed, it is the proper role of the AU to assist create one, probably with some assistance from the UN.

The AU must grow. It must be bold in addressing crisis situations in Africa. It must not fall into the impotency trap that the OAU fell into. Where obstacles obstruct further progress towards peace, the AU must help to remove it. When a basis for an agreement exists, it is the role of the AU to help facilitate it. Cooperation by parties to a conflict and their willingness to work towards peace can sometimes be nurtured by the African Union if it is able to assist with short-term stability while providing positive inducements for long-term reconciliation. Peace-making efforts must also encompass healing war-torn communities and addressing gross human rights violations. The UN Liaison Office at the African Union Headquarters in Addis seeks to consolidate cooperation between the AU and the UN and to facilitate the coordinated deployment of political efforts to prevent, contain and resolve conflicts in Africa. The selection of a mediator in situations of conflict must be very carefully considered and carried out with the closest possible consultation. In 1997, there was appointed a joint UN/AU Special Representative for the Great Lakes Region. This was a significant innovation which may also prove useful in other circumstances. Another example of how cooperation might be structured is the UN support for the mediation efforts of late former President Julius Nyerere of Tanzania with respect to Burundi.

Sanctions, as preventive or punitive measures, have the potential to be an effective tool in addressing conflicts. The multilateral threat of economic isolation may help to encourage political dialogue while the application of rigorous economic and political sanctions can diminish the capacity of the protagonists to sustain a prolonged fight. The imposition of an arms embargo can help to diminish the availability of arms with which to pursue a conflict by making the acquisition of weapons more difficult and more expensive. Greater use should be made of sanctions aimed at decision-makers and their families, including the freezing of personal and organizational assets as well as restrictions on travel. Better targeting of sanctions is necessary to ensure that they achieve their intended purpose. Where arms embargoes are imposed it is necessary for countries not only to refrain from official transactions but to seek to discourage their nationals or corporations from violating such sanctions.

Peacekeeping is the deployment of a military presence, with the consent of all parties concerned. Peacekeeping deployment aims at preventing, halting or resolving conflicts. UN peacekeeping operations are mandated by the Security Council under Charter VII of the UN Charter. Given that the nature of international conflict has drastically changed, current peacekeeping operations rely heavily on civilian and police components. Peacekeeping can be used not only to address conflict but also to prevent it. Preventive peacekeeping deployment could be a proactive response to the threat of conflict.

In 1989–1990, the UN deployed in Namibia a peacekeeping operation known as UNTAG. From 1989 to 1996, the UN also deployed in Angola three peacekeeping missions named as the UNAVEM I, II, III. The deployment of these missions was the beginning of a new era of complex, post-cold-war peacekeeping. Peacekeeping is apparently one of the most effective methods of resolving armed conflicts, but it is quite costly. However, in human, material and financial terms, the cost of peacekeeping operations is evidently far less than the cost of unchecked armed conflict. Yet, increasingly there appears to be a marked reluctance by both the UN and the AU to assume the political and financial responsibilities associated with mounting peacekeeping operations in trouble spots in Africa seemingly because of unavailability of identified and willing states and/or organizations ready to foot the bill.

*

This book runs through twelve chapters. It is divided into four parts. Part One discusses boundary and territorial conflicts. Part Two examines intra- and interstate conflicts. Part Three studies the new dimension of armed conflicts in Africa represented by domestic and transboundary terrorism. Part Four analyses indigenous and modern African conflict management and resolution frameworks.

NOTES

1. These are 'boundary', 'conflict', 'dispute', 'expansionism', 'frontier', 'international armed conflict', 'international dispute', 'non-international armed conflict' and 'territory'.
2. (1924) PCIJ, Series A, No. 2, p. 11.
3. Case No. IT-94-1-AR 72.
4. 'Zulus' Battle over Power, Culture Haunts Natal', *The Washington Post*, 11 April 1994.

Part One

BOUNDARY AND TERRITORIAL CONFLICTS

The sources of conflict between states over boundary and territory are varied. The commonest source is the imprecision of the frontier line between the states concerned as arbitrarily drawn at Berlin in 1884/1885 by the European colonizers during the Scramble for Africa. Imprecision of the frontier line is often due to an absence of a boundary treaty which would have clearly defined and described the boundary. In some cases, the legal validity of an existing border agreement is in doubt or is hotly contested. In some other cases, there are pending boundary-delimitation issues such as inadequate or incomplete delimitation, invalid delimitation due to factual errors on the ground as to the location of certain geographical features, delimitation in the form of a draft description but not subsequently followed up and finalized and failure to follow up a delimitation by carrying out demarcation on the ground. The chaotic boundary situation in Africa is captured in the following passage.

> Nearly all of the international boundaries in Africa have been delimited; that is to say, their theoretical location is defined by treaty or other legal process. Most of them were also demarcated on the ground, either by natural features, such as rivers, or by artificial marks. . . . [But] frequent discoveries [show] that the original demarcation has either been inadequately undertaken or allowed to fall into such decay that boundary lines are no longer visible. The most obvious occurrence of African delimitation that did not derive from agreement between two neighbouring sovereign states is found in the former French empire where internal administrative limits later emerged to become international boundaries. . . . Examples of delimitation that was not immediately followed and stabilized by demarcation are found in remote desert regions, such as the Chad-Sudan border, and in The Gambia whose original external boundaries were drawn on a map mainly as curvilinear lines that lay ten kilometres on each side,

and followed the sinuosities, of the river from which the country takes its name. Far more common are situations where colonial demarcation, performed rapidly and relatively inexpensively to meet the needs of the day, has failed through lack of maintenance to serve its intended purpose. The Nigeria/Benin boundary is something of a hybrid, for its was completely delimited by imperial treaty but only partially demarcated. Not only was 53 per cent of the total boundary left unmarked, but its physical establishment in the treaty location would now be a formidable task which, even if successfully accomplished from a technical point of view, might leave neither country satisfied with the outcome. (McEwen, 1991: 62)

Terrestrial and maritime boundary conflicts are a distinctive experience in post-colonial Africa and a common feature of African politics (Allcock et al., 1992; Boutros-Ghali, 1972). These conflicts often arise when adjacent or opposite states disagree on the course of the common boundary line separating them in the relevant sector or area, each claiming the contested terrestrial or maritime space. Where the conflict involves a claim to a substantial stretch of territory under the jurisdiction of another state or to the entirety of a contested territory, it is a territorial dispute (Oduntan, 2015; Touval, 1967). Where it involves a claim to some maritime area falling within the contested jurisdiction of adjacent or opposite coastal states, it is a maritime boundary dispute. More often than not, disputes arise not so much because the parties seek to obtain cartographical or survey certainty as to the exactitude of the course of the boundary line. In most cases, the disputes are triggered by matters such as expansionist ambitions, irredentist claims, identity and dignity questions (Brian, 2002), and, more especially, competition for resources. In a competition for resources, each side seeks to have direct access to, and control of, resources such as water, grazing land, fishing rights, minerals, onshore or offshore oil and gas.

One case of resource conflict arising from claims to access to water or to grazing pasture is the periodic clash over pasture and livestock between Somali Kitui herdsmen and Kenyan Kamba community along the Kitui and Tana River. Clashes of this nature do not involve a challenge to the territorial status quo. Nevertheless, it is an irritant that causes friction between Somalia and Kenya. In another case, this time in West Africa, there was a border incident between Mauritania and Senegal in the 1960s caused by repeated clashes between Mauritanian herdsmen and Senegalese farmers regarding cattle trespass and grazing on farmland (Kornprobst, 2002). The incident did not involve a challenge to the territorial status quo.

Resource conflicts have been going on in the Democratic Republic of the Congo since the 1970s. Implicated in these conflicts are foreign mineral extractive companies and the adjacent states of Burundi, Rwanda and Uganda

(*ACHPR Communication 227/99*).[1] Angola in the 1980s and Sierra Leone in the 1990s were theatres of long-drawn diamond conflicts. More recently, potential offshore oil and gas have fuelled maritime boundary delimitation conflicts between a number of states with adjacent or opposite coasts. Here too, oil exploration and exploitation companies are not innocent bystanders or onlookers. The Somali/Kenya maritime dispute is just one example of a conflict over oil and gas in the form of a dispute over maritime boundary delimitation. Other African maritime boundary disputes involve the following pairs of countries: Equatorial Guinea/Gabon, Eritrea/Djibouti, Ghana/Côte d'Ivoire, Guinea Bissau/Senegal, South Sudan/Sudan, Sudan/Egypt, Uganda/Kenya and Cameroon/Nigeria. Some of these disputes were referred for judicial settlement, others were settled through bilateral negotiations, while still others involved the threat or use of force but were eventually settled through third-party mediation.

NOTE

1. *Democratic Republic of Congo v. Burundi, Rwanda & Uganda*, ACHPR Communication 227/99.

Chapter 1

Claims and Conflicts over Land Territory and Land Boundaries

In the early years of Africa's decade of independence, the 1960s, some states made but later renounced expansionist claims to territory within a neighbouring state. Well-known expansionist claims that have been made in the continent are those of Libya to the Aouzou Strip in Chad, of Morocco to the Tindouf and Béchar regions in Algeria and to the whole of Mauritania and the Western Sahara (Reyner, 1963; Zartmam, 1965; Wild, 1966; De la Serre, 1966), of Ethiopia to Eritrea, and of Somalia to Djibouti, the Ogaden and Haud regions in Ethiopia, as well as to the North Frontier District in Kenya (Lewis, 1960, 1963; Drysdale, 1964; Touval, 1963; Lewis, 1963; Castagno, 1964; Mesfin, 1964). The basis for each of these claims was either ethnicity or historical ethnic allegiance. The territorial aggrandizement claim of the Cameroun Republic (formerly French Cameroun) to Ambazonia (formerly the trust territory of British Southern Cameroons) is absurdly said to be based on the German colonial territory of *Kamerun* (from 1884 to 1914) which became extinct in 1919 and out of which the international tutelage system created two separate and distinct territories, the mandated/trust territory of the British Cameroons and the mandated/trust territory of French Cameroun.

LAND-TERRITORY CONFLICTS

Four cases of claim to territory resulted in war. Morocco's claim to the Western Sahara resulted in a full-scale war with the SADR. The SADR was admitted in 1984 to the OAU and is thus a member of the AU.[1] Despite a 1975 International Court of Justice (ICJ) advisory opinion rejecting Moroccan claim to the territory as invalid in international law, Morocco continues to occupy the territory against stiff resistance by POLISARIO,

Western Sahara's liberation movement. Currently, there is a lull in the fighting. The UN recognizes the Western Sahara as a non-self-governing territory and its right to self-determination. Ethiopia's expansionist claims to Eritrea resulted in a thirty-year-long war which began in September 1961 and ended in May 1991 with Eritrean independence recognized by Ethiopia. From May 1998 to June 2000 both countries were again engaged in war, this time over a border dispute. The Western Sahara and Eritrea have always considered their respective national liberation wars as a self-determination struggle against colonialism by an adjacent expansionist African state, a colonization indistinguishable from European colonization. Somalia has always claimed Somali-inhabited areas in the Horn of Africa, that is, French Somaliland, the Haud and Ogaden regions in Ethiopia and the North Frontier District of Kenya. These areas are within the territory of other states. That notwithstanding, Somalia has pursued its irredentist claim arguing the need to 'recover' its ethnic people. Somalia subsequently renounced its claim to French Somaliland which achieved independence as Djibouti. But apparently, it has not given up its claim to other Somali-inhabited districts within the neighbouring states of Ethiopia and Kenya. Libya claimed the Aouzou Strip in Chad and fought a long war with that country, the matter being finally resolved by the ICJ in favour of Chad.

In all these cases, it seems the principle of territorial integrity of the country concerned was apparently not disputed, challenged or rejected as such. Each of the claimant states appeared to suggest they only sought to reinforce that principle by claiming territory they believe rightfully belonged to them in law. Morocco founded its claim to the Western Sahara on 'historical consolidation', that is, consolidation of territory that Morocco said historically belongs to Morocco. This contention was rejected by the ICJ.[2] Ethiopia founded its claim to Eritrea on the UN recognition of Eritrea as falling under the sovereignty of the Ethiopian Emperor, Haile Selassie. Eritrea rejected this and militarily imposed on Ethiopia a consensual agreement on Eritrea's independence. Libya founded its claim to the Aouzou Strip on the cession of the Strip by Chad to Libya but could not produce the instrument of cession. Somalia considered itself entitled to unite all Somali-speaking people and their territories in one Great Somali nation, a vision not dissimilar from the nineteenth-century agenda of Bismarck with regard to German unification and of Cavour with regard to Italian unification. But times have changed. Since the mid-twentieth century, the principle of self-determination has emerged as a legal norm, in fact, a rule of *jus cogens*. Self-determination trumps such emotional and fanciful claims as unification or ethnicity. It is emotionally fashionable in some sections of the continent to blame the territorial woes of the several African states on the European Scramble for Africa and the Berlin 1884/1885 partition of the continent among the principal European powers. But however arbitrary the partition may have been, the continental political organization, the (O)AU, has not rejected but, in fact, confirmed it by adopting as its foundational principle the intangibility of African borders as they were on the date of achievement of independence.

Early Territorial Claims

In the early 1960s, a number of newly independent African states nursed expansionist ambitions which were camouflaged as 'union' with an adjacent state or country. In West Africa, Nigeria toyed with the idea of union with its adjacent French-speaking neighbour, Benin Republic (Omoniyi, 1984–1985). The idea seemed particularly attractive as it was based on an appeal to the Yoruba ethnic community that sits astride Benin Republic and Western Nigeria. The Nigeria hypothetical claim may also have arisen from the uncertainty of the boundary alignment.

> Nigeria and Benin . . . share a land boundary approximately 770 kilometres in length, made up of three distinct sections: the Atlantic coast to the Okpara River (203 kilometres), the Okpara River thalweg (161 kilometres) and the Okpara to the Niger River (407 kilometres). From a legal point of view the boundary is clearly defined by two Anglo-French agreements of 1906 and 1914. In practice, however, the absence of sufficient original demarcation has caused confusion concerning the actual physical location of much of the boundary. The Okpara River section is regarded as self-demarcating and appears to present no special problem in its alignment. A re-demarcation of the boundary south of that river started in 1974. Between the Okpara and the Niger rivers the colonial treaty boundary was drawn as a series of artificial lines that were never properly traced or marked on the ground. In the northern part of this section, particularly, the uncertainty of boundary location creates jurisdictional problems that include a continuing controversy surrounding the sovereignty over a number of border villages. (McEwen, 1991)

Nigeria abandoned its hypothetical claim since ethnicity is a weak basis for the claim to territory. In February 2021, however, the *Premium Times* of Nigeria reported an intriguing meeting between the president of Benin and the president of Nigeria with their respective ministerial delegations. At the end of that meeting, the Nigerian Minister of Foreign Affairs was quoted to have suggested that Benin wanted to become Nigeria's thirty-seventh state. 'The President of Benin said as far as they are concerned, they want (not just saying like that) but in reality, Benin should be the 37th state of Nigeria.' That is what the Nigerian foreign minister was quoted to have said. The statement immediately raised eyebrows in both countries and was promptly retracted by the Nigerian Foreign Ministry which said the minister had been quoted out of context. According to the Foreign Ministry spokesman, what the Foreign Minister meant was that 'the President of Benin Republic said he would like the relations between the two countries to be so close as if Benin was the 37th state of Nigeria'. The Ministry clarified that 'Nigeria has never aspired to make the Republic of Benin or any other country a part of its territory'.

French-speaking Togo made a claim to neighbouring British Togoland on a similar appeal to ethnicity (Kornprobst, 2002). The Ewe ethnic community bestrides the two countries and also spills over into the east of Ghana. From the mid-1940s, Ewe nationalists demanded 'reunification' of their people in one state. The demand was ignored by Britain, France and the United Nations. On 9 May 1956, a plebiscite was held in British Togoland. The plebiscite offered the choice of remaining under trusteeship until neighbouring French Togoland had decided upon its future or to become part of the Gold Coast. The vote went in favour of integration with the Gold Coast, soon-to-be Ghana. Meanwhile, in French Togoland, a referendum was held on 28 October 1956. The choice was between becoming an autonomous region within the French Union or remaining a trusted territory. The vote went in favour of autonomy within the French Union. The result was rejected by the United Nations General Assembly because the referendum did not include the option of independence. The UN therefore decided to continue with the trusteeship.

In 1957, Ghana and British Togoland achieved independence as one state under the name and style of the Republic of Ghana. The claim of the Republic of Togo (former French Togoland) to British Togoland had no merit. First, in 1956 French Togoland and France had opposed one plebiscite for the two Togo and a joint tallying of the results. The French fear was that such a plebiscite would likely result in the vote going either in favour of independence or integration with Ghana because of the Ewe factor. The British therefore organized a plebiscite in British Togoland and the French a referendum in French Togoland, with the results in each case as earlier noted. Secondly, the Ewe tribe straddles eastern Ghana as well as British Togoland and French Togoland. If the Republic of Togo (former French Togoland) could claim ex-British Togoland on the basis of ethnicity, Ghana could also make, and indeed threatened to make, exactly the same claim over French Togoland. The hypothetical Togolese claim to ex-British Togoland was therefore not a strong enough reason for the war against Ghana, irrespective of whether militarily such an eventuality was feasible or not.

Spain was the colonial power in the Western Sahara since the Scramble for Africa in 1884–1885. In 1975, Spain relinquished control of the territory to a joint administration by Morocco and Mauritania and hurriedly left. A war erupted between POLISARIO, the liberation movement of the Western Sahara on the one hand and Morocco and Mauritania on the other hand. This was ironical because Morocco had earlier been involved in an unsuccessful armed conflict with Algeria over a border dispute and had also made an unsuccessful irredentist sovereignty claim to the whole of Mauritania itself on the basis of historical ethnic allegiance. (Wild, 1966; De la Serre, 1966). Morocco's claim was weak and could not be a *casu belli* justifying going to war against Mauritania. In 1979, Mauritania withdrew its claim to any part of the Western Sahara. The liberation war continued against Morocco which succeeded in securing de facto control over most of the territory. Morocco poured into the Western Sahara hundreds of thousands of Moroccan flag-waving 'civilians' in what was said to be a 'march' to reclaim the territory for Morocco.

Morocco's territorial claim to the Western Sahara is, however, hotly contested by the people of the Western Sahara. Morocco continues to face insurmountable legal and political resistance. It is doubtful that Morocco's claim can ever succeed in the face of the anti-colonial ideology in Africa, the decolonization agenda of the UN, the unquestionable right of the Saharawi people to self-determination, the principle of respect for the intangibility of frontiers inherited from colonization and the advisory opinion of the ICJ in the *Western Sahara* case that Morocco's sovereignty claim to that territory is invalid under international law as it is based on such purely political expression as history or purely moral expression as personal allegiance. Notwithstanding the fact that the UN considers the Western Sahara a non-self-governing territory, considers POLISARIO as the legitimate representative of the Saharawi people, and considers self-determination as a right to which the Saharawi people are entitled Morocco continues to occupy the Western Sahara to this day. Surprisingly, the political organs of the UN appear to be deadlocked on the issue.

An early claim to territory is the claim of the Cameroun Republic (former French Cameroun) to the British Northern Cameroons. The territorial claim to the British Northern Cameroons goes back to proceedings instituted in the ICJ by an Application of 30 May 1961 filed by the Cameroun Republic against the United Kingdom of Great Britain. In that application, the Government of Cameroun Republic requested the court to declare that, in the application of the Trusteeship Agreement for the Territory of the Cameroons under British Administration, the UK failed, with regard to the British Northern Cameroons, to respect certain obligations flowing from that agreement. The Cameroun Republic further claimed that the UK had violated the Trusteeship Agreement for the Territory of the Cameroons under the British Administration by creating such conditions that the Trusteeship had ended up with the attachment of the Northern Cameroons to Nigeria rather than to the Cameroun Republic, previously administered by France. The UK raised preliminary objections to the court's jurisdiction. The court found that to adjudicate on the merits would be devoid of purpose since, as the Cameroun Republic had itself recognized, its judgement thereon could not affect the decision of the General Assembly in Resolution 1608 (XV) of 21 April 1961 providing for the attachment of the Northern Cameroons to Nigeria in accordance with the results of a plebiscite supervised by the UN. Accordingly, by a judgement of 2 December 1963, the court found that it could not adjudicate upon the merits of the claim.

Cameroun Republic's suit was in fact an attempt by that country to claim as part of its territory the British Northern Cameroons on the basis of a self-assigned 'special interest' in a so-called 'reunification of all the peoples of the Cameroons'. The Cameroun Republic was however unable to identify who these so-called 'peoples of the Cameroons' were that it had appointed itself to 'reunify'. It could not exhibit the mandate from any such people requiring it to make this expansionist claim. The Northern British Cameroons, part of the separate and distinct UN Trust Territory of the British Cameroons, has always been ethnically, culturally, religiously and administratively welded to Northern Nigeria since 1916. In February 1961, it decided to remain, and in June the same year, it became under international law, part of Nigeria. UN General Assembly Resolution 1608 (XV) of 21 April 1961 decided that the Northern Cameroons shall join Nigeria on 1 June 1961 as part of Nigeria's Northern Region. The Cameroun Republic conceded in its pleadings that it was not requesting the court to transfer or restore to it the people and territory of the Northern Cameroons since it had at no time acquired and then lost them. It is the competent organ of the UN which decided that the British Northern Cameroons should join Nigeria on 1 June 1961 as part of the Northern Region of that country, and the Northern Cameroons did become part of the territory of Nigeria on 1 June 1961. No decision by the UN would change that fact. Therefore, any ruling by the court would serve no purpose. There was thus no need to make a pronouncement on the case as requested by the Republic of Cameroun. The court adjudged and declared that Cameroun's request for a declaratory judgement was legally devoid of purpose. It accordingly dismissed as without object the case instituted by the Republic of Cameroun against Britain[3] in a veiled claim to the territory of the Northern British Cameroons in the hope of annexing it.

In its judgement, the court first gave the historical background to the case. The court recalled that the Cameroons had formed part of the possessions to which Germany renounced her rights under the Treaty of Versailles, 1919, and which had been placed under the Mandates System of the League of Nations. It had been divided into two Mandates, the one administered by France and the other by the United Kingdom. The latter divided its territory into the Northern Cameroons, which was administered as part of Nigeria, and the Southern Cameroons, which was administered as a separate province of Nigeria. After the creation of the UN, the mandated territories of the Cameroons were placed under the international trusteeship system by Trusteeship Agreements approved by the General Assembly on 13 December 1946. The territory under the French administration attained independence as the Republic of Cameroun on 1 January 1960 and became a member of the UN on 20 September 1960. In the case of the territory under UK administration, the UNGA recommended that the Administering Authority organized plebiscites in order to ascertain the wishes of the inhabitants. Pursuant to these plebiscites the Southern Cameroons federated in free association with the Republic of Cameroun on 1 October 1961, and the Northern Cameroons joined on 1 June 1961 the Federation of Nigeria, which had itself become independent on 1 October 1960. On 21 April 1961, by resolution 1608 (XV) the UNGA endorsed the results of the plebiscites and decided that the Trusteeship Agreement concerning the Cameroons under UK administration should be terminated upon the two parts of the territory 'joining' the Republic of Cameroun and Nigeria, respectively. The Republic of Cameroun voted against the adoption of this resolution.

After giving that historical background, the court then marshalled the following line of argument. Resolution 1608 (XV) of 21 April 1961 by which the UNGA decided that the Trusteeship Agreement should be terminated with respect to the Northern Cameroons on 1 June 1961 had definitive legal effect. The Republic of Cameroun did not dispute that the decision of the UNGA would not be reversed or that the Trusteeship Agreement would not be revived by a judgement of the court on the merits, that the Northern Cameroons would not be joined to the Republic of Cameroun, that its union with Nigeria would not be invalidated or that the UK would have no right or authority to take any action with a view to satisfying the underlying desire of the Republic of Cameroun. The function of the court was to state the law, but its judgement must be capable of having some practical consequences. It might be contended that if, during the life of the Trusteeship, the Trustee was responsible for some act in violation of its terms that resulted in damage to another member of the UN or to one of its nationals, a claim for reparation would not be liquidated by the termination of the Trust, but the Application of Republic of Cameroun sought only a finding of a breach of the law and included no claim for reparation.

Even if it were a common ground that the Trusteeship Agreement was designed to provide a form of judicial protection that any member of the UN had a right to invoke in the general interest, the court could not agree that judicial protection survived the termination of the Trusteeship Agreement. In filing its application on 30 May 1961, the Republic of Cameroun had exercised a procedural right which appertained to it, but, after 1 June 1961, the Republic of Cameroun would no longer have had any right to ask the court to adjudicate at this stage upon questions affecting the rights of the inhabitants of the territory and the general interest in the successful functioning of the Trusteeship System. Republic of Cameroun's contention was that all it sought was a declaratory judgement of the court that prior to the termination of the Trusteeship Agreement, the UK had breached its provisions. The court reasoned that it might, in an appropriate case, make a declaratory judgement but such a judgement must have continuing applicability. In this case, there was a dispute about the interpretation and application of a treaty, but the treaty was no longer in force, and there could be no opportunity for a future act of interpretation or application in accordance with any judgement the court might render. Circumstances that had since arisen rendered any adjudication devoid of purpose. Under these conditions, for the court to proceed further in the case would not, in its opinion, be a proper discharge of its duties.

Later Territorial Claims

Other ethnic-based attempts to claim territory include the claim of Somalia to Djibouti and parts of Ethiopia and the claim of Libyan to the Aouzou Strip in Chad. In the Horn of Africa, Somalia dreamt of building a 'Greater Somalia' nation that would embrace all ethnic Somalis and the lands they inhabit, even if some ethnic Somalis are within the territories of other states. In pursuit of that self-appointed unification agenda, Somalia asserted its sovereignty claim to French Somaliland (Djibouti). It waged war against Ethiopia to reclaim the Somali-inhabited Ogaden and Haud regions. It asserted sovereignty claim to the North Frontier District of Kenya. This ambition drove Somalia into war against Ethiopia and into hostile relations with Kenya.

The dispute between Somalia and Ethiopia over the Ogaden led to a year-long war between them from 1977 to 1978. Soon after achieving independence in 1960, Somalia asserted territorial claims against both Ethiopia and Kenya. Both claims were based on Somali ethnic communities that spill over across the border into each of those countries. In the 1960s, Somalia asserted its claims militarily (Mariam, 1964) and pursued those claims right into the 1970s. In July 1977, it invaded Ethiopia to recover the adjacent regions of Ogaden and Haud which are home to ethnic Somalis. The invasion was a disaster. It unleashed a bitterly fought nine-month war (July 1977 to March 1978) which Somalia lost. Bizarrely, at the onset of the war, the Soviet Union switched its support from Somalia to Ethiopia, while the United States did the converse by switching its support from Ethiopia to Somalia. Egypt, as part of its long-standing policy of securing the unhindered flow of the River Nile, also supported Somalia by providing arms and military training. The OAU brokered a truce which eventually led to the end of the war and the retreat of Somali forces back across the border.

The British may have unwittingly encouraged Somalia to seek to bring together under one sovereign Somali nation all Somali-inhabited territories in East and North Africa. Britain's colonial territories in East Africa included British Somaliland and Kenya. Four days before granting Somaliland independence on 30 June 1960, the British government alluded to the unification of all Somali-inhabited areas of East Africa in one administrative region. The areas in question were British Somaliland (Somaliland), Italian Somaliland (Somalia), French Somaliland (Djibouti), the Ogaden region in Ethiopia and the Northern Frontier District in Kenya. An informal plebiscite in that district reflected the overwhelming desire of the region's population to join the newly formed Somali Republic constituted by Somalia and Somaliland. Britain changed its earlier position. It ignored the wishes of the people of the Northern Frontier district. It went ahead to grant administration of the region to Kenya. On the eve of Kenya's independence in August 1963, it became clear that the independent Republic of Kenya would not be willing to give up the Somali-inhabited region earlier transferred to Kenya by Britain (Castagno, 1964).

Since then, that region has continued to be a flashpoint of repeated conflicts between Somalia and Kenya, including targeted attacks deep inside Kenya by the Somali insurgency group known as Al-Shabaab: the 1998 US Embassy bombings in Nairobi, the 2002 Mombasa attacks, the 2013 Westgate shopping mall attack, the 2014 Mpekoni attack, the 2014 Gikomba bombings and the 2015 Garissa University College massacre of 147 people, the deadliest attack up to that date. Somalia has apparently not given up its dream of a Pan-Somalia (or Greater Somalia) that includes Eastern Ethiopia and the Northern Frontier District of Kenya. But it is yet to figure out how to achieve that dream. Militarily it cannot because it will not be able to prevail over Ethiopia and Kenya jointly or separately; legally, it cannot because of the international law principle *uti possidetis juris*, the African Union sacrosanct principle that the boundaries of an African state ossify on the date of its achievement of independence and the international law prohibition of war of aggression. The use of force by individual states as a means of settling disputes is impermissible under the UN Charter. It might well be the case that Somalia has to all intents and purposes renounced its territorial claims. This is more so as Somaliland has since 1991 separated from Somalia and is running its affairs as a separate independent state though so far deprived of *de jure* recognition.

The territorial dispute between Ethiopia and Eritrea over the border area of Badme led to a two-year war from 1998 to 2000, one of the deadliest interstate wars the continent has witnessed so far. Following Eritrea's successful war of national liberation against Ethiopia and its achievement of independence in April 1993, the hitherto presumptive internal boundary between the two became an international frontier. Both countries could not agree on the exact course of that frontier line in certain sectors. Colonial treaties between Ethiopia and Italy, the former colonial overlord of Eritrea, proved unhelpful as the treaties did not clearly delimit the precise frontier line. At the heart of the dispute over the course of the frontier line is the border area of Badme claimed by each side.

For two years, from May 1998 to June 2000, Eritrea and Ethiopia fought a bitter war over that piece of territory. The war left over 70,000 dead. Despite the savagery, intensity, duration and cost of the war, the end result was only a minor border adjustment. Following the (O)AU-mediated Algiers Agreement, the two parties presented their case to the Permanent Court of Arbitration. The UN Eritrea–Ethiopia Boundary Claims Commission established that Badme belongs to Eritrea and that under the Cease-Fire Agreement of 18 June 2000 Ethiopian armed forces were obligated to withdraw in 2000. Ethiopia was unhappy with this ruling and as of 2019 was still in occupation of the disputed territory. Intermittent skirmishes and the wrangling over the physical demarcation of the frontier between both countries go on.

The Eritrea-Ethiopian war does not call into question the principle of territorial integrity as such. If anything, it appears to have been fought to secure the certainty of the *frontier* so as to reinforce in a concrete way the principle of territorial integrity. The dispute arose because of imprecise boundary delineation, a fact that obscured sovereignty over certain localities in the border area. The nature of this dispute makes it different from a claim to territory extending well beyond the border area. Such an extensive claim is not a boundary but a territorial dispute. A territorial dispute puts into question the principle of territorial integrity. The sanctity of territorial boundaries as of the date of independence is a core principle in Africa. This principle entails the rejection of any attempt to put into question the principle of territorial integrity of African states or countries. Any attempt to do so bears the seed of destabilizing the entire continent by opening the door to any state that sees itself as militarily strong to grab territory from its perceived weaker neighbour or even grabbing the whole of that neighbouring state. That is why the following claims cannot succeed: the unfounded claim of Somalia to the Ogaden and the Kenyan Northern Frontier District; the baseless claim of Morocco to the Western Sahara and even to Mauritania as it once asserted; and the implausible territorial claim of Republic of Cameroun to Ambazonia (the former trust territory of the British Southern Cameroons). The principle of self-determination trumps each one of these expansionist claims.

In the Maghreb, Libya made a determined effort to wrestle the Aouzou Strip from Chad. This conflict was specifically over disputed territory in the border area claimed by Chad and Libya. The dispute saw a series of sporadic clashes in that area between the armies of both countries from 1978 to 1987. Libya claimed the Aouzou Strip as part of Libya on the basis of a 1935 Franco-Italian treaty. In 1935, Libya was under Italian colonization while Chad was a French colonial territory. The 1935 Franco-Italian treaty was signed by the parties but never ratified. The Libyan case was that on 28 November 1972, President François N'Garta Tombalbaye of Chad ceded the Aouzou Strip to Libya. In June 1973, Libyan troops then moved into the Strip and established an airbase, a civil administration and extended Libyan citizenship to the inhabitants of the area. From that moment, Libyan maps represented the area as part of Libya.

After a year of inconclusive talks, Chad and Libya submitted the dispute to the ICJ in September 1990. Libya was unable to exhibit the signed original copy of the 'agreement' of 1972 by which Chad is said to have ceded the Strip to Libya (Ricciardi, 1992). If indeed Chad ceded the Strip to Libya, then it means the sovereignty of the Strip belonged to Chad because Chad could not have ceded what it did not have. The onus was on Libya as the party asserted to show that there was indeed a cession of the Strip in 1972. Libya failed to do so. In its ruling delivered on 3 February 1994, the ICJ held that the Aouzou Strip belongs to Chad.[4] The court declared that once agreed, the boundary stands, for any other approach would vitiate the fundamental principle of the stability of boundaries. The formal and final transfer of the Strip from Libya back to Chad took place four months later, on 30 May 1994.

The conflict between South Sudan and Sudan was a territorial dispute in which the oil equation, as in maritime boundary disputes, was the very bone of contention. In early 2012, the military forces of both countries clashed in Unity state of South Sudan. In March of the same year, South Sudanese forces seized the Heglig oil fields in lands claimed by both Sudan and South Sudan in the province of South Kordofan. South Sudan withdrew from Heglig a few days later, on 20 March, and the Sudanese army entered the area two days later. The oil equation bedevils relations between South Sudan and Sudan. Border disputes also strain relations between both countries. The row over sovereignty of the 10,546 square kilometre Abyei border area is yet to be resolved. A promised referendum for the inhabitants of the region to decide whether to join Sudan or South Sudan is yet to take off. The area with a population of 125,000 inhabitants remains under 'special administrative status', effectively a Sudan-South Sudan condominium, as was agreed under the 2004 Protocol on the Resolution of the Abyei Conflict in the Comprehensive Peace Agreement of 5 January 2005.

Other unresolved resource disputes include a land dispute between the Dinka farmers in South Sudan and Misseriya Arab cattle-herders across the border. There is also a cattle-raiding feud between rival ethnic groups in the Jonglei state of South Sudan. To compound this seemingly endless situation of conflicts, in December 2013, barely two years after South Sudan achieved independence, a political power struggle between President Salva Kiir Mayardit and his sacked deputy Riek Machar Teny Dhurgon degenerated into a full-scale country-wide civil war pitching the country's two main ethnic groups, Dinka and Nuer. Sustained peace efforts by the AU and IGAD succeeded in ending the war and securing peace after two years of senseless killing, maiming, internal displacement of people and destruction of the country's basic and very limited infrastructure. The end of the civil war after two years of fighting was partly due to war fatigue and acceptance of the expedient of a national unity government promoted by IGAD and the AU. But peace did not last for long. Fighting soon resumed, the government of national unity collapsed and Riek Machar escaped into exile. Mediation efforts continued and peace of some sort has returned under a government of national unity in which Riek Machar got back his position of vice president, but then only as one of five vice presidents under the agreed unity government.

European Overseas Territories in Africa

The old European colonizers of Africa – Britain, France, Portugal and Spain – still occupy certain islands and mainland territories that arguably properly belong to Africa. The islands in question are located off Africa's coast and inhabited mainly by persons of European descent. They have been under the sovereignty of the named European powers before the Scramble for Africa. They are not claimed by any African state except for the Spanish exclaves claimed by Morocco, the Chagos Islands claimed by Mauritius and Mayotte (aka Mahoré) with a population of 250,000 inhabitants is claimed by Comoros. The Comoros claim Mayotte as a sovereign territory of Comoros and not of France.

British Overseas Possessions

Britain has three main island possessions in the South Atlantic Ocean. The islands in question belong to the continent of Africa but are important for British and American strategic and military interests. First, Tristan da Cunha is a 40 square mile principal island in a cluster of tiny islands that include the rugged volcanic 92-square-kilometre island of Gough which is uninhabited except for a handful of people who usually maintain the weather station there. Tristan da Cunha has a population of about 300 inhabitants and is dependent on the larger island of St Helena. Second, St Helena is 1,950 kilometres off the west coast of Africa. Its capital is Jamestown. It has an area of 160 square miles and an estimated population of about 8,000 inhabitants, descendants of sailors, settlers and slaves. The Island's economy is dependent on British grants and remittances from abroad. In 1815, the British defeated the French at the decisive battle of Waterloo. Britain then exiled the Corsican-born French Emperor Napoleon Bonaparte to St Helena where he lived from 16 October 1815 until his death on 5 May 1821.

Third, Ascension Island is 34 square miles in area and has a transient population of about 1,000 inhabitants mainly Britons, Americans and St Helenians. It is located 700 miles NW of St Helena through which it is administered. Ascension is a communications relay centre for Britain and has a US satellite tracking centre. Half the inhabitants of the island are communication workers. The island is about 1,500 miles from the coast of Angola. These three islands are far from each other but form a single territorial grouping under British sovereignty. On 9 May 2008, the UK lodged with the UN Commission on Limits of the Continental Shelf a submission in which it claimed a continental shelf beyond 200 nautical miles around the Ascension Island. The submission was declined on 15 April 2010.

Britain possesses a group of islands in the Indian Ocean known as the Chagos Archipelago but designated by it as the BIOT. Mauritius has for long claimed sovereignty over the Chagos Islands as part of the territory of Mauritius which Britain unlawfully excised in 1965 before granting Mauritius independence in 1968. The long-standing territorial dispute between Mauritius and Great Britain over the Chagos Archipelago (Anyangwe, 2000) was finally referred to the ICJ for an advisory opinion. In a case concerning the *Legal Consequences of the Separation of the Chagos Archipelago from Mauritius in 1965 (Request for Advisory Opinion)*,[5] the court ruled in remarkably forthright terms that the process of decolonization of Mauritius was not lawfully completed when that country acceded to independence. The court also ruled that the United Kingdom is under an obligation to bring to an end its administration of the Chagos Archipelago as rapidly as possible.

The genesis of the case can be traced to 2017. On 2 June 2017, the UNGA adopted resolution 71/292 in which it requested the ICJ to render an advisory opinion on the following questions:

(a) Was the process of decolonization of Mauritius lawfully completed when Mauritius was granted independence in 1968, following the separation of the Chagos Archipelago from Mauritius and having regard to international law, including obligations reflected in General Assembly resolutions 1514 (XV) of 14 December 1960, 2066 (XX) of 16 December 1965, 2232 (XXI) of 20 December 1966 and 2357 (XXII) of 19 December 1967?

(b) What are the consequences under international law, including obligations reflected in the aforementioned resolutions, arising from the continued administration by the United Kingdom of Great Britain and Northern Ireland of the Chagos Archipelago, including with respect to the inability of Mauritius to implement a programme for the resettlement on the Chagos Archipelago of its nationals, in particular those of Chagossian origin?

In its Advisory Opinion delivered on 25 February 2019, the court concluded that 'the process of decolonization of Mauritius was not lawfully completed when that country acceded to independence' and that 'the United Kingdom is under an obligation to bring to an end its administration of the Chagos Archipelago as rapidly as possible'. Before reaching this conclusion, the court first addressed the question of whether it possessed jurisdiction to give the advisory opinion requested by the UN General Assembly. Having established that it did have jurisdiction to render the advisory opinion requested, the court examined the question raised by a number of participants that it should nevertheless decline to exercise that jurisdiction as a matter of judicial discretion. On this question of jurisdiction, the court held that in light of its jurisprudence, there were 'no compelling reasons for it to decline to give the opinion requested by the General Assembly'. It also found that there was 'no need to reformulate the questions submitted to it for an advisory opinion in the proceedings'. It then proceeded to examine the factual circumstances surrounding the separation of the archipelago from Mauritius, as well as those relating to the removal of the Chagossians from this territory. Having done so, it went on to address the questions submitted to it by the General Assembly.

In examining the first question, the court turned to the nature, content and scope of the right to self-determination applicable to the process of decolonization of Mauritius. It recalled that respect for the principle of equal rights and self-determination of peoples is one of the purposes of the UN. It also recalled that the charter included provisions that would enable non-self-governing territories ultimately to govern themselves. It went on to note that 'the adoption of resolution 1514 (XV) represents a defining moment in the consolidation of State practice on decolonization' and that 'both State practice and *opinio juris* at the relevant time confirm the customary law character of the right to territorial integrity of a non-self-governing territory as a corollary of the right of self-determination'. The court considered that the peoples of non-self-governing territories are entitled to exercise their right to self-determination in relation to their territory as a whole, the integrity of which must be respected by the administering power. After having examined the functions of the UNGA in matters of decolonization, the court also considered, in its analysis of the international law applicable to the process of decolonization of Mauritius, the obligations reflected in UNGA resolutions mentioned in the first question before the court.

In the court's view,

> By inviting the United Kingdom to comply with its international obligations in conducting the process of decolonization of Mauritius, the General Assembly acted within the framework of the Charter and within the scope of the functions assigned to it to oversee the application of the right to self-determination.

After recalling the circumstances in which the colony of Mauritius agreed in principle to the detachment of the Chagos Archipelago, the court considered that this detachment was not based on the free and genuine expression of the will of the people concerned. It took the view that the obligations arising under international law and reflected in the resolutions adopted by the General Assembly during the process of decolonization of Mauritius required the United Kingdom, as the administering power, to respect the territorial integrity of that country, including the Chagos Archipelago. The court concluded that 'as a result of the Chagos Archipelago's unlawful detachment and its incorporation into a new colony, known as the BIOT, the process of decolonization of Mauritius was not lawfully completed when Mauritius acceded to independence in 1968'.

In addressing the second question, having established that the process of decolonization of Mauritius was not lawfully completed in 1968, the court examined the consequences, under international law, arising from the UK's continued administration of the Chagos Archipelago. In particular, it was of the opinion that the UK's continued administration of the Chagos Archipelago 'constitutes a wrongful act entailing the international responsibility of that State', that the UK 'has an obligation to bring to an end its administration of the Chagos Archipelago as rapidly as possible, and that all Member States must cooperate with the United Nations to complete the decolonization of Mauritius'. The court found that since respect for the right to self-determination is an obligation *erga omnes*, all states have a legal interest in protecting that right. It observed that it is for the UNGA to pronounce the modalities required to ensure the completion of the decolonization of Mauritius. It however considered that all Member States must cooperate with the UN to put those modalities into effect. As regards the resettlement on the Chagos Archipelago of Mauritian nationals, including those of Chagossian origin, the court was of the view that this is an issue relating to the protection of the human rights of those concerned, which should be addressed by the UNGA during the completion of the decolonization of Mauritius.

What this case clearly suggests is that the UN cannot completely divest itself of responsibility in connection with a colonial territory, be it a non-self-governing or a trust territory, until the territory in question has achieved complete independence in accordance with the Declaration on the Granting of Independence to Colonial Countries and Peoples. The ICJ therefore had no difficulty in rejecting Britain's claim of sovereignty over the Chagos Islands held by Britain as a dependent territory after detaching it from Mauritius at the time of that country's independence in 1965. The court determined that Britain is required under international law to complete the decolonization of Mauritius by handing back the Chagos Islands to Mauritius as rapidly as possible. It clarified that continued British occupation of the archipelago is illegal. The fact that the decision is an advisory opinion does not mean that it is useless and has no legal or political implications.

Speaking through a foreign office spokesperson, Britain stated that it is obvious that this is an advisory opinion and then went on to claim, incredulously, as reported by *The Guardian*, 25 February 2019, that 'the defence facilities on the British Indian Ocean Territory help to protect people here in Britain and around the world from terrorist threats, organized crime and piracy'.[6] The UK also went on to say, somewhat obdurately, that there is 'no doubt as to our sovereignty over the British Indian Ocean Territory (BIOT), which has been under continuous British sovereignty since 1814'. For its part, the Mauritian government welcomed, in the same *The Guardian* report, the ICJ ruling as a 'historic moment in efforts to bring colonialism to an end, and to promote human rights, self-determination and the international rule of law'.

Britain's refusal to abandon its sovereignty claim to the Chagos Islands impelled Mauritius to go to the International Tribunal for the Law of the Sea to press its claim to those islands. Mauritius did so by asking the tribunal to resolve its separate maritime dispute with the Maldives. The Maldives is the nearest island to the waters around the Chagos Archipelago. It had tried to fend off the involvement of the maritime court by saying that there was an existing sovereignty dispute between Britain and Mauritius over the Chagos Islands, which meant it did not need to negotiate with Mauritius. But by eight votes to one, the maritime court, in a one-hour judgement, rejected all the jurisdictional objections the Maldives had raised.

Speaking after this judgement, wrote *The Guardian*, 28 January 2021, the prime minister of Mauritius called on Britain to end its unlawful occupation of the Chagos Islands, declaring that

> the judgement of the Special Chamber of the International Tribunal for the Law of the Sea (ITLOS) is clear and unequivocal: Mauritius is sovereign over the Chagos archipelago. The UK must now bring itself into full compliance with international law – it must immediately terminate its unlawful occupation of the Chagos archipelago which the ICJ and now today ITLOS, have determined to

fall exclusively within the sovereignty of Mauritius. . . . [W]e call on the UK to announce . . . that it will bring itself into compliance with international law.[7]

The Guardian, 28 January 2021, further reported that Professor Philippe Sands QC, who represented Mauritius in the case, declared:

> This judgment is damning. It has said near unanimously there is no basis for the UK claim to the islands. The UK has to go away and reflect on what it intends to do, but its current position is untenable. . . . The maritime court has ruled that the ICJ judgment is legally depositive. If the UK persists in its current position it will be knowingly in breach of international law and its reputation damaged in a strategically vital part of the world.

The same *The Guardian* report noted that the International Tribunal for the Law of the Law will proceed to delimit the maritime boundary between Mauritius and Maldives, on the basis that the Chagos Archipelago is the territory of Mauritius.[8]

French Overseas Territories

One relic of European colonization of Africa is the continuing French rule over the Indian Ocean islands of Mayotte, Glorieuse, Europa, Tromelin and Reunion. These islands lie between Madagascar and the coast of Mozambique. According to France, the islands are parts of its *territoires Outre-Mer* (overseas territories). The inhabitants of those islands seem quite content to be accorded the dubious 'privilege' of being part of France. They argue that they are economically not viable to claim independence. However, it would appear that the Comoros is unhappy with French suzerainty over the Comoros Island of Mayotte which France separated from the rest of the Comoros before granting it independence. The case is similar to that of the UK's separation of the Chagos from the rest of Mauritius which was then granted independence. But the Comoros has so far not taken legal action against France as Mauritius has done against the UK.

France considers Mayotte (capital Mamoudzou) a French *département* and treats it as such even though culturally the archipelago is most closely related to neighbouring Comoros Islands. Mayotte became an official French colony in 1843 while the three other islands in the Comoros archipelago became French protectorates more than forty years later (Grande Comore in 1886, Anjouan in 1887 and Mahéli in 1892). From 1912 to 1946, all of the four Comoros Islands were grouped with Madagascar to form what was called the Madagascar and Dependencies colony. In 1946, the Comoros archipelago became a French overseas territory with its capital at Dzaoudzi,

Mayotte. In 1958, Mayotte and the other three islands adopted different institutional approaches. In 1968, each island set up its own institutions. An independence referendum was held on 22 December 1974 in the Comoros. Three of the four islands chose to become independent. Mayotte voted by a majority of 64% to remain part of the French Republic. On 6 July 1975, the Comorian authorities unilaterally declared their independence. On 8 February 1976, France organized a second referendum to determine whether Mayotte residents wished to become part of the new Comorian State. Mayotte voted by 99.4% to remain part of France. In 2011, following votes in 2000 and in 2009 by Mayotte to become an overseas department of France, the island became the fifth overseas department of France and therefore one of the EU's outermost regions.

It has since been argued that France complied with international legal principles on the question of Mayotte and that this could explain why the Islamic Republic of the Comoros has not fought to have Mayotte as part of its territory. The line of argument marshalled by France is this. Mayotte's decision to remain part of France complied with international law on decolonization. The island was not part of an independent state with borders recognized by the international community. It clearly and freely refused independence at the self-determination referendum which took place on 22 December 1974. Comoros was admitted to membership of the UN on 12 November 1975. France respects the will of the inhabitants of Mayotte and the territorial integrity of the Comorian State. In 1997, France refused a request by the Comorian island of Anjouan to become part of France. France argued that admitting Anjouan to membership of France would violate the territorial integrity of the Federal Islamic Republic of the Comoros Islands. Mayotte's absorption as part of the territory of France, the argument goes, results from the application of a fundamental international legal principle: a people's right to determine their own destiny or the right to self-determination. In the *East Timor-Portugal v. Australia* case, the ICJ indicated in its judgement of 30 June 1995 that self-determination is an *erga omnes* right (opposable against all) and a fundamental norm of contemporary international law pursuant to the UN Charter. This principle underpins the 1974 and 1976 self-determination referendums in which Mayotte voted to remain part of the French Republic, a decision that French authorities were obliged to accept.

The above line of argument is attractive and compelling. But it ignores the point whether it was necessary and advisable for France to have conducted those referendums with an option to continue colonial status and permanent integration in the territory of the colonial power. This point is critical in view of the UN decolonization agenda, the Declaration on the Granting of Independence to Colonial Peoples and Countries 1960 and the Declaration on Principles of International Law Concerning Friendly Relations and

Co-operation Among States in Accordance with the Charter to the United Nations 1970. The referendum choice at those referendums should simply have been independence as an autonomous state or union with the state of Comoros.

Spanish and Portuguese Overseas Territories

The two Iberian countries of Spain and Portugal have small colonial outposts in Africa. Portugal exercises sovereignty over the Island of Madeira as part of its territory. The Island is just a stone's throw off the coast of Morocco.

Spain exercises sovereignty over the Atlantic Ocean islands of the Canary, Las Palmas and Santa Cruz. Spain also has tiny exclaves situated on Morocco's Mediterranean coast: Ceuta (72,000 inhabitants, 19.7 square kilometre in area) and Mellila (67,000 inhabitants, 12.5 square kilometre in area). These two tiny exclaves, Ceuta and Mellila, are designated as Spanish North Africa. They are the sole foreign-ruled territory in the mainland African continent. Spain continues to reject Morocco's claim to both exclaves.

LAND BOUNDARY CONFLICTS

Terrestrial boundary disputes are more intense. They often result in military skirmishes. There are four possible explanations for this. First, people are more attached to land than to the sea. They are more attached to land because they inhabit the land and live off it. The land is an ancestral homeland. Water is the abode of the water spirits such as the mythical mermaid. Second, in international law, a basic principle in maritime delimitation is that the land dominates the sea. Third, where the frontier line is eventually determined in detail by the experts inevitably involves the transfer of some population and most likely some strategic physical feature or geopolitical assets such as a hill, a river or section of a river, an oasis or watering hole, or some piece of forest or pasture land. This is often exasperating and painful for affected local communities. That experience elicits resistance which often escalates into violence. Fourth, terrestrial boundary and territorial disputes easily evoke sentiments of national pride, dignity and honour which tend to be perceived as being at stake.

It is a trite comment that African boundaries were arbitrarily drawn by colonial powers with little or no consideration for the interest of ethnic communities (Boutros-Ghali, 1972; Allcock, 1992). Many boundary descriptions in Africa were imprecise. Some did not correspond with geographical and ethnological realities on the ground. Others used language and concepts which were far from clear. African territorial disputes involving land and maritime boundaries can thus be partly traced to the continent's colonial and 'post-colonial' history. It is estimated that about 70% of Africa's borders are imprecisely delimited. The absence of imprecision of boundary delimitation creates tension between adjacent countries seeking control of natural resources. It chills economic activities in the disputed frontier area, influences political and international relations between the states concerned and triggers disputes over land and/or maritime borders.

The early types of disputes that arose between newly decolonized African states were those over the precise location of the frontier line between the states concerned (Touval, 1967, 21: 102).

> In a broad sense many questions of title arise in the context of 'frontier disputes', but as a matter of principle the determination of the location in detail of the frontier line is distinct from the issue of title. Considerable dispositions of territory may take place in which the grantee enjoys the benefit of a title derived from the grant although no determination of the precise frontier line is made. On the other hand, precise determination of the frontier line may be a suspensive condition in a treaty of cession. The process of determination is carried out in accordance with a special body of rules, the best known being the *thalweg* principle. According to the doctrine of the *thalweg* in the case of a navigable river, the middle of the principal channel of navigation is accepted as the boundary. This and associated geographical doctrines are presumptions and principles of equity rather than mandatory rules. The practical aspects of frontiers must be emphasized. Agreement as to the precise details of a frontier, enshrined in a written instrument, is often followed by the separate procedure of demarcation, that is, the marking, literally, of the frontier on the ground by means of posts, stone pillars, and the like. A frontier may be legally definitive, for some purposes, and yet remain un-demarcated. Frontiers which are 'de facto', either because of the absence of demarcation or because of the presence of an unsettled territorial dispute, may nevertheless be accepted as the legal limit of sovereignty for some purposes, for example those of civil or criminal jurisdiction, nationality law, and the prohibition of unpermitted intrusion with or without the use of arms. (Brownlie, 2003)

A survey of postcolonial African countries shows that border disputes have remained a common feature of African politics. Many African countries achieved independence between 1960 and 1970, the so-called decade of independence in Africa. From that period onwards border disputes have been a regular feature of state interactions in the continent. Some of these disputes resulted in limited military clashes and were eventually settled through judicial process. Others were submitted right away for judicial settlement. Happily, none of these early land boundary disputes escalated into war. All of them appeared ultimately to have been resolved amicably. The parties respected the status quo and normalized their bilateral relations. Unlike cases of territorial disputes, Africa's border disputes sometimes result in short border skirmishes but do not escalate into full-scale war (Allcock, 1992).

Little Known Boundary Disputes

West Africa alone has known about a dozen obscure border disputes. There was a border dispute between Guinea, Côte d'Ivoire and Liberia in the region of Mount Nimba (aka Mount Richard-Molard); between Côte d'Ivoire and Liberia in the area between the Cess and Cavally rivers; between Mali and Mauritania in the Hodh desert border and also in the Savannah region from Djel Mael to Queneibe; between Niger and Burkina Faso (formerly Upper Volta) along their entire common border; between Ghana and Burkina Faso regarding a one-mile strip at their common border; between Ghana and Côte d'Ivoire about the Sanwi-inhabited area of Côte d'Ivoire; between Benin Republic (formerly Dahomey) and Niger over the island of Lete in the Niger River; between Nigeria and Benin Republic over Nigeria's claim to the Yoruba inhabited areas of that country; between Ghana and Togo regarding the irredentist claim by each country to the Ewe-inhabited areas of the other; between Benin and Niger as well as between Benin and Nigeria over border demarcation problems; and between Mauritania and Senegal over the common border around the River Senegal (Kornprobst, 2002).

The Mauritania-Senegal Border conflict from 1989 to 1991 was along the shared border of both countries. Mauritania and Senegal are former colonial territories of France. But while Mauritania sought reinforcement of its predominantly Arab identity by strengthening ties with the Arab world, Senegal remained very close to France, especially through its promotion of *Négritude* (the affirmation or consciousness of the value of black culture) and its attachment to the OIF, a French imitation of the Commonwealth. As a result, the two countries increasingly adopted divergent foreign policies. The armed conflict between them arose from disputes over the River Senegal border and grazing rights. The conflict was compounded by the multiple ethnicities in Mauritania – Fula, Arabs, Berbers, Toucouleur, Wolof and Soninké – and the fact that one ethnic community, the Wolof, is in Senegal as well (Marchesin, 2010; Dauré-Serfaty, 1993). These ethnicities have inhabited the Senegal river basin for centuries. The drought in the 1980s increased tension over arable land. When the Senegal river basin authority undertook the development of the area by constructing dams, the basin assumed greater importance because the waters of the dams altered the balance between herders and farmers by opening new parts of the valley to irrigation. Mauritania's 1983 land reforms strengthened the role of the state and undermined traditional agriculture. This exacerbated the problem of many farmers on both sides of the Mauritania/Senegal border. Relations between the two countries deteriorated, each hardening its stance against the other with each further incident. This created an explosive situation that the local media magnified by focusing heavily on the ethnic dimensions of the conflict.

On 9 April 1989, Fulani herdsmen and Mauritanian Soninké farmers in Senegal clashed over grazing rights in the Senegalese town of Diawara. The Mauritanian army invaded northern Senegal, occupied 1,000 square kilometre of territory, killed two Senegalese and seriously injured several others, and took a dozen prisoners. Riots broke out in Senegal during which shops of Mauritanian traders were looted and burnt, and some Mauritanians were killed by decapitation or setting ablaze. At the end of April, retaliatory riots also broke out in Nouakchott and other Mauritanian cities. Hundreds of Senegalese citizens were killed and others injured. Both countries began expelling nationals of the other. About 160,000 Mauritanians were repatriated from Senegal. In Mauritania, lynch mobs and police brutality against Senegalese saw about 70,000 Black Mauritanians of the Halpulaar minority in southern Mauritania forced across the River Senegal into Senegal even though they had no links with Senegal. Both sides then engaged in armed cross-border raids, forcing about 250,000 people to flee their homes. Violence did not dissipate until 1991–1992. Hundreds of people died in both countries.

The border between the two countries was closed and, on 21 August 1989, diplomatic relations were cut off. The OAU made a failed attempt to negotiate a reopening of the border. It was ultimately an initiative of Senegalese president Abdou Diouf who led to a treaty being signed on 18 July 1991 providing for the re-establishment of relations, which took place in April 1992 and the reopening of the border, which took place on 2 May 1992. In the course of the next decade, Mauritanian refugees slowly trickled back into the country. In June 2007, Mauritanian president Sidi Ould Cheik Abdallahi requested the UNHCR to help it repatriate Black Mauritanians who had been forced out during the war and were living in refugee camps in Mali and Senegal. Between January 2008 and March 2012, the UNHCR assisted in the repatriation of 24,272 Mauritanians from those 2 countries back to Mauritania. The period of conflict left a lasting impact on relations between Mauritania and Senegal, as well as domestic perceptions of each other. The armed black nationalist Mauritanian movement, FLAM, was founded in 1983 with Ibrahima Octar Sarr as leader, its main headquarters located in Dakar and its European headquarters in Paris (Kinne, 2001).

In the Horn of Africa, Eritrea and Djibouti had a dispute over the Ras Doumeira area (Sultanate of Raheita). A boundary dispute between the

Federal Democratic Republic of Ethiopia and the Republic of Sudan has been on since the nineteenth century. In 1902, while Sudan was still under British rule, the Ethiopia-Sudan 744-kilometre border was demarcated, based on a 1902 Anglo-Ethiopian treaty. The border was demarcated with the help of Charles Gwynn, a British royal engineer, without the presence of Ethiopia. The demarcation was rejected by Ethiopia as not clear and as mainly relying on natural landmarks such as mountains, trees and rivers. In 1972, negotiations between Ethiopia and Sudan failed to settle the question of the Baro (River) Salient and the fertile agricultural region of al-Fashaga. In the latter area, Ethiopia claims the land up to the Atbarah and Tekezé River while Sudan claims the border is further east.

In North Africa, Morocco asserted, but subsequently abandoned, claim to parts of western Algeria and to the whole of Mauritania. Libya and Tunisia referred their lateral maritime boundary dispute to the ICJ for resolution. In the Lake Chad Basin, the shrinkage of the surface water of the lake has led to conflict due to altered natural boundaries. Furthermore, territorial conflicts have emerged between riparian states and between sub-national states. For example, in 1983, Chad fought with Nigeria over the status of some of the islands that had emerged in the lake as a consequence of the lake's recession and fluctuating shorelines. The fighting caused eighty-four fatalities and was ended by a settlement between the two countries (Okpara Uche et al., 2014). The ambiguity of the legal status of the islands in the lake has rendered the islands a political no man's land lacking legally defined national affiliation. That no man's land has been occupied by the Boko Haram insurgent group, the joint countering of which is recognized by the riparian states as a shared problem.

In Southern Africa, there is the South Africa/Swaziland (Eswatini) dormant border dispute. Swaziland and Lesotho appear to be dissatisfied with their respective common borders with South Africa. Swaziland has made repeated calls for 'border adjustment' with South Africa. South Africa's response is that the aggrieved state is free to take the matter to the ICJ. However, neither Swaziland nor Lesotho has taken up the South African challenge to submit the matter to that court for international judicial determination (Anyangwe, 2004).

The border between Lesotho and South Africa is 909 kilometre long. It forms a complete loop as Lesotho is an enclave entirely surrounded by South Africa. Historically, the Basotho people formed a distinct polity in the 1820s under Moshoeshoe I, their first paramount chief. At that time Basotho territory included much of what is now the Free State province of South Africa. This territory was lost in the 1850s. In the 1860s, a series of wars were fought between the Basotho and the Boers of the Orange Free State. As a result of these wars, Moshoeshoe lost a great portion of the western lowlands. In 1868, Basutoland (as Lesotho was then called) became a British protectorate. From 1871 to 1884 it was under annexation by the Cape Colony but reverted to the status of a British protectorate and remained so until 1966 when independence was achieved as the Kingdom of Lesotho. Some consider Lesotho and Eswatini (Swaziland) as satellite states of South Africa. In Lesotho, some activists have urged Lesotho to accept annexation by South Africa. According to *The Guardian*, 6 June 2010, earlier in 2010, a trade unionist, Vuyani Tyhali, started a petition in support of annexation. He said,

> We have 30,000 signatures. Lesotho is not just landlocked – it is South Africa-locked. We were a labour reserve for apartheid South Africa. There is no reason for us to exist any longer as a nation with its own currency and army.[9]

The petition has made no headway. South Africa itself does not appear interested in annexation because it would then have to shoulder extra burdens and onerous responsibilities which the incorporation of Lesotho or Swaziland or both would certainly entail.

The border between Lesotho and the Orange Free State was defined in the 1869 Convention of Aliwal North. This treaty effectively reduced Moshoeshoe's kingdom to half its previous size by ceding away its western territories. The Lesotho-Orange Free State border was confirmed by the High Commissioner's notice of 13 May 1870, as amended by Government Notice No. 74 of 6 November 1871. In this notice, the boundaries of 'British Basutoland' were described as:

> From the junction of the Cornetspruit with the Orange River, along the centre of the former to the point nearest to Olifantsbeen; from that point, by Olifantsbeen, to the south point of Langeberg to its north-western extremity; from thence by a prolongation of the same, to the Caledon River to the heads of the Orange at the Mont aux Sources; thence westwards along the Drakensberg, between the Watershed of the Orange River and the St. John's River to the source of the Tees; down the centre of the river to its junction with the Orange River, and down the centre of the latter river to its junction with the Cornetspruit. (Brownlie, 1979: 1109; US State Department, 1974)

It would appear that South Africa and Lesotho established a consultative committee in 2019 to resolve border disputes. Seemingly, these disputes arise not from disagreement as to the boundary alignment but rather from misunderstandings that stem from the movement of people across their common border.

In the case of Swaziland, its call for border adjustment would appear to suggest that Swaziland does not recognize the territorial status quo. Many

African boundary disputes stem from competition for resources or the pursuit of irredentist policies based upon arguments of history and ethnicity. In the Swazi case, the ethnic equation is the primary plank in its claim. Prior to its independence in 1968, Swaziland formally notified South Africa that it would make representations for 'certain border adjustments' with that country after the achievement of independence by Swaziland (Anyangwe, 2004). The notification was probably intended to defeat a possible argument by South Africa that through recognition and acquiescence by conduct Swaziland has accepted their common frontier line as definitive. The Swazi note may therefore have been designed to prevent South Africa from pleading estoppel. It may also have been intended to serve as a reservation of rights regarding the border alignment. It is probably within this logic that both the 'citizenship' and 'territory' clauses in the Swazi Independence Constitution were repealed by the King's Proclamation of 1973. Claimed Swazi territories inhabited by acknowledged Swazi people were outside the Swazi boundaries as they stood at independence. The 'border adjustment' would rectify the two issues of territory and citizenship.

The Swazi claim would suggest the Swaziland denies that its borders were ossified on the date of its attainment of national independence. If that is the case, it would seem to contradict the well-known principle of *uti possidetis juris* and subscribed to by African states since 1964 when they solemnly pledged to respect the frontiers existing on the date of achievement of national independence. Swaziland achieved its independence within the framework of its current borders. Those borders are based upon reality, the validity of which Swaziland does not impugn. In fact, at independence, the territory of the Kingdom of Swaziland, as a successor state, devolved upon it on the basis of the pre-existing boundaries as established by the Anglo-Transvaal London Convention, which superseded the Convention of Pretoria, 1881. Swaziland would therefore appear, prima facie, to have a hopeless case. But boundaries can always be changed or adjusted by agreement consistent with international law. Moreover, *uti possidetis juris* does not affect disputes about demarcation; it does not affect frontiers that were in dispute during colonial times; it does not affect frontiers in dispute before the colonial intervention. The principle does not and cannot prevent all border disputes, nor can it erase existing agendas of border disputes. Boundary disputes have arisen and will arise in situations of obscure colonial boundaries, un-demarcated boundaries, of a boundary description that poses technical problems or of a boundary demarcation never accepted by one or both parties as a valid frontier.

Swaziland's claim appears to arise from technical and historical problems relating to the delimitation and demarcation of the Swaziland-South African border. However, by presenting the claim as a mere 'border adjustment' rather than as a 'boundary dispute' or a 'territorial dispute', it would seem the matter is perceived by Swaziland as a mere technical problem, a technical problem of a topographical and/or geometrical nature regarding the boundary description. It is probably significant that in 1981 the then South African homeland of KwaNgwane, Swazi-inhabited, rejected Swaziland's border adjustment claims as 'expansionist'. The homeland declared its intention to remain within South Africa, influenced no doubt by a calculation that the lot of those Swazis is better within South Africa than within Swaziland. In that same year, South Africa in effect challenged Swaziland to take the boundary dispute to the ICJ. Swaziland has so far not taken up the challenge. Quite apart from cost, a legal barrier is that Swaziland does not appear to have made any declaration, under Article 36(2) of the Statute of the ICJ, accepting the compulsory jurisdiction of the court. South Africa did, but withdrew it in 1967 (Anyangwe, 2004).

Notable Land Boundary Disputes

The disputes under this head were eventually settled through the judicial process after initial military skirmishes in some cases, as in the land and maritime boundary dispute between Cameroun and Nigeria that left an unspecified number of casualties, and the dispute between Burkina Faso and Mali over the Agacher Strip which left fifty people dead. The boundary dispute between Namibia and Botswana over the appurtenance of the tiny Sedudu/Kisikili Island in the Chobe River was submitted to the ICJ which ruled that the islet belonged to Botswana.

Botswana and Namibia: Legal Status of the Kasikili/Sedudu Island in the Chobe River

The dispute between Botswana and Namibia turned on the boundary between both countries around the disputed Island of Kasikili/Sedudu in the Chobe River, and the legal status of the island. The ICJ ruled that the boundary between the parties around the disputed island follows the line of deepest soundings in the northern channel of the Chobe River and that the island forms part of the territory of Botswana.[10] The central question, in that case, was the interpretation and application of the words 'main channel' of the River Chobe. It was common ground between both parties that the River Chobe is the border between the two countries in the disputed area. However, both differed strongly on exactly where the riverine boundary line had to be drawn in the area of the tiny 5 km^2 Kisikili/Sedudu Island. The Heligoland-Zanzibar treaty of 1 July 1890 between Britain and Germany determined the border between the colonial possessions of the two powers, parts of which are present-day Namibia and Botswana. But the treaty was not clear on the question of the ownership of the island. On this point, the treaty simply stipulated that the borderline through the Chobe River shall be along the 'centre of the main channel' of the river but without assigning meaning to that phrase. Namibia argued that the 'main channel' runs south of the island. Botswana made the opposite argument saying the 'main channel' runs north of the island. The success of either argument would give the state advancing its ownership of the disputed island irrespective of how the centre line of that channel eventually had to be drawn.

It is a principle of international law that the meaning of a treaty must be determined from within the four walls of the text of the treaty. Failing that, it is permissible, in the face of ambiguity, to have recourse to alternative methods of interpretation. The main channel of a bifurcated river could be the one that carries the most water (i.e., the most volume of flow), or the one with the deepest channel, or the one with the most navigable channel. Conflicting historical material, contested scientific evidence and the fact that the island is submerged for several months every year compounded the task of the court. To further complicate matters, the German text of the Heligoland-Zanzibar treaty referred to an imprecise concept, the 'thalweg' of the main channel. Unable to reach an agreement, both parties in 1996 signed a Special Agreement referring the dispute to the ICJ. The court was requested 'to determine on the basis of the Anglo-German treaty of 1 July 1890 and the rules and principles of international law, the boundary between Namibia and Botswana around Kasikili/Sedudu Island and the legal status of the island'. In order to resolve this problem, both Namibia and Botswana supported their respective positions by adducing voluminous scientific evidence and relying on conflicting colonial-era maps showing the island as within their own territory.

Namibia's case. Namibia contended that the interpretation of the relevant part of the treaty involved a question of scientific fact, calling for expertise in hydrology, geology and hydro-geomorphology. Botswana disagreed, arguing that scientific evidence was 'irrelevant and supererogatory' to the determination of the location of the river boundary and to the application to that situation of the words 'centre of the main channel' and 'thalweg'. This early skirmish in the forensic battle notwithstanding, both parties produced scientific evidence to shore up their respective case. The focus of Namibia's scientific evidence was on three items, namely, the volume of water carried by the Chobe River, the deposition of sediment in it and the geomorphology of the river. For Namibia, the main channel of a river is the one with the capacity to carry the largest flow, and in the case of the River Chobe the south channel carried substantially all of its annual flow. The scientific criterion defined that the main channel is the velocity of flow and so the main channel is the one that conveyed the largest proportion of the annual flow of the river. It followed from the available scientific evidence that the main channel is the southern channel. Further, the size of a river is measured by its ability to transport debris and the maximum sediment load it can carry. In normal hydrological practice, the size of the channel is measured by the flow volume. The relationship between flow volume and sediment resulted from the fact that the energy transporting the sediment load comes from the volume and velocity of the flow. There were clear indications of the movement of sediment and therefore flow through the southern channel.

Namibia went on to reject Botswana's scientific evidence based on a sedimentological study of the soils of the island which Botswana had carried out. It argued that the studies carried out by Botswana failed to take a sample of the material in the natural levee along the right bank of the northern channel which had fine material, readily erodible sand and not the black clay found in the upper layer of the core samples on the rest of the island. Regarding the geomorphology of the river, Namibia contended that major floods and frequent movements of the tributaries of the river cause the silting up of the southern channel thereby shifting the channel from the southern to the northern channel. The predominant downstream flow at the Island is along the course of the southern channel, the northern channel being a relic channel of a previous phase in the passage of the Zambezi River through its floodplain. The present course of the Chobe River around Kasikili/Sedudu Island had to be resolved in favour of the southern channel. For Namibia, the thalweg concept was irrelevant though even if the concept was thought to be relevant, the core element of this concept is the connection of the thalweg with the flow or current of the river, the factor of depth being derivative and secondary.

Botswana's case. Botswana strongly disputed Namibia's scientific evidence and conclusion. Its own scientific evidence came from two commissioned reports, a Joint Survey Report of 1985 by a team of experts in hydrology, geology and geomorphology, and a 1996 Report on the Sedimentological Study of the soils of the island and supplemented by flow measurements taken in 1997 and 1998. Both studies came to the conclusion that the northern channel is the main channel. Based on the scientific evidence of these geomorphological, hydrological and field studies, Botswana argued that the northern channel, by reason of the greater depth, width and bed profile, is the navigable channel capable of carrying the greater flow and hence the main channel of the river in the vicinity of the island. In the view of Botswana, these studies also provide convincing scientific support for the evolution of the present topography and comparative flows around the island. Botswana assailed Namibia's submission on this point as based on a misreading of the topography of the region, a misreading of the hydrological and geomorphological characteristics of the Chobe River and on erroneous conclusions drawn about sediments, bank erosion and sediment bars.

Botswana drew attention to sampling which, in its view, indicated that the sediment deposits showed no significant difference in the deposition of fresh sediment or their visual characteristics from the sediment deposition pattern of other zones on the island. It argued that the continuity of the northern channel with the direction of the Chobe upstream indicated strongly that the channel carried the bulk of flow and continued the thalweg of the upstream river. The existence of three small islands at the western exit of the southern channel, 'the crenelated nature' of the southern channel and its angle of exit, all suggest, in the view of Botswana, a hydraulically inefficient channel. For Botswana, the Report on the Sedimentological Study established inter alia that (i) a black top layer consisting of clay, silt and mud mixture extending to about 1.5 m depth was distributed evenly across all parts of the island and so its presence cannot be used to identify the path of the Chobe through the southern channel; (ii) the sand which underlay the island was not of fluvial origin as it was predominantly angular. If the river had brought the sand from afar, it would have been rounded out in transit; moreover, the many swamps through which the river system passed would have filtered out such sand fraction; (iii) the right bank of the northern channel was not composed of readily erodible material but by the same top peaty layer of material. Given this peaty material and the fact that the Chobe is a low-energy river the evidence of erosion of bank collapse of the right bank was limited.

Botswana further submitted that aeolian (wind formed) bars and sediment bars (channel features formed by fluvial deposition) were located at the mouth of the entrance to the southern channel. Photographs indicate that sand banks block the entrance to the southern channel, not the northern channel. The four loaf-like sand deposits on the meander loop of the southern channel were not such channel features and do not have the shape or orientation of channel bars. Sediment bars do not lie traverse in the direction of the flow as these 'deposits' do. Their peculiar shape suggests a wind-blown origin. Botswana submitted that the accepted scientific definition of the thalweg is 'the line of maximum depth along a river channel'. From the totality of the scientific evidence adduced, Botswana was able to conclude that in terms of the volume of flow and hydraulic characteristics (depth, surface width and velocity) and the sedimentology of the soils composing the disputed Island, the northern channel qualifies to be classified as the main channel of the Chobe River in the vicinity of Kasikili/Sedudu Island.

Ruling of the ICJ. In order to make a determination regarding the main channel at the bifurcation of the Chobe River, the ICJ considered the depth and the width of the northern and southern channels, the flow, the bed profile configuration and the navigability of each channel. After considering the figures submitted by both parties, as well as surveys carried out on the ground at different periods, the court concluded that the northern channel of the Chobe River around Kasikili/Sedudu Island must be regarded as its main channel. In the view of the court, the boundary between Botswana and Namibia around Kasikili/Sedudu Island follows the line of deepest soundings in the northern channel of the Chobe River and so the Island formed part of the territory of Botswana.

Burkina Faso and Mali: Disputed Alignment of the Frontier Line

In the dispute between Burkina Faso and Mali over a section of the frontier line in the Agacher area, the armies of both countries sporadically clashed from 1975 to 1983 until a ceasefire was eventually concluded thanks to the OAU. At issue was the delimitation of a sector of the common frontier between the two countries. This entailed ascertaining what frontier line had been inherited from the French colonial administration in that area. In resolving the dispute, the ICJ emphasized two fundamental principles applicable to the case: the principle of intangibility of frontiers inherited from colonization and the principle of *uti possidetis juris* which, though of general scope in matters of decolonization, is of exceptional importance for the African continent as it accords pre-eminence to legal title, defined by frontiers, over effective possession as a basis of sovereignty. The court observed that *uti possidetis juris* has exceptional importance for the African continent due to the fact that the primary aim of the principle is to secure respect for the territorial boundaries which existed at the time an African territory achieved independence.[11]

Cameroon and Nigeria: Territorial Claim to the Bakassi Peninsula

The land and maritime dispute between Cameroon and Nigeria ended up in the ICJ.[12] On 29 March 1994, Cameroun filed an application instituting a case before the ICJ against Nigeria. This case was initially framed as a dispute relating to the question of sovereignty over the Bakassi Peninsula but later expanded to include the delimitation of the entire land and maritime boundary between the parties from Lake Chad to the Gulf of Guinea. In 2002, the ICJ ruled on the entire Cameroon–Nigeria land and maritime boundary. The court held that the relevant instruments of delimitation were the Milne-Simon Declaration, 1916, legally confirmed in 1919 under the Treaty of Versailles, the Thomson-Marchand Declaration 1929–1930 and the Henderson-Fleuria Exchange of Notes 1931. It clarified that its task as far as the land boundary was concerned was not to delimit the boundary *de novo* or to demarcate it. Its task, as requested by the parties, was 'to specify definitively' the course of the maritime boundary and the land boundary, from Lake Chad down to the Gulf of Guinea, as fixed by the relevant instruments.

There are two aspects of the land dispute between the parties: first, territorial claim to the 1,000-square-kilometre Bakassi Peninsula in the Gulf of Guinea, a claim framed as a title to the peninsula; second, specification of the land boundary separating the parties to the dispute, as to the territorial claim to Bakassi. The peninsula is situated in the hollow of that Gulf. It is bounded by the River Akwayafe to the west and by the Rio del Rey to the east. The Anglo-German treaty of 11 March 1913 on the settlement of the frontier between the British Protectorate of Nigeria and the German *Schutzgebiet von Kamerun* provided that the frontier in that coastal area shall follow the *thalweg* of the Akwayafe River and that should the lower course of the river 'so change its mouth as to transfer it to the Rio del Rey, it is agreed that the area now known as the Bakassi Peninsula shall still remain German territory'. The treaty also provided that 'the boundary shall follow the centre of the navigable channel of the Akwayafe River as far as the 3-mile limit of territorial jurisdiction' and that for the purpose of defining this boundary 'the navigable channel of the Akwayafe River shall be considered to lie wholly to the east of the navigable channel of the Cross and Calabar Rivers'. These provisions proved easy to interpret in resolving ownership of the peninsula. It was clear that Bakassi lies to the German *Kamerun* side of the border. Nigeria's attempt to establish title over the peninsula on the basis of historical consolidation of title or prescriptive acquisition was rejected by the court as incapable of displacing Cameroon's conventional title.

Concerning the specification of the terrestrial boundary between both countries from Lake Chad down to the Gulf of Guinea, the court noted that the boundary had been delimited and approved by Britain and France. The court further noted that the Lake Chad sector had been demarcated from 1983 to 1991 by the Lake Chad Basin Commission. The court did not accept Nigeria's arguments based on Nigeria's presence in the disputed Lake Chad sector localities, historical consolidation of title and peaceful possession coupled with acts of administration. In the view of the court, historical consolidation of title is a controversial theory that cannot replace modes of acquisition of title recognized by international law. The court found that Cameroon was the holder of a pre-existing title over the disputed areas and that there had been no manifest acquiescence by Cameroon to the relinquishment of this title in favour of Nigeria. It thus held that sovereignty over settlements situated to the east of the boundary continued to lie with Cameroon.

Nigeria, Chad, Cameroun and Niger share Lake Chad, a freshwater lake. The lake has decreased dramatically in size from about an average of 4,000 square miles in the dry season in the 1960s to only 839 square miles presently.

Some of the reasons for this shrinkage include human actions relating to climate variations, increasing demands of the ever-expanding population in the area and animal overgrazing that has the effect of reducing vegetation in the region. The reasons for the shrinkage further include overgrazing that has the effect of reducing the ability of the ecosystem to recycle moisture bask into the atmosphere, droughts causing an increased demand for lake water to irrigate crops and desertification problems caused by the gradual southward push of the Sahara Desert. (Price, 2005). The land disputes in the lake region displaced fishermen as a result of drought and desertification. In order to avoid boundary disputes at the lake, there is a need for the riparian states to conclude a treaty on the delimitation of their respective areas.

Preference for Settlement by the ICJ rather than through Bilateral Diplomacy

Parties to some land disputes tried to resolve them through an initial appeal to force but realized its futility and subsequently opted for international judicial settlement. In some other cases, the parties concerned avoided violence and directly submitted their dispute for international judicial settlement. African states have now signed up to AU arrangements, including non-aggression pacts and commitments to peace such as the AU agreement in respect of the Great Lakes region. These arrangements seek to ensure that both intrastate and interstate disputes are resolved peaceably. More recently, there has been a flurry of AU/UN peacekeeping activities in trouble spots in Africa such as Congo Democratic Republic, Somalia, Central African Republic, Mali, Ivory Coast, South Sudan and the Darfur region of Sudan. This is a welcome development.

Litigation in the ICJ has been the preferred method of resolving interstate boundary disputes. But international litigation is expensive and long drawn.[13] The ICJ, of course, applies international law in resolving territorial and border disputes referred to it for settlement. The Eurocentric content of aspects of international law has always drawn sharp criticism from some scholars, especially those from the global south (Snyder & Sathirathai, 1987; Anand, 1966). Some other scholars too criticize the application of contemporary international law to the resolution of these African disputes (Oduntan, 2015). While these criticisms are valid, the fact of the matter is that African states accepted, as an incidence of their nascent statehood, the legitimacy of much of the corpus of international law although they also challenged some of its norms as unaccommodating of their political and economic interests as well as their ideas and values. The basic argument is that African countries were not participants in the development of rules of international law on account of the fact they were only 'recently' decolonized and became subjects of international law. This argument still retains much of its force with regards to customary international law, but it is probably less compelling regarding treaties concluded after African states attained statehood and participated in the framing of those instruments. For example, the international law of the sea applies in the resolution of disputes about maritime delimitation. Much of that law is contained in the 1982 United Nations Convention on the Law of the Sea. The African states that were independent at the time effectively participated in the ten-year-long discussions that led to the conclusion of that treaty. The rules of international law formulated in that instrument were not adopted on the basis of an established framework or philosophical assumptions earlier agreed upon in the absence of African states.

A land boundary dispute may also be resolved through bilateral diplomacy. However, this is seldom the case in Africa. Even where the parties have negotiated a bilateral agreement, all too often they tend to prefer a third party 'honest broker', as it were, who would underwrite the agreement as a kind of insurance that commitments made would be kept and implemented by each side. For example, the Greentree Agreement on the implementation of the ICJ decision in the *Cameroon v Nigeria case* was underwritten by the big powers in the manner of the grand old practice of guaranteed neutralization. There are two possible explanations why African states tend to shy away from resolving an interstate land boundary dispute through bilateral diplomatic negotiations. First, it is probably the case that some states lack legal and diplomatic negotiating capacity and skills and therefore feel ashamed having to resort to hiring skills from outside. Nevertheless, in this regard, not a few ex-French colonial territories depend on France to provide that expertise.

Second, a bilateral agreement concluded between heads of states often runs the risk of being impugned or denounced by the domestic constituency and ratification declined by parliament. Some examples suffice to illustrate the point. One, the Maroua Agreement on Cameroun's boundary with Nigeria negotiated between President Gowon of Nigeria and President Ahidjo of Cameroun in 1975 was denounced by Nigeria as invalid and its parliament declined to ratify it. It took the decision of the ICJ to hold that the agreement was valid as between both countries. Two, President Tombalbaye of Chad and President Gaddafi of Libya apparently concluded an agreement in terms of which the Aouzou Strip was ceded to Libya. The agreement was denounced by Chad as a Libyan forgery. The ICJ could not pronounce on the validity of the claimed cession since Libya was unable to produce the original copy of the agreement. Three, a Libya-Chad unification agreement concluded between President Goukouni and President Gaddafi was also rejected by Chad. Chad said the unification touted by Gaddafi was a disguised form of colonization of Chad by Libya. Four, the agreement concluded in 1935 between French prime minister Pierre Laval and Italian prime minister Benito

Mussolini respecting the boundary between Eritrea (Italian possession) and Djibouti (French possession) was declined ratification by the French Parliament and was therefore not enforceable.

NOTES

1. As of November 2020, the SADR has been recognised by eighty-four states, forty-five of which have since frozen or withdrawn or suspended recognition.
2. *Western Sahara Case*, Advisory Opinion, 16 October 1975, 1975 ICJ Rep.
3. *Case Concerning the Northern Cameroons (Cameroon v United Kingdom)*, Judgement of 21 December 1962, 1963 ICJ Rep.
4. *Case Concerning the Territorial Dispute (Libya v Chad)*, 1994 ICJ Rep 6.
5. ICJ Rep. 2018. Remarkably, many states participated in this case. Thirty-one Member States of the United Nations and the African Union filed written statements. Ten states and the African Union filed written comments on the written statements. Ten states and the African Union subsequently presented written comments on these written statements. Twenty-one states and the African Union participated in the oral proceedings, which took place from 3 September to 6 September 2018.
6. *The Guardian*, 25 February 2019: 'UN court rejects UK's claim of sovereignty over Chagos Islands'. The competence of the ICJ to give advisory opinions is not an exercise in futility devoid of implications. The court's advisory opinions do have weight. They have legal and political implications. Further, the British government's excuse about protection against terrorist threats does not explain why that presumed protection should involve Britain's colonization of other lands and peoples.
7. *The Guardian*, 28 January 2021.
8. *The Guardian*, 28 January 2021: 'Chagos Islands – UN court rejects UK claim to the Chagos Islands in favour of Mauritius'.
9. *The Guardian*, 6 June 2010: 'Lesotho's people plead with South Africa to annex their troubled country'. Lesotho is 30,000 square kilometre in area and has a population of about 2 million inhabitants.
10. *Case Concerning Kasikili/Sedudu Island (Botswana v Namibia)*, Judgment of 13 December 1999.
11. *Case Concerning the Frontier Dispute (Burkina Faso v Mali)*, Judgement of 22 December 1986, 1986 ICJ Rep 554.
12. *Case Concerning the Land and Maritime Boundary between Cameroon and Nigeria (Cameroon v Nigeria: Equatorial Guinea Intervening)*, Judgement of 10 October 2002.
13. A decision by the ICJ in cases of this nature takes between four and eight years on average, depending on how hotly contested the issues submitted for adjudication are. For example, it took the ICJ eight years to hear and rule on the land and maritime dispute between Cameroun and Nigeria and a further six years to implement the ruling: the case was instituted in 1994; the ruling was given in 2002 and it was only in 2008 that the decision was implemented.

Chapter 2

Disputes over Maritime Boundary

Water boundaries give rise to boundary delimitation difficulties in Africa. The most troublesome of water boundaries are river boundaries. The problem is always one of deciding what line in the river should be the boundary and how that line should be defined. It is now settled international law that in the case of a non-navigable river, the boundary line, in the absence of contrary treaty provisions, runs down in the middle of the river or down its principal arm if it has more than one, following the sinuosity of the river, that is to say, all turnings of both banks of the river. This line is known as the 'median line'. The median line principle was adopted for non-navigable rivers by the Versailles Peace Treaties of 1919–1920. In the case of a navigable river, the rule is that the boundary line runs through the middle line of the deepest navigable channel, that is, the *thalweg*. The *thalweg* is in effect the median line of the principal channel of navigation. Where a bridge spans a boundary river, state practice favours the median line of the river or the centre point of the bridge structure as the boundary line on the bridge. The reason for this is the need to preserve the equality of the riparian states with respect to their common interests in the integrity of the structure (Shearer, 1994). The choice of the boundary line is not a point directly above the *thalweg* because that point may shift in the course of time. Exceptionally, under treaty or by long-established peaceable occupation, a boundary line may sometimes lie along one bank of the river, while the whole bed is under the sovereignty of the other riparian state.

Concerning lakes and land-locked seas, the choice of the suitable boundary line depends on the depth, configuration and use of the particular lake or sea concerned. In a shallow lake or sea, the navigable channel, if any, may be taken as a convenient boundary. More generally, the boundary line will be the 'median line', as in the case of a river.

Many special apportionments have been made by treaty, but these have been of the most arbitrary character, and have followed no definite pattern or principle. As to bays or straits, no general rule for boundary delimitation can be given, as considerations of history and geography come into play. On many occasions, however, the 'median line' has been accepted as the boundary. (Shearer, 1994: 175)

Disputes concerning maritime delimitation are now settled in terms of the UNCLOS, the international legal instrument that largely governs matters relating to the sea. The convention is a treaty adopted on 30 April 1982 and entered into force on 16 November 1994. The adoption came after nine years of protracted negotiations to preserve the sea as a common heritage of all mankind and avoid the danger of what has been described as a 'scramble for the seas'. The convention deals with the high seas, the deep seabed and four maritime zones, namely, the territorial sea, the contiguous zone, the exclusive economic zone and the continental shelf.

In Africa as elsewhere, disputes concerning maritime boundary delimitation often arise from unregulated competition by littoral states for sea resources. Unlike other maritime states in Africa, those in the southern Africa region have so far registered no maritime boundary disputes. Coastal states in the other regions of Africa have a long history of maritime boundary disputes; in the Gulf of Guinea: Cameroun/Nigeria, Cameroun/Equatorial Guinea and Equatorial Guinea/Gabon; in West Africa: Côte d'Ivoire/Ghana, Guinea-Bissau/Guinea-Conakry and Guinea-Bissau/Senegal; in East Africa: Uganda/Kenya; in the Horn of Africa: Somalia/Kenya and Eritrea/Djibouti; and in North Africa: Egypt/Sudan and Libya/Tunisia. These maritime boundary disputes may be considered under four heads: shelf claims (Cameroun/Equatorial Guinea and Tunisia/Libya), location of the precise boundary alignment in the disputed maritime area (Cameroun/Nigeria, Cameroun/Equatorial Guinea, Uganda/Kenya, Equatorial Guinea/Gabon and Eritrea/Djibouti), maritime zone claims (Côte d'Ivoire/Ghana, Guinea-Bissau/Guinea-Conakry and Guinea-Bissau/Senegal) and lateral maritime boundary delimitation (Somalia/Kenya). In one case, Egypt/Sudan, the two countries concerned agreed on joint exploration and exploitation in the contested area.

Remarkably, the source of maritime boundary delimitation disputes has always been inherited colonial historical facts. It is invariably the case that the boundary description in the boundary treaty is imprecise. Newly decolonized states failed, in the early years of independence, to deal with the imprecise boundary question. This is particularly the case regarding maritime boundaries. These boundaries began attracting attention only after the importance of the ocean economy became evident. Some disputes have involved mere islets or a number of them. They have been fought with tenacity and dogged determination not because the islands or islets in themselves have any value (they may in fact be uninhabitable or uninhabited) but for the potential or known resources in and under the surrounding waters.

SHELF CLAIMS

Cameroun/Equatorial Guinea

An area of potential but avoidable dispute between Cameroun and Equatorial Guinea is that of the overlapping shelf claims of both coastal states. In May 2009, Equatorial Guinea, like Cameroun in the same year, submitted to the Law of the Sea Commission on Continental Shelf Limits preliminary information on its claim to the outer limits of the continental shelf beyond 200 nautical miles offshore its Annobon Island (also called Pagalu, capital San Antonio de Palé).[1] Equatorial Guinea claims a huge area of the sea surrounding Annobon. The area claimed is larger than the entire land and sea border of the rest of Equatorial Guinea. In its submission, Equatorial Guinea indicated that it was undertaking studies to determine other areas of the continental shelf beyond 200 nautical miles. Equatorial Guinea however acknowledged, as did Cameroun, the possible overlapping claims of neighbouring coastal states but stated that the information it submitted was without prejudice to any other maritime delimitations. It ratified the Law of the Sea Convention in January 1984. It is bound by the Part XI Agreement which deals with the 'Area', that is, the seabed and ocean floor and subsoil thereof. It has delimited its exclusive economic zone with São Tomé and Principe.

Cameroun has a maritime boundary with Equatorial Guinea and although both countries ratified the 1982 Convention on the Law of the Sea,[2] their respective common offshore boundaries in the Gulf of Guinea suffered neglect and incomplete delimitation until comparatively recent times. The impetus to complete the delimitation arose from awareness of enormous economic benefits derivable from offshore oil and gas exploitation in the area. Offshore oil and gas activities have prompted maritime delimitation in the whole of the Gulf of Guinea. Delimitation in the eastern end of the Gulf was complicated at one time by competing territorial and maritime claims between Cameroun and Nigeria in the Bakassi Peninsula. It was further complicated by the fact that further south of the peninsula into the sea, a possible maritime boundary must take into account the interests of Equatorial Guinea to the northwest of the Island of Bioko. Delimitation would be even more complicated when Ambazonia (formerly the trust territory of the British Southern Cameroons), sandwiched between Nigeria to the west and Cameroun to the east, accedes to independence.

Tunisia/Libya

A dispute arose between Tunisia and Libya concerning the delimitation of their common continental shelf in the disputed region. By a special agreement notified to the ICJ in December 1978, the court was asked to determine what principles and rules of international law were applicable to the delimitation as between Tunisia and the Libyan Arab Jamahiriya of the respective areas of continental shelf appertaining to each. The court considered arguments and evidence based on geology, physiography and bathymetry submitted by each party and on the basis of which each sought to support its claims to particular areas of the seabed as the natural prolongation of its land territory.

In a judgement of 24 February 1982, the court found that the area relevant for delimitation constitutes a single continental shelf as the natural prolongation of the land territory of both parties. The court further found that the two countries abutted on a common continental shelf and that physical criteria were therefore of no assistance to the purpose of delimitation.[3] It ruled that the applicable rules of international law had to be 'equitable principles', taking account of relevant circumstances such as the general configuration of the coast of the parties, the existence and position of islands in the area, the land frontier between the parties and the element of a reasonable degree of proportionality between the areas allotted and the lengths of the coastlines concerned.[4] The court noted that equity as a legal concept is a direct emanation of the idea of justice. It emphasized that the term 'equitable principles' cannot be interpreted in the abstract but only as referring to the principles and rules which may be appropriate in order to achieve an equitable result.

The court found that the application of the equidistance method could not, in the particular circumstance of the case, lead to an equitable result. With respect to the course to be taken by the delimitation line, it distinguished two sectors: near the shore, it considered, having taken note of some evidence of historical agreement as to the maritime boundary, that the delimitation (beginning at the boundary point of Ras Adjir) should run in a north-easterly direction at an angle of approximately 26°; further seawards, it considered that the line of delimitation should veer eastwards at a bearing of 52° to take into account the change of direction of the Tunisian coast to the north of the Gulf of Gabes and the existence of the Kerkennah Islands, to which a 'half-effect' was attributed.

During the course of the proceedings, Malta requested permission to intervene, claiming an interest of a legal nature under Article 62 of the court's statute. In view of the very character of the intervention for which permission was sought, the court considered that the interest of a legal nature that Malta had invoked could not be affected by the decision in the case and that the request was not one to which, under Article 62, the court might accede. It therefore rejected it.

Tunisia later filed an application for revision and interpretation of the above judgement. The application was submitted to the court by Tunisia. Tunisia took the view that the 1982 judgement gave rise to certain problems of implementation. The court had already had to deal with several requests for interpretation. But this was the first time an application for *revision* had come before it. The statute of the court states that a judgement may only be revised if there has been a discovery of some fact of such a nature as to be a decisive factor. Libya opposed Tunisia's twofold application, denying that there had been any problems with implementation of the kind invoked by Tunisia and argued that Tunisia's request for interpretation was merely an application for revision, in another guise. In its judgement of 10 December 1985, rendered unanimously, the court rejected the application for revision as inadmissible. It found admissible the request for interpretation of the judgement of 24 February 1982 so far as it related to the first sector of the delimitation laid down by the judgement, stated the interpretation which should be made in that respect, and found that the submission of Tunisia relating to that sector could not be upheld. The court found, moreover, that the request made by Tunisia for the correction of an error was without object and that there was no call for it to give a decision thereon. The court also found admissible the request for interpretation of the judgement of 24 February 1982 so far as it related to the most westerly point of the Gulf of Gabes in the second sector of the delimitation laid down by the judgement. The court indicated the interpretation which should be made in that respect and found that it could not uphold the submission made by Tunisia relating to that sector. In conclusion, the court found that no cause had arisen for it to order an expert survey for the purpose of ascertaining the precise coordinates of the most westerly point of the Gulf of Gabes.

LOCATION OF THE BOUNDARY LINE IN THE DISPUTED COASTAL AREA

Every state has a territory, the tangible attribute of its statehood. A state without territory is a legal impossibility. The territory of a state is the defined portion of the surface of the earth which is subject to that state's sovereignty (Lauterpacht, 1955: 451). It consists of the designated landmass, subsoil, the water enclosed in the landmass (i.e., internal waters), the land under the water, the territorial sea up to 12 nautical miles in breadth and airspace over the landmass and territorial sea. Soil may become relevant in international law in connection with title to territory, particularly in the context of river or maritime boundary between states with opposite or adjacent maritime coasts.

In the contemporary period, a state's claim to a specific portion of the land territory is likely to arise in the context of boundary disputes between bordering states. The operation of geographical processes such as sedimentation, accretion, avulsion, dereliction, reliction or erosion may provoke such a dispute. Dereliction occurs when water gradually recedes, exposing dry land in the process. Reliction, on the other hand, is the process of exposing dry land when a river leaves its old bed forming an entirely new one by a sudden inundation. Erosion is the loss of soil by the gradual encroachment of water (Beck, 1967). Accretion involves the gradual increase in the territory through the operation of nature. It is the process where the action of water causes the gradual and imperceptible deposit of soil in a certain place so that it becomes dry, fast land. For example, the gradual shifting of a river's course may lead, in the case of a boundary international river, to the additional territory through the formation of alluvial deposits and thus giving rise to a boundary dispute in that area. Fine-grained sediments may cause the silting up of the channel of a river and so bring about a river metamorphosis. If accretion occurs on a boundary river between two states, the international boundary between the two affected states may change over time, giving rise to a dispute as to where exactly the boundary line should be drawn. If the river is navigable, the middle of the river stream will constitute the boundary. In law, the river boundary line is often held to move with the channel if the channel shifts slowly due to a process of bank erosion and lateral accretion (Chorley et al., 1984).

Avulsion refers to a violent change, such as a sudden alteration in a river's course. In avulsion the water location changes suddenly or swiftly, as, for example, when a river leaves its old bed forming an entirely new one, inundating land in the process. The term avulsion also applies to the emergence of an island in territorial waters as a result of a volcano or a tsunami. Examples are the Island of Scutsey which appeared in Icelandic territorial waters on 14 November 1963 following a volcanic action; a newly formed island, 200 metres in diameter, in November 2013 in Japanese territorial waters; and the Hunga Tonga-Hunga Ha'apai Island which emerged from January 2015 to September 2017 in Tonga territorial waters in the South Pacific. In cases of avulsion, the international boundary will remain where it was originally established. Thus, the 'birth' of a new island in a state's territorial waters does not affect the breadth of the territorial sea. Similarly, in the case of a boundary river that suddenly changes its course, the boundary will remain along the old river bed, and what then changes would be the ownership of that portion of the river that has suddenly changed its course. It is generally the law that the boundary remains fixed if the change in the course of the river is abrupt and avulsive in nature (Chorley et al., 1984). In *Cameroon v. Nigeria*, the relevant treaty provided that a sudden change of the course of the River Akwayafe would not affect the ownership of the Bakassi Peninsula.

International rivers serve navigational and non-navigational purposes, including serving as delimitation of the boundary between riparian states. The relevant boundary treaty usually delimits exactly where the line of the water boundary passes. If there are any ambiguities in the treaty on this point, its interpretation would take into account any special characteristics of the international river. As a result, a determination is made regarding ownership of the disputed piece of territory. The disputed area where the disputed boundary line passes is often part of a lake or the mouth of a river or offshore waters. Invariably, what is at stake is sovereignty claim to an islet and perceived resources in and around it. A decision that the boundary alignment is on the east or west, north or south, bank of the river in effect gives sovereignty of the islet to one side or the other.

Cameroun/Equatorial Guinea

There is an unresolved sovereignty dispute between Cameroun and Equatorial Guinea over an island at the mouth of the Ntem River. A 20-kilometre section of that river downstream to its mouth constitutes the boundary between both countries. The dispute is a relatively minor one, scarcely causing a ripple internationally. However, for either country, it is nonetheless a dispute of some importance. This is not surprising. Long ago, the great American judge Justice Holmes remarked that a river is 'more than an amenity; it is a treasure. It offers a necessity of life that must be rationed among those who have power over it'.[5] A river is part of the national territory. It is an amenity for navigation, fish stock, farm land, flora, fauna, ecosystem, various water uses such as for drinking, for household and agricultural use, for recreation, for damning and for electricity.

Equatorial Guinea's jurisdiction in the northeast of the Gulf of Guinea radiates from Bioko Island and Rio Muni. Historically, Bioko and Rio Muni were never a single country. In 1956, Spain, the colonial power, amalgamated them as provinces of a single country to which it granted independence in 1968 as the Republic of Equatorial Guinea. Equatorial Guinea is now controlled by the Fang tribe from Rio Muni which has gradually subordinated and reduced the mainly Bubi people of Bioko Island[6] even though much of the country's hydrocarbon wealth comes from fields around that island. The country claims a territorial sea of 12 nautical miles[7] and an exclusive economic zone of 200 nautical miles.[8] The exclusive economic zone claim was a tactical preliminary move to join the *Cameroon v. Nigeria* case and influence the location of the Cameroun-Equatorial Guinea-Nigeria tripoint. Equatorial Guinea did in fact intervene in that case. In delimiting the maritime boundary between 'Cameroon' and Nigeria from the Bakassi Peninsula southwards into the sea, the ICJ gave partial effect to the Equatoguinean Island of Bioko.

The mainland enclave of Equatorial Guinea borders the Atlantic on areas claimed by Cameroun and Gabon. A dispute between Cameroun and Equatorial Guinea over the Ile de Dipikar, an island off the mouth of the Ntem River, remains unresolved. The River Ntem rises from Cameroun and flows wholly within Cameroun territory downstream to Yengué where it becomes a frontier river between Cameroun and Equatorial Guinea. It then continues its flow further downstream for about 20 kilometre to its mouth at the Atlantic Ocean at Campo Point. The disputed island is located at the mouth of the river. Cameroun maps show the whole length of the Ntem River from its source to its mouth as wholly within the territory of Cameroun as a national river. They depict the river boundary from Yengué to Campo Point as lying along the south bank of the river thus implying that this portion of the river, including the disputed island, also falls within Cameroun sovereignty. This is disputed by the other riparian state, Equatorial Guinea. The River Ntem is not navigable. But it has potential non-navigational uses such as irrigation, hydroelectric power, fishing, flood control, sand-harvesting and even small-scale fluvial mining for gold. Ownership of the island would clearly determine the boundary alignment along the river at that point. The present boundaries of the Equatoguinean mainland territory of Rio Muni were settled in 1900 by the Franco-Spanish Treaty of June 1900. But the treaty is silent on the appurtenance of this island.

Cameroun/Nigeria

The 'Cameroon'-Nigeria dispute over the Bakassi Peninsula caused prolonged friction and tension between both countries and attained a pitch that threatened international peace and security.[9] The Anglo-Germany Agreements of 11 March and 12 April 1913 describe the boundary line between the contiguous territories of Nigeria (British) and Kamerun (German) from Lake Chad down to the Bakassi Peninsula in the Gulf of Guinea at the Atlantic Ocean. A few months after the outbreak of World War I in 1914, the Kamerun territory, barely twenty-seven years as an entity, was overrun by Britain and France. In February 1916, pending the conclusion of World War I, both powers provisionally partitioned the German colonial territory along the Milner-Simon Line from Lake Chad down to the mouth of the River Mungo in the Gulf of Guinea at the Atlantic Ocean. France got away with the area to the east, becoming the mandated/trust territory of French Cameroun which was then administered along with the contiguous territories of French Equatorial Africa.

Britain took the area to the west of that line, becoming the mandated/trust territory of the British Cameroons (divided into two parts – the Southern Cameroons and the Northern Cameroons) and administered as though it formed an integral part of the adjacent British territory of Nigeria. The British Cameroons trust territory thus had a common boundary with Nigeria running from Lake Chad to the Bakassi Peninsula, described in the Anglo-German Agreements of 1913. It also had a common boundary with French Cameroun from Lake Chad to the River Mungo in the Gulf of Guinea, described in the Simon-Milner-Simon Line of 1916, a territorial alignment confirmed as permanent in 1919 and again in 1931 (Brownlie, 1979: 553). This territorial alignment was confirmed by both the League of Nations and the UN. It is thus the Southern Cameroons, formerly a trust territory under British administration, which has a maritime boundary with Nigeria at the Bakassi Peninsula and not Cameroun Republic, formerly French Cameroun, its coast being some 150 kilometre, as the crow flies, southeast from Bakassi.

The *'Cameroon' v. Nigeria* case was about two things: the specification of the land boundary between the two parties from Lake Chad down to the Bakassi Peninsula in the Gulf of Guinea and the delimitation of the maritime boundary in the Gulf of Guinea, as between the two parties.[10] As in the case of other boundary disputes in contemporary Africa, this dispute had its root in imprecise boundary delimitation by colonial treaties and the neglect by the nascent states to proceed to demarcation of the boundary line.

In January 1960, French Cameroun achieved independence under the name and style of *République du Cameroun* (variously translated in English as 'Republic of Cameroun' or 'Republic of Cameroon' or simply as 'Cameroon' or 'Cameroun'). In September 1961, Cameroun surreptitiously laid claim to the British Southern Cameroons (Ambazonia) as part of its territory. In October, the departing British colonial authority purportedly transferred powers to Cameroun which then assumed a contested colonial authority over Ambazonia. Cameroun then started issuing maps in 1973 that represented its territory as having a maritime boundary with Nigeria at the Bakassi Peninsula firmly located within Ambazonia. That peninsula is more than 400 kilometre by road to the northwest of its legitimate maritime boundary at the mouth of the Mungo River, adjacent to the Douala estuary. In spite of this controversial development, the people of Ambazonia always 'feel more linguistically linked to Nigeria' and have always known that 'they are the rightful owners of Bakassi' (Price, 2005). The cultural, historical, language, educational, social and economic ties between the peoples of Ambazonia and those of Nigeria have always been strong. These ties were woven over a period of half a century of the British administration of Ambazonia as an integral part of Nigeria.

Cameroun has always been fearful of what it considers as 'l'impérialisme potential du Nigeria' (Nigeria's potential imperialism). It has also always been fearful of the effect of the centrifugal forces that it dreads might be set in motion by continued strong ties between the people of Ambazonia and those of Nigeria. It adopted policies meant to deter people-to-people ties with Nigeria. It acted to frustrate trade links between the peoples of Ambazonia and those of Nigeria. It imposed a prohibitive tax on Nigerian goods entering Ambazonia. When these measures yielded no tangible results, Cameroun's military periodically sought and destroyed in situ any Nigerian products found in shops and markets in Ambazonia. This operation was expanded to include regular harassment of Nigerian traders and fishermen in the border area as well as of Nigerians entering or leaving Ambazonia.

These muscular actions and unceasing harassment against Nigerians led to intermittent clashes with Nigerian soldiers in the contested maritime area, especially following the killing there of some Nigerians by Cameroun soldiers, a killing for which Cameroun president Ahidjo apologized. Officially, the military skirmishes were said to be due to the imprecise nature of the maritime boundary. The Nigeria-Cameroun bilateral negotiations in Yaoundé, Kano and Maroua from 1971 to 1975 resulted in signed agreements aimed at resolving this problem. The boundary line drawn in the Maroua Agreement acknowledged the fact that Bakassi Peninsula lies to the east of the boundary line described in the 11 March 1913 Anglo-German Agreements. Following the overthrow of President Gowon shortly after signing the Maroua Agreement, subsequent Nigerian governments asserted Nigerian sovereignty over the peninsula, impugned the validity of the Maroua Agreement, denied the constitutional power of President Gowon to have signed the said agreement and pleaded the non-ratification of the agreement by Nigerian Parliament. Cameroun on the other hand asserted the validity and force of the agreement.

In the face of this disagreement, there continued to be friction between the two parties. Cameroun and Nigeria have always had an uneasy border relation in part because of the imprecision of the boundary alignment between the two countries and in part also because Yaoundé has always considered Abuja 'hegemonic and a very difficult neighbour'. The festering boundary and territorial disputes between Abuja and Yaoundé erupted into violence in May 1981 following the killing earlier in the year of five Nigerian soldiers by a Cameroun coastguard patrol and the continued harassment by Cameroun gendarmes of Nigerians moving in and out of Ambazonia. The Cameroun president apologized for the killings but not for the continued harassment of Nigerians. Intermittent border skirmishes between the military of both countries continued for about ten years. By December 1993, Nigerian troops had enough and simply moved in and occupied the peninsula, partly inhabited by a large number of Nigerian ethnic community, the Effik. Nigeria then quickly annexed the peninsula and consolidated its hold. It established there a Nigerian civil administration and constituted it into a Nigerian local government area. Cameroun reckoned that taking the peninsula militarily from Nigeria was clearly not feasible even if it counted on French military help, having intimated it was going to invoke its military 'cooperation' accord with France. There followed a long border war of attrition that was not finally resolved until thirteen years afterwards. Finally, Cameroun advisedly decided to have judicial recourse.

On 29 March 1994, Cameroun filed an application before the ICJ instituting proceedings against Nigeria. The case was initially framed as a dispute relating to the question of sovereignty over the Bakassi Peninsula, and hence a territorial dispute. The case was later expanded to include the delimitation of the entire land and maritime boundary between the parties from Lake Chad to the Gulf of Guinea. Nigeria's counter-memorial on the merits of the case was filed on 31 May 1999. In 2002, the ICJ ruled on the entire Cameroon–Nigeria land and maritime boundary in *Case Concerning the Land and Maritime Boundary between Cameroon and Nigeria (Cameroon v. Nigeria: Equatorial Guinea Intervening)*, Judgement of 10 October 2002. The court held that the relevant instruments of delimitation were the Milne-Simon Declaration 1916 approved at the Versailles Peace Conference in 1919, the Thomson-Marchand Declaration 1929–1930 and the Henderson-Fleurier Exchange of Notes 1931. It clarified that its task as far as the land boundary was concerned was not to delimit the boundary *de novo* or to demarcate it. Its task, as requested by the parties, was '*to specify definitively*' the course of the boundary as fixed by the relevant instruments.

On the question of sovereignty over the Bakassi Peninsula, Nigeria advanced a number of arguments: that the Anglo-German Agreement of 1913 was defective on the grounds that it was contrary to the preamble to the General Act of the Berlin Conference 1885, that the 1913 Agreement had in fact not been approved by the German parliament and that the agreement had been abrogated by Article 289 of the Treaty of Versailles 1919. Nigeria also impugned the legal validity of the Anglo-German Agreement on the ground of inconsistency with the principle *nemo dat quod non habet* as far as the Bakassi provisions of the agreement were concerned. Nigeria contended that 'title to sovereignty over Bakassi . . . was originally vested in the Kings and Chiefs of Old Calabar . . . [and was] in no way . . . transfer[red] . . . to Britain under the Anglo-Calabar Treaty of Protection 1884'. The court rejected these arguments.

> Britain had a clear understanding of the area ruled at different times by the kings and chiefs of Old Calabar and had in 1913 been in a position to determine its

boundary in Nigeria with Germany, including in the Bakassi Peninsula. Bakassi was covered by the terms of the Mandate over the British Cameroons and the separate status of the British Cameroons had been preserved by the British Order in Council of 1923. The territorial situation remained unchanged under the Trusteeship Agreements for the British Cameroons. Although the British Northern and Southern Cameroons were administered 'as if they formed part of Nigeria', the boundary between Bakassi and Nigeria remained an international boundary. Bakassi formed part of the Southern Cameroons under British Trusteeship. During negotiations between the parties on maritime issues, Nigeria had accepted the legal validity of the Anglo-German Agreement and had recognised Cameroon sovereignty over Bakassi Peninsula, the parties' common position being reflected in geographic patterns of their oil concessions up to 1991. The Anglo-German Agreement was therefore valid and applicable in its entirety. Historical consolidation cannot give Nigeria title over Bakassi where its occupation of the Peninsula is adverse to Cameroon's prior conventional title. Nigeria was unable to act *à titre de souverain* before late 1970s, as it did not then regard itself as having title to Bakassi. There was insufficient evidence after the late 1970s that Cameroon acquiesced in relinquishing its title in favour of Nigeria. Consequently, in accordance with the delimitation of the boundary as described in articles 18-20 of the Anglo-German Agreement, sovereignty over Bakassi lies with Cameroon. (*Cameroon v. Nigeria*, ICJ Judgement, 10 October 2002, Cause List No. 94, para. 238 et seq.)

The ICJ went on to specify definitively the maritime boundary between both parties, according to partial effect to the Equatoguinean Island of Bioko. It specified the maritime boundary between the parties in the following manner. First, the boundary in Bakassi follows the *thalweg* of the Akwayafe River, dividing the Mangrove islands near Ikang in the way shown on the map, as far as the straight line joining Bakassi Point and King Point. Second, up to point G shown on the sketch, the boundary of the maritime areas appertaining respectively to each party takes a course starting from the point of intersection of the centre of the navigable channel of the Akwayafe River with the straight line joining Bakassi Point and King Point. The boundary then follows the 'compromise line' drawn jointly by both parties and passes through twelve numbered points whose coordinates are as indicated by the court. Third, from point twelve, the boundary follows the line adopted by both parties, as corrected by the exchange of letters between them, and passes through points A to G. Fourth, from Point G, the boundary line between the maritime areas appertaining respectively to each party follows a loxodrome having an azimuth of 270° as far as the equidistance line passing through the midpoint of the line joining West Point and East Point. The boundary meets this equidistance line at a point X, with coordinates of 8° 21′ 20″ longitude E and 4° 17′ 00″ latitude north. Fifth, from point X, the boundary between the maritime areas appertaining respectively to each party follows a loxodrome having an azimuth of 187° 52′ 27″. The court thus agreed with Nigeria that the equidistant line between the parties provided an equitable result. It did not, however, specify a definite location off the coast of Equatorial Guinea where the maritime boundary between the two parties would terminate.

Implementation of this maritime boundary delimitation was for a time impeded by certain factors. First, the definition of the coordinates of the boundary was imprecise. Second, Nigeria went back on its earlier acceptance in September 2004 to withdraw from the peninsula. It argued that Nigerian public opinion opposed withdrawal. It also argued that Nigerians residents in the peninsula oppugn withdrawal on account of Yaoundé's dismal human rights record, are unwilling to relinquish their Nigerian citizenship to take up a Cameroun citizenship they regard as very weak and meaningless, reject the very idea that they could opt to be citizens of a French-speaking country and demand a plebiscite based on the right to self-determination. A third impediment to the implementation of the maritime boundary delimitation was a motion moved and adopted in Nigeria's parliament declaring as unconstitutional any handover of the peninsula. The Nigerian government itself indicated that many technical problems stood in the way of withdrawal. It contended that withdrawal would lead to the collapse of law and order in the peninsula, jeopardizing Nigeria's security and would be tantamount to giving Cameroun a free hand to continue its gross human rights abuses of Nigerian citizens. It further argued that withdrawal would pose a major obstacle to the potential development of offshore oil reserves near the Bakassi Peninsula.

In June 2006, Abuja and Yaoundé signed the Greentree Treaty. Underwritten by the Big Powers, the bilateral treaty agreed on a number of guarantees for Nigerians in the peninsula. Nigeria and Cameroun formed a Joint Border Commission to meet regularly to resolve differences bilaterally. The commission commenced demarcation in less contested sections of the boundary, starting in Lake Chad in the north. It reviewed the 2002 ruling on the entire border and bilaterally resolved all outstanding differences, including differences in the June 2006 Greentree Agreement that immediately ceded sovereignty of the Bakassi Peninsula to 'Cameroon' with a full phase-out of Nigerian control and repatriation of residents who wish to leave. The parties agreed maritime delimitation in March 2008 and Nigeria eventually withdrew its forces from the Bakassi Peninsula, after three decades of conflict and litigation.

Uganda/Kenya

Migingo is an islet in Lake Victoria claimed by both Uganda and Kenya. It is a tiny 2,000 square metres (0.20 hectres) island inhabited by about 130 fishermen. According to official maps since 1926 the islet belongs to Kenya. In 2008, the islet was claimed by both Kenya and Uganda. Uganda's claim appears to have been prompted by the lucrative fishing rights mostly for the valuable Nile perch and the fact that Ugandan waters come within about 500 metres to the west of the island. In July 2009, Uganda claimed much of the waters near Migingo as appertaining to Ugandan. But eventually, it officially conceded that the islet is Kenyan and withdrew its security presence from the island. A joint re-demarcation line of the maritime border was undertaken in 2009 to recover and place survey beacons on land, making delineation of the boundary on the lake more precise. The results of this work were released in late July 2009 confirming that the islet falls 510 metres on the Kenyan side of the line.

Equatorial Guinea/Gabon

Equatorial Guinea and Gabon, though small in size and population, are African major oil exporters. The oil output of Gabon and Equatorial Guinea are, respectively, about 250,000 and 350,000 barrels per day. This has not diminished each country's appetite for more oil fields. Gabon has an opposite shoreline with the Equatoguinean Island of Bioko and an adjacent coastline with that country's mainland territory of Rio Muni. The area that is the subject of the sovereignty dispute between both countries comprises the island of Mbanié and three small islands (Cocotiers, Conga and Corisco) located in Corisco Bay north of the Gabonese capital Libreville, near the border with Rio Muni. The offshore waters in that Bay are potentially oil-rich and believed to have reserves of several hundred thousand barrels of oil. Gabon and Equatorial Guinea are, respectively, former French and Spanish colonial territories. There appears to have been a French presence on the disputed islands before 1950. But that presence was ended in the mid-1950s when the Spanish colonial authorities in Equatorial Guinea removed the French from those islands without any protest from Paris.

The crux of the maritime and territorial dispute between Gabon and Equatorial Guinea relates to the different interpretation, by both states, of Article 7 of the Franco-Spanish Convention of 27 June 1900 on the frontier between Gabon and the Equatoguinean mainland territory of Rio Muni. The dispute surfaced in 1972 when Gabon extended its territorial sea. The matter then went dormant for twenty-three years. It was re-ignited in October 1995 when Equatoguinean authorities seized Gabonese fishing boats near Corisco Island. Four years later, in 1999, Equatorial Guinea claimed a 200 nautical miles Exclusive Economic Zone that extended south of the hypothetical median line shown on the map (Dzurek & Schofield, 2001). This extension used islands in the bay as baselines, thereby discounted part of Gabon's coastline at the southern entrance to Corisco Bay. Both countries eventually agreed to submit the maritime boundary dispute, and by implication the status of the Corisco Bay islands, to UN mediation. The Multilateral Investment Guarantee Agency (World Bank) helped broker an agreement which was signed in January 2004.

The resolution of the Corisco Bay dispute however still left unresolved the dispute relating to the other contested island, the tiny 30-hectre island of Mbanié with its potentially oil-rich surrounding waters. The territorial dispute over this island, located 30 kilometres from Pointe Mdombo, was in gestation for a long period of time. It resurfaced in 2003 when Ali Bongo, the then Gabonese defence minister, now president, visited the island of Mbanié and reasserted its appurtenance to Gabon. This action elicited swift reaction from Equatorial Guinea whose Prime Minister Candido Muatetema Rivas expressed over radio his government's deep concern and indignation at Gabon's 'illegal' occupation of the small island of Mbanié. Then in March 2004, in an act of brinksmanship, Gabon registered with the UN a document it claimed was a treaty delimiting the land and maritime boundary with Equatorial Guinea and which, it further claimed, entered into force the day it was signed. According to Gabon, it concluded an agreement with Equatorial Guinea in 1974 in which the latter recognized Mbanié as appertaining to Gabon.

Equatorial Guinea challenged the validity of the document. It refuted the Gabonese claim and raised objections with the UN, contending that no such treaty was ever signed by both countries. It conceded that it was in negotiations with Gabon for thirty years to establish a maritime boundary but maintained that those negotiations were fruitless. The UN simply proffered to Equatorial Guinea the piece of advice that Gabon's registration of the document conferred it legal status. Both countries are parties to the UNCLOS. But Gabon, imitating France, has opted out of compulsory dispute resolution for disputes concerning interpretation or application of Articles 15, 74 and 83 relating to sea boundary delimitations. The option of compulsory dispute resolution under that treaty was therefore out of the question. The president of Gabon did for a while canvass the possibility of referring the dispute to the ICJ. But both countries eventually agreed to submit it instead to the UN secretary general Kofi Anan who appointed a Canadian lawyer Mr Yvon Fortier as mediator. As an interim measure, both parties agreed to jointly exploit the area until the dispute is resolved. This has considerably reduced the possibility of confrontation in that oil-and-gas-producing Bay.

Interestingly, in this dispute Gabon has the support of France, its former colonial parent state, in part because Gabonese oil fields are controlled by France and mainly operated by the French multinational Total/Fina/Elf. On the other hand, Equatorial Guinea's offshore oilfields, discovered in 1995, are mostly operated by the US oil giants ExxonMobil, Amerada Hess and Marathon. Equatorial Guinea is thus seen as having the support of the United States which is concerned about the security of oil supplies from the turbulent Middle East and has made no secret of its ambition to import more oil from more reliable sources in the Gulf of Guinea.

Eritrea/ Djibouti

Eritrea, anciently part of the Ethiopian kingdom of Aksum, was colonized by Italy from 1890 until 1941, when it was captured by the British during the World War II. There followed a period of British and UN supervision which ended in 1952 with Eritrea being awarded to Ethiopia as part of a federation. But Ethiopia annexed Eritrea as a province in 1962, leading to a thirty-one-year-long struggle for independence which was declared on 24 May 1993. Regarding Djibouti, France took control of what became French Somaliland in stages between 1862 and 1900. French Somaliland became in 1945 an overseas territory of France and was renamed in 1967 as the French Territory of the Afars and the Issas. Ethnically, the Afars are related to Ethiopians and the Issas to Somalis. The territory achieved independence on 27 June 1977 as Djibouti. At one time, Ethiopia and Somalia asserted claim to the territory but each later renounced its claim to the area, though each accused the other of trying to gain control.

The international boundary between both countries was determined in a boundary agreement concluded in 1900 between Italy and France. The boundary alignment starts at Cape Doumeira (Ras Doumeira) at the Red Sea and runs for 1.5 kilometres along the watershed divide of the peninsula. The boundary agreement did not specify the appurtenance of Doumeira Island and its adjacent smaller islets, which was a serious lapse in the treaty. It demilitarized those islands without saying to which country they appertained. In January 1935, Italy and France signed the Laval-Mussolini Agreement wherein a substantial part of French Somaliland was transferred to Eritrea. But the actual boundary alignment at Ras Doumeira, a hill, was never fully demarcated. The Laval-Mussolini Agreement merely stipulated broadly that the northern slopes of the hill were Italian and the southern slopes were French. The shared adjacent maritime boundary between Eritrea and Djibouti is a mere 10.5 nautical miles long in the northern approaches to the Straight of Bab el Mandeb to a tripoint with the opposite state of Yemen. The delimitation of this frontier would give a lateral territorial sea boundary between both African countries (Dzurek & Schofield, 2001). But this has not yet been done because of the dispute relating to the sovereignty of the islands of Dumeira (Doumeira) and Callida in the Straight, just offshore the land boundary terminus. Eritrea does not accept a median line solution because the presence of these islands would deflect a median line to its disadvantage (Dzurek & Schofield, 2001).

The genesis of the 2008 dispute between both countries is a map produced by Eritrea in 1996 representing about 290 square kilometre of northern Djibouti as belonging to Eritrea. The area cartographically incorporated into Eritrea is a triangular portion of Djibouti along the coast near Ras Doumeira and Dar-Elwa. Djibouti promptly protested the Eritrean map. It also protested a claimed attack by Eritrean forces on Djibouti positions in the disputed area. Eritrea denied that any attack had occurred. Djibouti and Eritrea had twice previously clashed over this same border area. The controversial map would seem to have been based on the one drawn in 1935 by Italy on the basis of the 1935 Laval-Mussolini Agreement. The legal status of that agreement, binding or non-binding, was a matter of some serious doubt. The agreement appears not to have come into force for certain reasons (Dzurek & Schofield, 2001). It may not have been ratified by the French Senate. Even if it was ratified by the signatory states, the instruments of ratification were never exchanged. The entry into force of the agreement was additionally dependent on the completion of the Convention on Tunisian Nationality, which was not performed. Besides, in 1938, three years after signing the accord, Italy notified France that it did not consider the agreement as binding. Furthermore, in 1994, the ICJ in the *Chad v. Libya case* rejected as invalid the Laval-Mussolini Agreement.

The Eritrean map may well have been a simple cartographic error, though if this were the case the map should promptly have been withdrawn when the error was pointed out. Instead, in 1996 Eritrea merely stated that there had been no negotiations with Djibouti over the maritime boundary and that delimitation would be simple once good bilateral relations between both countries were established (Dzurek & Schofield, 2001). Eritrea has since been preoccupied with its war with Ethiopia and subsequent disengagement. It has therefore not been able to redirect its attention to the issue of its lateral maritime boundary with Djibouti. In April 1996, Djibouti and Eritrea had almost gone to war after a Djibouti official accused Eritrea of shelling Ras Doumeira, an accusation Eritrea denied. This time round, in June 2008, the armies of both countries had a military standoff for three days in the same disputed border region. Tension began in mid-April 2008 when Djibouti claimed that Eritrean forces had penetrated into Djiboutian territory and dug trenches on both sides of the border. Three weeks later the military forces of both countries clashed for three days at Ras Doumeira, with France providing logistical, medical and intelligence support to Djibouti. Djibouti dispatched to the UN a letter in which it called for UN intervention and claimed that new maps put out by Eritrea represented Ras Doumeira as part of Eritrean territory. Eritrea denied it had any problems with Djibouti. But Djibouti insisted that on 10 June 2008, a number of Eritrean troops deserted their positions and fled to the Djiboutian side and that Eritrean forces then started firing at Djiboutian forces demanding the return of the deserters. This account was dismissed by Eritrea as 'anti-Eritrean'. According to Djibouti, the three days of military clash left forty-four Djiboutian soldiers dead and fifty-fife wounded; hundred Eritrean soldiers killed and hundred captured; and twenty-one defected. These were high casualties for just three days of fighting.

The matter quickly drew international reaction. France, which has about 3,000 troops in Djibouti and a mutual defence agreement with the country, provided logistical, medical and intelligence support to the Djibouti army. It announced increased French military presence in and support for Djibouti. It made preparations to deploy a forward logistics base and a land force near Ras Doumeira. It stepped up its air surveillance over the border to monitor the activities of Eritrean forces. At the same time, however, the French called for a diplomatic settlement of the dispute. America, with some 2,000 military personnel in Djibouti, condemned Eritrea's 'military aggression' saying it represented an additional threat to peace and security in the already volatile Horn of Africa. It called on Eritrea to accept third-party mediation on the border dispute. Ethiopia, which at that time relied on Djibouti for access to the Red Sea since Eritrea's independence, declared that the military confrontation constituted a threat to the peace and security of the whole Horn of Africa. It ominously stated that Ethiopia would secure its trade corridor through Djibouti in the event of a conflict, a statement interpreted to mean it was prepared to fight alongside Djibouti against Eritrea. The League of Arab States called on Eritrea to withdraw from the disputed border region. The UNSC invited both sides to exercise maximum restraint and re-establish dialogue. The Peace and Security Council of the AU urged Eritrea and Djibouti to exercise the utmost restraint and to resolve the dispute through dialogue, including fully accepting and cooperating with an AU mission sent to the area.

The UNSC met on 28 June 2008, heard a briefing on the situation and sent a fact-finding mission to both countries. The mission afterwards issued a report in which it stated that the standoff between Djibouti and Eritrea could 'have a major negative impact on the entire region and the wider international community'. The report noted that Djibouti had pulled out of the disputed area but Eritrea had not. In its Resolution 1862 adopted on 14 January 2009, the UNSC urged dialogue between the two countries to solve their boundary difference peacefully. The council welcomed Djibouti's withdrawal to positions before 10 June 2008 and demanded that Eritrea make a similar withdrawal within five weeks of the resolution, which it eventually did. In early June 2010, Djibouti and Eritrea agreed to refer their dispute to Qatar for mediation, snubbing the African Union that nevertheless praised the move.

But the matter still awaits final resolution. According to a *Voice of America* report on 4 August 2018, Djibouti's Ambassador to the UN cautioned that

> There is no escaping the fact that the international boundary remains disputed, Eritrea continues to occupy Djiboutian territory . . . threat of force continues to emanate from the Eritrean side, and the risk of violent confrontation remains high. We urge Eritrea to resolve the border dispute peacefully with Djibouti . . . in a manner consistent with international law.

In September 2018, it was announced merely that Djibouti and Eritrea agreed to 'normalize' their relations.

MARITIME ZONE CLAIMS

Côte d'Ivoire/Ghana

Both countries are maritime neighbours with adjacent coasts and have overlapping maritime zone claims. Côte d'Ivoire had a decade-long political turmoil from which it recovered in 2011. It has since been seeking to develop its potentially lucrative offshore oil and gas sector. Ghana too has been actively exploring oil in its maritime zone claims, some of which overlap with those of Côte d'Ivoire. Oil companies are looking to redraw licensing blocks on these zones. Since the 1960s, relations between the two adjacent states have tended to oscillate between the frosty and the warm. In the 1980s, for example, relations went sour when Ghana accused Côte d'Ivoire of harbouring Ghanaian dissidents and political agitators. Relations later improved but deteriorated again following an ugly soccer incident in late 1993. In November that year, Côte d'Ivoire was eliminated by Ghana in a championship soccer match played in Kumasi, Ghana. According to media reports at the time, the Ivorian public reacted to the elimination by violently attacking Ghanaians living in Côte d'Ivoire, killing at least forty. Some 1,000 homes and businesses were looted. Many Ghanaians lost their property and more than 10,000 out of the approximately 1 million living in Côte d'Ivoire at the time were immediately evacuated by the Ghanaian government, while more than 30,000 others reportedly sought refuge in the Ghanaian embassy and the embassies of friendly countries. A twenty-member joint parity commission set up by both countries investigated the attacks, recommended compensation for victims and suggested ways of avoiding similar incidents in the future. By the end of the year, bilateral relations between both countries had been normalized, including resumption of soccer matches, thanks to Togolese mediation.

Ghana and Côte d'Ivoire share a 640-kilometre-long land boundary which though described on paper had never been demarcated. As early as 1974, both countries established a border commission to carry out demarcation, and, in 1989, after fifteen years of lack of progress, agreement was reached on demarcation of the course of the land border. However, delimitation of the lateral maritime boundary between both countries remained outstanding. In their separate April–May 2009 submission to the UN Commission on the limits of the continental shelf both countries stated that neither of them has signed any maritime boundary delimitation agreements with any of its neighbouring states. In 2010, Côte d'Ivoire took the maritime boundary demarcation question to the International Tribunal for the Law of the Sea (ITLOS).[11] Shortly afterwards, Ghana established a boundary commission to determine through negotiations the country's land and maritime boundaries with Côte d'Ivoire. A delegation from both countries met at the end of April 2010 and discussed delimitations according to international law but the outcome of the discussions was not made public. However, the fact that the presidents of both countries met in Abidjan on 15 July 2010 and again in 2012 at the behest of former UN secretary general, Kofi Annan, on the same boundary issue would suggest that previous negotiations on the subject were inconclusive. Progress on this matter was still slow, and the nature of the discussions was unclear.

Both countries eventually expressed their commitment to a peaceful solution of the dispute and chose the path of judicial settlement. They concluded a special agreement to submit the dispute concerning the maritime dispute between them in the Atlantic Ocean to a Special Chamber of the tribunal to be formed pursuant to Article 15, Paragraph 2, of the Statute of the Tribunal. In *Dispute Concerning Delimitation of the Maritime Boundary between Ghana and Côte d'Ivoire in the Atlantic Ocean (Ghana/Côte d'Ivoire)*, Case No. 23, the Special Chamber of the ITLOS in Hamburg, on 21 April 2015, declined the request of Côte d'Ivoire that Ghana be ordered to suspend all oil exploration and exploitation in the disputed maritime zone. It made an interim ruling to the effect that Ghana could continue production in a multi-billion-dollar offshore oil development in the disputed maritime zone but must not start any new drilling or exploration. The tribunal also ordered a number of provisional measures which both Ghana and Côte d'Ivoire were required to comply with, including continued cooperation until the tribunal gives its decision on the maritime boundary dispute, expected sometimes in late 2017 or early 2018. If precedent is anything to go by, the tribunal is likely to reiterate the principle of the equidistant maritime boundary, adjusting it, if need be, to produce an equitable result.

The final judgement in the maritime boundary delimitation case between Ghana and Côte d' Ivoire[12] was delivered by an ad hoc Special Chamber of the ITLOS on 23 September 2017. The decision addressed important legal questions relating not only to maritime boundary delimitation but also to the balancing of various rights and interests at the provisional measures stage and international responsibility for unilateral resource exploitation activities in disputed zones pending delimitation. The court made findings on tacit boundary agreements, delimitation methodology and international responsibility.

The attorney general and minister for justice of the Republic of Ghana, by letter dated 21 November 2014, transmitted to the president of the ITLOS the notification and the statement of the claim and grounds on which it is based, dated 19 September 2014 and addressed by Ghana to the Republic of Côte d'Ivoire, instituting arbitral proceedings under Annex VII to the UN Convention on the Law of the Sea in 'the dispute concerning the maritime boundary between Ghana and Côte d'Ivoire'. In its notification, Ghana sought the following relief:

> That the Tribunal delimit, in accordance with principles and the rules set forth in UNCLOS and international law, the complete course of the single maritime boundary dividing all the maritime areas appertaining to Ghana and to Côte d'Ivoire in the Atlantic Ocean, including the continental shelf beyond 200 miles.

Ghana further asked the tribunal 'to determine the precise geographical coordinates of the single maritime boundary in the Atlantic Ocean'. Ghana informed the tribunal that it reserved 'the right to supplement and/or amend its claim and the relief sought as necessary, and to make such other requests from the arbitral tribunal as may be necessary to preserve its rights under UNCLOS'.

In its Memorial and Reply, Ghana requested the Special Chamber to adjudge and declare that Ghana and Côte d'Ivoire have mutually recognized, agreed and applied an equidistance-based maritime boundary in the territorial sea, exclusive economic zone and continental shelf within 200 nautical miles; the maritime boundary in the continental shelf beyond 200 nautical miles follows an extended equidistance boundary along the same azimuth as the boundary within 200 nautical miles, to the limit of national jurisdiction; in accordance with international law, by reason of its representations and upon which Ghana has placed reliance, Côte d'Ivoire is estopped from objecting to the agreed maritime boundary; the land boundary terminus and starting point for the agreed maritime boundary is at Boundary Pillar 55 (BP 55); as per the parties' agreement in December 2013, the geographic coordinates of BP 55 are 05° 05'' 284" N and 03° 06' 21.8" W (in WGS 1984 datum); consequently, the maritime boundary between Ghana and Côte d'Ivoire in the Atlantic Ocean starts at BP 55, connects to the customary equidistance boundary mutually agreed by the parties at the outer limit of the territorial sea and follows the agreed boundary to a distance of 200 nautical miles. Beyond 200 nautical miles, the boundary continues along the same azimuth to the limit of national jurisdiction.

In its counter-memorial, Côte d'Ivoire requested the Special Chamber to reject all Ghana's requests and claims and to declare and adjudge that the sole maritime boundary between Ghana and Côte d' Ivoire follows the 168.7° azimuth line, which starts at BP 55 and extends to the outer limit of the Ivorian continental shelf; to declare and adjudge that the activities undertaken unilaterally by Ghana in the Ivorian maritime area, as delimited by this chamber, constitute a violation of the exclusive sovereign rights of Côte d'Ivoire over its continental shelf; the obligation to negotiate in good faith, pursuant to Article 83, Paragraph 1, of UNCLOS and customary law; the obligation not to jeopardize or hamper the conclusion of an agreement, as provided for by Article 83, Paragraph 3, of UNCLOS; and the provisional measures prescribed by this chamber by its order of 25 April 2015.

In terms of geography, the maritime area to be delimited in the present case lies in the Atlantic Ocean. Ghana and Côte d'Ivoire are adjacent states, bordering the Gulf of Guinea in West Africa. Ghana has a land boundary with Togo to the east, Burkina Faso to the north and Côte d'Ivoire to the west. Côte d'Ivoire shares a land boundary with Guinea to the west, Mali and Burkina Faso to the north and Ghana to the east. There are no islands in the area to be delimited. In terms of the subject matter of the dispute, Ghana made it clear that 'primarily, this is not a maritime delimitation case, but rather a request to declare the existence of the boundary'. It adds that 'it is only in the alternative that Ghana requests the Chamber to proceed to the delimitation of the maritime boundary'. For its part, Côte d'Ivoire declares that the dispute brought before the chamber 'essentially concerns the delimitation of the maritime boundary between Côte d'Ivoire and Ghana in the Atlantic Ocean'. According to Côte d'Ivoire, both parties agree that the chamber must determine a single delimitation line. Côte d'Ivoire observes that in its reply Ghana attempts a sudden redefinition of the dispute and no longer speaks of delimitation of the maritime boundary with Côte d'Ivoire, but of the 'demarcation' of that boundary, in the hope to persuade the chamber that the boundary has already been defined by agreement between the parties. Côte d'Ivoire explained that the chamber must make an actual delimitation consisting in 'resolving the overlapping claims by drawing a line of separation of the maritime areas concerned'.

The Special Chamber identified the legal basis, nature and scope of Ghana's claim for the delimitation of the territorial sea, exclusive economic zone and continental shelf within and beyond the 200 nautical miles as based on a tacit agreement which has been developed or confirmed as a result of the oil activities of both parties over the years. The chamber then proceeded to ascertain whether a tacit agreement exists, as Ghana argues and which Côte d'Ivoire challenges. The chamber considered oil activities (oil concessions, seismic surveys, drilling activities and the question of protest and concession maps), the legislation of the parties (observing in this regard that national legislation, as a unilateral act of a state, is of limited relevance to proving the existence of an agreed maritime boundary), representation to international institutions, bilateral exchanges and negotiations and other maritime activities (fisheries, movement of licensed fishing vehicles and oceanographic research).

In the view of the Special Chamber, oil practice, no matter how consistent it may be, cannot in itself establish the existence of a tacit agreement on a maritime boundary. Mutual, consistent and long-standing oil practice and the adjoining oil concession limits might reflect the existence of a maritime boundary or might be explained by other reasons. As the ICJ stated in Territorial and Maritime Dispute between Nicaragua and Honduras in the Caribbean Sea:

> A de facto line might in certain circumstances correspond to the existence of an agreed legal boundary or might be more in the nature of a provisional line or of a line for a specific, limited purpose, such as sharing a scarce resource. Even if there had been a provisional line found convenient for a period of time, this is to be distinguished from an international boundary. (*Nicaragua v. Honduras*, Judgement, para. 253)[13]

As the ICJ also stated with respect to oil concessions limits: 'these limits may have been simply the manifestation of the caution exercised by the Parties in granting their concessions'.[14] Thus, the proof of the existence of a maritime boundary requires more than the demonstration of long-standing oil practice or adjoining oil concession limits. As far as oil concession maps are concerned, the Special Chamber is not convinced that these maps show not only the limits of oil concessions but also maritime boundaries as Ghana claims. In the absence of a clear reference to an international maritime boundary on the maps, it is difficult to accept such depiction of a line on oil concession maps as an indication of an international maritime boundary.

After considering Ghana's invocation of estoppel in the present case, the Special Chamber ruled that Côte d'Ivoire has not demonstrated, by its words, conduct or silence, that it agreed to the maritime boundary based on equidistance. Having found that no tacit agreement on the maritime boundary between the parties exists and that the requirements of estoppel have not been met, the Special Chamber proceeded to the delimitation of the territorial sea, the exclusive economic zone and the continental shelf. The Special Chamber emphasized that under the convention different rules apply to the delimitation of the territorial seas and the delimitation of exclusive economic zones and continental shelves. The delimitation of the territorial sea is governed by Article 15 of the convention, which reads:

> Where the coasts of two States are opposite or adjacent to each other, neither of the two States is entitled, failing agreement between them to the contrary, to extend its territorial sea beyond the median line every point of which is equidistant from the nearest points on the baseline from which the breadth of the territorial seas of each of two States is measured. The above provision does not apply, however, where it is necessary by reason of historic title or other special circumstances to delimit the territorial seas of the two States in a which is at variance with therewith.

The Special Chamber noted that in delimiting the territorial sea it has to be borne in mind that the rights of the coastal states concerned are not functional but territorial since they entail sovereignty over the seabed, the superjacent waters and the air column above. This has been emphasized by the ICJ in *Qatar v. Bahrain*.[15] The Special Chamber notes that the parties, in requesting the Special Chamber to delimit a single maritime boundary for their territorial seas, exclusive economic zones and continental shelves, have implicitly agreed that the same delimitation methodology be used for these maritime spaces. On this basis, the Special Chamber considered it appropriate to use the same methodology for the delimitation of the parties' territorial seas, exclusive economic zones and continental shelves within and beyond 200 nautical miles.

The Special Chamber found that the international jurisprudence concerning the delimitation of maritime spaces in principle favours the equidistance/relevant circumstances methodology. It further found that the international decisions which adopted the angle bisector methodology were due to particular circumstances in each of the cases concerned. This international jurisprudence confirms that, in the absence of any compelling reasons that make it impossible or inappropriate to draw a provisional equidistance line, the equidistance/relevant circumstances methodology should be chosen for maritime delimitation. As the tribunal stated in *Bangladesh/Myanmar*,[16] 'each case is unique and requires specific treatment, the ultimate goal being to reach a solution that is equitable'. The Special Chamber considered it to be in contradiction of the principle of transparency and predictability to deviate, in this case, from a delimitation methodology which has been practised overwhelmingly by international courts and tribunals in recent decades.

The Special Chamber unanimously concluded that it has jurisdiction to delimit the maritime boundary between the parties in the territorial sea, in the exclusive economic zone and on the continental shelf, both within and beyond 200 nautical miles; that there is no tacit agreement between the parties to delimit their territorial sea, exclusive economic zone and continental shelf both within and beyond the 200 nautical miles , and rejects Ghana's claim that Côte d'Ivoire is estopped from objecting to the 'customary equidistance boundary'; decides that the single maritime boundary for the territorial sea, exclusive economic zone and the continental shelf within and beyond the 200 nautical miles starts at BP 55+ (with the coordinates specified by the special tribunal), and from the turning point F, the single maritime boundary continues as a geodetic line starting at an azimuth of $191°° 38' 06.7''$ until it reaches the outer limit of the continental shelf. The chamber also unanimously found that Ghana did not violate the sovereign rights of Côte d'Ivoire; that Ghana did not violate Article 83, Paragraphs 1 and 3 of the convention; and that Ghana did not violate the provisional measures prescribed by the Special Chamber in its order dated 25 April 2015.

Guinea-Bissau/Guinea-Conakry

Both countries are adjacent littoral states with a lateral maritime boundary. Guinea-Bissau is a former Portuguese colony and Guinea-Conakry a former French colony. On 12 May 1886, Portugal and France signed an agreement delimiting the land but not the maritime boundary of the two Guineas.

In the 1980s, Guinea-Bissau sought to settle through international arbitration its maritime boundaries with its adjacent neighbours, Senegal to the north and Guinea-Conakry to the south. In the arbitration case between Guinea-Bissau and Guinea-Conakry, the arbitration tribunal was called upon by both states to draw a single line dividing their territorial sea, the continental shelf and the exclusive economic zone. In its arbitral award, the tribunal declined to use the equidistance method in drawing the dividing line in the latter two maritime zones declaring that to do so would produce an unsatisfactory result because the effect in the instant case would be to exaggerate the importance of insignificant coastal features.[17]

In the absence of a maritime boundary delimitation in that Franco-Portuguese Agreement, both parties requested the arbitration tribunal to draw a single line dividing the following three overlapping maritime zones of both countries: the territorial sea, the exclusive economic zone and the continental shelf. In dealing with the case, the arbitration tribunal applied its mind to the ordinary meaning of the terms in the agreement in their context and in the light of the object and purpose of the Franco-Portuguese Agreement, subsequent practice of the parties, the *travaux préparatoires* and circumstances in which the agreement was concluded, the nature of the coastline of both countries, the general configuration of the West African coastline, the unity of the continental shelf, proportionality between the areas to be apportioned and the length of the coasts, methods of delimitation, equidistance and parallels of latitude.

In its arbitral award in *Case Concerning the Delimitation of the Maritime Boundary between Guinea and Guinea-Bissau*, 14 February 1985, the tribunal noted that using the equidistance method in drawing the dividing line in the exclusive economic zone and the continental shelf would be unsatisfactory since it would have the effect, in the instant case, of exaggerating the importance of insignificant coastline features. The tribunal went on to observe further that the evidence with regard to the geological and geomorphological features of the continental shelf was unsatisfactory and that the concepts of natural prolongation and economic factors, based as they were upon an evaluation of data that was constantly changing, were in the circumstances of little assistance. The tribunal emphasized that the aim of any maritime delimitation process is to achieve an equitable solution having regard to the relevant circumstances. The tribunal specified the line delimiting the maritime areas appertaining respectively to Guinea-Bissau and Guinea-Conakry as taking the following course: the line starts from the intersection of the thalweg of the River Cajet and the meridian of 15° 06' 30" longitude west; joins loxodromes A, B and C indicated in the award; and then a loxodrome having an azimuth of 236° from point C as indicated, up to the external limit of each state's maritime areas recognized under general international law.

This case is the first of only two African maritime boundary disputes so far referred to arbitration. The Guinea-Guinea-Bissau example has not been followed by other African states that have been faced with maritime boundary delimitation disputes. The matters which the court took into consideration such as the general configuration of the West African coastline, the unity of the continental shelf and proportionality between the areas to be apportioned and the length of the coasts will probably have a direct effect on the neighbouring countries of Senegal and Sierra Leone (Aquarone, 1995).

Guinea-Bissau/Senegal

Access to fish stock in the maritime zones of the adjacent coastal states of Guinea-Bissau and Senegal was for some years a source of dispute between both countries over areas in the overlapping maritime zones claimed by both. The legitimate economy of Guinea-Bissau relies heavily on farming and fishing. Similarly, the Senegalese coast is a rich fishing ground and generations of Senegalese communities depend on fishing to make a living. The once-abundant fish stocks in the Senegal-Guinea-Bissau waters have attracted a spate of unregulated and illegal fishing, especially by unauthorized industrial fishing ships. In January 2014, for example, the *Oleg Naydenov*, a Russian trawler was seized for illegal fishing and its crew arrested by the Senegalese Navy supported by the French. The trawler had sixty-two Russians and twenty-three Guinea-Bissau citizens on board and claimed to be fishing in Guinea-Bissau waters. Russia was fined under Senegalese law to pay 400 million CFA (about US$727,000), and the trawler's cargo was confiscated.

The *Guinea-Bissau v. Senegal arbitration case* also had its roots in the colonial past of both countries. In 1960, France and Portugal concluded an agreement defining the maritime boundary between France's possession of Senegal and the Portuguese colony Guinea-Bissau. After the accession to independence of Senegal and Guinea-Bissau, a dispute arose between the two states concerning the delimitation of their maritime territories. The two states submitted this dispute to an arbitration tribunal which had to decide whether the agreement of 1960 had the force of law between the parties; and in the event of a negative answer, to define the course of the line delimiting the maritime territories of the two states. On 31 July 1989, the arbitration tribunal ruled that the agreement of 1960 had force of law in relation to the parties.

A month later, on 23 August 1989, Guinea-Bissau instituted proceedings in the ICJ against Senegal concerning the existence and validity of the arbitral award of 31 July 1989, arguing that one of the two arbitrators making up the appearance of a majority in favour of the text of the award had, by a declaration appended to it, expressed a view in contradiction with the one apparently adopted by the vote. On 18 January 1990, Guinea-Bissau stated to the court that the Senegalese Navy had taken certain actions in a maritime area which Guinea-Bissau regarded as an area disputed between the parties. Guinea-Bissau therefore requested the court to indicate, in order to safeguard the rights of each of the parties, the following provisional measures, namely, that the parties should abstain in the disputed area from any act or action of any kind whatever, during the whole duration of the proceedings until the decision is given by the court. The court declined to grant the request. In the view of the court the subject matter of the request for provisional measures was not the same as that of the proceedings before the court on the merits of the case. The request for provisional measures sought to protect the respective rights of the parties in the maritime areas in question. But the Application of 23 August 1989 asked the court to declare the award of 31 July 1989 to be inexistent or, subsidiarily, null and void and thus inapplicable. The court pointed out that the requested provisional measures could not be subsumed under the court's judgement on the merits as is required by Article 41 of the statute of the court. Moreover, the decision of the court on the merits stating the invalidity of the award would not entail any decision as to the applicant's claim in respect of the disputed maritime delimitation. The necessary link between the subject matter of the request for interim measures and the request on the merits was therefore lacking.[18]

While the proceedings on the merits were still pending before the court, Guinea-Bissau brought a new claim against Senegal on 12 March 1991 concerning the delimitation of the maritime areas between the two states. Guinea-Bissau claimed that the basic dispute concerns the conflicting claims of the parties to control exploration and exploitation of maritime areas and that the purpose of the measures requested is to preserve the integrity of the maritime area concerned. The ICJ found guidance in the UN Convention on the Law of the Sea, 10 December 1982, especially in Part V on the Exclusive Economic Zone and in Part V on the Continental Shelf. Both the Government of Guinea-Bissau (25 August 1986) and the Government of Senegal (25 October 1984) have signed and ratified this convention. Article 74, Paragraph 1, of the convention, dealing with the delimitation of the exclusive economic zone between neighbouring coastal states provides that the delimitation of the zone 'shall be effected by agreement'. Identical provisions are found in Article 83 of the Convention on the Delimitation of the Continental Shelf. Though the convention had not yet entered into force at the time of the arbitration, the ICJ opined that Articles 74 and 83 of the treaty give expression to governing principles of international law in this field. Those articles entail that coastal states should conclude agreements, where necessary, concerning the allowable catch of fish stocks, the distribution of this catch between the states concerned, the issuance of fisheries licences, the character and modes of fishing gear, the protection of spawning grounds, the maintenance of the necessary contacts between the relevant national fisheries authorities together with other means for the rational and peaceful exploitation of these vital resources of the oceans.[19]

The arbitration award in the matter between Guinea-Bissau and Senegal was given on 31 July 1989. A Franco-Portuguese Agreement of 26 April 1960 had defined the maritime boundary between Senegal (still a French colonial territory at the time) and Guinea-Bissau (then a Portuguese colonial territory). After independence, a dispute arose between both states over the delimitation of their maritime zones. Guinea-Bissau insisted on delimitation without reference to the 1960 agreement, disputing its validity and its opposability to Guinea-Bissau. The three-member arbitration panel to which the matter was eventually submitted decided that the 1960 Franco-Portuguese Agreement relating to the maritime boundary has the force of law in the relation between Guinea-Bissau and Senegal with regard solely to the area mentioned in the agreement. Guinea-Bissau rejected the award challenging its validity in law. The challenge was brought before the ICJ which held that the award was valid and binding on both parties, which were obliged to apply it.[20]

LATERAL MARITIME BOUNDARY

Somalia/Kenya

Somalia and Kenya are adjacent states on the coast of East Africa. Somalia is located in the Horn of Africa. It borders Kenya to the southwest, Ethiopia to the west and Djibouti to the northwest. Somalia's coastline faces the Gulf of Aden to the north and the Indian Ocean to the east. Kenya shares a land boundary with Somalia to the northeast, Ethiopia to the north, South Sudan to the northwest, Uganda to the west and Tanzania to the south. Its coastline faces the Indian Ocean. Both states are parties to UNCLOS.

On 28 August 2014, Somalia instituted proceedings in the ICJ against Kenya 'concerning maritime delimitation in the Indian Ocean'. On 16 October 2014, the ICJ made an order fixing time-limits for the filing of the initial pleadings, memorials and counter-memorials. A year later, on 9 October 2015, it made another order fixing time-limits for the filing by Somalia of its written statement of observations and submissions on the preliminary objections raised by Kenya. The dispute between Somalia and Kenya goes back to 2009. It relates to the delimitation of the lateral maritime boundary between the two states from the terminus of their common land boundary seawards.

Somalia's contention is that its lateral maritime boundary with Kenya continues diagonally south of Kiunga into the sea in alignment with the course of the land boundary. Kenya, on the other hand, contends that the maritime boundary runs horizontally (i.e., perpendicular) to the land boundary into the sea similar to the alignment of its sea border with Tanzania and that according to the agreed convention that governs the offshore boundaries on the East African coast, the boundary in international waters is due east from the point of the line on land boundary. At stake is an area of the Indian Ocean about 100,000 square kilometre, forming a triangle east of the Kenya coast with potentially lucrative oil and gas reserves. Thus, at the heart of the dispute is a disagreement over resources on the seabed in that area which is also home to a Kenyan naval base at Manda Bay, a facility used by the US Navy in combating sea piracy in the Indian Ocean.

There are about forty-four oil and gas exploration blocks in or near this area. In 2012, Kenya leased eight of these offshore blocks in the Indian Ocean to the French Total and Eni oil exploration companies, including one company which discovered gas in the Lamu Basin. Seven of the eight blocks are located in a contested area that is roughly the size of Malawi. According to Somalia which is Kenya's adjacent neighbour to the north, in leasing those blocks to oil companies, Kenya contravened Somali Law No. 37 which defines Mogadishu's territorial sea, its contiguous zone, its exclusive economic zone and its continental shelf, and therefore its sovereignty. In 2014, the Somali government announced its completion of surveys of the disputed area and its plan to start issuing offshore oil and gas exploration licences as from 2015. This action by Somalia heightened tension in the area and between the two countries.

In order to mollify Somali anger, Kenya had initiated in 2009 a memorandum of understanding (MOU) with the then Somali Transitional Federal Government. The memorandum would have committed both parties to negotiate the dispute out-of-court and with the help of the UN Commission on the Limits of the Continental Shelf. But the document was rejected by the Somali Parliament. Kenya thus failed in its quest to have the matter settled by negotiation or through third-party arbitration. For Somalia, the conflict over the maritime demarcation goes far deeper than just the question of the ocean economy. For it, the conflict also has to do with national pride and dignity. Accordingly, Somalia insisted that only the ICJ would resolve the dispute as 'Kenya has violated its territorial waters' and both sides had exhausted all diplomatic channels. Should the matter get to the merit stage, it might take years before a final ruling on the dispute is made. Kenya and Somalia have not been able to hammer out any interim agreement on joint exploration and exploitation in the contested maritime area as some other countries have done. In the circumstances the ICJ would, on request, be inclined to order a number of provisional measures which both countries would be required to comply with, including continued cooperation until the court gives its final decision on the maritime boundary dispute.

Under Article 76, Paragraph 8, of UNCLOS, a state party to the convention intending to establish the outer limit of its continental shelf beyond 200 nautical miles shall submit information on such limits to the Commission on the Limits of the Continental Shelf (CLCS). The role of the commission is to make recommendation to coastal states on matters related to the establishment of the outer limits of their continental shelf beyond 200 nautical miles. With regard to disputed maritime areas, under Annex I of the CLCS Rules of Procedure, titled 'Submissions in case of a dispute between states with opposite or adjacent coasts or in other cases of unresolved land or maritime disputes', the commission requires the prior consent of all states concerned before it will consider submissions regarding such areas.

The MOU between Somalia and Kenya dated 7 April 2009 was signed 'to grant to each country No-Objection in respect of submissions on the Outer Limits of the Continental Shelf beyond 200 Nautical Miles to the Commission on the Limits of the Continental Shelf'. In June 2009, the MOU was submitted by Kenya to the secretariat of the UN for registration and publication pursuant to Article 102 of the charter of the UN. The secretariat registered it on 11 June 2009 and published it in the UN Treaty Series. In the following years, both parties raised and withdrew objections to the consideration of each other's submissions by the CLCS. As noted earlier, on 28 August 2014, Somalia instituted proceedings against Kenya before the court, requesting the court to determine, on the basis of international law, the complete course of the single maritime boundary dividing all the maritime areas appertaining to Somalia and to Kenya in the Indian Ocean, including the continental shelf beyond 200 nautical miles. As basis for the court's jurisdiction, Somalia invoked the declarations recognizing the court's jurisdiction as compulsory made by the two states.

Kenya, however, raised two preliminary objections: one concerning the jurisdiction of the court and the other the admissibility of the application. Regarding the first preliminary objection, Kenya argued that the court lacks jurisdiction to entertain the present case as a result of one of the reservations to its declaration accepting the compulsory jurisdiction of the court. The reservation in question, Kenya argued, excludes disputes in regard to which the parties have agreed 'to have recourse to some other method or methods of settlement'. Kenya asserts that the MOU constitutes an agreement to have recourse to another method of settlement. It adds that the relevant provisions of UNCLOS on dispute settlement also amount to an agreement on the method of settlement. The first preliminary objection thus required the court to deal with two issues: the legal status of the MOU under international law and the interpretation of the MOU. Regarding the second preliminary objection, Kenya claimed that Somalia's application is inadmissible because the parties had agreed in the MOU to negotiate delimitation of the disputed boundary and to do so only after completion of CLCS review of the parties' submissions. Kenya also stated that the application is inadmissible because Somalia breached the MOU by objecting to CLCS consideration of Kenya's submission, only to consent again immediately before filing its memorial. According to Kenya, the withdrawal of consent was a breach of Somalia's obligations under the MOU that gave rise to significant costs and delays. Kenya also contended that a state 'seeking relief before the court must come with clean hands' and that Somalia has not done so.

On 2 February 2017, the ICJ handed down its judgement on preliminary objection.[21] On the first preliminary objection regarding the legal status of the MOU, the court pointed out the fact that the MOU was registered with the UN without Somalia protesting the registration until almost five years afterwards, that the MOU made express provision for it to enter into force upon signature and that Somalia's signature of the MOU expressed its consent to be bound by the MOU under international law. The court concluded that the MOU is a valid treaty that entered into force upon signature and is binding on the parties under international law. On the matter of interpretation of the MOU, the court considered that although both states are not parties to the Vienna

Convention on the Law of Treaties (VCLT), 1969, nevertheless the court applies the rules on interpretation to be found in Articles 31 and 32 of the VCLT, which it has consistently considered to be reflective of customary international law. In line with Article 32, the court examined the travaux préparatoires, however limited, and the circumstances in which the MOU was concluded, which it considered confirmed that the MOU was not intended to establish a procedure for the settlement of the maritime boundary dispute between the parties. The court concluded that the MOU did not constitute an agreement 'to have recourse to some other method or methods of settlement' within the meaning of Kenya's reservations to its Article 36, Paragraph 2, declaration, and consequently this case did not, by virtue of the MOU, fall outside the scope of Kenya's consent to the court's jurisdiction. In light of the court's conclusion that neither the MOU nor Part XV of UNCLOS falls within the scope of the reservation to Kenya's optional clause declaration, the court found that Kenya's preliminary objection to the jurisdiction of the court must be rejected.

On the second preliminary objection (the admissibility of Somalia's application), the court having previously found that the MOU did not contain an agreement to negotiate delimitation of the disputed boundary, and to do so only after completion of the CLCS review of the parties' submissions, held that it must also reject this aspect of Kenya's second preliminary objection. The court observed the fact that an applicant may have breached a treaty at issue in the case does not per se affect the admissibility of its application. The court further note that Somalia was neither relying on the MOU as an instrument conferring jurisdiction on the court nor as a source of substantive law governing the merits of this case. Thus, Somalia's objection to CLCS consideration of Kenya's submission does not render the application inadmissible. In the light of the foregoing, the court found that the preliminary objection to the admissibility of Somalia's application must be rejected.

The ICJ thus rejected Kenya's preliminary objections and held that it has jurisdiction to entertain the application filed by Somalia on 28 August 2014 and that the application is admissible. This in effect meant the matter may proceed to the merit phase. The court set out important rules concerning the law of treaties. It embraced a more objective definition of treaties. It identified the significance of context and *travaux préparatoires* in treaty interpretation. The court further established itself as the default adjudicator in Law of the Sea disputes unless the reservation to its jurisdiction is sufficiently precise.

This matter took an unexpected turn, the first in the history of the ICJ, when on 14 March 2021, Kenya withdrew from the ICJ case saying it will no longer take part in the hearings. Kenya accused the ICJ of bias. The alleged bias was that the court insisted on a virtual hearing of the case. In doing so, the court ruled against Kenya's request for delay due to the coronavirus pandemic and also against Kenya's request to be given time to brief a new legal team. An element of Kenya's allegation of bias by the court was the fact that Judge Abdulqawi Ahmed Yusuf, a Somali national, was a member of the ICJ panel. Kenya demanded that he recuses himself. Somalia on the other hand accused Kenya of interfering in its internal affairs by backing the administration of the Jubbaland region against the Somali federal government. It may be recalled that this case was instituted by Somalia in 2014 and that it concerns a 160,000 square kilometre triangle in the Indian Ocean. Somalia contends that the maritime frontier should follow in the same direction as the land border. But Kenya argues that the frontier has always been taken in a horizontal line from the point where the two countries meet at the coast.

SOME PECULIAR ASPECTS OF MARITIME BOUNDARY DISPUTES

Maritime boundary delimitation disputes lack the 'ideational' aspect of terrestrial boundary or territorial disputes (Kornprobst, 2002). Land boundary can be pointed out. Land provides food. Land is the abode of the ancestors, and it is where the dead are buried. By contrast, maritime boundaries are less visible and less tangible. They are more difficult and more costly to police. They tend to be more remote and less tangible to the people of the coastal state, except perhaps to local littoral communities who are, in any event, concerned only with the waters within their immediate vicinity than with waters so many nautical miles away. The sea is constantly in undulant motion. It is merciless and can easily kill. It is the abode of water spirits and unknown creatures. There is thus less popular emotional attachment to maritime boundaries than there is to land boundaries. Maritime boundaries have therefore seldom provoked interstate wars. Unlike intrastate conflicts and terrestrial boundary or territorial interstate conflicts, maritime boundary delimitation disputes seldom escalate into war, not to talk of a full-scale war even when, as sometimes happens, each side gets overt or covert support from a third state. No African coastal state has the capacity and ability to project sea power. The navies of African coastal states are 'baby navies' not fitted to engage in naval battles. In any event, the threat or use of force by individual states as a means of settling disputes is impermissible under the UN Charter, though this prohibition is not always respected.

Impact of Coastal Geography

Many areas of the oceans fall within the maritime zones of one state only. This follows from the principle of international law that the land dominates the sea, meaning that maritime rights derive from the coastal state's sovereignty over land. Maritime zones are well defined under the UN Convention on the Law of the Sea. In principle, then, states ought to be able to reach agreement quite easily on maritime delimitation. But, geography can at times present problems. In order to resolve geographical problems that at times arise, international law ordains that 'special' or 'relevant' circumstances may be taken into account in delimiting the territorial sea or the continental shelf/ exclusive economic zone.[22] There is no legal limit as to what constitutes 'special' or 'relevant' circumstances.[23] However, 'only those that are pertinent to the institution of the continental shelf as it has developed within the law and to the application of equitable principles to its determination' qualify to be taken into account.[24] Ecological, geological, sedimental and geomorphological characteristics as well as coastal geographic configuration have been held to constitute 'special circumstances' in a number of cases. In *Delimitation of the Maritime Boundary in the Gulf of Maine Area* (1984), for example, the chamber of the ICJ considered coastal geographic configuration 'and other relevant circumstances' as factors to be taken into account in the delimitation of the exclusive economic zone and the continental shelf.

Similarly, in *Case Concerning Maritime and Territorial Dispute between Nicaragua and Honduras in the Caribbean Sea (Nicaragua v. Honduras)* (2007), the court considered the geography of the coastline to be a special circumstance to be taken into account. The land boundary between Nicaragua and Honduras ends at Cape Gracias à Dios, a sharply convex territorial projection abutting upon a concave coastline on either side to the north and southwest. The court reasoned that since the pair of base points to be identified on either bank of the boundary River Coco would assume a considerable dominance in constructing the equidistance line, and that given the close proximity of these base points to each other, 'any variation or error in situating them would become disproportionately magnified in the resulting equidistance line'. Moreover, said the court, continued sedimental accretion at sea brought about by River Coco caused its delta to exhibit a very active morpho-dynamism, especially as it travels out from the coast. Under the circumstances, the court considered that these factors taken together had the result that any equidistance line constructed at the present time could become arbitrary and unreasonable in the near future. The court then decided that it would not be sufficient simply to adjust the provisional equidistance line but that 'special circumstances' required the use of a different method of delimitation known as the bisector method, meaning the line formed by bisecting the angle created by a linear approximation of coastlines.

One crucial aspect of coastal geography that the court has held to be a 'relevant circumstance' is the configuration of the coastline, for example, the concave or convex nature of the coast.[25] In three cases, *North Sea*

Continental Shelf, Tunisia v. Libya and *Gulf of Maine*, the court was prepared to consider the geomorphology of the area to be delimited as a 'relevant circumstance' where it could be shown that there are features interrupting the continuity of the continental shelf; but in all three cases though it found no such discontinuities. However, in *Libya v. Malta* it held that

> since the development of the law enables a state to claim that the continental shelf appertaining to it extends up to as far as 200 miles from its coast, whatever the geological characteristics of the corresponding seabed and subsoil, there is no reason to ascribe any role to geological or geophysical factors within that distance either in verifying the legal title of the states concerned or in proceeding to a delimitation as between their claims.

The court went on to state that in so far as the areas to be delimited are situated at a distance of under 200 miles from the coasts in question, 'title depended solely on the distance from the coasts of the claimant states of any area of sea-bed claimed by way of continental shelf, and the geological or geomorphological characteristics of those areas are completely immaterial'. In other words, a state is by law entitled to claim an exclusive economic zone of up to 200 nautical miles from the territorial sea baseline whatever be the geology and geomorphology of the seabed of that 200-miles zone. Geological and geomorphological factors have no part to play in the establishment of title over that 200 nautical miles maritime zone. Those factors could not therefore be taken into account as a relevant circumstance for the purpose of delimiting the maritime zones of Libya and Malta as the distance between the coasts of the two countries is less than 400 nautical miles, so that no geographical feature can lie more than 200 miles from each other. In the past, the court has recognized the relevance of geophysical characteristics of an area of delimitation if they assist in identifying a line of separation between the continental shelves of the parties.

But such jurisprudence appears to ascribe a role to geophysical or geological factors in delimitation only where the warrant for doing so can be found in a regime of the title that it allots those factors a place (Jiuyong, 2010). What this means is that it is not possible to generalize by asserting that the various possible 'special' or 'relevant' circumstances are applicable for all maritime zones. Ecological characteristics may be relevant circumstances in the context of delimiting the exclusive economic zone but may not be so relevant in the context of the continental shelf, and geological characteristics may be relevant to the continental shelf but not to the exclusive economic zone.

Chapter 2

MARKED PREFERENCE FOR INTERNATIONAL JUDICIAL SETTLEMENT OF MARITIME DISPUTES

State practice in the continent shows a marked preference for the settlement of maritime boundary disputes by international judicial process, including international arbitration. In a few instances, states concerned accept mediation or simply negotiate a peaceful settlement bilaterally. In some other instances, recourse to any of these methods would have been preceded by appeals made by an inter-governmental political organization (UN, AU, IGAD and LAS) for a peaceful settlement of the dispute. This happened in the Eritrea/Djibouti dispute. In still some other instances, an offer of good offices by a respected international personality or a third state is made to and accepted by the parties concerned, resulting in a mediated settlement. This happened in the Equatorial Guinea/Gabon dispute and also in the Ghana/Côte d'Ivoire dispute. Qatar undertook mediation in the dispute between Eritrea and Djibouti, and Togo in the antagonistic relations between Ghana and Côte d'Ivoire.

However, it has to be appreciated that judicial settlement costs time and money. It costs a lot of money to litigate before an international forum and it takes years for the outcome to be known. One reason why some states opt for the judicial settlement route, as most states do in terrestrial disputes, rather than bilateral negotiation and settlement, is probably because legal issues involved in maritime boundary delimitation are highly technical and require certified expertise for resolution according to law. That expertise is seen as residing in an international tribunal. Furthermore, poor interstate relations can make it difficult to agree on a mutually acceptable mediator. Poor, strained and frosty interstate relations may in fact trigger a dispute. They may make it difficult to engage in fruitful bilateral negotiations or to reach an early acceptable compromise, even with the intervention of a third-party mediator. Further still, a maritime boundary delimitation dispute may be referred to an international judicial tribunal (ICJ, ITLOS or arbitration) because of the well-founded belief that a multi-judge international forum is a neutral highly competent and trustworthy arbiter. The stakes are higher when interested oil companies hover in the background, making a quick out-of-court settlement difficult. For this reason, also, a party may prefer judicial settlement and commence proceedings against the other party.

Disputes referred to arbitration for settlement are those that lend themselves to the possibility of legal resolution through arbitration, apart from settlement by the ICJ or ITLOS. A notable arbitration case is that which involved Guinea-Bissau and its two adjacent neighbours, Senegal to the north and then Guinea-Conakry to the south. When a dispute arises between states that have friendly and good neighbourly relations, as in the case of Guinea-Bissau and its neighbours, that fact makes it easier to refer the dispute to arbitration, which is comparatively less costly and less time consuming. Guinea-Bissau maintains good relations with both its neighbours in part because of the massive support both countries gave Guinea-Bissau in its long independence struggle. It was therefore easier for both parties to meet and agree to draw up a special agreement, a *compromis d' arbitrage*, in terms of which they voluntarily submitted their dispute to an ad hoc court of arbitration. The international arbitration tribunal, as required by the special agreement conferring it jurisdiction, made an award in the form of a described line on the basis of which adequate demarcation could then take place.

The African Standby Force which went operational in late 2015 under the AU Peace and Security Council (PSC) process has not been triggered in any of the maritime boundary disputes, except in the case of the Eritrea/Djibouti dispute. Part of the reason is that those disputes have seldom involved the use of military forces. In the Eritrea-Djibouti conflict, the AU PSC urged the parties to exercise restraint and to settle their dispute by peaceful means through dialogue. There was nothing new about such a bare call which, in any event, states in conflict are notorious for ignoring. Still, AU member states have committed themselves to facilitate early action by the PSC. They have also pledged to facilitate peace-making and peacebuilding in conflict-torn countries (Murithi, 2006; Mwanasali, 2006). To this end, the African Union has adopted a two-pronged approach: conflict prevention through political means and facilitation of peace-making and peacebuilding in war-torn countries (AHSI, 2004). This approach is more relevant in the context of terrestrial conflicts than in maritime boundary delimitation disputes.

The African PSC process was established in July 2002 when the African Union adopted the protocol relating to the establishment of the PSC as part of its response to conflicts in the continent and, in fact, made its first foray in peacekeeping by mounting such an operation in Chad (Mays, 2002). In terms of the protocol, Member States commit themselves to facilitate early action by the PSC which acts on early warning information provided to it by a continental early warning system. On receipt of that information, the PSC then intervenes to prevent conflicts through peacekeeping by the African Standby Force (Anyangwe, 2006).

Maritime boundary delimitation disputes involve a law that is highly technical and for that reason is more often than not referred to international arbitration or adjudication. Most African states lack expertise in this area of international law and rely on outside assistance in this regard. The ICJ Vice-President Abdulqawi Ahmed Yusuf lamented this fact in a declaration appended to the judgement of 2 February 2017 in *Case Concerning Maritime Delimitation in the Indian Ocean (Somalia v. Kenya) – Preliminary Objections*.

He made the following pointed observation:

2. The Memorandum of Understanding ('MOU') in this case was drafted, as a matter of fact, by Ambassador Hans Wilhelm Longva of Norway in the context of assistance provided by Norway to African States, which enabled them to make submissions or submit preliminary information to the Commission on the Limits of the Continental Shelf ('CLCS') within the time-limits prescribed by the States parties to the UN Convention on the Law of the Sea.

3. Many African States lack the requisite geological, geophysical, and hydrological technical expertise to compile a submission to the CLCS; in this respect, Norway's assistance was invaluable. However, this technical assistance should be distinguished from the drafting and conclusion of the MOU, which is a legal and policy matter that could have easily been directly negotiated by the two neighbouring States.

4. More than 50 years after their independence, it is surprising that Somalia and Kenya are in dispute over an agreement that they neither negotiated nor drafted. International law in the twenty-first century is more important than ever; its effects pervade the daily lives of people throughout the world. As the scope of international law has increased, so too has the importance of ensuring that each State actively participates in the creation of international legal instruments and rules which affect its peoples and resources, and understands the obligations which it takes on.

5. No Government can afford today to put its signature to a bilateral legal instrument which it has neither carefully negotiated nor to which it has hardly contributed. This applies especially to African Governments, which, due to their painful historical experience with international legal agreements concluded with foreign powers, should pay particular attention to the contents of such agreements.

When a government hotly contests a maritime boundary, it is often the case that it does so out of the expectation of deriving large revenue from the potential resources of the contested maritime area it claims as part of its territory. But, tragically, as the example of oil-producing states in the Gulf of Guinea shows, there is very little benefit that accrues to the ordinary people from offshore oil and gas revenues. For this reason, the generality of the people considers maritime boundary disputes as remote to their needs and circumstances. There are more maritime boundary disputes in West Africa and the Gulf of Guinea than there are elsewhere in Africa. A possible reason is that there are sixteen coastal states in those two regions and the coastline of each of those state is generally comparatively shorter than that of each coastal state in the rest of Africa, except for the coastline of Eritrea, Djibouti and Tunisia. The coastline of Angola, Egypt, Namibia, South Africa, Mozambique and Somalia, for example, is very extensive. Moreover, the maritime boundaries of most coastal states in southern, east and north Africa appear to have been settled quite early and therefore give rise to no maritime boundary delimitation disputes.

WEALTH SHARING

States involved in a maritime delimitation dispute sometimes accept a temporary or interim solution that allows each party access to maritime resources. This is an emerging trend. The issue is often dealt with in conjunction with other issues during peace or other negotiation processes. An example of this trend is the various protocols signed during negotiations for the end of the conflict in southern Sudan. Oil exploration loomed very large in the South Sudan/Sudan resource conflict because many of the oil fields are located near the historical boundary between the two countries and have been a source of controversy on account of potential revenue earnings. On 7 January 2004, the two sides signed the protocol on wealth sharing. Under the protocol, 50% of net oil revenue derived from oil-producing wells in southern Sudan were allocated to the government of southern Sudan at the beginning of the pre-interim period. The remaining 50% went to the national government and the states in northern Sudan. In the case of some boundary areas, a share of revenues was distributed directly to representatives of the local communities. The Protocol on the Resolution of Conflict in Abyei, signed on 26 May 2004, stipulated that the local inhabitants would be citizens of both Sudan and South Sudan. Net oil revenues would be divided six ways during the interim period: 50% for the national government, 42% for the government of South Sudan and 2% each for Bahr el Ghazal region, Western Kordofan, Ngok Dinka people and Misseriya people.

This wealth sharing idea is conceptually not dissimilar from the 'joint exploration and exploitation' or the 'joint exploitation area' arrangement adopted by some countries as an interim arrangement while waiting for the final resolution of their maritime boundary delimitation dispute. In the Ghana-Côte d'Ivoire dispute, however, the Special Chamber of the ITLOS made an interim ruling to the effect that Ghana could continue production in the multi-billion-dollar offshore oil development in the disputed maritime zone but must not start any new drilling or exploration. The goal in these temporary arrangements is the rational and peaceful exploitation of these vital resources of the ocean, pending final resolution of the dispute which could take many years.

Egypt v. Sudan

Sudan has an adjacent maritime boundary with Egypt. But it is a mere 90 nautical miles boundary to a tripoint with Saudi Arabia. It is delimited and is not the source of any dispute between both countries. Sudan's coast (in the Red Sea) is approximately 270 to 330 miles long. It is the opposite part of the coast of Saudi Arabia. But it would appear the Sudan-Saudi Arabia maritime boundary has not yet been constructed, though on the view of commentators 'the Sudanese inshore island archipelago of the Sawakin Group balances the Saudi Arabian inshore island archipelago on the Farasan Bank such that a median line solution would appear equitable' (Colson & Smith, 2005). But pending the construction of such a line, should there be agreement, Sudan and Egypt access the resources of the Central Red Sea area on the basis of a signed 1974 agreement on the joint exploration and exploitation of the resources of the seabed and subsoil in that sector of the Red Sea. This 1974 regime of joint exploration and exploitation of resources was quite prescient and is one that was endorsed in 1982 by the UN Convention on the Law of the Sea where states are not yet agreed on the delimitation line of their common maritime boundary.

NOTES

1. Available at www.jag.navy.mil/organization/documents/mcrm/equatorial-guinea_2014.pdf (accessed 26/5/2015).
2. United Nations Division for Ocean Affairs and the Law of the Sea (1998) (37) Law of the Sea Bulletin 6.
3. *Case Concerning the Continental Shelf (Tunisia v. Libyan Arab Jamahiriya)*, ICJ Reports, Judgement of 24 February 1982.
4. *Tunisia/Libya Continental Shelf case, ICJ Reports, 1982.*
5. 283 US 336 (1931).
6. Available at http://oilprice.com/Geopolitics/International/Tension-Builds-In-The-Gulfposted 2 April 2010 (accessed 20 Jan 2016).
7. Act No. 15/1984 of Nov 1984 on the territorial sea and the exclusive economic zone.
8. Act No. 15/1984 on the Territorial Sea and exclusive economic zone and Act No 1/1999 on the exclusive economic zone.
9. A long-standing aim of international law is the early pacific settlement of disputes, and in a manner fair and just to the parties involved. In this era of the UN Charter, the use of force by individual states as a means of settling disputes is impermissible. Amicable settlement is the only available means. One amicable settlement method is by a properly constituted international judicial tribunal, applying rules of law. At present, the only *general* organ of judicial settlement (apart from a regional judicial tribunal and a specialized tribunal such as the International Tribunal for the Law of the Sea) available in the international community is the International Court of Justice at The Hague.
10. The two hotly contested issues in that case were the maritime boundary and the status of Bakassi Peninsula, a 1,000 square kilometre of densely populated swamp

land which lies between two Rivers, the Akwayafe and the Rio del Rey. Both issues in fact involved the maritime boundary between Nigeria and the former trust territory of the British Southern Cameroons.

11. The International Tribunal for the Law of the Sea (https://www.itlos.org) is governed by its statute appended as Annex VI of the UN Convention on the Law of the Sea, 1982. The jurisdiction of the tribunal comprises all disputes and all applications submitted to it in accordance with the Convention on the Law of the Sea. It also includes all matters specifically provided for in any other agreement which confers jurisdiction on the tribunal (statute, Article 21). The Tribunal has jurisdiction to deal with disputes (contentious jurisdiction) and legal questions (advisory jurisdiction) submitted to it. To date, at least twenty-nine cases have been submitted to the tribunal, including the following cases involving a number of African states: The M/V 'SAIGA' Case (Saint Vincent and the Grenadines v. Guinea), the first case submitted to the tribunal on 13 November 1997; The M/V 'SAIGA' (No. 2) Case (Saint Vincent and the Grenadines v. Guinea); The 'Monte Confurco' Case (Seychelles v. France);The 'Juno Trader' Case (Saint Vincent and the Grenadines v. Guinea-Bissau);The M/V 'Virginia G' Case (Panama/Guinea-Bissau); The 'ARA Libertad' Case (Argentina v. Ghana); Dispute Concerning Delimitation of the Maritime Boundary between Ghana and Côte d'Ivoire in the Atlantic Ocean (Ghana/Côte d'Ivoire); The M/T 'San Padre Pio' Case (Switzerland v. Nigeria; The M/T 'San Padre Pio' (No. 2) Case (Switzerland v. Nigeria; and Dispute Concerning delimitation of the maritime boundary between Mauritius and Maldives in the Indian Ocean (Mauritius/Maldives). Judgements and orders delivered in cases submitted to the tribunal are reproduced in the series *Reports of Judgements, Advisory Opinions and Orders*.

12. *Delimitation of the Maritime Boundary in the Atlantic Ocean (Ghana/Côte d'Ivoire)*, Case No. 23, Judgement, ITLOS Reports 2017, p. 4; see also, Dispute Concerning Delimitation of the Maritime Boundary between Ghana and Côte d'Ivoire in the Atlantic Ocean (Ghana/Côte d'Ivoire), ITLOS, 21 April 2015.

13. *Nicaragua v. Honduras*, Judgement, ICJ Reports 2007 (II), p. 659, at p. 735, para. 253.

14. *Sovereignty over Pulua Ligitan and Pulua Sipadan (Indonesia /Malaysia)*, Judgement, ICJ Reports 2002, p. 625, at p. 664, para. 79.

15. *Maritime Delimitation and Territorial Questions between Qatar and Bahrain (Qatar v. Bahrain)*, Merits, Judgement, ICJ Reports 2001, p. 40, at p.93, paras 173–174.

16. *Delimitation of the Maritime Boundary in the Bay of Bengal (Bangladesh/ Myanmar)*, Judgement, ITLOS Reports 2012, p. 4, at p. 86, para. 317.

17. *Case Concerning the Delimitation of the Maritime Boundary between Guinea and Guinea-Bissau*, 14 February 1985, Reports of International Arbitral Awards (RIAA), vol. XIX, pp. 149–196; see also *Guinea-Guinea-Bissau Maritime Boundary Arbitration* of 1985, 1986 77 ILR 635.

18. *Case Concerning the Arbitral Award of 31 July 1989 (Guinea-Bissau v. Senegal)*, Order of 2 March 1990; see also *Guinea-Bissau v. Senegal (Interim Measures of Protection)*, Order of 2 March 1990.

19. *Case Concerning the Arbitral Award of 31 July 1989 (Guinea-Bissau v. Senegal)*, Judgement of 12 November 1991.

20. *Guinea-Bissau v. Senegal*, Judgement of 12 November 1991.

21. *Case Concerning Maritime Delimitation in the Indian Ocean (Somalia v. Kenya)*; see also *Case Concerning Maritime Delimitation in the Indian Ocean (Somalia v. Kenya) – Preliminary Objections*, Judgement, 2 February 2017.

22. UNCLOS, art 15, 74(1), 83(1); *Maritime Delimitation and Territorial Questions between Qatar and Bahrain*, 2001; *Maritime Delimitation in the Area between Greenland and Jan Mayen*, 1993.

23. *North Sea Continental Shelf cases*, ICJ Reports, 1969.

24. *Libya v. Malta Continental Shelf case*, ICJ Reports, 1985.

25. *North Sea Continental Shelf cases*, ICJ Reports, 1969.

Part Two

ARMED CONFLICTS WITHIN AND BETWEEN STATES

An armed conflict within the territory of a state is variously denoted as an intrastate armed conflict, a non-international armed conflict, an internal armed conflict or a civil war. The first two expressions are somewhat pedantic terms apt to be found in works on international humanitarian law. The last two terminologies are in common use and most often interchangeable. An armed confrontation within a state does not make it less of a war. From the point of view of a government in power, a rebellion or revolution may appear as a heinous crime to be repressed by all means at the disposal of 'the forces of law and order'. Yet, as Schwarzenberger notes, if a revolt develops into a prolonged civil war and revolutionaries establish effective control over large areas, such a state of affairs is, for all practical purposes, indistinguishable from war. This is in fact how third states tend to view the situation. In international law, if the recognized government no longer exercises any effective control over portions of its territory and the revolutionaries are able and willing to abide by international humanitarian law, the latter qualify sooner or later for recognition as insurgents or belligerents. Even the legitimate government itself may find it advisable and in its own interest to recognize its rebels as belligerents. The implication of a legitimate government recognizing its rebels as belligerents is that it must then apply international humanitarian war in all its relations with the rebels (Schwarzenberger, 1976: 172–173).

Decolonization from white rule did not come easily. Many African countries fought anti-colonial wars to obtain national liberation. This was the case in countries where the colonial power rejected consensual decolonization. In East Africa, independence was by and large achieved consensually except in the case of Kenya. In West Africa too, independence was obtained without waging a war of national liberation except in two cases, that of Guinea Bissau and Cape Verde. Algeria and Libya in North Africa, and Angola, Mozambique, Namibia and Zimbabwe in Southern Africa all snatched independence from obstinate colonial powers after protracted wars of independence. Achievement of independence did not, however, inoculate the continent against disputes and violent conflicts. Year after year since independence, one African country after the other has experienced armed conflicts. These conflicts have left millions of people dead and thousands maimed. There is the added agony of indignity and humiliation inflicted on hundreds and thousands of others by the sheer violence unleashed on them. Armed conflicts have caused forced internal displacement of large populations and massive refugee flows to neighbouring countries. They have also caused massive infrastructural and agricultural destruction and engendered a general climate of fear and insecurity. Agricultural productivity and other economic activity have all been rolled back.

AFRICA AS A CHRONIC UNSTABLE SPACE

The African continent continues to be synonymous with war, destruction, famine, refugees, starvation, instability and chaos and remains a chronically unstable space. The resultant hostile and inimical environment deters investment and other development initiatives. The economic impact of Africa's conflicts is incalculable. For example, it is reckoned that the Algerian civil war that started in 1991 had by 2001 claimed 100,000 lives and caused economic losses of up to $20 billion.[1] In 1998, the UN secretary general Kofi Annan submitted to the Security Council a report that is still relevant today. In that report, he observed that although Africa had started to make significant economic and political progress in recent years, nevertheless progress remained threatened or impeded by conflict in many parts of the continent. He noted that since 1970 up to the time of the report, more than thirty wars have been fought in Africa, most of them intrastate in origin, and that these conflicts have seriously undermined Africa's efforts to ensure long term stability, prosperity and peace of its peoples (Annan, 1998).

The reasons that account for so many internal armed conflicts in Africa include historical legacies such as the border problem, colonial relations instituted by colonization, and Cold War confrontation that got African countries sucked into rival ideologies. They also include political corruption, lack of respect for the rule of law, human rights violations and the legacy of European colonization. Other causes are Cold War proxy wars supporting and arming dictatorships in Africa. It is estimated that in the year 2000, $1.5 billion worth of weapons shipped to Africa came from the United States alone (Hartung & Moix, 2000). Contrary to what it might seem, ethnic diversity does not necessarily lead to civil war. In fact, ethnic diversity is actually less likely to cause civil war, as long as there is no weaponization of ethnicity or ethnic polarization between very large ethnic groups (Elbadawi & Sambanis, 2000). Failed policies and politics, lack of credible institutions, failed institutions, high levels of poverty and the 'resource curse' are further advanced as reasons for conflicts in Africa. However, contrary to what theoreticians of the much-criticized 'greed and grief' thesis appear to suggest, poverty in itself does not necessarily lead to intrastate or interstate conflict. The 'greed and grief' theory has already been mentioned in the general introduction to this book and need not detain us here.

The proliferation of small arms in the region helps fuel many conflicts. Africa is an attractive and profitable dumping ground for nations and arms manufacturers eager to get rid of weapon stocks made superfluous by the end of the Cold War or by technological developments (Stohl, 1999). Corporate interests and activities in Africa enrich African and foreign elites while at the same time contribute to exploitation, conflict, and poverty for ordinary people. A theoretical explanation of war and peace is the 'diversionary theory'. According to this theory, a country faced with serious domestic political, social or economic problems will seek to divert attention by appealing to patriotism and aggressively reviving a dormant dispute or asserting an old claim with its neighbour or unleashing the military on part of its population (Mambo & Schofield, 2007). The 'diversionary theory' offers a plausible explanation for the border war between Morocco and Algeria in 1963 and Cameroun's colonial war in Ambazonia since 2017.

'WAR AND PEACE' THEORY

Some international relations commentators posit that a balance of military power between states is a guarantee of peace. In their view, a preponderance of power by one state or an alliance of states protects that state or alliance of states against attack, given the superior military capabilities of the state or alliance. Defence alliances such as the North Atlantic Treaty Organization and the Warsaw Pact are premised on such thinking. This logic explains why states with means always equip themselves with sophisticated military resources, including the acquisition of nuclear weapons which is the ultimate weapon of human destruction. The powerful state is thus in a position to attack a weak state and impose terms. This militarization strategy deters a weak state from challenging a strong state. Historically, however, it is always a strong and not a weak state that always challenges another state. Interestingly, this theoretical power-based explanation of war and peace seems inapplicable in Africa. In the Horn of Africa, for example, the 'fear of the strong state' theory is in fact turned on its head. There, it is the perceived weaker state that tends to attack the perceived stronger one.

One reason for this asymmetrical or 'unequal' war is that in each case the 'weaker' state has the backing of an external power. When Somalia attacked Ethiopia, Somalia was backed by the Soviet Union. When war broke out between Djibouti (weaker state) and Eritrea (stronger state), Djibouti, which has remained a quasi-protectorate of France, was supported militarily by France. When Eritrea (weaker state) went to war against Ethiopia (stronger state), it had external support. When Cameroun (weaker state) went to war with Nigeria (stronger state) over the Bakassi Peninsula it did so in the full knowledge of the fact that France will provide, and did provide, backing and support by way of arms, logistical support and military advisory and intelligence. The element of external support plays a key role in these conflicts. That support was a factor in the East-West rivalry, the strategic interest of external powers. Some see the role of external powers as a deterring and stabilizing hand; others think it encourages foolhardiness and a readiness to act without restraint as in the case of Cameroun's colonial war against Ambazonia which began in 2017.

There is a further explanation why the apparently weaker state attacks its stronger neighbour. This has to do with identity, pride and dignity (Brian, 2002), the 'small-man' or 'under-dog' syndrome. The weaker state engages the stronger state in war because it feels abused or insulted or bullied by it. The weaker state might also feel that if it does not stand up to its stronger neighbour, it might with time lose much of its territory or an economically endowed or strategic part of it or, in fact, become extinct. The attack brings these matters out in the open and are then resolved in the context of a negotiated settlement signed by the parties and perhaps underwritten by the UN or by one or more of the big powers.

INTRASTATE WARS

Two main sources of civil wars in Africa may be identified – decolonization and bad governance – and these have to do with 'grief' and not 'greed'. Some civil wars start under circumstances that are historical, having to do with decolonization.[2] In many instances, no sooner was independence achieved than the nascent state became embroiled in a civil war. Some other civil wars start under circumstances that have to do with enduring ethnic tension within the state, often provoked by post-colonial bad governance issues. Bad governance issues include electoral malpractices, deeply flawed constitutional orders, highly authoritarian and oppressive regimes, and gross human rights violations.[3] Circumstances of decolonization and of bad governance are compounded by what has fittingly been denoted as 'the ethnicization of power' within the state (Rothchild, 1997). The incentive to pick up arms in either case often has to do with altruism or national interest but without, however, discounting the bonus represented by the capture of political power in the state. Many civil wars usually arise from power struggle, often in the form of an armed insurgency, to remove an established government by force of arms. In some other cases, rival armed organizations fight against each other in order to seize the ultimate prize which is power in the state.

The post-conflict period is always very challenging. Countries that have gone through a civil war experience many post-conflict challenges. One of the biggest challenges is how to deal with tens of thousands of IDPs, returning refugees, orphaned children, persons who have become widows and widowers as a result of war and amputees and other persons disabled by war. Other challenges include the disarming of thousands of combatants and militias, integrating them into the regular army and into the wider society, getting rid of weapons that may still be in possession of individuals and the destruction of bombs and landmines that may still be lying around or buried and unexploded (Özerdem, 2008). There might also be an outbreak of disease which the country's weak, post-conflict health infrastructure might be unable to cope with.

INTERSTATE WARS

Regarding interstate conflicts in Africa, no matter how they may be camouflaged or presented, they are basically about resources – perceived economic resources in contested territory or a claim to ethnic communities (a critical human resource) within the borders of another state. These conflicts often take the form of disputes over territory or frontiers (Anyangwe, 2003; Allcock et al., 1992; Boutros-Ghali, 1972; Touval, 1967; Oduntan, 2015) and, more often than not, result in war. This is a clear indication that such quarrels are not just about some non-descript barren piece of real estate or some innocuous crooked line on the ground. Africa's interstate armed conflicts have, with the exception of the war between Ethiopia and Eritrea, eventually been referred by the parties concerned to the international judicial process for resolution of the bone of contention. This would suggest that in the matter of armed conflicts caused by border disputes or territorial claims, African states show a marked preference for judicial settlement, rather than settlement by multilateral diplomacy, direct negotiation, mediation or conciliation. In the case of dormant disputes, however, the tendency appears to be to have recourse to bilateral and multilateral diplomacy (Anyangwe, 2003: 29–30).

Since 1980, no less than twenty-eight African states have experienced war, with sixteen of them having been embroiled in interstate conflicts.[4] Some were involved in post-independence armed conflicts with a non-African state: Egyptian forces fought Britain, France and Israel in the Suez Canal crisis; Ugandan soldiers fought Israeli commandos during the Israeli raid on Entebbe; Somali forces fought American soldiers in the US Operation Enduring Freedom in the Horn of Africa; Libyan forces fought Americans and Europeans in their aerial war against Libya; countless French military interventions in Africa in the Democratic Republic of Congo, and its former colonial territories in Africa.[5] Some other states have been subjected to armed violence led, sponsored or promoted by some Western powers in their declared war against terrorism or Islamic fundamentalism or simply to safeguard what they consider as their turf or sphere of influence.

NOTES

1. Washington Times, 14 July 2001.

2. Angola, Cameroun, Chad, Congo Brazzaville, Congo Kinshasa, Côte d'Ivoire, Mozambique, Nigeria and Zimbabwe, for example.

3. For example, Algeria, Burundi, Cameroun, Chad, Central African Republic, Congo-Brazzaville, Côte d'Ivoire, Djibouti, Ethiopia, Guinea Bissau, Kenya, Liberia, Libya, Mali, Niger, Rwanda, Senegal, Sierra Leone, Somalia, South Sudan and Sudan.

4. Algeria, Burkina Faso, Chad, Djibouti, Egypt, Eritrea, Ethiopia, Libya, Mali, Mauritania, Morocco, Somalia, Sudan, Tanzania, Uganda and Western Sahara.

5. Burkina Faso, Burundi, Cameroun, Chad, Central African Republic, Comoros, Congo Brazzaville, Côte d'Ivoire, Djibouti, Gabon, Guinea Conakry, Mali, Mauritania, Rwanda and Togo.

Chapter 3

Sources of Civil Wars
Colonial Hangover

Non-international armed conflicts are civil wars. They range from full-scale armed confrontations to unarmed but widespread uprisings or disturbances. African countries have experienced, and some continue to experience, major episodes of internal violent armed conflicts entailing very high military expenditure at the expense of other sectors. Armed conflicts cause environmental damage, entail social and economic waste and aggravate health issues. They also cause mass starvation, massive refugee flow, internal displacements and mass killings.[1] Of the current fifty-four states in Africa, twenty-seven have had civil wars, some as early as the 1950s and 1960s.[2]

Another form of violence in Africa consists of an endless cycle of military coup d'états often causing death and destruction, particularly in circumstances of resistance to the coup (Anyangwe, 2012). The coup phenomenon continues to plague the AU which has tried, with limited success, to end it by using ineffective weapons of suspension and targeted sanctions. The most recent military coups d'état took place in Mali on 18 August 2020, in Chad on 21 April 2021 and in Guinea on 5 September 2021. Bizarrely, the Chadian chairperson of the AU Commission Moussa Faki Mahamat eagerly condemned the coup in Mali but failed to condemn the one in Chad and also the one in Guinea.

'FRIENDS TODAY, ENEMIES TOMORROW'

Liberation wars fought in Africa have an inglorious chapter. In one scenario, after liberation was achieved, former liberators turned their weapons against each other so as to grab and monopolize power. In Angola and Zimbabwe, war broke out between rival liberation movements shortly after independence was achieved. In another scenario, yesterday's comrades-in-arms plotted and eliminated their comrades. In Guinea-Bissau, after independence was achieved and the former liberation movement acceded to power, a bitter and murderous struggle for power ensured, entailing coup d'état, civil strife and serious loss of lives. In the process of such inter-movement or intra-movement fighting, the entire country got sucked in, polarized along ethnic lines and ending in massive death and destruction. Friends of yesterday simply became enemies after independence was achieved. Fortunately, this phenomenon was something of an exception.

Angola

Almost immediately upon achieving independence in 1975 following a fourteen-year war of liberation, civil war broke out in Angola spearheaded by Jonas Savimbi's UNITA and Holden Roberto's FNLA, on the one hand, and Agostinho Neto's MPLA, on the other hand. The war claimed about half a million lives. It officially ended in 1991 but fighting resumed in 1992 when Unita rejected the results of the multi-party elections of that year and returned to the bush. In 2005, Unita was defeated, and Savimbi was killed. The country returned to normalcy. The official ending of the civil war in 1991 and its resumption in 1992 illustrates the point made by analysts that some conflicts go in abeyance and are temporarily frozen, typically due to external intervention, but only to reignite later (Croker et al., 2005).

A four-century-old Portuguese colonization of Angola began in 1575 (James III, 2011). In 1961, Angola's armed three liberation movements launched a war of independence to free the country. The movements were the MPLA led by Agostinho Neto and later José Eduardo dos Santos, the FNLA led by Holden Roberto and UNITA led by Jonas Savimbi who had earlier broken from the FNLA. After fourteen years of war, Portugal sued for peace. The Alvor Accord signed in Lisbon on 15 January 1975 between Portugal and the three liberation movements ended Angola's war of independence. Surprisingly, the departing colonial power did not oversee the formation of a government in Luanda and did not transfer powers to any or all of the movements. Portugal instead withdrew from Angola leaving the country without a government, without transfer of powers and without a proclamation of independence having been made (Heimer, 1979). This serious dereliction created a power vacuum which the three-armed liberation movements, all of them based in the capital Luanda at that time, started fighting to fill.

In July 1975, the MPLA forced the FNLA out of Luanda. The FNLA withdrew to its ethnic base of Bakongo in the north along the border with Zaire. Unita took the cue and withdrew to its Ovimbundu ethnic stronghold in the south along the border with Zambia. Apartheid South Africa and Zaire sent in troops to support Unita and FNLA. Cuban intervention in support of Neto enabled the MPLA to consolidate power in Luanda. On 11 November 1975, eleven months after the end of the war of independence, Neto formerly declared Angola independent under the name and style of the People's Republic of Angola, with Luanda as its capital. Unita also declared the same country independent as the Socialist Republic of Angola, with Huambo as its capital. The FNLA too made its own declaration of independence calling the country the Democratic Republic of Angola, with headquarters in Ambriz. From far away Paris, the Front for the Liberation of the Enclave of Cabinda (Flec) proclaimed the independence of the Republic of Cabinda (Heimer, 1979).

A few days later, on 23 November 1975, Savimba and Roberto announced the formation of a coalition government based in Huambo with both of them as co-presidents but failed to get international recognition. The stage was thus set for the civil war that quickly consumed the entire country and lasted three decades. The failure of Savimbi and Roberto to get international recognition was in stark contrast to Neto and his MPLA government. On 9 December 1975, the OAU collectively recognized the MPLA government, confirming its 1969 recognition of the MPLA as the only true representative of the Angolan people. A year later, in 1976, Neto's government was formally recognized by the OAU as the legitimate government of independent Angola. The United States initially vetoed Angola's membership of the UN on 23 June 1976, but that veto was subsequently overcome, and Angola eventually became a member of the UN by the end of the year. Zambia, a Savimbi supporter, then forbade Unita from launching attacks against the Angolan government from its territory.

Before 1975, the liberation movements had been united in the common objective of ending Portuguese colonial rule. But upon achieving that goal, they turned their guns against each other in a bitter struggle to capture political power in the state. The civil war pitted the MPLA against both the FNLA and UNITA. The struggle for power was exacerbated by the fact that the movements had mutually incompatible and untrusting leaderships, were ethnically based and had different political ideologies. The MPLA espoused socialism and posed as Marxist-Leninist. UNITA and FNLA subscribed to capitalism and presented themselves as anti-communists. The MPLA was essentially a multiracial and urban movement drawing its support largely from the Ambundu ethnic group in the large cities of Huambo, Benguela, Luanda and its environs. The FNLA was rural-based and drew support mainly from the Bakongo people of northern Angola bordering Zaire. UNITA was also rural-based but drew its support from mainly the Ovimbundu people of the Angolan central highlands bordering Zambia. Moreover, there had emerged in the early 1970s a division based on skin colour between *assimilados* and *indigenas* but which somehow masked the inter-ethnic conflict between the various native tribes (Heimer, 1979). Mutually untrusting leadership, opposing ethnicity and antagonistic ideology were three factors that played out with devastating effect in the thirty-year *Guerra Civil Angolana* which eventually saw the victory of the MPLA in 2005.

Many analysts consider the civil war to have been a surrogate Cold War theatre on account of the large-scale direct and indirect military intervention in the war by opposing powers. The Soviet Union, East Germany, Romania and Cuba were on the side of the MPLA. The United States, Apartheid South Africa, China and Zaire were on the side of Unita and FNLA (Scherrer, 2002). When José Eduardo dos Santos was sworn in as president of Angola following the death of Neto in September 1979, he undertook to end the civil war by signing non-aggression pacts with Zaire and Zambia. He also participated in ceasefire agreements with his opponents. In the 1980s, the civil war escalated in intensity and witnessed increased international support by allies of both sides. When apartheid South Africa threatened to use nuclear weapons, Cuba threatened to retaliate with nerve gas. A ceasefire was eventually signed in New York by the warring parties in 1988, prompting the UN to create the UNAVEM, a peacekeeping force that began arriving in Angola in January 1989. The arrival of UNAVEM did not stop fighting on the ground. A ceasefire signed by Dos Santos and Savimbi in Gbadolite, Zaire, at a meeting convened by Mobutu in June 1989 was later rejected by Savimbi who then resumed the armed conflict. Meanwhile, peace efforts continued.

On 31 May 1991, Dos Santos and Savimbi met again, this time in Lisbon, and signed three ceasefire agreements – the Bicesse Accords, which provided for multi-party democracy and a transition under UNAVEM II, presidential elections in 1992 and the demobilization and integration of rebel forces into the national army. But UNITA did not disarm. Savimbi lost the 1992 presidential election, claimed that it had been rigged, and resumed fighting. A meeting convened in 1993 in Addis Ababa to restore peace failed, and fighting resumed with even greater intensity. UNITA initially gained the upper hand in the fighting through indiscriminate shelling of besieged cities while MPLA government countered by making use of airpower, causing high civilian casualties. On 31 October 1994, the Lusaka Protocol was signed reaffirming the Bicesse Accords. But this peace agreement fared no better than the previous ones (Pazzanita, 1991). Between 1988 and 1994, at least five ceasefire agreements and peace accords were concluded with UNITA: one in New York in 1988 that prompted the establishment of the UNAVEM; one in Gbadolite, Zaire, in 1989; one in Lisbon, the Lisbon Bicesse Accords in 1991 which provided for a multi-party transition under UNAVEM II and presidential elections in 1992 as well as the demobilization and integration of rebel forces into the national army; one in Addis Ababa in 1993 known as the Addis Ababa Peace Initiative; and a final one in Zambia, the Lusaka Protocol in 1994 which reaffirmed the Bicesse Accords. However, each one of these peace accords was denounced soon afterwards by UNITA, and each denunciation was followed by a resumption and intensification of the civil war. This insincerity interrogates the motivations of an insurgency in signing peace agreements to end an armed conflict (Mutwol, 2009).

The Angolan peace initiatives collapsed for reasons that included the following: mutual distrust between the two warring parties, continued importation of arms by both sides, an unrealistic emphasis on maintaining a balance of power between the two sides and weak international monitoring of the implementation of the agreement. When the government of national unity and reconciliation established in 1997 also collapsed and fighting resumed for the nth time, Dos Santos became convinced that the only way to ultimately achieve peace was through intensification of the war. In 1999, he launched a massive offensive code named 'Operation Restore'. UNITA initially gained the upper hand in the fighting through indiscriminate shelling of besieged cities. The MPLA government countered by making use of air power, causing high civilian casualties. Government forces also used a strategy that consisted in isolating UNITA from its rural base by forcing civilians in the countryside to relocate to major cities. This strategy enabled the MPLA to destroy 80% of Unita's militant wing. Several UNITA commanders became dissatisfied with Savimbi's leadership. They broke away and formed a group, UNITA *Renovada*. In 1999 and 2000, thousands of UNITA supporters deserted. By 2001, government forces were in control of virtually the entire country. Following the killing of Savimbi in Moxico province on 22 February 2005, the remnants of UNITA signed a Memorandum of Understanding with the government on 4 April 2005 as an addendum to the Lusaka Protocol. UNITA's new leadership declared the guerrilla movement a political party and officially demobilized its guerrillas in August 2005.

The Angolan civil war left some half a million people dead, over a million internally displaced, thousands of orphans and thousands of amputees and other disabled persons. It devastated the country's health, road, school and other infrastructure. It severely damaged the state's public administration and economic enterprises. It deeply divided the country's ethnic groups. It cost the country billions and billions of US dollars. It informed the country's later involvement in the Namibian war of independence against apartheid South Africa, its involvement in the civil war in Congo Brazzaville during Pascal Lissouba's presidency and its involvement in the civil war in the Democratic Republic of Congo during Laurent Kabila's presidency.

Guinea-Bissau

The country was colonized by the Portuguese in the nineteenth century. It fought a thirteen-year national liberation war against Portugal and finally gained independence on 10 September 1974. Six years after decolonization, the army under Bernardo Vieira seized power in 1980. An army uprising against Vieira in 1998 triggered a civil war. Senegal and Guinea-Conakry intervened on the side of the Vieira government. A peace accord signed in November 1998 collapsed. A few months later, in May 1999, the rebels overthrew Vieira. Civilian rule returned to the country but in 2003 there was another coup. Vieira won a presidential runoff election held in 2005 and returned to power but was murdered in 2009 by a group of rebel soldiers. Political violence continued, albeit of low intensity. The violence cost the lives of 655 persons and displaced 350,000 people. Calm has since returned to the troubled country.

Zimbabwe

In Zimbabwe (formerly the British colony of Rhodesia) elections were held in 1980 to usher the new independent state of Zimbabwe after a grim nearly two-decade war of independence (1964–1980) that left more than 20,000 people dead (10,450 freedom fighters, 1,361 Rhodesian security forces and 7,790 black and 468 white civilians). The election saw the victory of Robert Mugabe's ZANU party and he became prime minister. Joshua Nkomo, leader of ZAPU party, was given a series of cabinet positions. In April 1980, the British colony of Southern Rhodesia was formally renamed Zimbabwe, and the name of the country's capital was changed from Salisbury to Harare.

In 1980 and again in 1981, there was an armed clash between two forces, Mugabe's ZANLA and Nkomo's ZIPRA. In 1983, Mugabe dismissed Nkomo from the cabinet. The dismissal triggered bitter fighting between supporters of Nkomo's ZAPU and Mugabe's ZANU in two Ndebele ethnic regions of the country, Matabeleland and the Midlands. Ndebele rebels mounted armed resistance to the government. The government's response was a robust military crackdown by Zimbabwe's North Korean-trained Fifth Brigade (Stiff, 2000; Hill, 2005). The operation was locally called *Gukurahundi*, a Shona word that means 'the early rain which washes away the chaff before the spring rains'. Gukurahundi became known as the Matabeleland Massacres. Zanu initially presented *Gukurahundi* as an ideological strategy aimed at carrying the war into major settlements and individual homesteads. It recruited mainly from the majority Shona people, whereas ZAPU had its greatest support among the minority Ndebele.

In early 1983, the Fifth Brigade, a counter-insurgency infantry brigade, commanded by Colonel Perrance Shiri, began a crackdown on dissidents in Matabeleland North Province, a homeland of the Ndebele. Thousands of Ndebele were reportedly detained by government forces, some marched to re-education camps and some others were summarily executed. The Gukurahundi operation ended with the crushing of the armed resistance in 1985. It is reckoned to have left about 20,000 people dead, most of them victims of public executions (Eppel, 2008; Nyarota, 2006). Violence between ZANLA and ZIPRA forces continued until December 1987 when the two groups agreed to merge into one political party. Mugabe and Nkomo signed the Unity Accord which effectively merged ZAPU and ZANU into ZANU-PF, with Mugabe as leader of the party. Mugabe became president of Zimbabwe and abolished the office of prime minister to avoid two centres of power in the country. At various times between 1992 and 2000, Zimbabwe government officials, including Mugabe, apologized for the execution and torture of civilians by the Fifth Brigade, some describing the action as 'eternal hell' and others as 'a moment of madness'. Mugabe announced an amnesty for all dissidents, and Nkomo called on them to lay down their arms. The amnesty was extended to include all members of the security forces who had committed human rights violations. In the 1990s, the disturbances were finally at an end, bringing relief nationwide. Joshua Nkomo died on 1 July 1999 and Robert Mugabe on 6 September 2019.

RELIGION

Religion, whether Muslim or Christian, is seldom a divisive factor in Africa. But there are cases in which the immediate cause of civil war has been the religious factor. This is especially the case when religion is instrumentalized, weaponized or manipulated by elites fighting for political power or seeking to establish religious hegemony in the state. That is what Islamic jihadists, some Christian 'fundamentalist' or 'born again' groups (such as the LRA in Uganda) seek to do. In Somalia, Al-Shabaab has for years been waging an insurgency to overthrow the government in Somalia and replace it with a radical Islamic regime. In Uganda, the Lord's Resistance Army has been fighting a bush war for decades to overthrow Yoweri Museveni, who had himself come to power by the sword, and establish in Uganda a government based on the Biblical Ten Commandments.

Algeria

Some 150,000 to 200,000 people are estimated to have died in Algeria as a consequence of civil commotion which erupted on 26 December 1991 and morphed in February 1992 into a civil war that lasted until 2002 (Martinez, 2000; Souaidia, 2001). The immediate cause of the war was the declaration of a state of emergency by the government in reaction to the victory of the FIS in the first round of parliamentary elections, a victory that put the FIS in a commanding position to accede to power. The strength of the Algerian Islamic movement was principally a consequence of government policies in the 1970s. Government excluded the 'Arabization' of a rapidly expanding secondary school system and the recruitment of Iraqi, Egyptian and Palestinian teachers trained in modern Islamic theological centres. Furthermore, certain factors combined to undercut the FNL government's legitimacy. These factors were: rapid population increases, government indebtedness which followed the 1985 collapse of oil prices and an increase in unemployment of 200,000 more people per year in the 1980s. In 1989, there were food riots in the country. In the wake of these riots, a new constitution was adopted providing for the establishment of a multi-party system. Thirty new parties were created, most of which had some kind of affiliation to the notion of Islam as a state religion. The largest party, the FIS, was outspoken in its antipathy not just to the secular government but also to liberal democracy (Willis, 1996). Militarized Islamic opposition movements were active in several other North African countries, including Egypt and Libya.

In cancelling the elections and declaring a state of emergency, the government of Abdelaziz Bouteflika claimed that an FIS victory and accession to power would end democracy in Algeria (Willis, 1996). The ensuing violence pitted the government against the FIS and lasted eleven years. It left thousands of Algerians dead and hundreds of others injured. It caused infrastructural destruction and cost billions of dollars. Repeated mediation efforts in 1994 and 1995 by the Rome-based Saint *Egidio* Catholic Association failed. The government boycotted peace talks in Rome arguing, unconvincingly, that the Algerian problem could only be resolved by Algerians in Algeria. As a result, the FIS that had been prepared to lay down its arms and pursue its objectives in a peaceful and democratic way carried on with its insurgency (Quandt, 1998). More deaths were caused as the government was bent on military victory. The conflict ended indeed with a government victory, following the surrender of the Islamic Salvation Army and the 2002 defeat of the Armed Islamic Movement. Some 5,000 people died in Algeria as a consequence of the civil war which began in February 1992 after the declaration of a state of emergency by the government in reaction to the victory of the FIS in the first round of parliamentary elections.

Chad

France colonized Chad around 1900 and incorporated it as part of French Equatorial Africa. In a single move, France hurriedly granted the country independence on 11 August 1960, together with other sub-Sahara French colonial territories. Independence was obtained under the leadership of François Tombalbaye, but the Muslim north resented his policies. The resentment culminated in the outbreak in 1965 of civil war in which northern Muslim rebels fought against animists, the Christian south government and French troops stationed in the country to protect the regime in place. Numerous ceasefires and peace pacts over a period of fifteen years yielded nothing. In 1979, Muslim rebels captured the capital, N'Djaména, and put an end to the south's hegemony, forcing President Goukouni Oueddei to flee the country. But the rebel commanders fought among themselves for power until 1982 when Hissène Habré defeated his rivals. In 1978, Libya invaded Chad hoping to seize the Aouzou Strip. The Chad-Libya war went on for ten years. In 1987, France intervened militarily in the war by launching *Opération Epervier* which stopped the Libyan advance.

In 1990, Habré was overthrown by a Libyan-supported insurgency known as the Patriotic Salvation Movement led by Idriss Deby Itno who then assumed power as president. Some stability returned to the country thereafter but this did not mean an end to violence by rebel groups seeking to capture power. Rebel activity along the common border with Sudan intensified. It escalated in 2006 as Chadian rebels, along with Sudanese Janjaweed militants, attacked civilians. In February 2008, about 700 civilians died in N'Djaména when more than 200 Chadian rebels stormed the capital and clashed with government forces supported by French troops. Chad's intermittent periods of civil war since independence have left thousands of people dead and not less than 157,000 internally displaced persons. Idriss Deby was assassinated in April 2021 when he was about to celebrate his 'election' victory to the sixth term of office. With the support of France, Deby's son, a soldier, seized power and put in place a military council under him to rule the country. Another rebel insurgency advancing on Ndjamena and just 150 kilometre from the capital made some noise but soon 'disappeared'.

Central African Republic

France seized and colonized in 1894 the territory then known as Ubangi-Shari. Under the 1911 Treaty of Fez, France ceded roughly 300,000 square kilometre portion of the Sangha and Lobaye basin of Ubangi-Shari to the German Empire. After World War I, France re-annexed the Sangha and Lobaye basin and re-incorporated them as part of Ubangi-Shari. The establishment in 1908 of French Equatorial Africa saw Ubangi-Shari being administered from Brazzaville. In 1958, Bathelemy Boganda declared the establishment of the Central African Republic under the French Union and served as its first prime minister. He died in a plane crash on 29 March 1959. His cousin David Dacko took over and became the country's first president when the country formally gained independence from France on 13 August 1960.

Dacko dismissed his political rivals, including former Prime Minister Abel Goumba whom he forced into exile in France. After suppressing all political parties, Dacko declared a one-party state in November 1962. Three years later, on 31 December 1965, he was overthrown by Colonel Jean-Bedel Bokassa, his cousin. Bokassa declared the constitution suspended and the National Assembly dissolved. He instituted a one-man rule and in 1972 declared himself President for Life. As if that was not enough, four years later, on 4 December 1976, he crowned himself in an extravagant ceremony, Napoleon-Bonaparte-style, as Emperor Bokassa I of what he decreed as the Central African Empire.

Bokassa did not take kindly to school children who protested against his decree of imposing compulsory purchase of school uniforms from a company owned by one of his wives. The government violently suppressed the protest, killing hundred schoolchildren. In September 1979, France overthrew Bokassa and reinstated David Dacko to power. Dacko abolished the empire and restored the name the Central African Republic. But he lasted less than two years for, on 1 September 1981, he was overthrown in a coup d'état by General André Kolingba. In 1993, Ange-Félix Patassé defeated Kolingba in elections held with the help of the international community. On 28 May 2001, rebels stormed strategic buildings in Bangui in an unsuccessful coup attempt. The attempt failed largely because Patassé was able to bring in 300 troops of the Congolese rebel leader Jean-Pierre Bemba and Libyan soldiers. Patassé came to suspect that General François Bozizé was involved in another coup attempt against him. Bozizé then fled with loyal troops to Chad. In March 2003, Bozizé launched a surprise attack against Patassé, who was out of the country at the time. Libyan troops and some 1,000 soldiers of Bemba's Congolese rebel organization failed to stop the rebels. Bozizé's forces succeeded in overthrowing Patassé.

In 2004, forces opposed to Bozizé took up arms against the government. The Sirte Agreement in February 2007 and the Birao Peace Agreement in April 2011 called, inter alia, for a cessation of hostilities, the billeting of rebel forces and their integration with the national army, and the liberation of political prisoners. Some rebel groups did not sign the agreement and fighting continued. In 2012, Séléka, a coalition of rebel groups, took over towns in the north of the country and in January 2013 eventually reached a peace deal involving a power-sharing with Bizozé's government. But the deal soon broke down and the rebels seized the capital in March that year. Bizozé fled the country. Michel Djotodia took over as president. A UN peacekeeping force of 3,000 troops bolstered the 6,000 African Union soldiers and 2,000 French troops. In September 2013, Djotodia officially disbanded Séléka but many rebels refused to disarm. As part of a deal negotiated at a regional summit in neighbouring Chad, Djotodia resigned in January 2014 and Catherine Samba-Panza was elected by the National Transitional Council as interim president. This was followed by a peace deal signed in Congo Brazzaville in July 2014. On 14 December 2015, Séléka rebel leaders declared the independent Republic of Logone. Elections were held in March 2016 at which Faustin Archange Touadéra was declared the winner and was sworn in as president

The Central African Republic, the theatre of another African civil war, is a classic example of the military and rival armed groups fighting for power. The Séléka revolt was presented as a struggle between Christians and Muslims. But after the overthrow of Bozizé in December 2013, the armed rebel groups started fighting for power. France sent in troops under 'Opération Sangaris' ostensibly to establish peace but that military intervention turned out to be an operation designed to facilitate French continuing dispossession of the country's mineral resources. After two years of civil war, AU and UN peacekeepers were able to bring precarious stability to the country by the end of 2015. As a result of the civil war, about one-fifth of the population became IDP and thousands of others fled to Cameroun and Chad. In 2015, there were sixty-nine allegations of child rape and other sexual offences by peacekeepers. In March 2016, the UN began investigating those claims. It was also reported that a UN peacekeeper made four girls to engage in bestiality by forcing them to have sex with a dog. There have been repeated allegations of child sex abuse by international troops in the Central African Republic. As of 2021, the country remains the scene of a civil war, albeit low-keyed.

Côte d'Ivoire

Ivory Coast's downslide to the civil war started in 1993 when Henri Konan Bedié became president following the death that year of President Felix Houphouet-Boigny, Ivory Coast's president at independence in 1960. In 1999, Alassane Ouattara, a Muslim, decided to run for president in 2000. His plan to challenge Bedié split the country along ethnic and religious lines. The reason for the split was that a hastily drafted law by Bedié's government and approved in a referendum required both parents of a presidential candidate to be born within the Ivory Coast. This excluded the northern presidential candidate Alassane Ouattara from the race. Ivoirians assert with confidence that he is a native of Burkina Faso who had generously been accepted in Côte d'Ivoire by late president Houphouet-Boigny. In December 1999, Bedié was overthrown by a military coup and General Robert Guei became the president. Presidential elections were held in October 2000 with Guei and Gbagbo as candidates. Guei announced that he had beaten Laurent Gbagbo in the presidential race. He went on to proclaim himself the elected president. A popular uprising forced Guei to flee the country. He was replaced by Laurent Gbagbo, the presumptive winner of the elections. Fighting broke out between President Gbagbo's mainly southern Christian supporters and followers of his opponent, Alassane Ouattara, who are mostly Muslims from the north. The following year, 2001, the two men meet and agree to work towards reconciliation.

The period from 2002 to 2007 is reckoned as that of the first Ivorian civil war. In 2002, Ouattara's RDR party was given four ministerial posts in a new government. But barely a month later soldiers in Abidjan mutinied, unhappy at being demobilized. The mutiny developed into a full-scale rebellion. The rebel soldiers seized control of the northern half of the country. The following year, an agreement was reached stipulating that rebel members be included in a new government. But violence continued. A year later the first contingent of a UN peacekeeping force was deployed. Shortly afterwards, as the violence continued, the Ivorian air force attacked rebel positions. French forces entered the fray after nine of their soldiers were killed in an air strike. The French bombed and destroyed on the ground the entire Ivorian air force. This disproportionate French action triggered anti-French protests. The UN imposed an arms embargo on Côte d'Ivoire. Following talks that were held in South Africa in 2005, government and rebels declared an immediate and final end to hostilities. Planned elections in October 2005 were shelved. The UN extended Gbagbo's mandate for a further year. Under a power-sharing peace deal mediated by Burkina Faso in March 2007, 'New Forces' leader Guillaume Soro was named prime minister. As part of the process of returning the northern part of the country to state control and reuniting the country, rebel soldiers pulled back from frontline positions and handed over ten northern zones to civilian administrators.

The second Ivorian civil war was a five-month conflict from December 2010 to April 2011. In December 2010, Ouattara took over as president after the election commission controversially declared him the winner of the presidential election held in November that year. Gbagbo refused to accept the result. Dispute between the Ouattara and Gbagbo camps escalated into violence. In April 2011, Ouattara's forces captured Gbagbo and eventually handed him over to the International Criminal Court in November to face charges of crimes against humanity. A jihadist Al-Qaeda attack on the Abidjan beach resort in March 2016 left eighteen people dead, bringing the number of people killed in the civil war in Ivory Coast to about 3,000 and the number of displaced persons at 500,000. In January 2019, the ICC acquitted Gbagbo of the charges preferred against him. In November 2020, Ouattara was 're-elected' for a controversial third term. In mid-June 2021, Gbagbo returned to Abidjan to a rousing public welcome.

Senegal

The Casamance region is located in the southern region of Senegal. It is connected in the East to Senegal but separated from the rest of Senegal by The Gambia. The principal inhabitants of the region are members of the Jola ethnic group and many are Christians or animists, unlike the majority of Senegalese who are Muslims. The people of the region argue that they do not benefit sufficiently from the region's richness and that Dakar, the capital, reaps most of the profit from the region's products. In the 1980s, the region engaged in peaceful demonstrations for independence which was met with arrests and military clampdowns. In the 1990s, the Movement of Democratic Forces of Casamance (MFDC) led by Father Augustin Diamacoune Senghor began reprisal attacks against military buildings in the region prompting the military to attack MFDC bases. Several ceasefire attempts failed and violence continued. By 2001, at least 500 people were dead in battle.

Father Senghor and President Abdoulaye Wade agreed on a peace deal that provided for prisoner release, the return of refugees and the clearance of land mines. The agreement however did not bring autonomy for Casamance. Some in the MFDC regarded this as a betrayal. They split and formed a rival faction. The two factions then started fighting each other. A short-lived truce was signed in 2004. In 2006 fighting resumed, prompting thousands of civilians to flee across the border to The Gambia. Father Senghor died in January 2007. Fighting between the insurgents and the Senegalese army continued until 2012 with casualties on both sides, sometimes in double digits. In April 2012, newly sworn-in president Macky Sall proposed to involve the leaders of Gambia and Guinea-Bissau in efforts to find a solution to the long-running Casamance conflict. Some low-level violence took place in 2013. But in 2014, the leader of the MFDC Salif Sadio sued for peace and declared a unilateral ceasefire. This came about as a result of secret talks held at the Vatican between the MFDC and the government of Senegal led by Macky Sall. The total number of people killed in this insurgency would probably be about 550.

The Casamance rebellion in Senegal displaced 20,000 persons as refugees. The Casamance Province of Senegal was governed by Portugal before the 1884 African Berlin Congress. Its population is drawn from communities which straddle the border with Guinea-Bissau where the insurgent MFDC was based until its expulsion by troops of Guinea-Bissau in 1997. Support for the Casamance separatists had promoted divisions within the army of Guinea-Bissau, following the dismissal of its pro-Casamance chief of staff. These tensions sparked off an army mutiny in the country in June 1997, which ECOWAS worked to resolve.

Somalia

Major General Mohammed Siad Barre overthrew by coup d'état and assassinated President Abdirashid Ali Shermarke, Somali's second president after Mukhtar Mohamed Hussein. That was on 21 October 1969. As president of Somalia, Barre espoused the concept of a 'Greater Somalia (Soomaaliweyn)'. Greater Somalia encompasses Somalia, Djibouti, the Ogaden in Ethiopia and Kenya's former northeastern province. These are regions of the Horn of Africa inhabited by ethnic Somalis and have historically been the majority population. In pursuit of this expansionist ambition, Barre made a failed attempt to seize Somali-inhabited regions within the territory of adjacent countries. He started the Ogaden war which began in 1976 and ended in 1978 when Somali troops were ultimately pushed out of the Ogaden. In the 1970s, Barre espoused a pan-African vision. During his presidency, Somalia trained Burundi's Air Force (1974), protected the borders of Tanzania and Uganda (1972–1978), defended Mozambique from Portugal (1975), flew jets for Zambia (1978), trained South African freedom fighters and backed Eritrea's war of independence.

From 1980 to 1990, various Somali clan-based insurgency groups fought to overthrow Barre's authoritarian regime. The insurgency groups were the Somali Salvation Democratic Front – SSDF, the United Somali Congress – USC, the Somali National Movement – SNM and the Somali Patriotic Movement – SPM. The SNM in particular was supported by Mengistu Haile Mariam's Dergue regime in Ethiopia. In January 1986, Barre and Mengistu met in Djibouti to normalize relations between their respective countries. Under an agreement signed in 1988, Barre disbanded his clandestine anti-Ethiopian organization, the Western Somali Liberation Front. In turn, Mengistu was expected to disarm the SNM active on the Ethiopian side of the border. But in response to the agreement, the SNM relocated to Northern Somalia.

As the insurgency intensified, Barre sent punitive expeditions to insurgent strongholds and even bombarded them. But these actions failed to stop the insurgency. Siad Barre's dictatorial regime was eventually overthrown in January 1991. Somalia plunged into chaos and deeper civil war on 26 January 1991 when Barre fled Mogadishu, and his regime collapsed. Media reports at the time indicated that Barre fled in an army tank filled with reserves from the Somalian Central Bank, including gold and foreign currency estimated to have been worth $27 million. He first fled to his family's stronghold from where he made a failed bid in May 1991 to retake power. He eventually moved to Nairobi and then to Lagos, Nigeria, where he died on 2 January 1995 of a heart attack.

The military overthrow of President Siad Barre was followed by warfare between military factions led by General Mohamed Farah Aidid and interim president Ali Mahdi Mohamed. As in Liberia, the organization of state structures around regionally organized patronage networks based on kinship and clan systems make it especially susceptible to fragmentation with the removal of external support for a central authority. Notwithstanding the presence of UN-authorized peacekeeping force, totalling 35,000 soldiers at one stage, intermittent fighting between various clan-based military factions continued unabated. By the end of 1992, famine attributed to military operations had killed a quarter of all Somali children under the age of five. Following the collapse of the Barre regime, various armed groups began fighting each other to fill the power vacuum left by the collapsed regime. In the south, ex-Italian Somaliland, armed factions led by USC commanders General Mohamed Farah Aidid and Ali Mahdi Mohamed, in particular, clashed as each sought to exert authority over the other. In the northern, ex-British Somaliland revived its three days of independence achieved in 1960, declared itself the Republic of Somaliland and established normalcy and a functioning government.

Somalia had no central government. An estimated 350,000 Somalis were dead due to disease, starvation or civil war. This prompted the UN in 1992 to adopt Resolutions 733 and 746 creating 'UNOSOM I' to provide humanitarian relief. This UN-approved military mission was code-named 'Operation Restore Hope' and was led by the United States. Its purpose was to help the starving country by protecting food shipments from being seized by the warlords and to help restore order in Somalia. 'UNOSOM I' military observers arrived in Mogadishu in July 1992 and were immediately followed by peacekeepers. Between 1993 and 1995, 'UNOSOM I' successfully mediated some reconciliation between the warring clan leaders or warlords. But the various factions soon started fighting for control over the capital Mogadishu. In 1993, one of the rebel factions shot down two US helicopters, resulting in the death of eighteen US soldiers. Hundreds of Somalis were killed in the battle that ensued. US troops made an unsuccessful attempt to apprehend rebel faction leader Mohamed Farah Aideed. In 1994, the US formally ended its mission to Somalia. That mission cost the US $1.7 billion, with a death toll of 43 soldiers and 153 wounded. UN peacekeepers also suffered significant casualties and were withdrawn in March 1995.

There was some return to customary and religious law in most regions, one of which declared itself in 1998 the autonomous region of Puntland. Pockets of conflicts continued as the various factions battled for control of more territory, including the capital. By the year 2000 fighting had reduced in intensity but not over yet. A series of conferences in Djibouti achieved some limited success in reconciling the parties. A Transitional National Government was established, followed in 2004 by a Transitional Federal Government (TFG). The TFG became Somalia's internationally recognized government. In an effort at reconciliation, representatives of the TFG and the newly formed Islamic Courts Union (ICU) representatives held several rounds of unsuccessful talks in Khartoum under the auspices of the Arab League.

In 2006, Ethiopian troops entered Somalia and seized most of the south from the ICU. The ICU then splintered into more radical groups, notably Al-Shabaab which has since been fighting not only the Somali government but also 'AMISOM', the AU-mandated peacekeeping force. Al-Shabaab is fighting for control of Somalia. It launched deadly terrorist attacks deep inside Kenya (McGregor, 2007). By January 2009, Al-Shabaab and other militias had forced Ethiopian troops to retreat from Somali territory which it had seized and occupied since 2006. A federal government was established in August 2012. This was the first permanent central government in the country since the start of the civil war in 1980. With the help of AMISOM, the federal government re-captured all of Somalia's major urban centres. However, Al-Shabaab continued to control many rural areas where a number of their operatives had reportedly 'melted' into local communities in order to effectively exploit any mistakes by the central authorities. In August 2014, the Somali government launched 'Operation Indian Ocean' to mop up the remaining insurgent-held areas in the countryside. But Al-Shabaab remains undefeated and has resorted to detonating explosives and using suicide bombers. The use of suicide bombers and explosives has a devastating effect on Somali troops, AMISOM forces and local civilians. Fighting continues, including suicide bomb attacks. Necrometrics estimate that around half a million people have been killed in Somalia since the start of the civil war in that country to about 2020. Of this number, at least 3,000 are AU soldiers killed in that country over the past few years. In addition, about 3.5 million Somalis suffer from war and famine.

Sudan

Sudan achieved independence from Britain on 1 January 1956. It has since known several military coups up to Omar al-Bashir's coup in 1989. It has also gone through three periods of civil war, 18 August 1955 to 27 March 1972, April 1983 to January 2005 and the war in Darfur which began in 2003 but is now low-keyed. From 1955 to 1972 and again from 1983 to 2005, the marginalized people of the southern part of the country, largely Christians and followers of traditional religions, fought the Khartoum government dominated by Arab-Muslim northern Sudanese. The civil war from 1955 to 1972 was wagged by the south against the north by a southern insurgency known as the 'Anya Nya' (Akol & McCall, 2020). That insurgency gained regional self-government for South Sudan under an agreement reached in Addis Ababa in 1978. In 1983, civil war between north and south of Sudan broke out again, the south led by John Garang's SPLM. The civil war and related famine cost an estimated 2 million lives and displaced millions of southerners. A peace agreement was signed in 2005 which offered power-sharing and autonomy for South Sudan to be followed by an independence referendum, which eventually took place in 2011, and South Sudan attained independence on 9 July 2011. Meanwhile, another rebellion broke out in western Sudan in the Darfur region from 2003 to 2011. By 2009, this theatre of the Sudanese civil war had claimed the lives of 300,000 people and displaced another 2.7 million people, the presence of thousands of AU and UN peacekeepers notwithstanding.

Sudan's dual society is divided between a more Arabized Northern Sudan and a Christian-led South Sudan. The broad contrasts between the Arab and the African ethnic and cultural aspects of Sudan play a major role in the country's internal conflict. The different peoples of Sudan view themselves from different angles. Some visualize their country as linking the Arab and the African worlds. Others feel that Sudan must choose between those two worlds. The identity of the country is further complicated by the fact that more than half of the population views itself as Africans even though the country's majority speaks Arabic, and Sudan's official language is Arabic. The Muslim Arab minority dominates the political and economic life and seeks to integrate the country into the Arab/Islamic world. Non-Arabs and non-Muslims, by contrast, tend to look towards Africa for their symbol of identity.

The civil war in Sudan started prior to the country's independence during the last days of the Anglo-Egyptian condominium colonial administration from 1898 to 1956. Violence erupted in 1955 when the southern part of the Torit garrison mutinied and was joined by southern civilians, police and prison guards. For a period of two weeks, Equatorial Province in South Sudan became the dying field for northerners, most of whom were civilians, including women and children. Government reprisal was brutal, though many mutineers had fled into the bush or to neighbouring countries. Sudan's situation and the north-south polarization worsened when Ibrahim Abboad, a military officer, was in power from 1958 to 1964. Abboad generally forced the Arabization of education and administration in the south of Sudan. The north-south divide dominates Sudanese politics, despite substantial cultural and ethnic diversity within each. It also explains the extensive external intervention in the Sudanese civil war. Additionally, the Southern Policy of the colonial administration which divided the country into northern and southern Sudan had the objective of eventually partitioning the country into two prior to independence. By the time the Southern Policy was abandoned, the two entities, North Sudan and South Sudan, had developed different identities and different rates of social and economic development and were already drifting apart. The south was far less developed relative to the north.

When Abboad came to power, he promoted Islamization, insulated the south and restricted the operation of Christian churches and schools. This created severe internal conflict between southern Sudanese and the government in Khartoum. This protest escalated into a full-scale rebellion in the early 1960s. The southern Sudan further demanded the separation of the south as an independent state. This rebellion came to an end in 1969 after another government took over and recognized the historical and cultural differences. This culminated in the Addis Ababa Accord of 1972. However, in 1983, the civil war resumed due to Numeri's continual violations of the Addis Ababa Accord. Furthermore, Numeri instituted Islamic law in September 1983. This had the effect of turning non-Muslims into second-class citizens and imposed religious penalties. The southerners were angered over the re-division and Islamic laws. This promoted their continued economic backwardness contrary to the development of the south which they expected to follow the Addis Ababa Accord. This subsequently reinforced their disappointment. Renewed armed rebellion was triggered by the forcible suppression on 16 May 1983 of absorbed forces from Anya Nya. These soldiers resisted orders to be transferred north. The mutineers regrouped in Ethiopia where Colonel John Garang de Mabior, an officer in Khartoum, joined them. He welded them into the SPLM whose immediate demands included an end to Islamic law and the overthrow of Numeri. Garang further sought to re-structure the overall political system in order to eliminate ethnic discrimination and redistribute power to the marginalized peoples and regions.

The case of Sudan shows that apart from religion as the immediate cause of conflict, there were other underlying issues such as unequal sharing of power, ethnic discrimination and unequal rates of development.

ETHNICITY

Ethnic-based conflicts leading to civil wars have erupted in Burundi, Cameroun (where the anti-colonial war was continued to unseat what was characterized as 'a French-installed puppet regime that made Cameroun a vassal state of France'), Congo Brazzaville, Congo-Kinshasa, Djibouti, Kenya, Liberia, Mozambique, Rwanda and South Sudan.

Burundi

Burundi and Rwanda constituted a single trust territory, known as Ruanda-Urundi, under Belgian administration. In 1962, the territory voted to divide into the two sovereign states of Rwanda and Burundi. Burundi thus gained its independence from Belgium in 1962. Following periodic assassinations and coup d'états going back to the mid-1960s, the country relapsed into a civil war in which Tutsi and Hutu, the country's two main ethnic groups, engaged in communal self-destruction. In 1993, Burundi held its first multi-party democratic elections since independence. The elections were won by Melchior Ndadaye, a Hutu. But he was assassinated on October 21 that year by Tutsi extremists. A few months later Ndadaye's successor, Cyprien Ntaryamira, a Hutu also, was assassinated in the same plane crash with Rwandan president Juvenal Habyarimana. These treasonable killings provoked year-long armed violence between Hutu and Tutsi, leaving some 100,000 people dead and marking the onset of a protracted civil war that only ended in 2006.

Ntaryamira's successor, Sylvester Ntibantunganya, took over the reins of power in April 1994 at the height of an influx of hundreds of thousands of Rwandan refugees and increased violence between armed Hutu and Tutsi groups. Ntibantunganya was barely two years in power when Major Pierre Buyoya, a Tutsi, seized power by coup d'état in 1996. Hutu armed rebels retaliated by killing about 300 Tutsis in July of that year, followed by revenge killing of 126 Hutu refugees by Tutsi soldiers in January 1997. The civil war continued despite ceasefire talks in Tanzania and the efforts of the international community to create a peace process. A ceasefire and power-sharing accord were signed by three Tutsi armed groups and the government. Leading Hutu armed groups refused to sign the accord. The civil war then continued. Twenty Tutsis and one British woman were killed on 28 December 2000, in what became known as the Titanic Express massacre. In April 2001, there was an attempted coup against Buyoya. Shaken, Buyoya put in place a transitional government in October. But there was no end in sight to the civil war. Three hundred boys were kidnapped from Museuma College in November 2001 and 500 Hutu militias were killed when they attacked the Tutsi army on Christmas day 2001. Fighting intensified for several months. On 9 September 2002, an attack at Itaba saw the massacre of hundreds of unarmed civilians. Fighting reduced in 2003 although a rebel attack on Bujumbura left 300 dead and 15,000 displaced.

That year saw the establishment of a 2,500-strong African Union peacekeeping mission in Burundi at Bujumbura under South African Major General Sipho Binda. A ceasefire agreement was signed at the end of the year. In 2004, a Hutu rebel group claimed responsibility for killing 160 Congolese Tutsi refugees in a UN camp at Gatumba near the Congo border in Burundi. A few months later, UN and government forces began to disarm thousands of Burundi soldiers and former rebels. In 2005, President Buyoya signed a law initiating a new national army, consisting of Tutsi military forces and Hutu militias. The constitution was approved by voters in a referendum. The Hutu

CNDD-FDD won the parliamentary elections that were organized and later, Pierre Nkurunziza, from the FDD and a former leader of a Hutu rebel group, was elected president by the two Hutu-dominated houses of parliament as the ninth president of Burundi.

On 15 April 2006, the mid-night-to-dawn curfew imposed since 1993 was lifted, signalling the formal end of the civil war. Matters continued to look promising after Burundi's last rebel group, the FNL, signed a ceasefire deal in Tanzania. As part of the agreement, members of the FNL were to be assembled, demobilized and integrated into the national army. There was a brief resumption of combat in April 2008 when FNL rebels shelled the capital, Bujumbura, killing at least thirty-three. Another violent conflict started in April 2015 when President Pierre Nkurunziza announced a controversial plan to run for a third term, which he went on to win. The violence killed more than 400 people and displaced more than 250,000 from their homes and thousands more fled to Tanzania as refugees. The 2005 estimated death toll stood at 300,000. Nkurunziza left office in May 2020 when his third term came to an end. He suddenly died in June of the same year, reportedly of COVID-19. He was succeeded by Evariste Ndayishimiye.

Cameroun

Present-day Cameroun, formerly French Cameroun, was part of Kamerun, Germany's colonial territory in central Africa from 1884 to 1916. When World War I broke out, British-led troops invaded *Kamerun* from the adjacent British territory of Nigeria, and Franco-Belgian troops invaded from the adjacent French Equatorial African group of territories. Following the collapse of German resistance in Kamerun in March 1916, Britain and France provisionally divided the territory along what came to be known as the Milner-Simon Line, pending the end of the war. Britain took a narrow strip of territory on Nigeria's border from Lake Chad down to the Gulf of Guinea, designating it as the British Cameroons. This partition was confirmed in 1919 at the Versailles Peace Conference. The British Cameroons were split into two parts, the southern Cameroons and the northern Cameroons, both administered as part of Nigeria, the former from Enugu, eastern Nigeria, and the latter from Kaduna, northern Nigeria.

France was allowed to keep the rest of the Kamerun territory. It detached two parts therefrom and incorporated them into neighbouring French colonial territories. The area known as the *Duckbill* was incorporated into Chad. The *NeuKamerun*, in the southeast, was fragmented into three. One part was absorbed into Ubangui-Shari (later known as the Central African Republic), another was incorporated into Congo Brazzaville and a third was fused into Gabon. The territory left after the *Duckbill* and the *NeuKamerun* had been detached was then held as French Cameroun which practically became part of French Equatorial Africa, a 1910–1958 federation of French colonial possessions in central Africa. The headquarters of these possessions was Brazzaville, from where all of the constituent colonies of the unitary entity were administered. An amendment to the 1958 constitution of France which established the Fifth Republic separated the territories into their constituent parts, each becoming an autonomous colony within the French community.

French Cameroun gained independence from France on 1 January 1960 under the name and style of *République du Cameroun*, that is, *Cameroun* for short. André Marie Mbida was prime minister for a short while in 1958 before being removed by the French who then appointed Ahmadou Ahidjo, a Peuhl or Hausa, to take over. It was under Ahidjo that France granted independence to the territory. The civil war in that country began in 1955 and lasted until January 1971 (Deltombe et al., 2011). In 1948, a political party, the *Union des Population du Cameroun* (UPC), was created, basically by persons of Bassa and Bamiléké ethnicities, to fight for immediate independence for French Cameroun, and it immediately found itself at loggerheads with the French colonial authorities. In 1955, there was an uprising in Douala, the biggest town in the territory. The French blamed the revolt on the UPC, proceeded to declare the party a proscribed terrorist organization and intensified the repression of its members. Tens of thousands of French Cameroun people escaped and sought refuge in the British southern Cameroons. The UPC leadership itself escaped there as well. That is where Felix Moumié, Ernest Oundié and Abel Kinguè first sought refuge. Later, when the British declared their presence undesirable they moved to Ghana. The UPC leader Mpodol Ruben Um Nyobe, however, decided to stay back and to launch a guerrilla war against the French from the forest of his native Sanaga-Maritime district.

Cameroun fought the UPC-armed insurgency with the help of French soldiers who had seen action in French Indochina where France suffered a humiliating defeat at Dien Bien Phu. The French also enlisted native African soldiers from French Equatorial Africa. Um Nyobe was betrayed by his own ethnic people. He was shot in the back by French troops and killed in September 1958 in his forest hideout near his Boumnyebel village. The French colonial authorities childishly announced that 'Um Nyobe died having on his person proof of his adherence to witchcraft and to communism' (Deltombe et al., 2011: 278). The killing of Um Nyobe failed to signal the end of the anti-colonial war against the French. Félix-Roland Moumié took over the leadership of the UPC in exile but was killed in Geneva through thallium poisoning by the French in October 1960. Ernest Ouandié took over the mantle of the guerrilla war. He concentrated his efforts especially in the forest of the Moungo localities and the Bamiléké highlands in the western part of French Cameroun.

The French brought in their military aircraft. They bombarded suspected localities of guerrilla fighters. They acted with unparalleled cruelty. They systematically burnt down homes and villages in areas suspected to be supporting the guerrillas. They systematically carried out cordon and search operations in areas they chose, terribly abusing civilians in the process, committing gross human rights abuses and violating international humanitarian law. They herded whole communities into hurriedly established 'security villages' under military control, allowing no one out or in. These 'zones de pacification, ZOPAC' (pacification areas) were established in December 1957. The French decapitated captured guerrillas and suspected guerrillas and then systematically exhibited their heads on stakes along the road to terrorize local people into refraining from supporting the guerrillas in any way. This savagery failed to end the independence struggle. The French then decided to politically cut the ground under the feet of the UPC. They appointed Ahidjo Prime Minister in February 1958. In their view, Ahidjo was a lesser evil of all French Cameroun politicians. They therefore hurriedly granted what in their own words was a mere 'fictitious independence' (Messmer, 1998) to French Cameroun with Ahmadou Ahidjo as its French-appointed president.

The UPC considered Ahidjo a French lackey. It rejected the transfer of power to him as they saw him as a mere puppet of France. It vowed to carry on with the insurgency against 'the puppet government' until genuine independence was achieved. The struggle in effect became an insurgency against the new Cameroun government. The country was on the brink of anarchy (Italiaander, 1961: 176). The French sent in massive troop deployment and its air force to support the shaky Yaoundé government which lacked popular support. French military action was particularly savage. Heads were decapitated and displayed along the road to terrorize the people (Deltombe, 2011). Thousands of people continued to be rooted from their communities and herded into so-called protective areas under French military surveillance. Despite the lavish French military, financial and diplomatic support to prop up Ahidjo's government, the armed insurgency continued for another ten years. At the end of 1970, the exhausted remnants of the insurgents gave themselves up. In January 1971, they were put through the motion of a show trial and quickly given the pre-determined death sentence. The leaders were taken to their ethnic communities where they were publicly executed by firing squad in the enforced presence of the local people (Deltombe et al., 2011). The exact number of people killed by the French is difficult to ascertain. But some sources speak of a genocide that saw the killing of at least 500,000 people, arguably the first genocide case in post-white-colonial Africa.

Congo Brazzaville

In 1958, Rev. Father Fulbert Youlou, a laicized Roman Catholic priest, became mayor of Brazzaville and head of the Congolese Territorial Assembly based in Pointe-Noire. Oppangault was Youlou's opponent in that Assembly and kept calling for war. Ethnically motivated political tension and hostility towards Youlou remained high in Pointe-Noire prompting him to move the capital from Pointe-Noire to Brazzaville. This measure gave rise to a three-day uprising which was instigated by workers and rival political parties. In the riot, houses were burnt, thousands of people were killed and many more wounded. The French army intervened and quelled the riot. On 8 December 1958, Youlou became prime minister. In February 1959, antagonism between two Congolese ethnic groups, the Mbochi on the one hand and the Lari-Kongo on the other hand, resulted in a series of riots in Brazzaville which the French army also quelled. When Congo achieved independence on 15 August 1960, Youlou became president, proclaiming himself to be 'rightist' and anti-communist. His rule was marked by bloody repressions, and several riots against his regime. One such riot took place from the 13th to the 15th August 1963 when a protesting mob marched on the Presidential Palace, demanding his resignation. The mob shouted, 'we want freedom', 'the Youlou dictatorship must fall'. When Youlou unsuccessfully appealed to De Gaulle for French military intervention to quell the uprising, he announced his resignation as president of the Republic, as mayor of Brazzaville and as member of the National Assembly.

The Congolese army seized power and held it for four months. It arrested Youlou and held him prisoner in a military camp and later transferred him and his family to another military camp. Four months later, on 19 December 1963, the military transferred power to a civilian government headed by Alphonse Massamba-Débat whose regime was politically the opposite of Youlou's. It was leftist in leaning. Massamba-Débat was cozy with China and the Soviet Union. He invited several hundred Cuban army troops into the country to train his country's militia units. On the night of 14 to 15 February 1965, three prominent Congolese were kidnapped and the mutilated bodies of two of them were later found by the Congo River. The persons were: Lazare Matsocota, the state prosecutor; Joseph Pouabou, president of the Supreme Court; and Massoueme Anselme, director of the information agency. On 25 March 1965, Massamba-Débat helped Youlou to flee to Congo Leopoldville where he was immediately granted political asylum by Moise Tshombe. Three months later, on 8 June 1965, Youlou was tried in absentia in Brazzaville. He was accused of genocide, misappropriation of public funds and of using for his personal purpose a Heron warplane 'donated' by France. He was sentenced to death and an order was made for the confiscation of all his properties. Twenty-four years later, in 1991, Youlou's memory was rehabilitated by the sovereign national conference and his confiscated properties were returned to his family.

Meanwhile, however, in 1966 and again in 1967 pro-Youlists, led by Youlou's nephew, Captain Felix Mouzabakani, attempted to seize power by coup d'état. But the attempt in each case was foiled by the Cuban troops Massamba-Débat had brought in to train his militias. Hundreds of people lost their lives in those coup attempts. Captain Marien Ngouabi, a Marxist, carried out a bloodless coup which ousted the government of Massamba-Débat in September 1968. Ngouabi became president on 31 December 1968. He denounced the Youlist coup plots that took place in 1966 and 1967. But the Youlist made yet other coup attempts, one in November 1968 and another in March 1970. In the meantime, Youlou had left Congo Leopoldville and landed in France. He requested to be allowed to settle in France. France turned down his request and instead sent him to Spain where he was well received by the Franco regime. He lived in Spain on a French pension of 500,000 French francs until his death from hepatitis on 5 May 1972 in Madrid. The socialist and revolutionary regime which Ngouabi instituted in Congo was held responsible for all the country's economic woes and several attempts were made to get rid of him. Ngouabi survived yet another coup attempt in 1972. Perhaps in an effort to mollify the Youlists, Ngouabi in December that year allowed the return of Youlou's body to Brazzaville where it was laid in state for three days before being taken to his home village and buried without any official ceremony. Five years later, on 16 March 1977, Ngouabi was assassinated. Joachim Yhombi-Opango took over as president but was forced out of office in 1979 in a coup led by Denis Sassou Nguesso. In 1990, the wind of democracy started blowing all over Africa. People went into the streets calling for a sovereign national conference to usher in a new era of multi-party democracy. A sovereign national conference was put in place in Brazzaville. It framed a new constitution for the country and decided that multi-party elections be held in 1992.

Pascal Lissouba and Denis Sassou Nguesso who had shed their military uniform and became a civilian stood for the presidential elections. Lissouba beat Nguesso and became Congo's first elected president. As presidential elections scheduled for July 1997 approached, tension mounted between the Lissouba and the Nguesso camps. President Lissouba's government forces surrounded Sassou's compound in Brazzaville on 5 June 1997. Sassou ordered members of his private militia, known as 'Cobras', to resist the government forces. Pascal Lissouba's 'Zulu' militia and Bernard Kolelas' 'Ninja' militias combined to fight Nguessou's 'Cobra' militias aided by Angolan troops. So began a four-month savage armed conflict that destroyed or damaged much of Brazzaville and caused tens of thousands of civilian deaths. The civil war in fact pitted Pascal Lissouba's ethnic group against Sassou Nguessou's. Lissouba is from the Bakongo ethnicity in the south of the country while Denis Sassou Nguessou is from the Bangala ethnicity in the north of the country. The entry of Angolan forces in the civil war on the side of Sassou Nguessou's militias gave an international dimension to the war. It was proved decisive in tilting the balance of firepower in favour of Nguessou. In mid-October 1997, the Lissouba government fell. Sassou declared himself president. Lissouba fled the country into exile. Sassou Nguessou considered him a fugitive on the run and in 1999 had him tried in absentia for high treason and given thirty years.

Following the presidential elections of 2002, at which Lissouba and Bernard Kolelas were prevented from competing, fighting restarted in the Poole region between government forces and rebels led by Pastor Ntumi. A peace treaty to end the conflict was signed in April 2003 and the Ninjas were disbanded. In March 2016, Guy-Brice Parfait Kolelas, son of Bernard Kolelas, stood for the presidential election against President Sassou Nguessou and was declared to have got only 15% of the vote. Fighting broke out again in the capital in protest at Sassou Ngouesso's fraudulent manipulation of the presidential elections of that year to maintain himself in power. Nguessou attacked the Poole region, where the Ninja rebels of the civil war used to be based. This led to a revival of the Ninja rebels who raided Brazzaville on 4 April 2016, attacking an army position and four police stations. Nguesso ordered airstrikes on suspected Ninja areas in the southeastern Poole region, causing deaths and destroying churches, schools and medical facilities. According to reports, helicopters dropped thirty bombs on residential areas, including the town of Vindza where the target was a house which used to be the residence of Pastor Frederic Ntumi, the leader of the Ninja militia group.

Djibouti

The territory previously known as Italian Somaliland and later the French territory of Afars and Issas achieved independence from France on 27 June 1977 as Djibouti. The RPP, an Issa ethnic-based political party led by Hassan Gouled Aptidon, formed the government. Aptidon ill-advisedly excluded representation in the government of the Afars, the country's other ethnic group. The Afars created the FRUD and launched an insurgency against the government. Civil war broke out in November 1991 when Afar rebels laid siege to the towns north of the country, capturing all the military posts in that part of the country. A month later, government troops moved into the Afar-inhabited district of the capital, opened fire on crowds and killed at least fifty-nine people. In February 1992, France despatched troops to fight alongside government forces while at the same time incongruously posing as mediator between the government and the rebels. The rebels rightly did not see France as an honest broker but nevertheless declared a unilateral ceasefire. Two rounds of peace talks, one in November 1992 and another one in May 1993, failed and fighting resumed.

The government enlarged its armed forces from 5,000 to 20,000 men and, with French help, launched an offensive on 5 July 1993, recapturing much of rebel-held territory. Dozens of persons were killed and hundreds wounded. Thousands of Djiboutians fled to neighbouring Ethiopia. President Hassan Gouled Aptidon was prevailed upon to reshuffle his government and to have a careful balance between Afars and Issas. The FRUD then split into two because of disagreement over discussions with the government. Eighteen months later, on 26 December 1994, a faction of FRUD signed a peace agreement with the government. The constitution was revised, and seven FRUD leaders joined the government in 1995. This effectively brought the civil war to an end, though the other faction of FRUD carried on with the insurgency in the form of small-scale low-level armed resistance, eventually signing its own peace agreement with the government in 2001.

Kenya

Kenya achieved independence from Britain on 12 December 1963 under the leadership of Jomo Kenyatta. Independence was achieved after a four-year bitter anti-colonial guerrilla warfare known as the Mau Mau Uprising. The Mau Mau was a militant African nationalist movement that originated in the 1950s among the Kikuyu people of Kenya and which advocated violent resistance to British rule in Kenya. It was associated with ritual oaths common to the Kikuyu. In 1950, the British authorities banned the movement and declared the freedom fighters 'terrorists' responsible for a campaign of sabotage and assassination. The colonial authorities declared a state of emergency in October 1952 and began four years of military operations, code-named Operation Jack Scott, against freedom fighters. By the end of 1956, a large number of people had been hanged, and more than 11,000 freedom fighters and 100 Europeans had been killed in the fighting. Also killed were 2,000 Kenyans who collaborated with the British by fighting on the British side against fellow Kenyans. More than 150,000 other Kikuyu were herded into concentration camps where the British tortured them horribly and made intensive efforts to brainwash them to abandon their nationalist aspirations. Despite this massive British crackdown, Kikuyu resistance spearheaded the Kenya independence movement. Jomo Kenyatta who, in 1953 was jailed for ten years for leading the Mau Mau movement, became prime minister of an independent Kenya in 1963. In 2003, the colonial ban on the Mau Mau was lifted by the Kenyan government.

In the early 1990s, under Daniel Arap Moi's presidency, the country suffered widespread unemployment and high inflation. Tribal clashes in the western provinces (Kikuyu against Luo) claimed thousands of lives and left tens of thousands homeless. Elections held in 1992 and 1997 were marred by irregularities and violence. A year later, on 7 August 1998, a truck-bomb explosion at the US Embassy, carried out by Al-Qaeda, killed more than 200 people and injured another 5,000. Kibaki succeeded Moi in 2002 and was controversially declared the winner over his challenger Raila Odinga in the 2007 presidential election. A huge ethnic violence exploded, again pitting Kikuyu (Kibaki's tribe) against Luo (Odinga's tribe). When a spokesman of Kibaki's government claimed that Odinga's supporters were engaged in ethnic cleansing, Odinga countered that Kibaki's camp was guilty of genocide. Several weeks of violence left 1,500 people dead and 600,000 displaced. Under a power-sharing deal mediated by the then UN secretary general Kofi Anan, Kibaki remained president while Odinga took the newly created post of prime minister. In 2008, a Truth, Justice and Reconciliation Commission was established as provided in the National Accord and Reconciliation Act passed by Kenya's Parliament. Apart from sporadic ethnic violence experienced by Kenya from time to time, there has been no post-independence major strife that could be termed a civil war.

Liberia

Liberia was founded in 1847 by freed American slaves. From then until Master Sergeant Samuel Doe's coup, indigenous Liberian tribes were excluded from power. Samuel Doe was from one of the indigenous Liberian tribes, the Krahn. For that reason, his toppling of President William Tolbert and taking over as president enjoyed popular support from the indigenous tribes. But within five years Doe started cracking down on any form of opposition, driven by a constant fear of a counter-coup against him. Moreover, he gave preferential treatment to his own ethnic group. Disillusionment with his rule quickly set in. Civil war started in 1989 and ended in 1997 but resumed two years later in 1999 until 2003, claiming over 250,000 lives. The source of the war can be traced to two events, the coup d'état which Doe carried out against the elected government of Liberia in 1980 and the 1985 presidential election which Doe rigged in order to stay in power. Perhaps because of its duration, its many ethnic-based rebel groups, the utter savagery of the conflict and the fact that neighbouring countries were sucked into the conflict, the Liberian civil war is well-documented in detail (Huband, 1998; Ellis, 2007; Hoffman, 2007; Moran, 2008; Gerdes, 2013).

In 1985, Thomas Quiwonkpa, the sacked commander of the Liberian military forces, attempted to overthrow Doe from Sierra Leone where he had taken refuge but was killed in the process. Doe exacted gruesome revenge against the Gio and Mano tribes in the north of the country where Quiwonkpa and his co-plotters came from. Four years later, Charles Taylor also set out to overthrow Doe. Taylor was a sacked Doe minister who had escaped from a US prison in Massachusetts and had undergone training in Libya before relocating to Côte d'Ivoire. There he raised a rebel army, the NPFL, consisting mainly of ethnic Gio and Mano who felt persecuted by Doe's regime. On the Christmas Eve of 1989, the hundred-man NPFL led by Taylor invaded the north of Liberia from Côte d'Ivoire with the set objective of toppling the Doe government. The Liberian Army retaliated against the civilian population of the region, attacking and killing unarmed civilians and burning entire villages in a scorch-earth policy. Many people fled as refugees to Guinea and Côte d'Ivoire. Many others joined the rebels. The guerrillas were soon fighting not only against the Liberian Army but also against Doe's ethnic Krahn, sympathetic to his regime. The civil war became distinctively ethnic, Gio/Mano against Krahn. Thousands of civilians were massacred on both sides. Hundreds of thousands fled their homes. By early 1990, Taylor was at the door of Monrovia and in July the same year, Prince Johnson who had split from the NPFL to create an independent rebel group, quickly took control of parts of Monrovia. This prompted the US Navy to evacuate foreign nationals and diplomats.

The ECOWAS deployed a joint military intervention force which later included troops from Tanzania and Uganda, as well as ECOMOG under Nigerian leadership. The mandate of ECOMOG was to impose a ceasefire, help Liberians establish an interim government until elections could be held, stop the killing of innocent civilians, ensure the safe evacuation of foreign nationals and prevent the conflict from spreading into adjacent states, countries which share a complex history of state, economic and ethno-linguistic social relations with Liberia. In September 1990, Doe was captured by Prince Johnson's rebel forces and brutally tortured before being killed and dismembered. The remnants of Doe's Army took refuge in Guinea and Sierra Leone where they formed the ULIMO in June 1991. In a pattern of the rise and splintering of rebel groups throughout the civil war, a plethora of armed groups emerged at various stages of the conflict, each fighting to capture power in the capital, to settle local scores and to have some economic gain. Several unsuccessful attempts were made to have a ceasefire in place and to secure peace. Between 1990 and 1991, a series of peace-making meetings were held in Bamako, Banjul, Lomé and Yamoussoukro. But they failed (Mutwol, 2009).

From June to August 1991, ULIMO fought alongside the Sierra Leonean Army against the RUF rebels. In September, ULIMO invaded Liberia, subsequently splitting into two ethnic factions, one Krahn-based and the other

Mandingo-based. A year later, in October 1992, Taylor attacked Monrovia with the help of Burkinabe soldiers. The attack was repulsed by ECOMOG which drove Taylor's rebels beyond the capital's suburbs. In 1993, ECOWAS brokered a peace agreement in Cotonou, Benin. The UN established UNOMIL to support ECOMOG in implementing the Cotonou peace agreement.

Renewed armed hostilities broke out in May 1994 and continued until August. The humanitarian situation had become disastrous. One million eight hundred thousand Liberians were in need of humanitarian assistance. An agreement between rebel leaders was reached in Akosombo, Ghana, in September 1994 to supplement the Cotonou agreement (Mutwol, 2009). But disagreements soon ensued and fighting broke out yet again. One year later, the main factions signed an agreement brokered by Ghanaian president Jerry Rawlings. ECOWAS, the UN, the United States, the EU, and the OAU sponsored a conference at which Charles Taylor agreed to a ceasefire and a timetable to demobilize and disarm his forces. But heavy fighting broke out again in April 1996. An accord was reached at Abuja, Nigeria, to end the fighting, to disarm and demobilize by 1997 and to hold elections that year. The elections were duly held. Taylor and his National Patriotic Party won and took over power in August 1997. Hopes that the bloodshed in Liberia would thereby end were dashed as violent events flared up with new rebel groups mushrooming and launching attacks here and there in 1999, some with the aim of destabilizing the government and others with the aim of gaining control of the local diamond fields. Taylor himself threw in his lot with guerrillas in neighbouring countries and funnelled 'blood diamonds' and 'blood timber' into small arms purchases for the rebel armies he supported.

After a two-year interregnum, the civil war resumed in 1999 when a Guinea-backed rebel group, LURD, emerged in northern Liberia. The new rebel group captured various locations and eventually laid siege to the capital. In early 2003, a second rebel group, MDL, this one backed by Côte d'Ivoire, emerged in the south and scored major victories against government forces. Liberia was now apparently free from any audacious group and neighbouring state. By mid-2003, Charles Taylor's government controlled only a third of the country. Fighting ended by August 2003 thanks to the intervention of ECOMOG which stopped the rebel siege of Monrovia. The warring factions met in Accra where a Comprehensive Peace Agreement was signed by the parties on 18 August 2003 marking the political end of the conflict and the beginning of the country's transition to democracy under the National Transitional Government of Liberia led by interim president Gyude Bryant until the general election of 2005.

In the midst of all these happenings, a group of Liberian women headed by Leymah Gbowee formed an organization called 'Women of Liberia Mass Action for Peace'. In 2003, they marched to State House and insisted on having a meeting with President Charles Taylor. They did and were able to secure from him a promise to attend the ongoing peace talks in Accra. During that peace process, a delegation of the women organized nonviolent protests outside the venue of the meeting and the Presidential Palace. They continued to apply pressure on the warring factions to reach a peace agreement. Through the joint efforts of these 3,000-plus Christian and Muslim women, peace eventually came to Liberia after fourteen years of civil war. Their action played no small part in helping bring to power the country's first female president, Ellen Johnson Sirleaf.

Taylor was forced to resign as president of Liberia and to go into exile in Nigeria. The special court for Sierra Leone, set up jointly by the government of Sierra Leone and the UN to try persons guilty of atrocities during the civil war in Sierra Leone, indicted Taylor for actively supporting the rebel RUF and its atrocities in Sierra Leone. An international warrant was issued for his arrest. General elections were held in Liberia in 2005 and were won by Ellen Johnson Sirleaf, initially a strong supporter of Charles Taylor. The interim president handed over power to the incoming president in January 2006 who in the same year established the LTRC to promote national peace, security, unity and reconciliation. That same year, Charles Taylor was arrested on the Nigeria-Cameroon border as he tried to escape. He was transferred to The Hague where he was tried for crimes against humanity and war crimes by the special court for Sierra Leone. In 2013, he was sentenced to 50 years of imprisonment.

The Liberian civil war was one of Africa's bloodiest war. It claimed the lives of more than 250,000 Liberians. It uprooted thousands who became internally displaced persons. It forced a million people to flee to refugee camps in the neighbouring countries. Entire villages were emptied as people fled. The various armed groups recruited children into military service as soldiers or ammunition porters and used them to commit atrocities, to rape and to murder people of all ages. Moreover, as part of Liberia's wartime culture, child soldiers (Beah, 2007) like other combatants were routinely forced to take narcotic drugs as a means of control, for it was generally believed by rebel leaders that taking narcotic drugs such as cocaine made soldiers more effective in battle. Liberia's civil war uprooted most of its people and destroyed the country's basic and economic infrastructure. The war involved all of Liberia's neighbours. It contributed to the arrest of the democratization process that was steadily gaining ground throughout west Africa at the beginning of the 1990s. It destabilized the region, facilitating the recruitment of armed militias and the availability of small arms.

Interestingly, mysticism and human sacrifice played a significant part in the Liberian civil war. Liberia became mythically 'a land of magic soldiers' (Bergner, 2003). It is said that some rebel leaders consulted oracles and witch doctors before planning battle strategy or engaging in battle and that they wore charms that reportedly made them invisible to the enemy or their body bullet proof. Many combatants also wore protective charms when going into battle so as to be invincible and fearless and to cast a spell of confusion, weakness and ineffectiveness on their enemies. Others claimed to be guided by prophetic dreams and visions assuring them of victory. The tale is told of one Liberian warlord, twenty-year-old Joshua Milton Blahyi (nom de guerre: General Butt Naked) in 1991, who is said to have declared war on Charles Taylor bizarrely after receiving a phone call from none other than the devil himself. The same Blahyi is said to have admitted to murdering children as a sacrifice to the devil in hopes of being protected against bullets. Another aspect of the notoriety of the Liberian civil war is the reported practice of human sacrifice and ritualistic killings by the various warring factions. The gleefully ritualistic manner in which Samuel Doe was killed and dismembered, the entire ritual being video-taped, lends support to the view that ritual killings appeared to have been much resorted to during the war. It is unlikely that the killing and dismemberment of Doe by Prince Johnson and his rebel group in such a cold ritualistic manner was a first- or last-time practice. Throughout the Liberian civil war, it appeared to have been accepted practice to sacrifice, eat, murder or maim individuals in order to attain prowess in battle. Eating the heart of an enemy army general was seen as a means of attaining power, presumably the supposed power of an army general. The alleged cannibalism of the then Emperor Bokassa of the Central African Republic and of the then-president Idi Amin of Uganda would seem to have been prompted by these same satanic beliefs.

Mozambique

In April 1974, the authoritarian government in Portugal was overthrown by the *Movimento das Forças Armadas* (the Armed Forces Movement). The movement pledged a return of civil liberties in Portugal and an end to fighting against national liberation movements in the colonies. By September that year, FRELIMO was able to extract from the Lisbon coup makers a firm commitment to grant independence to Mozambique and transfer power to FRELIMO within a year. Nine months after the coup in Lisbon, on the 25th of June 1975, Mozambique achieved independence, with Samora Machel as president of the new state. Portugal thus ended its colonial rule in Mozambique in 1975 after unsuccessfully fighting against the Mozambican armed independence movement known as the Front for the Liberation of Mozambique (FRELIMO). However, barely two years after independence, in 1977, Mozambique was plunged into a bitterly fought civil war that lasted fifteen-and-a-half years. By the time the war ended in 1992, about 1 million people had died from fighting and starvation, five million civilians had been displaced and thousands had become amputees by landmines.

In 1977, white-ruled Rhodesia and apartheid South Africa created, sponsored, funded and equipped a puppet organization known as RENAMO to undermine the capacity of the nascent Mozambique state to support nationalist forces fighting to liberate South Africa and Rhodesia from white minority rule and apartheid. The civil war began when RENAMO started military operations against FRELIMO and also against the Mozambique-based ZANLA. RENAMO carried out raids against towns and important infrastructure. The rebel movement abducted civilians and forced them to join its ranks. It made very extensive use of children as soldiers and porters (carrying goods and ammunition) and of women as sex slaves and producers of food for RENAMO. It mined roads, schools and health centres. It also made extensive use of landmines in order to terrify the population, stall the economy and destroy the civil services.

In turn, FRELIMO also used land mines to defend important infrastructure from sabotage by RENAMO which by the mid-1980s controlled much of the countryside and carried out raids virtually anywhere in the country except for the major cities. FRELIMO also created and fortified communal villages called *aldeamentos* where much of the rural population was relocated. Throughout the 1980s, there was a stalemate in the war despite external intervention and support on both sides. FRELIMO was initially supported by the Soviet Union. But before long additional support came from Tanzania, Zimbabwe, France, the UK and the United States, RENAMO was created, backed and supported by Rhodesia and apartheid South Africa and additionally had the support of Kenya and West Germany. Malawi's president Hastings Banda, in an act of duplicity, supported both sides. He used the Malawi young pioneers to back RENAMO and the Malawi armed forces to back the FRELIMO government. After Zimbabwe became independent, apartheid South Africa replaced Rhodesia as RENAMO's main supporter, using Malawi as a conduit for South African aid to reach RENAMO.

Economically ruined by the civil war, and in order to alleviate the economic misery and famine in the country, a reluctant President Machel signed a non-aggression pact with South Africa, known as the Nkomati Accord. One of the conditions given by Dhlakama of RENAMO for *halting* the insurgency against the FRELIMO government was that there had to be created a new national military. Chissano accepted Dhlakama's commitment to negotiations though not on conditions he laid down. Since Chissano was not certain of whom he should be talking to within RENAMO, he requested a group of clerics to access the most appropriate point of contact. America also acted as behind-the-scenes facilitator in the mediation process. Chissano's efforts to engage RENAMO in the peace process were endorsed in early 1989 by 700 delegations of Mozambicans. The willingness to talk about peace came from the people themselves through their leaders and this meant the people themselves took ownership of the process and therefore had a vested interest in its maintenance. Imposed 'peace settlements' simply give some respite to the conflict and are later resumed because the 'settlement' invariably collapses and fighting resumes. If people are not owners of a peace process, they will not feel obliged to go along with it.

For the formal negotiation process to begin, Chissano invited Daniel Arap Moi of Kenya to Maputo on 21 July 1989 and asked him to serve as a mediator. Chissano asked Robert Mugabe of Zimbabwe to share the mediatory role with Moi. The initial meeting co-chaired by Mugabe and Moi was held from 10 to 14 August 1989 in Nairobi, with Dhlalama heading the RENAMO delegation. During this meeting, Chissano asked the Mozambican clerics who had initially contacted RENAMO to present on FRELIMO's behalf a twelve-point statement of principles. RENAMO was also compelled to issue its own sixteen-point statement of principles. The purpose of each of these documents was a demand for recognition of legitimacy by the two parties involved. This was followed by the presentation of a seven-point peace proposal to Dhlakama in Nairobi on 8 December 1989 by a US diplomat in an effort to end the stalemate. The seven-point peace proposal synthesized the major demands of each party. The proposal further stated that FRELIMO should be recognized as the legitimate government of Mozambique and that all grievances should be resolved through democratic and peaceful means. The ceasefire ended three months after which Chissano told President Bush that he was prepared to begin unconditional talks with the insurgents.

In 1990, the FRELIMO government and RENAMO held the first direct talks since the inception of the civil war in 1977. The church's involvement in the peace process became paramount at the time Archbishop Jaime Goncalves became intimately involved in the process. This assured RENAMO that their interests would be fairly treated as RENAMO shared many common areas of interest with the church. This compelled RENAMO leader to agree to begin the negotiations. The success in laying the groundwork for negotiations was to a large extent that of the catholic church and Saint Egidio which were the only institutions that had the trust of both RENAMO and FRELIMO. Furthermore, the mediators had a deeper understanding of the dynamics between the two warring factions. The results of this were evident in the five rounds of talks in Rome between July 1990 and January 1991, where RENAMO and FRELIMO agreed on a partial ceasefire, and a mechanism to monitor the agreement called the JVC was established. This was a building block for ceasefire.

A new constitution was adopted in November 1990. It made provision for political pluralism, periodic elections and guaranteed democratic rights. Thanks to the mediation efforts of the Community of Sant'Egidio, supported by the UN, the Rome General Peace Accords were negotiated by both parties. On 4 October 1992, the accords were signed in Rome by President Chissano and RENAMO leader Afonso Dhlakama. The agreement took effect on the 15th of October 1992. A 7,500-UN peacekeeping force, ONUMOZ, arrived in Mozambique and oversaw a two-year transition to democracy. International observers numbering 2,400 took part in supervising the elections held in October 1994. The last ONUMOZ contingents departed in early 1995. The Mozambique civil war lasted from 1977 to 1992, claiming over a million lives and also rendering some 5 million people homeless. Halo Trust, a de-mining group funded by the United States and the United Kingdom, began operating in Mozambique in 1993, recruiting local workers to remove land mines scattered throughout the country. In September 2015, the country was finally declared to be free of land mines, although with RENAMO taking back to the bush in mid-2013 and several reported killings since then, there were fears that the landmines might soon be back. But security experts considered RENAMO a spent force highly unlikely to be able to return to the military strength and external funding and support it had during the civil war. There were nevertheless fears that were the fighting to resume, it would cause great damage to Mozambique's economy currently expanding at around 7% a year. What has now recently emerged in Mozambique is an Islamic insurgency in the province of Cabo Dalgado. Occasionally the ISIL-backed insurgency causes havoc. But so far, the government has been able to contain it with the support of countries like Tanzania, Rwanda, South Africa and Zambia.

The church's involvement worked in Mozambique. But it failed in Congo-Kinshasa, Sudan, Angola and Uganda. In each of these countries, various peace accords were signed but violated several times. The conflicts in Liberia, Sierra Leone and Guinea-Bissau demonstrated the limits of these church interventions and peace agreements. Other 'peace' methods have also been used but without continent-wide attraction and success. The truth and reconciliation method worked in South Africa but failed in Zimbabwe. The expedient of a 'sovereign national conference' worked in Benin but failed in Congo-Kinshasa and was rejected in Cameroon by the regime.

A number of things were done to make the Mozambique peace process a success. Among these were the pre-negotiation stage, an understanding of the root causes, identifying all the actors or aggrieved parties, identifying the facilitators, setting a realistic timetable and sustaining the efforts. The aim of the pre-negotiation stage was to bring the parties into the negotiation process with the purpose of outlining the logistical framework and time framework for negotiations and setting ambitious yet realistic goals for each stage of the initial negotiation. The intent of pre-negotiation phase is to reduce intractability, to formulate and to design a process which can bring parties to the negotiating table and to bring the trust and confidence-building necessary for a successful negotiation. In the Mozambican case, President Chissano worked towards this in the following ways. He enticed foreign governments to terminate or reduce aid that was being given to RENAMO, and he negotiated with his South African counterpart to withdraw support to RENAMO. On the part of his party, FRELIMO, Chissano established a conducive political ground characterized by the publication of a draft constitution (Reynolds & Kuperman, 2015). The new constitution was drafted by the people and acceptable to all political parties and civil society. It was endorsed by a referendum at which each province casts at least 70% affirmative votes. Chissano also identified influential presidents and clerics as mediators and co-mediators.

Rwanda

The civil war in Rwanda, from October 1990 to August 1993 and then from April to July 1994, left 5,000 killed in the fighting and 800,000 dead as a result of the ensuing genocide. It was a war between the Hutu-led government of President Juvenal Habyarimana and the Tutsi rebel RPF. The RPF was formed by Tutsi refugees in Uganda who had joined Museveni's insurgency against Amin and then against Obote. Asa a mark of gratitude to the RPF for its assistance, Museveni undertook to return the Tutsi refugees to Rwanda by any means possible. In October 1990, the RPF invaded Rwanda from Uganda with the knowledge and support of President Museveni. In 1993, after three years of fighting, the Rwandan government, the rebels and the government signed the Arusha Accords creating a power-sharing government between Tutsi and Hutu. Within eight months of signing the accords, President Habyarimana was assassinated when the plane in which he was travelling from France was shot down over Kigali as it approached the airport to land. The death was blamed on the RPF which had resumed its offensive against Habyarimana's government forces.

When news of the RPF offensive broke, France and Belgium sent troops to Kigali to assist the Rwanda government military in fighting the invasion. The Belgian presence was short lived because its laws prevented the army from intervening in a civil war. France, by contrast, supported the regime and gave significant military and financial assistance. In a military operation code-named Noroit, France deployed 125 soldiers, who had been based in the Central African Republic, to support the Rwandan government. Zairian president Mobutu also assisted Habyarimana, sending several hundred troops of the elite Special Presidential Division. In October, the French increased their troop numbers to 600. With French and Zairian assistance, the Rwandan government forces enjoyed a major advantage, and they gradually regained all the ground the RPF had taken. The rebels were eventually pushed back to the Ugandan border on 30 October and were in complete disarray. Many soldiers deserted, some crossed back into Uganda, while others went into hiding in the Akagera National Park. The Rwandan government announced that they had won the war.

But by 1991, Kagame restarted the war by carrying out hit and run style guerrilla war. Low-intensity fighting dragged on with neither side managing to inflict any major defeat on the other. Over the next few months, there were numerous attempts at ceasefire, though they achieved little and the fighting continued until 13 July 1992 when a ceasefire agreement was signed in Arusha, Tanzania. The agreement fixed a timetable for an end to the fighting. It also fixed a timetable for political talks that would lead to a peace accord and power-sharing. It authorized a neutral military observer group under the auspices of the OAU. The ceasefire took effect on 31 July 1992, and political talks began on 30 September the same year. Over the course of the following months, negotiations continued, though without any serious breakthroughs and with the tension on both sides mounting (Mutwol, 2009).

The RPF launched a major offensive on 8 February 1993 when reports filtered out that Tutsis had been massacred. The RPF offensive prompted France to send several hundred French troops to the country along with large amounts of ammunition for the artillery of the Rwandan Armed Forces. The arrival of these French troops in Kigali seriously changed the military situation on the ground. On 20 February, the RPF declared a unilateral ceasefire and over the following months pulled its forces back. As of that date, over 1.5 million civilians, mostly Hutu, had left their homes. An uneasy peace was once again entered into, which would last until 7 April 1994. Over the following months, the peace process developed. On 6 April 1994, President Habyarimana was returning from negotiations in Dar es Salaam when his presidential jet was shot down, killing all inside. Interahamwe, a Hutu militia organization, and the presidential guard began to kill opposition politicians and prominent Tutsi. Over the following days, it became clear that the target of these killings was the entire Tutsi population along with certain moderate Hutu. The Rwanda Genocide had begun and would last three months, costing the lives of hundreds of thousands of people, about 937,000 according to the RPF. The RPF renewed its offensive in the south. In June, the RPF pushed the government forces west through the southern region, along the border with

Burundi. It captured the town of Butare on 2 July and stopped further advance when French troops from *Opération Turquoise* arrived and blocked its path.

With the fall of Kigali, Rwanda's government forces began to disintegrate. By 3 July government forces completely ran out of ammunition and withdrew from the capital, taking with them the majority of the civilian population. The following day, after a three-month-long battle, the RPF moved in and captured the entire capital. French forces from *Opération Turquoise* controlled a large area of the southwest. The area was given over to the RPF on 21 August 1994. The RPF took complete control of the country. It established a government under its leader, Paul Kagame. The assassination of Habyarimana had sparked the revenged massacre of 800,000 mainly Tutsis by Hutus in what became known as the Rwanda Genocide. Ousted from power by the RPF, the remnants of the Habyarimana government formed a Hutus government-in-exile, using refugee camps in the DRC to harass the new RPF government.

Although the Tutsi rebels defeated the Hutu regime and ended the genocide in July 1994, approximately two million Hutu refugees – some who participated in the genocide and feared Tutsi retaliation – fled to neighbouring Burundi, Tanzania, Uganda and Zaire. Thousands died in epidemics of cholera and dysentery that swept the refugee camps. The international community responded with one of the largest humanitarian relief efforts ever mounted. The RDR, composed of Hutu troops and militia members, began to militarize the camps, using them as bases to overthrow the new RPF-dominated government. The remnants of the Democratic Forces for the Liberation of Rwanda (FDLR) and possibly other Hutu militants maintain a presence in eastern Congo. But they are currently not strong enough to pose a threat to the Kagame government.

South Sudan

Barely two years after independence, the nascent Republic of South Sudan plunged into civil war in December 2013 until the end of 2015. The internal war left about 50,000 people dead, some 2 million people displaced, and 255,000 have fled as refugees to neighbouring Ethiopia, Kenya, Uganda and Sudan. Trouble started when President Salva Kiir Mayardit, from the Dinka tribe, sacked his deputy Riek Machar Teny Dhurgon from the Nuer tribe. The reason given for the dismissal was that a mutiny by some Nuer soldiers was actually an attempted coup d'état by Machar. The civil war prompted by Machar's dismissal as deputy president quickly took an ethnic colouration because Salva Kiir and Riek Machar come from different tribes, the Dinka and the Nuer, respectively, with a long history of conflict. The government of South Sudan appealed to Uganda for military help. Uganda deployed its troops to Juba to assist in securing the airport and evacuating Ugandan citizens.

By end of December 2013, the civil war had intensified and become vicious. Reports of atrocities and massacres continued throughout the war with reports of ethnic targeting. In January 2014, American Marines landed in Juba and evacuated US citizens from South Sudan. Ugandan forces joined in the fight on the side of the government. Five ceasefire agreements were signed by the warring parties between January 2014 and February 2015, but each was broken as soon as it was signed. Another peace agreement mediated by IGAD and supported by the UN, the AU, China, the EU, the United States, United Kingdom and Norway was signed in late August 2015. The agreement secured a commitment from the government of South Sudan that Riek Machar would be re-instated as the vice president of the country. Machar was duly appointed by Kiir as first vice president of South Sudan on 21 February 2020 and sworn in two days afterwards.

Two months later, Uganda announced the voluntary withdrawal of its soldiers from South Sudan, as stipulated in the peace agreement signed in August 2015. On Christmas Eve 2015, Salvar Kiir announced he was going forward with a plan to increase the number of states from ten to twenty-eight and then, five days later, swore in all new governors appointed by him and considered loyal to him. On 11 April, UNICEF warned that the conflict in South Sudan had triggered a serious risk of famine that would kill up to 50,000 children within months if immediate action was not taken. In November 2014, the International Crisis Group estimated the death toll could be between 50,000 and 100,000. In March 2016, some aid workers and officials estimated the death toll could be as high as 300,000 and over 2 million people displaced.

NOTES

1. Known mass killings (massacres, pogroms or genocide) in the continent include the Herero genocide in Namibia from 1904 to 1907, the Sétif and Guelma massacre in Algeria in 1945, the Batepa massacre in Sao Tome & Principe in 1953, the Bamileke pogrom in French Cameroun in the 1950s and 1960s, the Ibo pogrom in Northern Nigeria in 1966, the Sharpeville massacre in South Africa in 1966 and the Garissa massacre in Kenya in 1980 and again in 2015. Other mass killings include the Wagalla massacre in Kenya in 1984. Yet other mass killings include the Ebubu massacre in 1961, Tombel massacre in 1966, Bamenda and Ndu killings in 1990, the Bui killings and the Buea University killings in 1993 and 1994, and the scores of massacres since 2017 in Santa, Ngarbu, Ekona, Bali, Kumba, Muyuka, all of these

killings, characterized as genocide, perpetrated by Cameroun Republic in occupied Ambazonia. There is also the Rwanda genocide in 1994, the massacres committed during the Eritrean liberation war, the Titanic Express massacre in Burundi in 2000, the Itaba massacre in Burundi in 2002, the Darfur killings in Sudan in 2003, the Gatumba massacre in Burundi in 2004 and the Turbi village massacre in Kenya in 2005.

2. Algeria, Angola, Burundi, Cameroun, Central African Republic, Chad, Congo (Brazzaville), Congo (Kinshasa), Côte d'Ivoire, Djibouti, Eritrea, Ethiopia, Guinea-Bissau, Kenya, Liberia, Libya, Mali, Mozambique, Niger, Nigeria, Rwanda, Sierra Leone, Somalia, South Sudan, Sudan, Uganda and Zimbabwe.

Chapter 4

Sources of Civil Wars
Despotism, Overstay in Power and Historical Discontent

Many African states continue to rely on centralized and highly personalized forms of government.

> They lack democratic institutions and have fallen into a pattern of corruption, a pattern of governance based on personal rule and ethnicity, and a pattern of gross human rights abuses. The African ruler tends to see himself as ruler for life. In order to cling on to power indefinitely he has no scruples manipulating elections and diverting the military and the police to focus instead on protecting him, his family and his rogue regime. He has no scruple manipulating ethnicity, manipulating the document that passes for a constitution, and harassing and torturing dissidents and political opponents. . . . [M]ost African militaries are simply regime or tribal armed militia, their sworn allegiance being to the incumbent ruler rather than to the nation represented by the flag, and so do not qualify to be called a 'national' army. Overdue stay in power is one of the sources of conflicts in Africa and a key contributory factor to corruption, graft and patronage. . . . In Africa, participation of citizens in the government of their country is more abstract than real; the citizens have been disempowered and are unable to change by peaceful means those who rule over them. . . . The concept of separation of powers has little meaning in many African states. There is only one office and one power that matters – that of the ruler. All else is mere decoration. The ruler issues decrees that override constitutional provisions, parliamentary deliberations, and court decisions. The 'legislature' is a mere rubber stamp, the judiciary a dependent and timid organ, and both lack power to control executive excesses. The ruler uses and controls the national purse as if it were his private bank account. (Anyangwe, 2012: 177–178)

In many African states, the promise that independence would usher peace, freedom, development and a better life for all soon became a mirage. More than half a century after decolonization, it is not yet *uhuru*. Here and there, 'pirates' have captured the state. Personal dictatorships, 'one-party' dictatorships, military dictatorships, a warlord culture and a species of governance anchored on ethnicity and terrorization of 'the other' have since emerged and taken root in some countries. In not a few countries, the ruler has in effect hijacked the state and converted it into his personal fiefdom, based on patron-client relations and systemic corruption. Ensconced in state house, some of these rulers embrace the authoritarian nature of colonial governance, complete with its trappings and illiberal laws, as well as its patronizing and self-serving logic. State apparatus, state power and state resources have become instruments in the distribution of patrimony, patronage and graft to relatives, tribesmen, friends and political confederates. In Africa, the ruler bestrides the state like a colossus. It is this inauspicious situation that has given rise here and there to the lucrative business of coup-making, popular uprisings and insurgencies. More often than not, the violence inevitably leads to civil war.

Africa is the least developed part of the global south despite its immense wealth in human, mineral, oil, gas, agricultural and other natural resources. Most African countries lack basic functioning infrastructure, electricity and water. The security of persons and property is not fully guaranteed and protected. This reality forces people to fall back on family, tribe and ethnic community for protection and guarantee of their safety. People live in fear of their lives and property. Africa's numerous and interminable violent conflicts all share a similar pattern. In one scenario, ethnically based opposing armed groups fight each other or the government (itself largely ethnically based) to capture political power, not necessarily for the general good. In another scenario, some so-called leader assumes power under dubious or controversial circumstances such as by coup d'état, by oligarchic succession or appointment, by hereditary succession or by fraudulent 'electoral victory'. The 'leader' then quickly entrenches himself in power and becomes accountable to no one. Together with his tribe, the 'leader' captures the state and takes it hostage, converts the military into his private security outfit and transforms the state's resources into his personal property for the benefit of himself, his family, his tribe and his cronies. Out of frustration, someone starts an insurgency to remove that leader from power and 'save' the country. The 'leader' deploys the so-called national military forces. Mutual killing, destruction and chaos then ensue.

It is traditional to blame the inauspicious governance environment in Africa on post-independence neo-colonialist forces, European and American secret and secretive outfits (Freemason, Rosicrucian and Illuminati) and the predatory French instrument known as *Françafrique*. This conveniently ignores survival strategies developed by African rulers themselves to stay long in power and to loot and plunder their respective countries. These strategies include hoarding political power, ethnic capture of the state, weaponization of ethnicity, terrorization of the people using the police and army, purposefully weakening state institutions, frequent tinkering with and manipulation of the constitution, operating a patronage system and promoting belief in occult or mystical protection.

A number of violent intra-state conflicts have thus taken the form of armed insurgencies seeking to overthrow an existing dictatorship, or to liberate an oppressed people or simply to procure the secession of part of a state as the only solution to decades of subjugation, oppression and human rights abuse by the country's government. In Mali, the Azawad insurgency sought and still seeks to create an Azawad republic. In Niger, the Tuareg insurgency seeks autonomy for Tuareg-inhabited parts of Niger. The Azawadi and the Tuareg discontent appear to have been manipulated and instrumentalized by France against Mali and Niger, respectively. Later happenings showed French soldiers fighting alongside Islamic jihadists in both countries and French soldiers mining and stealing gold in the north of Mali. In the Sinai, an Islamic state insurgency seeks to overthrow Egypt's Abdel Fattah Al-Sisi who had himself come to power by a violent military coup. In Somalia, Al-Shaabab seeks to overthrow the Somali government and replace it with a radical Islamic regime. In Uganda, the Lord's Resistance Army has been fighting for decades to overthrow Museveni who had himself come to power by the sword. Periodically, insurgencies emerge in Burundi, Central African Republic, Chad, Congo Kinshasa, Rwanda and Somalia, all aimed at regime overthrow. Another form of violence in Africa consists of endless military coup d'états often causing death and destruction (Anyangwe, 2012). Disputed elections and legitimate demands for constitutional reforms often trigger conflicts. Conflicts of this type led to successful popular insurrections in Burkina Faso, Egypt, Libya, Sudan and Tunisia, and failed ones in Algeria, Burundi, Cameroun and Togo.

From the earliest coups in the 1950s to about 1980, fifty-nine African leaders were toppled or assassinated. Not a single one of them was voted out of office. Only four voluntarily and peacefully gave up power – Leopold Sedar Senghor in Senegal (1981), Ahmadou Ahidjo in Cameroun (1982), Julius Nyerere in Tanzania (1985) and Siaka Stevens in Sierra Leone (1985). Until 1991, no incumbent African leader ever lost an election. Mugabe in Zimbabwe (before his death in 2019) and Idris Deby in Chad (before his death in 2021) were in power for at least thirty years. Dos Santos in Angola, Biya in Cameroun, Sassou Nguessou in Congo-Brazzaville, Ali Bongo in Gabon, Museveni in Uganda and Obiang Nguema in Equatorial Guinea have each been in power for at least thirty years and for more than forty years in the case of Biya. Each has rejected presidential term limits and valiantly 'obtained' one election victory after the other. Some African civil wars therefore have their origin in revolts against flawed elections. Others stem from unmet persistent demands for constitutional reforms in reaction to autocratic phenomena such as the elimination of presidential term limits, and oligarchic or hereditary succession to power. Since 1991, only four incumbents have lost an election and conceded defeat without any fuss: in Benin President Ahmed Kerekou lost to Nicéphore Soglo in 1991, in Senegal President Abdou Diouf lost to Abdoulaye Wade in 2000, in Zambia President Rupiah Banda lost to Michael Sata in 2011, in São Tomé & Príncipe President Patrice Trovoada lost to Pinto da Costa in 2011.

In Ethiopia, Mali, Nigeria, Niger and Sudan, civil war ensued following military action by the central government to suppress a secessionist bid – in Ethiopia to suppress the Oromo secessionist bid, in Mali to suppress the Tuareg attempt at secession and in Nigeria to thwart the attempt by Biafra to break away. In 2012, Tuaregs proclaimed an independent Azawad state in the northern two-thirds of Mali with Goa as its capital. The secessionist bid was put down after two years of civil war in which French and Chadian armies were at the forefront of the fight against the Tuaregs and their Jihadist allies, the French later switching sides. Other violent intra-state conflicts have taken the form of armed insurgencies seeking to overthrow an existing dictatorship, or to liberate an oppressed people or simply to procure the secession of part of a state following decades of subjugation, oppression and human rights abuse by the country's government. Mali experiences a cyclical Azawadi insurgency seeking to carve out an Azawad republic in northern Mali. A Tuareg insurgency in Niger seeks autonomy for Tuareg-inhabited parts of Niger. In the Sinai, the Islamic state insurgency seeks to overthrow Egypt's Abdel Fattah Al-Sisi.

PERSONAL RULE AND OVERSTAY IN POWER

Overstay in power invariably leads to despotism, rule by terror, bad constitutional order, tribalization of politics and patrimonial system of governance. This is a common phenomenon in Africa and to which African countries respond differently. But generally, military coups have tended to be seen as the remedy for overstay in power. The coup expedient is resorted to by well-meaning soldiers to end power abuse. Such remedial coups are sometimes preceded by popular uprisings, giving the military the needed justification to intervene and remove the despot, restore law and order and institute or restore democracy. In some cases, however, the military once in power abused it, inviting another coup. The coup-upon-coup phenomenon often triggers violence, ushering in an endless cycle of military coup d'états. This often causes death and destruction, particularly when the coup encounters resistance (Anyangwe, 2012). The coup phenomenon continues to plague the continent.

Only in a few states has overstay in power led to the overthrow of incumbents, consequent upon a population uprising. The success of such uprisings in engineering the overthrow of sit-tight presidents is illustrated by what has been characterized as the 'Arab Spring' in North Africa. Popular uprisings in Benin and Burkina Faso also saw the overthrow of incumbents. But they failed in Cameroun under Biya. Biya is old, incapacitated and generally reckoned to be an uninspired and uninspiring individual, a despot and an indivisible symbol of the corrupt government. Popular uprisings also failed in Uganda under dull and uninspiring Museveni; in Equatorial Guinea under dictator Teodoro Nguema; in Ivory Coast under very controversial Ouattara; in Guinea-Conakry under Alpha Condé (later removed by coup d'état); in Gabon under physically incapacitated Ali Bongo; in Congo-Brazzaville under dictator Sassou Nguessou; and in Chad under Idriss Deby who was finally removed through assassination after thirty years in power.

African rulers who, as of the end of 2021, long overstayed their welcome in power include Paul Barthelemy Mvondo Biya of Cameroun Republic (forty-six years in power), Teodoro Obiang Nguema of Equatorial Guinea (forty-one years in power), Yoweri Museveni (thirty-six years in power), Denis Sassou Nguessou (thirty years in power), Ali Bongo (thirty years in power) and Idriss Deby (thirty years in power before his assassination). The case of Libya's Muammar Gaddafi (forty-two years in power, 1969–2011), Tunisia's Ben Ali (twenty-three years in power, 1989–2011) and Egypt's Hosni Mubarak (thirty years in power, 19812011) illustrate how personal rule and overstay in power could lead to popular revolt and even civil war.

Egypt

Hosni Mubarak, an Air Force commander and Egyptian vice president under Sadat became president of Egypt following the assassination of President Anwar Sadat by Islamist extremists in 1981. For thirty years, from 1981 to 2011, he ruled Egypt high-handedly like a latter-day pharaoh and even tried to make his son, Gamal, succeed him as president of Egypt. He was an autocratic, an uninspired and uninspiring ruler who claimed that Egyptians cannot handle democracy. He relentlessly pursued Islamist groups using police tactics to suppress any move towards democracy.

> He had no agenda or vision for Egypt's future. . . . He paid no attention to mounting social and economic problems under which Egypt was slowly submerging . . . The Egyptian education system was already a disaster. . . . The Nile River's life-giving waters were threatened by a huge dam that Ethiopia was planning at its source. But Mubarak had paid no attention to Egypt's relations with Africa. (Ottaway, 2020)

Mubarak once appeared invincible. He survived multiple assassination attempts. He held power for three decades, longer than anyone since Muhammad Ali Pasha, the founder of the modern Egyptian state. But in the end, he was the architect of his own downfall. First, his edifice of power turned out to be fragile and dated, built on the strong-arm rule, cronyism and an alliance with the west. Second, he tried to position his son, Gamal, treated by Mubarak's regime as a prince of the state but detested by the military, to succeed him after he retired. Third, he failed to take seriously the threat posed by the massive street protests against his rule. The protests started on 25 January 2011 in Cairo and spread all over the country. In next-door Tunisia, President Zine al-Abidin Ben Ali was overthrown by street protests after the Tunisian military issued a statement saying it recognized 'the legitimacy of the people's demands' and promised not to use force against 'this great people'. Mindful of that, one of Mubarak's advisers even tried, to no avail, to scare him into resigning, telling him he was facing a 'Ceausescu moment', if he did not (Ottaway, 2020). Fourth, the social and economic situation in Egypt was dire. The causes of the popular uprising against Mubarak also included corruption, under-development, unemployment, unfair distribution of wealth and Israeli presence.

In spite of all this, Mubarak still did not believe he was in danger of losing power. The Egyptian military thought otherwise. It forced him to transfer power to the Supreme Council of the Armed Forces which seized power on the morning of 11 February after eighteen days of continuing street protests in what became known as the Arab Spring. Mubarak was flown to his home in Sharm el-Sheikh on the Red Sea. In August 2011, he was wheeled into a courtroom on a hospital gurney, placed in the defendants' cage to answer charges of financial corruption and conspiracy in the killing of more than 800 Egyptian protesters. He was convicted and sentenced to life imprisonment in June 2012. An appeals court overturned the verdict and ordered a retrial, and he was ultimately exonerated. But he was eventually taken to the Maadi Military Hospital in Cairo where he died in February 2020 at the age of ninety-one, leaving no particular vision and no noted achievement (Slackman, 2020). Ironically, after Mubarak spent thirty years relentlessly persecuting Islamists, it was the Muslim Brotherhood leader Mohammed Morsi who was elected president of Egypt in June 2012, becoming the first Islamist leader in Egypt's 6,000-year-old history. Morsi was however deposed on 3 July 2013 in a military coup led by his Defence Minister Abdel Fattah al-Sisi. He died in prison on 17 June 2019.

Libya

In 1969, Colonel Mu'ammar Al-Gaddafi and Major Jalloud deposed King Idris and seized power. The country remained peaceful until February 2011 when a popular uprising broke out against Gaddafi. That signalled the beginning of Libya's civil war which went through two periods, throughout that year, 2011, and from 2014 to 2015. The February 2011 uprising took place in the context of the 'Arab Spring'. Gaddafi's savage repression of the revolt, using warplanes to drop bombs on the unarmed protesters, led to two major developments. The peaceful protest turned into an anti-Gaddafi insurgency to topple the regime. A national transitional council assumed power as an interim authority in the rebel-controlled areas with headquarters in Benghazi. The UNSC adopted a resolution by which NATO was authorized to take all necessary measures to ensure the protection of Libyan civilians against Gaddafi's armed onslaught. A NATO-led coalition intervened, ostensibly to protect civilians against attacks by government forces but, in reality, to overthrow Muammar Gaddafi and his regime. On 19 March 2011, a multi-state NATO coalition enthusiastically led by France began a military intervention in Libya ostensibly to implement UN Security Council Resolution 1973 in response to events during the first Libyan civil war.

Libyan insurgents quickly developed military capability backed by NATO bombings of Gaddafi military targets. In June 2011, the International Criminal Court quickly issued an arrest warrant against Gaddafi and top members of his regime. After eight months of fighting, Gaddafi's forces were defeated in October 2011. Gaddafi and his son, a military commander, were captured and summarily executed by their captors on 20 October 2011. The Libyan Arab Jamahiriya he had established since 1969 was at an end. Some semblance of stability followed. Various armed militia groups soon emerged and violent confrontations using ground and air forces soon ensued as rival factions competed for power. The situation quickly degenerated into renewed full-blown civil war in 2014 which continued until January 2015 when the two main factions, one based in Tripoli and Misrata and the other in Tobruk, agreed on a ceasefire. The war claimed the lives of about 4,300. Fighting between the armed factions resumed, with no end in sight and no unified consensus government in sight. On 10 March 2021, a provisional government of national unity led by Fayez al-Sarraj was formed to unify the rival government of national accord based in Tripoli and the Second Al-Thani Cabinet based in Tobruk. There is a military stalemate, and the fight now is over elections originally slated for December 2021 but now postponed to a date yet to be announced.

Tunisia

On 7 November 1987, Ben Ali, Tunisia's interior minister, seized power in a bloodless palace coup from the country's increasingly erratic founding father Habib Bourguiba referred to by Tunisians as 'the Supreme Fighter'. Ben Ali announced that a team of doctors had declared Bourguiba mentally unfit to govern and that, as the recently appointed prime minister, he was assuming power. There was no opposition to the coup. Bourguiba had been dynamic, fiercely intelligent and his image ubiquitous. Ben Ali was dull, uncharismatic and merely one of the faceless cronies who would each day watch the president take his daily swim in the Mediterranean.

Ben Ali took power with the familiar promise to move Tunisia towards democracy. But when he organized the country's first multi-candidate election in 1999, he won with a farcical 99.44% of the vote. This earned him the nickname 'Mr 99%', although he was also known as 'Ben à Vie' ('Ben-for-life', meaning 'president for life'). Ben Ali's offer to the Tunisian people was stability, foreign investment, jobs and improved living standards. The price was near-zero tolerance of dissent, a slavish media and an all-inquiring police force. He crushed the Islamic movement at the start of the 1990s. But thousands of human rights activists, politicians and journalists were caught up in the crackdown, many of them tortured and sent to back-breaking labour. The Tunisian economy took a downturn, joblessness rose and prices shot up. Added to this was personal and family corruption, especially that of Ben Ali's second wife, Leila Trabelsi, loathed by many Tunisians for helping her extended family to acquire huge economic holdings across Tunisia.

Ben Ali ruled Tunisia with an iron fist for twenty-three years. During his rule, unemployment remained high and crony capitalism became firmly embedded. The country's record on democracy and human rights was woeful. The regime was dictatorial and massively repressive, especially towards the conclusion of Ben Ali's twenty-three-year iron grip on the country. The spontaneous protests that toppled Ben Ali first erupted in December 2010. They followed the self-immolation of a young street trader, Mohamed Bouazizi. Rioting quickly spread across the country, with young Tunisians using social media to organize demonstrations. What sealed Ali's fate was army withdrawal of support and its refusal to fire on protesters. At that point, Ben Ali fled into exile in Saudi Arabia in January 2011. In June 2011, a Tunisian court convicted him and his wife of embezzlement and sentenced both in absentia to thirty-five years in prison. Ben Ali died in mid-September 2019. He was the first autocrat to fall during the popular uprisings that spread across the Middle East in early 2011.

HISTORICAL DISCONTENT

It is not unusual in an African state to find a situation where a region or an ethnic community nurse serious grievances for years against the state – the governance of the state, the structure of the state and power monopoly by one ethnic group. Such grievances often arise from severe abuse, discrimination, political, economic and developmental marginalization of the region concerned. Over the years, the enduring nature of the plight of the community and the failure to address it deepens and worsens the discontent, pushing the ethnic group concerned to seek an alternative solution. In the face of government deafness and dumbness to appeals for the redress of grievances, the commonest remedy often sought by the affected region is either to opt out of the country (Katanga in Congo Kinshasa, Biafra in Nigeria, Oromo in Ethiopia, Azawad in Mali, South Sudan in Sudan, Somaliland in Somalia, Casamance in Senegal, Caprivi in Namibia, Barotseland in Zambia and Volta Region in Ghana) or to fight for regional autonomy (Tigray in Ethiopia and Tuaregs in Niger) or even to overthrow the existing regime and impose one expected to be amenable to its demands (Sierra Leone, Uganda and Liberia).

Congo Kinshasa

Belgium, the departing colonial power, granted independence to the Belgian Congo but immediately afterwards stoked the fires of civil war that soon consumed the country. The Congo (successively known as Congo Leopoldville, Congo Kinshasa, Zaire and currently the Democratic Republic of Congo) plunged into civil war immediately after independence on 30 June 1960. The civil war was provoked by the rebellion against the elected government of Patrice Lumumba by two key Congolese political persons, Joseph Kasa-Vubu and Moise Tshombe with his white-mercenaries-assisted Katangese gendarmes. Congo's civil wars have been fought mainly in the east, home to Congo's several revolts and insurgencies since decolonization. The country's endemic political instability since independence always has the effect of channelling country-wide discontent into outright rebellions and insurgencies.

In the ensuing 1960 chaos provoked by the rebellion of Kasavubu and Tshombe, Sergeant Mobuto seized power with Belgian support. Prime Minister Lumumba was taken hostage and then assassinated. His body was dissolved in acid by the Belgians. Since then and to this day the Congo has known alternating periods of insurgency and a measure of some stability. Periodically, revolts and insurgencies emerge in the country, such as the Simba and Kwilu Rebellions and the Kivbu Uprising in the east that made several attempts to overthrow Mobutu. In the south, Tshombe's Katanga made an unsuccessful secessionist bid. By the 1970s, the eastern insurgencies had been defeated with the help of Belgium and the material support of the American Central Intelligence Agency (CIA). But from 1996 to 1997, Laurent-Desiré Kabila, who had led an unsuccessful Maoist cross-border insurgency from the late 1960s to the 1980s against Mobutu, resurfaced in the east at the head of another insurgency. Kabila quickly swept across Zaire with the help of Rwanda and Uganda, overthrew Mobutu, captured power, gave the country a new flag and changed the Mobutu-era name Zaire to the Democratic Republic of Congo. Since then, the country has known several UN and AU peacekeeping missions and alternating periods of insurgency and a veneer of some stability.

Ethiopia

On 12 September 1974, a military junta headed by Aman Andom staged a coup in Ethiopia. The junta put in place a 'committee' or 'council' to coordinate the workings of the various branches of the country's security. The council was known as the Dergue, meaning the Coordinating Committee of the Armed Forces, Police and Territorial Army. It became the Marxist Provisional Military Government of Ethiopia. That same year General Andom was replaced with Gereral Tafari Benti who was executed in February 1977 along with Colonel Atnafu Abate. On 21 March 1975, the junta removed Emperor Haile Selassie from power, abolished the monarchy and the Ethiopian Empire and proclaimed the People's Democratic Republic of Ethiopia. From 1977 to 1987, the Dergue was led by Mengistu Haile Mariam. In 1987, the Dergue formally civilianized the administration and dissolved itself but its key members remained in key government posts until 1991 when the Dergue fell.

The Dergue instituted a violent regime of terror, torture and killings that prompted various insurgencies to emerge across all of Ethiopia's fourteen regions. This marked the onset of civil war in the country. Insurgencies sprung up across the cities and villages. They targeted Dergue supporters for assassination in what became known as the 'White Terror'. They were spearheaded by a coalition of multi-ethnic rebel groups under the banner of the EPRDF. Allies of the coalition were guerrilla movements in Eritrea, the EPLF led by Isaias Afwerki; in Tigray, the TPLF led by Meles Zenawi; and in Oromo, the OLF. The Dergue responded to the 'White Terror' with its own strain of violence, known as the 'Red Terror', in which death squads were used to murder rebel sympathizers. The Dergue was driven by Marxist ideology and was perceived as an Amhara elite that wanted to subjugate the Tigray and Eritrean peoples. By contrast, the Eritrean and Tigray guerrillas were driven by the desire for self-determination.

Both sides resorted to urban guerrilla warfare, executions, forced deportations, assassinations, torture and imprisonment of tens of thousands without due process of law. The Dergue additionally used helicopter gunships and MiGs to bombard rebel strongholds, killing thousands of civilians. The situation was compounded by the Dergue's brutal rule, which was further exacerbated by an unsuccessful invasion by Somalia to annex the Somali-inhabited

Ogaden region of Ethiopia. Also, drought and famine in the mid-1980s left an estimated half-a-million people dead. The EPLRDF surrounded Addis Ababa in May 1991 and the Dergue surrendered. American diplomats intervened and advised the acting president of Ethiopia Tesfaye G. Kidan to allow EPLRDF to occupy the city (which it did on 28 May 1991) in order to avoid bloodshed and wanton destruction of property. American diplomats also facilitated the flight of Mengistu from the country as the battle for Addis Ababa threatened to commence.

The civil war lasted seventeen years, ending with the overthrow of the Dergue, the arrest of its prominent officials, seventy-two of whom were found guilty of genocide in December 2006, while twenty-five, including Mengistu Haile Mariam, leader of the Dergue government, were tried in absentia. At least 1.4 million people perished in the civil war, tens of thousands were internally displaced and others escaped as refugees to neighbouring countries. At the end of the civil war, Eritrea asserted its independence from Ethiopia and the region of Tigray achieved a large measure of autonomy within Ethiopia. Afewerki, the leader of the Eritrean People's Liberation Front, became president of independent Eritrea while Meles Zenawi, leader of the Tigrayan People's Liberation Front, became prime minister of Ethiopia, shorn of Eritrea.

In November 2020, fourteen years after the end of Ethiopia's seventeen-year civil war, the long-simmering tension between Prime Minister Abiy Ahmed's government in Addis Ababa and leaders from the Tigray region in the north erupted into open violence. Ethiopia faced the spectre of yet another civil war. The clash between Tigrayan forces and the national military has left hundreds of people dead and tens of thousands have fled as refugees to neighbouring Sudan. In early November 2020, Abiy said Tigrayans had attacked a national military base. He said he then responded by bombing Tigray, destroying weaponry near the regional capital of Mekele and also by sending troops to Tigray province governed by the TPLF, a political party that once held influence across Ethiopia. Tigrayan forces retaliated by firing missiles at targets in Eritrea, saying that Eritrea sent troops and tanks across the border into Tigray to support the Ethiopian government.

The root cause of this latest round of armed domestic violence in Ethiopia can be traced to Abiy's dismantling of the long-standing coalition led for years by TPLF and replacing it with his Prosperity Party. This move in effect created a situation where the TPLF had to join the Prosperity Party and submit to Abiy's programme, or not, in which case they were out. The TPLF opted not to join. Further, Abiy postponed the 2020 elections in Ethiopia, citing concerns over the Corona-19 virus transmission. Tigrayan officials rejected the postponement and went ahead to hold the election in Tigray in September 2020. Abiy refused to recognize the results of that election. The stage was set for both sides to discount the other, each having grounds to declare the other illegitimate. Furthermore, in October 2020, lawmakers in Addis Ababa approved a plan to withhold federal funding for Tigray.

The international community was concerned that a further escalation of the conflict could destabilize the Horn of Africa and lead to mass displacement of Ethiopia's 110 million people. The Tigrayan missile attack on targets inside Eritrea added an international element to the conflict. Eritrea, led by Isaias Afewerki, was once a part of Ethiopia but gained independence in 1993 after a thirty-year struggle that began in 1963. From 1998 to 2000, Ethiopia and Eritrea fought in a civil war that left tens of thousands of people dead. The two countries remained enemies for the next eighteen years. Observers noted that involvement of the Eritrean military would be bad for Abiy because it would make him look like he needed the Eritreans to control his own territory. About 96,000 Eritrean refugees live in Tigray, sparking fears of being displaced yet again.

Foreign countries urged Abiy to pursue peace talks. Uganda and Kenya called for dialogue to resolve the conflict. Rwanda's president Paul Kagame offered to act as a mediator and flew to Addis Ababa where he met Abiy Ahmed and the Tigrayan region president, Derbretsion Gebremichael. A number of US Senators sent a collective letter to the American secretary of state asking him to 'engage directly' with Abiy and 'continue pressing all parties to agree to an immediate ceasefire, the de-escalation of tensions, protection of civilians, humanitarian access, and respect for international humanitarian law' (*Washington Post*, 19 November 2020). In March 2021, the Ethiopian prime minister admitted that in November 2020 Eritrean forces crossed into Tigray to support Ethiopia in its war against the Tigray province. He said Eritrea did so to protect its border, a curious way of a country protecting its border by invading another country that posed no threat to its border. The Ethiopian prime minister also acknowledged gross human rights abuses by armed parties but without identifying those suspected of carrying out the atrocities. However, human rights bodies allege that Eritrean soldiers killed more than a hundred people in the Ethiopian town of Axum. Eritrea withdrew its forces from Tigray at the end of March 2021. As of February 2022, the civil war has in fact intensified as Ethiopian fighter jets make regular sorties, bombarding the Tigrayan capital and other targets.

Mali

Mali was previously known as the French Soudan. Under Modibo Keita, it was established on 24 November as the Soudanese Republic, gained independence from France on 20 June 1960 and was proclaimed on 22

September 1960 as the Republic of Mali. Keita was ousted from power in 1968 in a military coup led by Colonel Moussa Traoré who remained in power until 1991 when there was a popular uprising against him. Colonel Amadou Toumani Touré intervened and removed Traoré from power. He gave the country a new constitution, put in place multi-party politics and organized free and fair municipal, parliamentary and presidential elections. In April 1992, Alpha Oumar Konaré won the presidential poll. Toumani Touré transferred power to him as the country's new president and went back to the barracks. But he contested the presidential election of 2002, won and became Mali's president. In January 2012, Tuareg insurgent groups in northern Mali took up arms against President Amadou Toumani Touré's government. One group, the MNLA, fought to establish an independent homeland, known as Azawad, for the Tuareg people. Another group, the FNLA, fought for greater autonomy for northern Mali.

In March 2012, just before the presidential elections were due in the country, Toumani Touré was ousted from power in an apparently bloodless coup led by Captain Amadou Sanogo who claimed that the president had failed to put down the Tuareg insurgency in the north of Mali and had failed to provide the military with adequate weapons to defeat the insurgency. After holding power for twenty-three days, the coup makers appointed the Speaker of the country's National Assembly Dioncounda Traoré as interim president.

By April 2012, the MNLA had taken control of the whole of northern Mali and was able to proclaim the 'Independent State of Azawad' with Goa as its capital. Another Tuareg-dominated group, the Islamic Ansar Dine (*Defenders of Faith*), initially fought alongside the MNLA against the government. However, because it did not seek independence but rather the imposition of Islamic law across Mali, it started fighting against the MNLA for control of northern Mali. By the end of 2012, Malian forces had been completely driven out of northern Mali. The government requested foreign, especially French, intervention. On 20 December 2012, the UN passed a resolution authorizing the deployment of an African-led International Support Mission in Mali (AFISMA) for an initial period of one year. The MNLA, driven out of most of its territory by Islamist groups, relinquished its previous goal of Azawadi independence in favour of a request for self-rule within Mali and began talks with the Malian government.

In January 2013, France, Britain, Denmark, Canada and ECOWAS forces (including those of Chad) entered the war against the Islamists, using air power to bomb Islamist positions and military equipment. France would later send in ground troops to join ECOWAS and Malian ground forces in the fight against the jihadists and started retaking the big cities from them. In February 2013, the French began operation *Panther* intended to subdue the region. The Islamists launched a guerrilla phase of the war, using suicide bombers, kidnapping, hostage-taking and cross-border incursions into neighbouring countries, particularly Algeria and Niger. The United States announced sending about hundred American troops to Niger to help the French in Mali by conducting surveillance against Al-Qaeda and providing Air Force logistics specialists, intelligence analysts and security officers. A peace deal between the government and Tuareg rebels was signed on 18 June 2013, but the MNLA ended the ceasefire in September of the same year after government forces opened fire on unarmed protesters.

In May 2012, Amnesty documented instances of gang rape, extrajudicial executions and the use of child soldiers by both Tuareg and Islamist groups. The World Food Programme issued a report referring to widespread looting of warehouses, hospitals, hotels and government offices. UNESCO reported damage or destruction of a number of historical and UNESCO World Heritage sites in Timbuktu on the grounds that they were idolatrous. Many Tuaregs and Arabs who lived in Bamako and elsewhere in southern Mali became victims of ethnic attacks by black Malians, even though many of them were hostile to Azawad separatism as well as the Islamists. Human Rights Watch and the International Federation of Human Rights reported several instances of extrajudicial and summary killings and other human rights abuses committed by the Malian army especially against ethnic Tuaregs and Arabs, as well as people suspected of being militants, with bodies subsequently being hastily buried in makeshift graves and wells.

Some victims were reportedly killed for not having identity documents or for their ethnicity. The government and the rebels finally signed a ceasefire on 20 February 2015 and agreed to tackle the causes of lasting tensions in the country. The government ill-advisedly continues to reject autonomy for the aggrieved northern Mali Tuareg community. However, it seems willing to consider 'devolved local powers'. The one-and-a-half-year Mali civil war left about 2,000 people dead, 144,000 refugees and 230,000 internally displaced persons. The secessionist bid was put down after two years of civil war in which the French army was at the forefront of the fight against the Tuaregs. The rebellion does not appear to be over as the French army stayed in northern Mali supposedly to counter the rebels and while also engaging, according to some reports, in resource looting and plundering in northern Mali. There have been popular revolts calling on the French military to leave. The new military government of Colonel Assimi Goïta ordered the French out of Mali. In January 2022, the government issued a six-month to five-year tentative transitional period of military rule. ECOWAS responded by adopting a wide range of sanctions against Mali. France submitted a draft resolution to the UN Security Council urging it to support the ECOWAS sanctions against Mali. Russia and China veto the resolution. There were concerns that France was seeking to re-enact the Libya, Syria, Ivory Coast and Iraq scenarios where UNSC resolutions were used as cover to effect regime change in those countries and, in the case of Libya and Iraq, kill their leaders. Mali has since invited Russians to Mali. It has ditched the French *colonies françaises africaines* (cfa) currency imposed by France on Francophone African countries. It has created its own currency known as the 'wari'; declared Bambara as Mali's official language replacing French; closed French schools in Mali; and served notice of its intention to exit ECOWAS.

Niger

Around the nineteenth century, Tuaregs invaded the area today known as Niger, coming from the Sahara in the north. A century later, between 1900 and 1922, the French defeated Tuareg fighters and established the French colony of Niger which eventually achieved independence on 13 August 1960. After decades of grievances about marginalization and discrimination, the Tuaregs envisaged an autonomous Tuareg homeland within Niger as the solution to their problem. In 1990, they launched an armed insurgency against the government to achieve that goal. After five years of civil war, a peace accord was signed with the government in 1995 ending the fighting. Following the assassination of the country's president in 1999 and with no progress on the homeland issue, the Tuareg insurgency resumed and has continued, even if intermittently.

Nigeria

In 1914, the United Kingdom amalgamated its differently structured and administered territories of Muslim northern Nigeria and non-Muslim Southern Nigeria where Christian missionaries were very active. The rationale for the amalgamation was a so-called 'administrative convenience'. From the onset, the newly amalgamated polity was bedevilled by a huge educational and developmental disparity, rabid ethnic rivalry and a pronounced trust deficit. This situation was compounded by the subsequent emergence of political parties, all of which were ethnically and regionally based – the NPC in the Hausa-Fulani North, the AG in the Yoruba West and the Mid-West, and the NCNC in the Ibo-dominated East. At independence, Nigeria became a lopsided four-state Federation (North, West, Mid-West and East) in which strong centrifugal forces were constantly at play pulling away from the centre towards the regional base of each major political party. All the political leaders had strong and firm political bases in the regions and fought hard for maximum powers for the regions, thus weakening the government at the centre. This was facilitated in no small measure by the type of federal constitution then in force and also the spirit in which it was applied by those in charge of the country. In the five years and three months interval between the achievement of independence on 1 October 1960 and the first coup of 15 January 1966, Nigeria experienced a number of turbulent episodes, a harbinger of what was to come.

First, when the Anglo-Nigerian defence pact signed at independence (very much like France's secret defence pacts imposed on its former colonies at independence) became known to the public in 1962, students and the general public carried out demonstrations denouncing the defence pact as an unequal treaty. The Nigerian Parliament abrogated it in December of that year. Second, Nigeria's first post-colonial general census conducted in 1962 gave figures for the northern region that were so inflated and highly improbable that they were publicly rejected, and a second census in 1963 gave figures that were only grudgingly accepted. Third, the Tiv people of the Middle Belt in northern Nigeria were unhappy with Hausa-Fulani-dominated NPC rule of the North and openly rioted from 1962 to 1965. Fourth, the 1964 general election in the country was so rigged that the principal political officeholders started urging the military to stage a coup d'état and seize power from the civil authorities. The formation of a broad-based government temporarily calmed matters down. A year later, in 1965, election rigging in Western Nigeria was so brazen that law and order broke down and a state of anarchy set in. The prevailing situation was one of precarious peace and stability on account of the country's politics, ethnography, geography, history, culture and demography. The scene was thus set for the four-year tragedy that would befall Nigeria: the coup in January 1966, the counter-coup in July 1966 and the bloody and destructive civil war that broke out on 6 July 1967 and lasted until 15 January 1970 (Madiebo, 1980).

The immediate cause of the Nigerian civil war was the ethnically motivated and executed coup and counter-coup of 1966. On 15 January 1966, Ibo military officers staged a coup that was particularly bloody, targeting Hausa-Fulani and Yoruba politicians and military officers. The political leadership of northern and western regions was killed by the coup makers. Six months later, officers of northern origin staged a revenge counter-coup, giving free rein to Northerners to carry out the pogrom that ensued. The Eastern Region's military government of Lt. Col. Ojukwu ordered Ibos from the rest of Nigeria to return to the Eastern Region. There followed an Ibo exodus from the North and other parts of Nigeria. Both coups altered the political equation in the country and destroyed the fragile trust and *modus vivendi* among the major ethnic groups, the Hausa-Fulani in the North, the Yoruba in the West and Mid-West, and the Ibo in the East. In order to break the power monopoly of these big ethnic blocs and to give smaller ethnic groups a stake in the governance of Nigeria, the country was divided in May 1967 into twelve states from the original four states. Ojukwu reacted to the creation of states by declaring the Eastern Region an independent state of 'Biafra' with himself as 'Head of State'. Lagos considered this an act of illegal secession and stated its intention to reintegrate and reunify the country.

Several meetings were held to resolve the issue peacefully but without success. On 6 July 1967, there began a thirty-month civil war characterized by carnage, starvation, mercenary activity and foreign involvement. In 1968, the Ibos proclaimed the old Eastern Region of Nigeria the Republic of Biafra with Enugu as its capital. It took two-and-a-half years of civil war to put down the secessionist bid. The secessionist regime claimed to be fighting for the survival of the Ibo people. The federal government declared that it was fighting to suppress the secession and to keep Nigeria one. Early in 1967, peace negotiations between the Supreme Military Council of the Federal Republic of Nigeria and the Eastern Region Military Governor, Lt. Col. Ojukwu, failed to yield fruits. Another peace talk called under the auspices of Gen. Ankrah of Ghana in Aburi, Ghana, also failed as Ojukwu continued to argue that to stay together at all, the regions of Nigeria first needed to draw apart. A flurry of other conciliatory efforts by eminent Nigerians, Emperor Hallie Selassie of Ethiopia, Dr Martin Luther King and even the OAU all proved abortive.

By the end of April 1969, the rebel enclave had been drastically reduced in size thanks in part to the role of the Nigerian Air Force and the Navy. Colonel Benjamin Adekunle who commanded the Third Marine Commando quickly became a household name not only for his bravery in leading his men but also for his daring amphibious landings in the strategic oil-producing Delta area and capturing the key coastal towns of Bonny, Port Harcourt and Calabar. His *nom de guerre* was 'Black Scorpion'. The folk tale has it that he had 'juju' powers that made him invincible and bulletproof. Federal forces embarked on a strategic envelopment of the remaining Biafran enclave. Biafra appealed unsuccessfully to the OAU whose Member States generally did not want to support secessionist movements. By Christmas of 1969, it was clear that the end of the civil war was in sight. Realizing the hopelessness of the situation, on 10 January 1970 Ojukwu fled the enclave to Ivory Coast with his immediate family members. The Commander of the Biafran Army, Maj. Gen. Effiong, who took over the administration of the remaining enclave, surrendered to the federal government on 14 January 1970 and signed the surrender and renunciation of secession papers (Obasanjo, 1980). That brought an end to the war, to the secessionist bid and to bloodshed.

During the war, each side had an odd mix of supporters who ordinarily would not do business together. Nigeria was supported by Britain, Egypt, Sudan, the Soviet Union, Chad, Niger, the United States, Syria, Algeria, Saudi Arabia and Bulgaria. 'Biafra', on the other hand, was supported by France, Portugal, Spain, apartheid South Africa, Rhodesia, Tanzania, Gabon,

Ivory Coast, Haiti, Zambia, West Germany, Switzerland and mercenary outfits. Well-known mercenaries who fought on the Biafran side were the German Rolf Steiner, the Welshman Taffy Williams and the Swedish Count Carl Gustav von Rosen. It is estimated that on both sides about 75,000 military and militia died while some 3 million civilians lost their lives, 2 million of them from famine and disease (Njoku, 1987).

Sierra Leone

The civil war in Sierra Leone began in March 1991 and ended in January 2002. It lasted for eleven years, the second-longest violent conflict in Africa after the Angolan civil war which lasted for twenty-seven years. The Sierra Leone civil war began when an armed insurgency group, the RUF, attempted to overthrow Joseph Momoh's government (Abdullah, 2004). The RUF recruited thousands of youths (Denov, 2010) deeply disenchanted by the post-independence systemic corruption, mismanagement, economic collapse, loot of government property and infrastructural decay in the country. It was led by Foday Sankoh and was supported by forces from Charles Taylor's insurgency in neighbouring Liberia (Keen, 2005; Gberie, 2005). More than twenty years of bad governance, poverty, corruption and oppression created the circumstances for the rise of the RUF, as ordinary people yearned for change. The RUF failed to overthrow the government. But the Sierra Leone army was so ineffective against the rebels that within a year the RUF was in control of the diamond-rich areas in the east and south of the country. This precipitated a coup d'état in April 1992. The military made some gains in pushing the rebels back to the Liberian border but was unable to defeat the RUF.

In 1995, the government contracted at $1.8 million per month a South African mercenary outfit deceptively denoted as Executive Outcomes (EO) to repel the RUF, which it did. In 1996, a civilian government was put in place in Freetown. A peace deal signed in Abidjan in March of that year was not honoured and fighting resumed (Mutwol, 2009). This prompted another coup by RUF-assisted disgruntled soldiers who established the AFRC as the government of Sierra Leone led by Paul Koroma. RUF joined with AFRC and captured Freetown with ease. The AFRC/RUF government then declared the war won and over. But the announcement appeared to have been a licence for the wave of looting, rape and revenge killings that followed. This widespread criminality was tellingly described as 'operation pay yourself'.

President Kabba escaped by helicopter for exile in nearby Guinea. The coup was universally condemned, the OAU, ECOWAS and the UN taking the lead. ECOMOG forces demanded that the new junta return power peacefully to the Kabbah government or risk sanctions and increased military presence. When this demand was ignored, ECOMOG forces intervened and retook Freetown on behalf of the ousted Kabba government. But it found it difficult to pacify the regions beyond Freetown. Diplomatic intervention by world leaders in January 1999 led to the signing in March 1999 of the Lomé Peace Accord between the government and the RUF. Sankoh, the RUF leader, was pardoned for treason, given the Vice Presidency of the country and chairmanship of the commission overseeing the country's diamond mines in return for a commitment to peace, disarmament and demobilization under international supervision. The disarmament, demobilization and reintegration programme offered to former rebel combatants, food, clothing and shelter in exchange for them handing in their weapons. By 2002, camps set up under the DDR process had collected over 45,000 weapons and sheltered over 70,000 former combatants (Özerdem, 2008).

In spite of the success of the DDR programme, many rebels refused to commit to the peace process. By May 2000, the RUF again began advancing towards Freetown, captured over 500 UNAMSIL peacekeepers and held them hostage. UNAMSIL was on the brink of collapse. In the face of the UN peace mission faltering, Britain intervened, in Blair's second military adventure after Kosovo, to support the weak government of President Ahmad Tejan Kabbah. Britain launched Operation Palliser (Dorman, 2009; Koroma, 2004; Woods & Reese, 2008). The deployment consisted of a 1200-man ground force supported by air and sea power. The objective of the operation was to evacuate foreign nationals and establish order in the country. The UN passed a resolution demanding the government of Liberia to expel all RUF members, to end financial support for the RUF and to halt the illicit diamond trade. British forces went after the rebels. Guinea carried out cross-border bombing raids of bases held by RUF and Guinean rebels. The combination of these factors led to the quick defeat of the rebels who sued for peace and signed a new peace deal. President Kabba declared the civil war over on 18 January 2002. In the same year, the government set up a Truth and Reconciliation Commission to facilitate post-war healing and, with the assistance of the UN, a Special Court for Sierra Leone to try persons who perpetrated the most serious crimes during the civil war.

The war left about 300,000 dead, thousands of amputees, and 2.5 million people displaced internally and externally. Several countries intervened in the war. Government allies were Kamajors militia, CDF, Britain, ECOMOG forces, EO mercenaries, Guinea, United States and UNAMSIL. Allies of the RUF were West Side Boys militia, AFRC, NPFL, Liberia, Libya and Burkina Faso. The RUF was able to sustain the war for so long, seemingly against all odds, because of its control of diamond areas and access to easily extractable diamonds which it was able to sell to finance its war effort. Diamonds were thus significant in motivating and sustaining the civil war (Hirsch, 2000; Lujala, 2005). But so too was gold mining and cash crop farming using forced labour. Looting was another prominent feature of the civil war, including looting of diamonds, currency, household items, food, livestock, cars and international aid shipments (Jalloh, 2001). The RUF was extremely brutal against civilians and in many cases cut off people's limbs. But government soldiers were equally brutal and indiscriminate in their 'mopping up' operations and treatment of rebels and the civilian population suspected of being in sympathy with the rebels. Civilians then relied on a militia force known as the Kamajors for their protection and the protection of their family and home (Allie, 2005).

Chapter 5

Noticeable Features of Africa's Civil Wars

Wars are usually won by armies with the best soldiers, the best equipment, the most powerful weapons and the sharpest generals. Sometimes smaller and weaker forces triumph over bigger armed forces, but this is the exception to the rule. Major post-colonial wars in Africa have been civil wars in about half the number of countries in the continent (Elbadawi & Sambanis, 2000). Whenever states pursue opposing or incompatible goals, there is always a risk of clash of interest at some point in their relations inter se. This could lead to conflict which is then resolved peacefully or by force. The states involved may take appropriate measures to contain or mitigate the conflict and thereby prevent its escalation. They may even suffer the conflict to escalate and then negotiate a mutually acceptable accommodation.

Some of Africa's conflicts have arisen out of expansionist or territorial aggrandizement ambitions of certain states seeking to enlarge their territory by forcibly grabbing an adjacent territory. Ethiopia sought to grab Eritrea. Libya sought to grab the Auozou Strip in Chad. Morocco sought to grab Mauritania. Morocco also sought and still seeks to grab the western Sahara. Somalia sought to grab all neighbouring Somali-inhabited territories within the lawful territory of other states. Currently, French-speaking Cameroun is trying its luck to grab the contiguous English-speaking territory of Ambazonia which was a similar former mandated Category B territory and later UN trust territory. Expansionist wars are not internal or civil wars. Each such war involves a claim to territory not within the boundary of the expansionist state on its achievement of independence.

A conflict may or may not involve an appeal to force. Where the parties have recourse to arms, the violence unleashed is characterized as either an intrastate or an interstate armed conflict. Resort to war is perversely claimed to be justifiable and unavoidable as the only realistic means of ending an enduring state of conflict, achieving a lasting settlement and imposing peace; even if from the point of view of the vanquished such a peace settlement is an unhappy and precarious one.

ELITE, COMMUNAL AND REVOLUTIONARY CONFLICTS

Students of conflicts identify at least five conflict types, namely, elite, factional, communal and mass, revolutionary and foreign intervention (Oyeniyi, 2011). Elite conflicts are those within the political leadership. The key means of dealing with elite demands have often been through the manipulation of appointments and policy shifts. Often, increasing the number of bureaucratic posts and distributing them are used as means of appeasement. This practice partly accounts for the bloated state machinery with inordinately high personnel cost. It also explains why the political leadership creates numerous state corporations, many state representations abroad, multiple political structures and a multiplicity of territorial units. These posts are used as strategies of appeasement and patronage. Factional disputes and conflicts emerge when contending elites mobilized their constituents to vie with other groups for scarce state-controlled resources. Ethno-regional inequalities intensify competition and conflict among various interests.

Communal and mass conflicts as well as inter-ethnic animosity call into question not only the legitimacy of specific regimes but also the essentials of state power. They challenge the state's territorial integrity. They protest the existing distribution of power. They foreground the promotion of sub-national identities by calling for adequate representation in all state structures, the protection of minority rights, the granting of real autonomy or for even outright secession. Revolutionary conflicts are mass or popular uprisings that seek to oust and replace the existing regime and political order as happened in Sudan, Burkina Faso, Mali, Zimbabwe, Egypt, Tunisia, Algeria, Libya and The Gambia.

Since the colonial period, there has been a series of self-interested foreign interventions (Zartman, 1985) and ruthless exploitation of African conflicts by especially France. During the cold war, the two superpowers, the United States and the former USSR, carved out spheres of influence in the continent and often acted through their respective proxies. High levels of intervention tended to prolong and intensify domestic conflicts. The introduction of the well-equipped troops of external power, foreign boots on the ground, usually increases the level of firepower, escalates the conflict and dramatically increases the number of casualties and the extent of infrastructural destruction.

NO CLEAR PATHWAY FOR CONFLICT MANAGEMENT

African states consider internal conflicts as matters essentially within their domestic jurisdiction. They generally tend to frown on third-party intercession, even if on humanitarian grounds. When a state objects to third-party intercession on the ground of 'non-interference in internal affairs', all the outside world does is to voice concern when the death toll and refugee flows from such conflicts escalate and attain a level that pricks the conscience of the world. A high threshold of killings and refugee flows has the effect of prompting international action as in the case of Darfur in Sudan or of the Central African Republic.

Every war ends on the battlefield as a result of the enemy's *debellatio* or in the conference room. Even the victor in war must eventually sit down with the vanquished in a conference to sign the formal ending of hostilities and the peace settlement that would have been reached. It is therefore surprising that aggrieved parties so instinctively and readily resort to coercive action rather than to the negotiation table. Surprisingly also, there is no clear pathway for managing conflict by way of de-escalating it or facilitating bargaining between the parties involved. In fact, one notes a near-total absence, at both state and continent-wide levels, of institutionalized mechanisms, structures or institutions for peaceful resolution of conflicts. At state level, most countries do not have credible mechanisms for the peaceful transfer of political power. States experiencing a serious crisis may receive an offer of ad hoc mediation. Such an offer is apt to be made by an eminent personality, a respected clergyman, an intergovernmental organization or a nongovernmental entity with stature and clout. At times the offer is rebuffed by one party or by all the parties to the conflict. At times also, mediation is undertaken but without success.

A society in the throes of a serious conflict simply positions itself for self-destruction if it has no credible mechanisms for the pacific settlement of disputes. It also opens itself to self-destruction if parties to the conflict are not willing to resolve their dispute amicably or to negotiate in a spirit of give-and-take or to bargain and compromise. Dialog or negotiation is not possible where the parties are not interested in engaging in good-faith talks. Where there is a third-party offer of mediation to broker a peaceful settlement, the mediator must be, and be perceived as, an honest broker. The mediator manages the conflict using a variety of appropriate strategies that could be non-coercive such as offers of fiscal rewards, promises, guarantees and developmental aid (Emmanuel, 2016); or coercive such as diplomatic pressure, sanctions or military intervention. UN involvement in the management of Africa's civil wars has mainly consisted of mounting peace enforcement and peacekeeping operations at some stage in the course of the conflict. These operations have never stopped state and non-state actors from pursuing their respective war aims.

In Africa generally, the leadership of a state that is in the throes of a conflict tries to manage it in the way it sees fit, constrained by neither law nor morality. In most cases, those who eventually gain the upper hand in power struggle jail or execute their 'defeated' opponents or refer them to the International Criminal Court (ICC) for trial on charges of crimes against humanity. For example, Alassane Ouattara's referral of Gbagbo, Joseph Kabila's referral of Jean-Pierre Bemba, Liberia's referral of Charles Taylor and Sudan's referral of Omar Bashir.

In the 61 years between 1960 and 2020, 118 African leaders were overthrown (Anyangwe, 2012) and of that number 74 were murdered, jailed or forced into exile. In Côte d'Ivoire, Alassane Ouattara referred his defeated opponent, Laurent Gbagbo, to the ICC. In Cameroun, there was a very bloody power tussle between former president Ahidjo and his self-designated oligarchic successor Mr. Paul Biya, appointed head of state by radio announcement in 1982. The conflict between the two men for pre-eminence in the state ended with Biya having Ahidjo (who had escaped to exile in Senegal) tried and sentenced to death in absentia. Biya then executed hundreds of persons from Ahidjo's ethnic community following a failed coup attempt which Biya claimed was masterminded by Ahidjo, his benefactor.

In Liberia, President Samuel Doe was defeated by the multiple insurgencies against him and was brutally murdered by his victorious enemies. Doe himself had come to power in a particularly bloody coup that saw the assassination of the country's president, William Tolbert, and the public execution of his ministers on the beach in Monrovia. In Angola, after fighting a vicious civil war against Dos Santos and the MPLA government, Jonas Savimbi who headed the rebel UNITA insurgency was killed by execution style. In Congo-Brazzaville, ex-president Sassou Nguessou defeated his successor, President Pascal Lissouba, in a particularly savage ethnic-based civil war and seized power again. Nguessou had Lissouba tried for high treason in absentia and given a thirty-year sentence. In Congo-Kinshasa, President Mobutu was defeated by an insurgency led by Joseph Kabila. Mobutu escaped into exile where he died. In Egypt, Abdel Fattah Khalil Al-Sisi staged a coup on 3 July 2013 and had arrested and sentenced to death the Head of State Mohamed Morsi under whom he served as defence minister.

In July 2002, the African Union adopted the protocol relating to the establishment of the PSC as part of its response to conflicts in the continent. In terms of the protocol, Member States commit themselves to facilitate early action by the PSC. The PSC acts on early warning information provided by a continental early warning system. It acts and intervenes to prevent conflicts through peacekeeping by an African Standby Force (Anyangwe, 2006: 43).

That force went operational in late 2015. At the core of the commitments to make, keep and build peace in Africa is the pledge by African states to facilitate peacemaking and peace-building in war-torn countries (Murithi, 2006; Mwanasali, 2006). In this endeavour, the African Union has adopted a two-pronged approach: conflict prevention through political means and facilitation of peacemaking and peace-building in war-torn countries. But this has not borne much fruit as much of this remains on paper. The African Union's record on conflict prevention and conflict mediation is still mediocre. Instead, it is Africa's regional organizations such as ECOWAS, SADC and so on that have assumed effective peacemaking, peacekeeping and stabilization functions in their respective regions.[1] In particular, ECOWAS took on conventional security tasks in the civil wars in West Africa (Brown, 2015).

International documents on post-conflict situations always stress peace, reconstruction and political stability but are silent on reconciliation. It is not clear why this is the case. But it could be a recognition of the reality on the ground that reconciliation cannot be decreed. That is probably why even the Millennium Development Goals are silent on post-conflict reconciliation in the transition from conflict to peace. The African Union through NEPAD has developed an African Post-Conflict Reconstruction Policy Framework. The Framework emphasizes the link between peace, security, peace-building and the humanitarian and development dimensions of post-conflict reconstruction. But no explicit reference is made to reconciliation. The UN Millennium Declaration adopted in 2000 is likewise silent on reconciliation. It only speaks of 'encouraging and sustaining regional and sub-regional mechanisms for conflict prevention and the promotion of political stability, and ensuring reliable resource flows for peace support operations'. Similarly, the UN Peace-building Commission established in December 2005 is silent on the issue of post-conflict reconciliation (Murithi, 2006). It focusses attention on post-conflict reconstruction and institution building which it sees as the foundation for sustainable peace, security and development. UN experience in peace-building is confined to the following three clusters of issues: security (disarmament, demobilization and the creation of a professional force), state-institution building (restoration of constitutional order and strengthening of the rule of law) and development (short-term development projects and short-term budgetary support) (Ozerdem, 2008). The benign neglect of reconciliation in these peace frameworks is difficult to explain.

Students of conflicts believe conflicts are not inevitable and that they can be prevented and mitigated. To that end, a number of preventive strategies have been suggested. One is the establishment of an early warning system. The system consists in feeding certain types of information into databases to provide early warning of possible future conflicts. It is not dissimilar from that of preventive diplomacy whereby information gathering, monitoring and the provision of databases can be utilized by governments, international agencies, humanitarian organizations and the media for action to prevent conflicts breaking-out or escalating. The success of the system may be doubted. It has failed to anticipate and prevent conflicts in the continent.

Africa itself needs to develop appropriate and realistic policies towards averting conflicts in the continent such as by developing new ways of conflict management. After all, the mere presence of many ethnic groups in a country does not by itself necessarily bring about internal instability, animosity and conflicts. What makes the difference between stable plural societies and unstable ones is usually the responsibility of the leadership to the fact of multi-nationality or ethnicity. Preventive deployment of UN peace enforcement is also another suggested prevention strategy. Boutros Boutros-Ghali, the UN secretary-general submitted to the UN in 1992 a report titled *Agenda for Peace*. In it he proposed 'preventive deployment' of peace-keepers. He further proposed what may be termed a mitigation strategy consisting of the creation of peace enforcement units, a rapid reaction UN force to enable action without the need to seek new troops for each mission, heavily armed peace-enforcers for dangerous missions and the strengthening of regional peacekeeping bodies to lighten the burden on the UN. The document called for increased UN military capacity financed by levies on international arms sales and air travel, and a more proactive, assertive approach to peacekeeping. It declared that 'the time for absolute and exclusive sovereignty' has passed. But African states still make a song and dance about it.

Suggested mitigation strategies include skills training in matters such as mediation, involvement in the healing process, establishing ceasefires and zones of peace, and disarming armed actors engaged in conflict. Such skills are critical. They are very useful because processes such as mediation, negotiation or peacekeeping require attitudinal changes in the actors involved.

TEPID EFFORTS AT CONFLICT MEDIATION

Until recently, intra- and interstate conflicts in Africa tended to involve various levels of military force in the false belief that the conflicts could be resolved through force or threat of force. But good sense invariably prevails. Resort is always finally had to some formal method of conflict resolution such as mediation or arbitration. However, attempts at conflict resolution through arbitration have always failed. Even mediation and Joint/Mixed Commissions, enthusiastically promoted by the OAU in the 1960s, 1970s and 1980s, have met with only limited success. The AU's reaction to African conflicts, within and between states, has understandably often been tardy, hesitant and even absent as the AU's culpable indifference to the armed conflict in

Ambazonia eloquently shows. Admittedly, the continental organization is not a supranational government. It has no standing military force. It lacks resources. Its decision-making is by consensus. It subscribes to the somewhat controversial principle of non-interference in the domestic affairs of Member States. Controversial because even the AU constitutional text acknowledges that there are some well-defined limited instances, namely, war crimes, genocide and crimes against humanity, in which it may legitimately intervene,[2] at least by issuing a condemnatory statement. Regional intergovernmental organizations have, by contrast, registered a measure of success in managing some of these conflicts. For example, ECOWAS, IGAD and SADC have been influential in resolving some domestic conflicts. These play a key role in arbitrating disputes, ending conflicts and re-establishing peace, working in cooperation with the AU, the UN and sometimes a European power.

The Church

Recourse to mediation by religious personages in situations of civil war appeared conventional at one time. The services of internal religious authorities were pressed into service to resolve internal conflicts in a number of countries. However, the church's political role in this regard, proclaiming justice and peace in the name of Jesus Christ, has often not been successful. In South Africa, Archbishop Desmond Tutu got politically involved in peace mediation between blacks and the racist white bastion. But it was only in the context of the TRC that his voice was effective. In Zaire, the efforts of Archbishops Monsengwo Pasinya and Monsenguro to broker a peace deal between the Mobutu regime and the opposition failed to bring peace to that tormented country. Similar efforts elsewhere fared no better. Efforts by Rev José Chipenda, through the UN and the OAU, to bring peace to Rwanda; by the Catholic Bishops to bring peace to Sierra Leone; by Christian Cardinal Tumi and Presbyterian Church Moderator Henry Awasom to bring peace to an agonizing Cameroun in a situation of no peace no war; by Archbishop Francisco Viti for peace in Huambo and by extension in the whole of Angola; by the Saint Egidio Catholic Association for peace in Algeria, all failed. Similar church efforts by a retired Anglican bishop in Northern Uganda to end the LRA insurgency in that country did not succeed. The only success of note by the church in this regard was that of the Saint Egido Catholic Association which successfully mediated in the Mozambique civil war, playing a crucial role in ending RENAMO's bush war against the FRELIMO government.

Intergovernmental Organizations

Efforts by intergovernmental organizations to broker peace have not registered spectacular results either. For example, the OAU mediation effort to end the

Nigerian civil war and its effort to broker peace between Egypt and Israel following the Six-Day War produced no results. In circumstances where rival political groups fight for power in the state, mediators often promoted and strongly recommended the formation of a so-called 'government of national unity' as a solution to the contest for power. This expedient was fashionable at one time. But it soon proved to be a dismal failure in every conflict-torn country where it was touted as a remedy. It failed in Togo, Rwanda, DRC, Burundi, Angola, Uganda, Zimbabwe, Chad and Somalia. It seems to have had only some measure of success in South Sudan and Libya. Nowadays no one seriously promotes 'government of national unity' as a solution to a country torn by a power conflict.

In 2015, UN and AU peace mediators seeking an end to the civil wars in Libya and in South Sudan pushed in vain for 'a government of national unity deal' between the warring factions in both countries. The joint efforts of the AU and IGAD, backed by muscular states such as America, Britain and Norway, succeeded in August 2015 in brokering a ceasefire and a peace deal in the Southern Sudan civil war. The war began in December 2013 when President Salva Kiir dismissed his Deputy Riek Machar, accusing him of planning a coup. This action set in motion a cycle of revenge killings that quickly split the country along ethnic lines, Dinka against Nuer. Despite hiccups, overall, the ceasefire and peace deal held leading to reasonable hopes that South Sudan's government of national unity (known as the Revitalized Transitional Government of National Unity under the terms of a peace agreement that came into effect on 22 February 2020) will entrench peace and begin the arduous task of national reconstruction.

It may be hypothesized that the overall failure of mediation efforts in Africa's conflicts is because such efforts do not come at the ripe moment (Zartman, 1985). The ripe moment for mediation engagement is when the situation is ripe for a settlement. A situation is ripe for a settlement when the parties have both arrived at the conclusion that they will probably be better off with a settlement than without one. An attempt to get a mediation going before the time is propitious will most likely fail, especially if the mediation is ambitious and conducted with much fanfare as is often the case. Mediation is thus likely to succeed if it comes at the right time. The right time is to get the mediation going early enough, that is, well before the parties get so far into the conflict that 'winning' becomes a matter of pride and an end in itself. Another right time to launch a mediation is to do so at a much more later stage when the parties have slugged it out and seem weary of fighting. At that point peace mediation offers them a face-saving opportunity to get out of the war and at the same time still appear undefeated.

The timing of proffering an offer to mediate is crucial. Where the aim in view is to anticipate and prevent a looming conflict, the offer to mediate would be made as soon as there are early warning signs of an impending violent conflict. But where the conflict has already broken out and the idea is to quash it or at least prevent it from escalating, the good time to make an offer to mediate is when the conflict is ripe for mediation, that is to say, when the conflict has reached a stage where the parties are prepared to acknowledge that mediation is in the best interest of everyone concerned. Mediation has so far not seriously been pursued in the Ambazonia/Cameroun armed conflict because of the apparent perception that the time is not yet ripe for any serious engagement since Cameroun continues to believe, unrealistically, that it can win the war and impose terms.

The AU sometimes gets involved in mediation efforts. It has recently supplemented that effort with peacekeeping activities in some instances. International peacekeeping efforts are laudable. But they are increasingly tainted by rogue and racist peacekeepers. Peacekeepers have been accused of involvement in resource trafficking in the Democratic Republic of Congo, Central African Republic and Sierra Leone. They have also been accused of sexual abuse and bestiality. In election-based conflict, mediators invariably promote a power-sharing government variously denoted as 'national unity', 'broad-based' or 'transitional' government. This is an indication that the conflict is simply a tussle for power by the parties concerned. The warring parties buy into that expedient but then only for the purpose of having a breathing space to better prepare for the next round of fighting. The so-called power-sharing government always invariably collapses and fighting resumes until one side is vanquished. The expedient of power-sharing often does not work as a cohesive government, nor has it perforce brought unity, peace and stability.

THE POLITICS OF ETHNICITY

Africa's civil wars are mostly the direct consequence of tribal politics and the 'ethnicization' of deadly power struggles by rival armed militia, political groups and military factions within the state (Fearon, 2003). Having political power in Africa is additionally a very lucrative form of business. In every African state, political power trumps all other centres of power in the country and enables control of other human beings. More importantly, political power gives unimpeded access to the nation's purse. The money is then used for oneself, one's own family and one's own ethnic group in the hope of avoiding the poverty curse. Moreover, people find strength, security and safety within their ethnic groups. Significantly, overthrown African rulers who escape death always take refuge in their ethnic district. Few are the African states that guarantee country-wide security and safety for everyone in the state. Few are the African leaders who command broad national followership.

The direct nexus between power struggle and the ethnographic and demographic structure of the country exacerbates ethnic animosity between the ethnic groups to which the leading contenders for power belong. Since some ethnic groups straddle state frontiers, the risk of civil war in one country increases dramatically when there is a civil war in an adjacent state. The genocide in Rwanda exported killings to the adjacent states of Burundi, Congo-Kinshasa and Uganda. Guinea, Sierra Leone, Ivory Coast and Mali were easily sucked into the civil war in Liberia. On the other hand, an unstable country benefits from a stable neighbour. Violence-prone Chad and Central African Republic benefited from a Cameroun that passed for a peaceful and stable country until that myth was exploded from 2016 onwards when it went the way of all French Equatorial African states by sinking into armed conflict. Somalia benefits from a stable Kenya and Burundi from a stable Tanzania.

Some civil wars have taken the form of an ethnically based armed insurgency against an established government in order to overthrow it. The purpose of seeking regime overthrow is to seize political power on behalf of a marginalized ethnic group or to procure the secession of a part of the country. In every African state that has experienced a civil war, the conflict tends to be directly linked to the ethnography of the country and to the struggle for power by the political elite and even the military. The most prevalent types of civil wars plaguing Africa are thus those caused by ethnic rivalry and political power struggles. In many instances, ethnic rivalry and political struggles degenerate into a civil war entailing very high military expenditure to the detriment of other sectors, a heavy loss of lives, environmental damage, social and economic waste and an aggravation of health issues (UNEP, 2001). Power struggles between political elites within the state often easily translate into ethnic animosity between the ethnic groups of the leading contenders for power (Rothchild, 1999). Ethnic animosity itself is generally kindled and sustained by the political power elites. When so kindled, ethnic animosity degenerates into violence, occasioning gross human rights abuses. It easily translates into a civil war which all too often takes the form of ethnic wars because of the demographic and ethnographic structure of African states (Rothchild, 1999).

The reason why power struggles quickly take the form of ethnic struggles is that political parties in Africa tend to be ethnically based. They are ethnic-based because in Africa people find strength, security and safety among their own, that is, within their ethnic groups. Few are the African leaders who command a broad national appeal and followership. Furthermore, power struggles are deadly in Africa because accession to political power trumps all other centres of power in the country and gives access not only to control of other human beings but, more importantly, gives unimpeded access to the nation's purse and other wealth for the person who captures power, for his family and for his ethnic group. Political parties are generally ethnic or regionally based. As a result, a power struggle between political parties invariably becomes a violent power struggle between ethnic groups represented by the political parties and easily degenerates into an ethnic civil war. The elites who initiate these wars are normally not the ones who reap the more violent reaction or destruction. It is the common man used as cannon fodder or expendable people for the attainment and sustenance of power, wealth and prosperity. At the end of the day, the continent's problems are due to leadership mismanagement.

THE HABIT OF INTERVENTION BY OUTSIDE POWERS

Outside powers, notoriously France, all too often intervene in African conflicts, on request or on their own accord. They engineer violent conflicts, give logistical support, provide weapons (Stohl, 1999) and prolong butchery, suffering and destruction. It is doubtful that outside powers always intervene in Africa's deadly conflicts out of altruistic or humanitarian considerations. More often than not they intervene to satisfy their political, economic, diplomatic or strategic interests. Third-party intervention may be driven by the need to protect at-risk people while remaining unbiased (Dorman, 2009). Intervention may also be for the purpose of helping the warring parties reach an agreement or assisting them in the implementation of one. But that is often a delicate task. Sometimes a state next door intervenes by supporting one of the parties, depending on its perceived interests. An outside ally would usually provide logistical support, weapons (Stohl, 1999) and even troops (Dorman, 2009).

Arms-supplying countries and companies take unconscionable advantage of Africa's civil wars to make a huge fortune out of them. In 2014, the UN adopted an arms control instrument from a humanitarian and human rights perspective. The instrument, the *Arms Trade Treaty*, aims at preventing the illicit trade in conventional arms and their diversion. It is considered a contribution to international and regional peace, security and stability. The focus of the document is on illicit trade and does not prohibit sovereign transfer of arms. The effectiveness of the treaty may be doubted. The treaty has made no difference to the civil war situation in Africa.

Third-party military assistance to one or both sides of a civil war simply protracts the conflict and prolongs the suffering of civilians. French intervention in Côte d'Ivoire and Mali, and NATO intervention in Libya, exacerbated the loss of lives in those countries. Third-party military assistance also occasions widespread and massive destruction, especially when the Air Force or Navy is pressed into service by the government side as in the civil wars in Angola, Congo-Brazzaville, Ethiopia, Libya, Somalia and Nigeria where the Navy played a key role in the victory of government forces. Third-party military assistance further has the effect of inducing a bad faith approach to peace initiatives in that it encourages intransigence which in turn leads to the collapse of peace initiatives. Without active outside involvement, it is doubtful that any civil war would last more than a few months, at most.

CHILD SOLDIERS

The conduct of civil wars in Africa continues to evolve. Both sides resort to a variety of small arms and to civil militia groups as additional forces. These militias often replace regular armies on the battlefield. Both sides also conscript child soldiers, boys and girls (Beah, 2007; Denov, 2010; Abdullah, 2004; Hoffman, 2007); boys as combatants and ammunition porters, and girls as sex slaves, cooks and fetchers of food, wood and water. For example, estimates by human rights organizations (HRW, 2004) indicate that the Angolan government had 3,000 child soldiers. UNITA had 6,000 child soldiers who married off between 5,000 and 8,000 underage girls to UNITA guerrillas. Some underage girls were used to forage for food for the guerrillas. Some others were handed over as 'trophies' to commanders after victories in battle. The commanders then sexually abused the girls.

In civil wars, insurgents make use of readily available modern technology and guerrilla tactics. Rebel forces use small arms, especially the AK47, automatic machine guns, grenades and explosives. Government forces, on the other hand, have a wide array of weapons, including artillery and tanks. In some instances, government forces deploy the Navy and even the Air Force. Aerial bombardment by government forces in Angola, Congo-Brazzaville, Nigeria, Somalia, Libya and Ethiopia caused huge civilian casualties. Arms-supplying countries and companies make a huge fortune out of civil wars in Africa (Hartung & Moix, 2000; Stohl, 1999). Allegations of starvation as a method of war are sometimes heard. But the case of starvation-related deaths during the civil war in Ethiopia and Mozambique appeared to have been the result of the severe drought experienced by each country at the time. International Humanitarian Law places limitations on the means and methods that may be used to injure and subdue the enemy. One way in which it constrains the waging of war is by prohibiting the killing of civilians and other at-risk persons. Another constraint on the waging of war is the prohibition of the use of weapons or methods of warfare that cause unnecessary losses or excessive suffering.

APPEAL TO RELIGION AND OCCULTISM

Religion, magic, witchcraft and occultism play a significant role in Africa's civil wars (Bergner, 2003; Ellis, 2007). These persistent themes sensationally flourish as a part of popular oral culture. There is not much literature on possible occult roots of civil wars in Africa or about some conflicts and certain situations being the product of arcane and demonic influence. However, one book, an edited collection of essays (Nicolini, 2006) investigates the reputed influence of witchcraft in processes of warfare and peace-building. Drawing from West, East, and Southern African country case studies, the investigation concludes that witchcraft and magic played an important historical role in political and military conflicts. The book notes that African anti-colonial resistance movements invoked the supernatural in political mobilization and that in fact witchcraft and magic have been invoked in many African power struggles through time.

Christianity and Islam proclaim messianic messages. Christians and Muslims pray to God for victory over their enemies who do exactly the same thing. Others appeal to esoteric forces for protection in battle and for victory over their enemies. Many combatants in the civil war in Nigeria, Liberia, Côte d'Ivoire and Sierra Leone appealed to and believed in mystical forces capable of making them invisible and invincible, or otherwise protecting them in combat. They purport to manipulate spells and portions and direct them towards their enemies. Some commanders reportedly had the ability to simply disappear in the face of an enemy or used certain herbs or magical portions that made their entire body bulletproof, affording a protection far better and less cumbersome than the helmet and bulletproof vest worn by 'ordinary' soldiers. For example, Col. Benjamin Adekunle who commanded the Nigerian Third Marine Commando quickly got the *nom de guerre* 'Black Scorpion'. He became a household name for bravery in always leading his men in battle and for his daring amphibious landings in the strategic oil-producing Delta area. Leading his men in battle had the same effect as what Wellington famously said about Napoleon that his presence on the battlefield 'was worth forty thousand men'. Col. Adekunle captured the key coastal towns of Bonny, Port Harcourt and Calabar and effectively enforced the naval blockade of the Biafran enclave. He is said to have been able to achieve these daring feats because he had 'juju' powers that made him invincible whenever he chose to and his body bulletproof.

Some other field commanders wore charms or amulets to protect themselves from being hurt. Reportedly, they readily made human sacrifices, drank human blood and ate human parts, especially the heart, for that purpose as well. The Liberian civil war is particularly edifying in this regard (Ellis, 2007; Gerdes, 2013). Mysticism and human sacrifice played a significant part in that war. According to anecdotal accounts, some rebel leaders consulted oracles and witch doctors before planning battle strategy or engaging in battle. Combatants wore protective charms that reportedly made them invisible to the enemy or made their bodies impenetrable by the bullet. Others chewed magical herbs that gave them lion-hearted bravery. They blew magical powder towards the enemy rendering them confused, weak and ineffective.

There were others who claimed guidance from prophetic dreams and visions assuring them of victory in battle. The story is told of one Liberian warlord Joshua Milton Blahyi who is said to have declared war on Charles Taylor bizarrely after receiving a phone call from none other than the devil himself (Bergner, 2003; Ellis, 2007; Gerdes, 2013). The same Blahyi is said to have admitted to murdering children as a sacrifice to the devil in hopes of being protected against bullets. Human sacrifice, ritualistic killings and cannibalism reportedly appear to have been notorious practices by the rebel groups during the Liberian civil war. The gleefully ritualistic manner in which Samuel Doe was killed and dismembered, the entire ritual being video-taped, would seem to lend support to such practices. It would seem that throughout the Liberian civil war it was an accepted practice to sacrifice, eat, murder or maim individuals in order to attain prowess in battle. Eating the heart of an enemy army general was seen as a means of attaining power, presumably the reputed power of an army general. It might however be the case that some of these extreme bloody measures perpetrated by various groups as they advanced and captured territory could have been done in order to remove political opposition and terrorize the population into submission.

Anecdotes about the role of religion, magic or occultism in violent struggles is a familiar one. In the Ambazonian national liberation struggle, guerrillas use 'odeshi' and the Bible to 'fortify' themselves. During the World Wars, Japanese soldiers used protective bands tied around the forehead or arms. The Mau Mau in Kenya, the UPC *marquisards* in Cameroun, RUF and Komajor militias in Sierra Leone, rebel militias in Côte d'Ivoire, members of the Lenshina sect in Zambia, the Lord's Resistance Army in Uganda and the Mayi Mayi militias in Congo all resorted to one form or another of magic or ritual in their various struggles. In fact, militias of the Simba Rebellion in Congo used magic to initiate themselves. They believed that by following a moral code they could become invulnerable to bullets. They are also said to have made extensive use of witchcraft to protect themselves and demoralize their enemies.

In a less religious context, some civil war field commanders believed that drug-taking inhibits fear in combatants. Commanders therefore encouraged drug-taking before battle to give the fighters Dutch courage. The reality of warfare, however, is that wars are usually won by armies with the most soldiers fired for legitimate reasons and a compelling motive for fighting, the best equipment suitable for the war theatre, the most powerful weapons and the sharpest generals. Admittedly, sometimes smaller and weaker forces triumph over bigger armed forces. But that is usually because of the very powerful motivation that drives them, their deep knowledge of their environment, the use of the local geography and weather to their advantage, their skill, bravery and toughness.

FUNDING CIVIL WARS

Conflict diamonds in Sierra Leone, Angola and Liberia constituted the key resource that sustained the civil wars in those countries for so long (Hirsch, 2000; Jalloh, 2001; Lujala, 2005; Pazzanita, 1991). For example, UNITA was able to mine and sell diamonds abroad through intermediaries to provide funding for the war to continue. It is estimated that despite international sanctions UNITA sold, from 1992 to1998, at least $3.72 billion worth of diamonds to fund its war effort. Charles Taylor's war in Liberia was largely funded by conflict timber, as well as blood diamonds and gold which he obtained through the Revolutionary United Front rebels in Sierra Leone. These rebels themselves funded their civil war effort particularly through the sale of blood diamonds and the looting of commercial banks and the central bank. In several parts of Africa, timber has become associated with violent conflict (Thomson & Kanaan, 2003; Verbelen, 2002; Global Witness, 2002; McNeely, 2002; Le Billon, 2003). Revenues from trade in 'conflict timber' are channelled towards activities that perpetuate conflict, such as the purchase of weapons. Moreover, in some cases, the exploitation of timber is itself a direct cause of conflict because of disputes over ownership of forest resources and the distribution of benefits (Dfid, 2001). More dramatically perhaps, military intervention in another country (often through proxies) is motivated by a desire to control the timber trade in that country. Timber is a commodity that can easily be harvested, used as fuelwood or transformed into cash to perpetuate conflict. Other sources of funding for civil wars include bank robberies by members of an insurgency, and hostage taking for ransom as when ships and crew members are seized by Somali insurgents off the coast of the Horn of Africa or by Niger Delta militants in the Gulf of Guinea.

IMPACT OF CIVIL WAR ON THE COUNTRY CONCERNED

The most devastating form of post-colonial violence in Africa is intriguingly the civil war, the one in Angola being the longest (Pazzanita, 1991). Africa's post-colonial civil wars always leave behind millions of persons dead, widowed, orphaned, injured (including amputee non-combatants), uprooted as refugees and internally displaced persons, and demobilized child soldiers (Huggins, 2002). They have also caused massive destruction of infrastructure and the environment, increased the health burden of affected countries, arrested or stunted development and exacerbated ethnic tensions and animosity. By the time the Mozambique civil war ended in 1992, about 1 million people had died from fighting and starvation, 5 million civilians had been displaced and thousands had become amputees by landmines. The war in Angola displaced 4.28 million people internally and reduced overall life expectancy to less than forty years of age. It provoked an exodus from the rural areas to the towns, causing an urban population explosion that represents slightly more than half of the population of Angola. Many young Angolans are still reluctant to go to a rural life that they never knew. There were about 15 million landmines laid in Angola by the end of the civil war. These made landmine victims. The de-mining operations continued more than ten years after the war.

Armed conflicts, whether within or between states, may have multiple, long- and short-term impacts on development, and on environmental and human well-being. The affects, even of internal conflicts, are felt at various spatial levels, within the immediate area of conflict, and often in neighbouring countries. Conflict may undercut or destroy environmental, physical, human and social capital, diminishing available opportunities for sustainable development. Conflict impacts human well-being, reducing quality of life, the capabilities of people to live the kinds of lives they value and the real choices they have. It results in the loss of lives, livelihoods and opportunity, as well as of human dignity and fundamental human rights. War aggravates poverty and hunger, and consequently promotes continued dependence on food aid. The destruction and decay of infrastructure not only affects the provision of essential services but leads to a breakdown in communication, through the loss of roads and telecommunications (UNEP, 2001).

The destruction and decay of infrastructure not only affects the provision of essential services but leads to a breakdown in communication through the loss of roads and telecommunications. This increases the extent of isolation already experienced by rural communities. It further diminishes their sense of citizenship and contributes to a shrinking of civil society. Infrastructural decay results in the loss of market and other economic opportunities. The

British Department for International Development reports that in the twenty years from 1980 to 2000, Africa lost over 50% of its infrastructure as a result of conflict (Dfid, 2001). For example, in South Sudan there is no viable road network, and Angola and the Democratic Republic of Congo are entirely dependent on transport by air due to the collapse of infrastructure. At the local level, controversies over resource access can be a factor in the formation of armed groups, which are often linked to larger national or international 'political' conflicts or economic interests. This may result in the militarization of the local socioeconomic space, including increasingly bloody competition over economic infrastructure and resources, extraction systems and trade networks.

The displacement of people is a major social and economic cost of serious conflict, in the short term as well as in post-conflict periods. Typically, the casualties of modern armed conflicts are civilians. Because conflict often takes on ethnic overtones, and because modern African conflicts generally involve militias and guerrillas rather than regular troops, it is all too easy for civilians to be targeted just because they share the same ethnic or cultural identity as an 'enemy group'. Since 1960, more than 8 million people have died directly or indirectly as a result of war in Africa. As of 2021, injuries caused by war have become the eighth most important factor placing a disease burden on society. In a significant number of conflicts, violence has taken new forms, with the deliberate targeting of civilians and an increasing incidence of mutilations, violent rituals and rape. As a result of the targeting of civilians, large areas can become de-populated. Output of agricultural or pastoral production is reduced, thus affecting local livelihoods and the national economy. Northern Uganda, where almost 2 million people are displaced on a regular basis, is a case in point. One major, and often lingering effect of such violence, is damage to the social fabric, including informal networks of trust and support, undermining governance and often natural resource management. Children are a major target of conflict and violence. In a significant number of conflicts, including in Uganda, Rwanda, Sierra Leone, Angola and Mozambique there has been the forced recruitment of child soldiers through, among other things, abductions. In 2001, there were estimated to be 200,000 child soldiers in Africa. Children may be killed or maimed by one group in order to undermine the morale of the other side. As a result of violent conflict, there has also been an increase in the number of street children (UN, 1999).

Displacements impact directly on neighbouring countries as refugees flee across international boundaries. Around conflict areas, there are often extended zones of 'bounded instability' which experience sporadic violence. Long-term situations of 'neither peace nor war' can therefore ensue. International border zones are especially conflict-affected. Typically, these zones of friction are the most politically and economically marginalized, with weak state administrative structures. Displacements of people also have direct impacts on receiving communities and countries. The burden placed on local infrastructures such as schools, hospitals and sanitation facilities may be considerable and difficult to bear. Conflict also has macro-level impacts. These include a decline in state capacity, associated with a shrinking revenue base and reduced public spending, and economic stagnation as a result of a fall in exports, hyper-inflation, exchange rate depreciation, disinvestment and capital flight. Countries bordering conflict zones may need to increase security expenditure in military and non-military sectors. Additionally, they may incur new costs in relation to refugees and losses from deteriorating regional trade. A further feature of conflict is the collapse of public institutions or the inability of these institutions to cope.

Increased urbanization can be a factor. In Angola, for example, a combination of war-related factors resulted in rapid and unplanned urbanization. The population of the capital city, Luanda, doubled in ten years from 1990 to 2001, and the proportion of the total population living in the capital is the highest of any country in sub-Saharan Africa. Between 1.3 million and 2 million people fled their homes from 1992 to 1994, moving primarily to urban areas. Between 1998 and 2002, when hostilities ended, an additional 3.3 million persons were forced to flee their homes. In Luanda, Maputo, Addis Ababa and Kinshasa, urbanization rates increased rapidly because of the war, with, for example, rates of 40% in Maputo Province in 1991. In other conflicting countries, one sees a similar phenomenon, though less dramatic, such as in Monrovia, Freetown, Mogadishu and Abidjan. Infrastructural deterioration is particularly significant due to a loss of investment as well as a reduced ability to maintain these structures. This has implications for health, communications, education and overall well-being.

NOTES

1. ECOWAS is the sixteen-member Economic Community of West African States; IGAD, the seven-member Inter-Governmental Authority on Development; and SADC, the sixteen-member Southern Africa Development Community.

2. Article 4 h, Constitutive Act of the African Union. The organization is yet to activate this provision of its constitutional text.

Chapter 6

Causes of Interstate Wars in Africa

A state may go to war against another state for one or more reasons. The strategic end of all war, whatever the reason or motive for it, is to break the enemy's will to resist and to impose the victor's will on the vanquished by force.

Africa's interstate wars exhibit interesting characteristics. Some of them were sponsored or led by non-African states either in the context of 'war against terrorism' or simply to safeguard their turf or sphere of influence. There have been countless French military interventions in Africa in former French colonial territories and in the former Belgian colony of Congo Kinshasa. Countries like Burundi, Congo Kinshasa, Chad, Eritrea, Ethiopia and Somalia have known war for so long that their soldiers have become hardened warriors. So habituated to armed conflict are these countries that they have slowly developed something of a war culture that readily predisposes them to go to war. Ironically, these countries are not among the wealthiest in the continent and yet they still find resources to go to war.

With the exception of third-party mediation in the Ethiopia-Eritrea war, one discerns no demonstrated interest in mediating Africa's interstate armed conflicts. This is intriguing. The reason could be that mediation is likely to be successful only where the parties are willing to accept it and to abide by commitments made during mediation. Apparently, for reasons of national pride, African states involved in an interstate armed conflict appear not to be enthusiastic about mediation to resolve the conflict. When a war starts, each party hopes to achieve its strategic objectives. The onset of war is too early a stage at which to offer mediation. The moment is not yet ripe for third-party mediation and the parties will not accept it since hopes of victory are high on each side. Tactically, therefore, it is always better to let the parties 'fight it out' to the point of a stalemate when victory by either side does not seem likely or when both sides are tired or when both sides have suffered heavy losses far beyond what each anticipated.

Intervention is therefore more likely to be receptive at the point when the parties have fought for quite some time. But Africa's interstate wars are never long-drawn-out. They are generally of short duration. They hardly last for more than a few months of continuous fighting. Where the war lasts for more than a year, the parties often tend to observe a long period of ceasefire before resuming fighting. The war between Libya and Chad over the Aouzou Strip lasted for ten years. But there was no continuous fighting for ten years. Rather, there was a series of intermittent fighting over a period of ten years. The Libya-Chad conflict was in the end referred to the ICJ for resolution of the bone of contention that prompted war. The Ethiopia-Eritrea war was referred to arbitration. In both cases, the continental intergovernmental political organization merely encouraged the referral.

Egypt found itself having to fight Britain-France-Israel in order to assert full control over its national territory and a critical national resource, to wit, the Suez Canal. Egyptian national dignity and pride were at stake. Egypt also fought Israel in what became known as 'the Six-Day War', to assert leadership of the Arab World and solidarity with Palestinians to reclaim Arab lands forcibly occupied by Israel. The Morocco-Algeria war was a straightforward war to assert a claim over disputed territory. The Western Sahara-Mauritania war was analytically a colonial war in that while Mauritania fought to 'grab' the Western Sahara, the Western Sahara fought to thwart attempts at colonial annexation and occupation. Idem with the Western Sahara-Morocco war which suffered a lull for decades until November 2020 when the Western Sahara announced it will resume hostilities against Morocco. The Ethiopia-Eritrea and the Burkina Faso-Mali wars were also straightforward violent conflicts in which each side staked its claim to contested territory along a sector of their common border. In all the wars over territory, it would seem the motive was not just mere territorial aggrandizement as such but a strategic move to secure certainty of the borderline in the disputed area and to appropriate territory believed to have mineral, oil or other resources.

Africa's interstate armed conflicts, except for those involving a power from outside Africa, have been fought over either territory or boundary and have spanned the period from the 1960s to recent times. Most of these wars have involved states in North Africa and the Horn of Africa. The reason for this appears to be that these regions of the African continent, in particular the Horn of Africa, including Sudan, are the melting pot of ethnic, religious and border conflicts, as well as civil wars, secessionist wars, expansionist claims, high military expenditure, migration and refugees and famine.

Additionally, during the Cold War period, these two African regions were of particular strategic importance to both the Soviet Union and the United States. Each power jockeyed to have and maintain a foothold in the area. Although criminal anarchy has now emerged as a real strategic danger in the Horn of Africa, Western powers still consider the region of great importance for their strategic interests. These powers are very much involved in the fight there against terrorism and maritime piracy in order to safeguard the Indian Ocean and the Gulf of Aden shipping sea lanes and to maintain military facilities used for launching various military operations elsewhere.

Incredibly, eight countries already have military bases in small Djibouti (23,200 square kilometre in area with 920,000 inhabitants) at very little distance from each other. The eight countries are America, Britain, China, France, Germany, Italy, Saudi Arabia and Spain with three more (Russia, Japan and India) seeking to establish military bases in that country as well. Djibouti is geographically located at the mouth of the Red Sea close to the Strait of Bab-el-Mandab, the oil-rich Arabian Peninsula, the entrance to the strategic shipping lane of the Gulf of Aden and the Indian Ocean. Not far from there are the Gulf of Oman and the Persian Gulf, linked by the equally strategic Strait of Hormuz. The rise of sea piracy in the area heightened the geostrategic and geo-economic relevance of Djibouti. The significance of the country is further increased by the weak security environments in Yemen and Somalia, especially in the context of the fight against Al-Shabab jihadists in Somalia, counter-piracy operations in the Gulf of Aden and the Saudi-Iran competition over Yemen. Students of security studies believe that the military build-up in small Djibouti poses a threat to the country's ability to make independent decisions on political, economic and social policies. It poses a risk to the security of the country and its people. It is apt to result in the decline of the legitimacy of the country's government since it may increasingly be perceived as a puppet government surrounded and propped up by multiple global actors.

Africa's interstate wars are few, of short duration and tend to cause fewer deaths and less destruction than civil wars. This is partly due to the restraint shown by the belligerents, timely third-party mediation in one or two cases and the localized nature of the conflict. Most of these wars have involved states in North Africa and the Horn of Africa. Interstate wars in Africa have been fought to claim territory on the border area, to claim an ethnic people together with the territory they inhabit falling within the borders of another state, to effect regime change in an adjacent state, to assert independence from colonial rule and oppression, or to defend the country from aggression by a power from outside the continent. These wars thus fall into five distinct categories.

Chapter 6

DISPUTE OVER BOUNDARY ALIGNMENT AND CLAIM TO TERRITORY IN THE BORDER ZONE

Most of Africa's interstate conflicts have been fought over either boundary alignment or a stretch of territory in the border area believed to be rich in natural resources. The departing colonial powers left nascent African states with ill-defined frontiers. In 1964, the continental intergovernmental organization, the OAU, sought to obviate the danger of boundary and territorial disputes in the continent by enunciating two basic norms – that of respect for the intangibility of frontiers inherited from colonization as of the date of achievement of independence (*uti possidetis*) and that of respect for the territorial integrity of Member States. If these two norms had not been enunciated, seemingly powerful states would have been tempted to colonize presumed weaker neighbours in the grand old European colonization style and for the same reasons as did European powers.

The principle of intangibility of frontiers means that borders inherited from colonization on the date of achievement of independence must stay as they are and cannot be changed unilaterally. This norm together with that of territorial integrity of a state forms the bases of the continental opposition to unilateral secession and to territorial aggrandizement. The territorial integrity of a state refers to the territorial framework that the state inherited from colonization on the date of independence. And yet, two African territories colonized by their respective neighbours have still not been decolonized: the annexation and colonization, covertly in 1961 and formally in 1972, of the erstwhile UN Trust Territory of the British Southern Cameroons (Ambazonia) by the adjacent French-speaking State of Cameroun and the annexation and occupation of the Western Sahara by Morocco. Colonization has thus not been completely eradicated from the African continent. African states may have reached a consensus on the norm of territorial integrity. However, proclaiming or even asserting the integrity of state territory has little meaning if the spatial configuration or alignment of the state territory is unclear. Consensus on a norm is one thing, survey or cartographical consensus is another thing. In many instances, the exact boundary alignment of state borders in Africa is not too clear. A boundary may have been described on paper but the description is not subsequently followed by delimitation and demarcation by the colonial authorities or the newly independent African states. Boundary delimitation assumed importance and urgency only from the 1980s because of competition for potential resources in the land and/or maritime border area.

Interestingly, however, not the entire course of the border alignment has been put into question. In many instances, disputes have arisen over only a small section of the border alignment. When one looks closely one realizes that the section in dispute is considered by the parties as potentially rich in economic resources. In Burkina Faso/Mali, the territorial claim that provoked war between the two countries in 1985 concerned the Agacher Strip, a sector along their common border thought to be rich in minerals. Barely a year after its war with Egypt, Libya was at war with Chad over the Aouzou Strip, a war that dragged on for ten years, from 1978 to 1987. The Aouzou Strip belongs to Chad and is along its common border with Libya and is believed to be potentially rich in minerals. The immediate cause of the war was the Libyan annexation of the territory and the extension of Libyan citizenship to its inhabitants. In 1963, Morocco went to war against Algeria, in what became known as the Sand War, to claim the Tindouf and Béchar border areas. Djibouti and Eritrea fought a brief four-day border war from 10 to 13 June 2008 over a small piece of land in the Ras Doumeira area.

Soon after achieving independence, the new state of Eritrea aggressively contested its boundaries not only with South Yemen and Djibouti but with Ethiopia as well. In May 1998, its military occupied the Yigran triangle, a barren 400-square kilometre region of desert. Ethiopia responded by armed attacks on Eritrean positions. There followed large-scale tank and artillery battles between both countries and mounted bombing raids on each other's towns. So began the war that was to last two years, from 6 May 1998 to 25 May 2000, in a dispute over the exact alignment of their common border. Ten years later, on 1 January 2010, both countries were again involved in a border skirmish over the Badme piece of territory on their common border. The violent conflict between Sudan and South Sudan involved competing for claims to the oil-rich Abyei region. Six pairs of countries have therefore gone to war over a sector of the boundary alignment and over claim to territory in the immediate vicinity of the disputed border – Burkina Faso-Mali, Libya-Chad, Morocco-Algeria, Ethiopia-Eritrea, Djibouti-Eritrea and Sudan-South Sudan. In chapter one, a detailed account was given of these six pairs of countries. This chapter focuses on the causes and not the course of the conduct of these wars.

Morocco-Algeria

The first African interstate war was the Sand War fought between Algeria and Morocco for three weeks from September 1963 to February 1964 (Torres-Garcia, 1963). The war was triggered by Morocco's attempt to seize the Algerian southwest border regions of Tindouf and Béchar in its irredentist quest for 'Greater Morocco'. Morocco claimed that those areas had formed part of Morocco until 1952 when France detached and incorporated them into French Algeria. France had seized Algeria in the nineteenth century and proclaimed it an integral part of France. In 1912, France occupied Morocco, declaring it a French protectorate. The boundary between Algeria and Morocco in the Tindouf/Béchar area remained undefined and was never delineated. France considered the area part of an internal boundary of its two adjoining possessions (Algeria and Morocco) which did not need to be precise (Heggoy, 1970). This attitude changed when oil, iron and manganese were discovered in that area. France then decided in 1952 to define more precisely the boundary between the adjacent colonial territories of Algeria and Morocco. In defining that boundary, France placed the Tindouf and Colomb-Béchar regions within the territory of Algeria. The Algerian War of Independence, from 1 November 1954 to 19 March 1962, had been fought in part to ensure that France did not, before leaving Algeria, excise the Sahara regions of the emerging Algerian state. Morocco chose to press its territorial claim when Algeria was still reeling from its successful War of Independence. Algeria had achieved independence barely eighteen months earlier and scarcely had full control over its territory. Algeria rejected Morocco's historical or political claims to 'Greater Morocco', calling the territorial claim expansionist and an attempt to undo Algeria's hard-won independence and territorial integrity.

The Algeria-Morocco war began when, on 25 September 1963, soldiers on both sides of the border zone began firing at each other. These skirmishes escalated into a full-blown confrontation. There was intense fighting around the Algerian oasis town of Tindouf and the Moroccan town of Figuig. The Algerian army consisted mainly of the erstwhile guerrilla army of the National Liberation Front that had just freed Algeria from French colonial rule and oppression. It had little heavy equipment but made up for that shortcoming with tens of thousands of battle-experienced, tough and ready veterans. The Moroccan army was equipped with modern weapons supplied principally by France. It was also superior on the battlefield. But it was unable to penetrate into Algeria. It built fortified sand walls embedded with land mines and electronic warning systems to counter the Algerian hit-and-run attacks. Both sides had external support, Morocco from France and the United States; Algeria from Cuba and Egypt. The war reached a stalemate.

The guns went silent after the OAU and the Arab League intervened. The OAU eventually managed to arrange a formal ceasefire on 20 February 1964. Following mediation by the Arab League, a peace agreement was reached and a demilitarized zone was established. The Sand War resulted in no territorial changes being made. Morocco abandoned its territorial claims to Tindouf and Béchar after OAU mediation (Touval, 1967; Wild, 1966). The war claimed about 500 lives. It prompted the OAU to adopt the fundamental principle of intangibility of African borders as obtained on the date of achievement of independence and to emphasize the principle of territorial integrity of states. It sowed the seeds of the continuing hostile rivalry between revolutionary Algeria and the conservative Morocco Kingdom. Negotiations to delimit and demarcate the border in the Tindouf area started in 1969 and were finalized only in 1972. The war also influenced Algeria's policy regarding the conflict in the Western Sahara. Algeria backs the People's Front for the Liberation of Sequiet el-Hamra and Rio de Oro (POLISARIO) and recognizes the POLISARIO-proclaimed independent Saharawi Arab Democratic Republic (SADR), partly to curb Moroccan expansionism in the wake of the attempt to annex Tindouf.

Burkina Faso-Mali

Burkina Faso (known as Upper Volta until 1985) and Mali are two neighbouring Francophone countries that were part of the *territoires français d'outre-mer* in West Africa. The territorial administrative organization of these French territories consisted of a hierarchy of administrative units known in French as *colonies, cercles, subdivisions, cantons* and *villages*. This means the boundary between both countries was considered a mere internal administrative boundary not requiring any precise delineation and demarcation. In particular, the boundary in the Agacher Strip sector was obscure. Already, way back in 1959–1960, there was a dispute relating to the common border between the *territoire outre-mer* of *le Soudan Français* (which became Mali at independence in 1960) and *la Haute Volta* (which became Upper Volta at independence in 1960 and then Burkina Faso in 1984).

In November 1974, the president of Upper Volta, Lt Col Sangoulé Lamizana, ordered the deployment of his army at the border with Mali along the Agacher Strip, a 160-kilometre-long strip of land bordering both countries. The president of Mali, Col. Moussa Traoré, responded by ordering the Malian army to annex the Strip. From 25th November to 15th of December 1974 the armed forces of both countries engaged in a few border skirmishes. An exchange of small arms fire took place along the Strip. This was the first armed conflict along that piece of borderland located in northern Burkina Faso and south-eastern Mali. There were no military operations, no significant fighting, and casualties on both sides were minimal. It is not clear what prompted the military skirmishes. But observers consider this to be an example of a 'diversion war' deliberately provoked by the military regimes of both countries to divert attention from domestic problems. The Strip was thought to contain substantial natural resources which both sides hoped to exploit to help improve the dire economic situations in their respective countries. Mediation was unsuccessfully attempted by Togolese president Gnassingbé Eyadéma and Niger president Seyni Kounché. Sporadic clashes continued into January 1975. In the end, the guns went silent and neither side emerged victoriously. An OAU mediation commission recommended that a neutral technical commission undertakes demarcation of the boundary in the disputed area. The recommendation was accepted by both sides in June 1975. The technical team never published its demarcation report. The relations between both countries became one of 'no war no peace'. The dispute over the Agacher Strip went dormant.

Ten years later, in 1985, that dormant dispute erupted into a war. The relations between both countries had deteriorated to such an extent that each accused the other of escalating tensions. Burkina Faso accused Mali of preparing for an invasion. Mali ridiculously accused Burkina Faso of violating its sovereignty, the alleged violation being the fact that some Burkinabé national census agents visited Fula camps in Mali in late 1985. At this point, Burkinabé ground troops were sent to the Agacher Strip to assert Burkinabé sovereignty over the area. Mali publicly denounced the act and requested African leaders to pressure Burkinabé president Thomas Sankara. When Burkinabé soldiers did not leave the area, tensions grew further. On 25 December 1985, Malian soldiers launched several ground attacks against Burkinabé border posts and police stations. The Burkinabé army responded by mobilizing soldiers in the region and launching counterattacks. But Mali was able to capture many villages and outposts. An attempt by Libya to negotiate a ceasefire failed. Mali called its Air Force into action. A marketplace in Ouahigouya was hit causing a number of civilian deaths. A second ceasefire attempt on 29 December 1985 sponsored by Nigeria and Libya also failed. A third truce a day later, on the 30th of December, sponsored by a West African group known as the *Non-Aggression and Defense Aid Agreement* (ANAD), was signed by both sides on the same day. That brought to an end the second Agacher Strip conflict, known locally as the 'Christmas War' because it started on Christmas day and ended on 30th December. The five-day war is said to have caused as many as 300 deaths.

In mid-January 1986, a *Non-Aggression and Defense Aid Agreement* summit was held in Yamoussoukro, Ivory Coast. At that summit, both countries agreed to withdraw their troops to pre-war positions as required by the provisional measures indicated by the ICJ to which the dispute had been referred in 1983. Prisoners of War were exchanged in February and full diplomatic relations were restored in June. But the land frontier dispute remained unresolved. Both countries had signed a special agreement in September 1983 agreeing to submit the dispute relating to the delimitation of their common frontier to a special chamber of the ICJ consisting of five judges. The chamber had to ascertain and indicate the frontier line between Burkina Faso and Mali. The judgement of the court, delivered on 22 December 1986, stressed two fundamental rules applicable to the case, the principle of intangibility of frontiers inherited from colonization and the principle of *uti possidetis juris*. The result was the division of the 3,000 square kilometre of disputed territory almost equally between the parties. Mali received the western portion and Burkina Faso the eastern.[1]

Chad-Libya

Chadian society and politics centre upon the ever-present north-south divide. This corresponds roughly with Muslim-Christian and Arab-African divisions. During French colonial rule in Chad, only the southern parts of the country were effectively governed and developed to any greater extent. With independence from France in 1960, political power in Chad also became entrenched firmly within the spheres of southern political parties. Soon after independence, the southern leaders instituted one-party rule under François N'Garta Tombalbaye's presidency (1960–1975) and a campaign of marginalization of the northern region.[2] In response to these policies northern Muslims initiated in 1965 the first episode of Chad's intermittent lengthy civil war.

The civil war grew in intensity and scope over the years, involving several different rebel movements between 1965 and 1981 when rebel leader Hissén Habré of the FAN (*Forces Armées du Nord*) captured the capital and seized power. Taking advantage of the chaotic 1970s in Chad, Libya invaded and annexed in 1975 Chad's territory of the Aouzou Strip. Habré's ascent to power did not however end the civil war in Chad. Several rebel groups opposed his rule because he did not even attempt to reform Chadian society but instead concentrated power in the hands of himself and his northern kinsmen. Further episodes of civil war thus followed between 1982 and 1990, when Habré was ousted from power in a coup by Idriss Déby, another northerner. Meanwhile, in 1983 Chad fought a brief war with Nigeria over the status of some of the islands in Lake Chad where both countries have borders. A settlement between the two countries ended the dispute and the fighting. Four years later, in 1987, Chad was also embroiled in a short war with Libya over the Aouzou Strip. In that war, many rebel groups rallied to the side of Habré and Chad in a bid to expel the Libyans.

The Libya-Chad war over the Aouzou Strip dragged on for ten years. This war was specifically over disputed territory in the border area, the Aouzou Strip claimed by Libya as part of its territory. The dispute saw a series of sporadic clashes in that area between the armies of both countries from 1978 to 1987. Libya claimed the Aouzou Strip as part of the territory of Libya on the basis of a 1935 Franco-Italian treaty. At that time Libya was under Italian colonization and Chad under French colonization. The treaty in question was signed but never ratified. The Libyan case was that on 28 November 1972, President Tombalbaye of Chad ceded the Aouzou Strip to Libya. In June 1973, Libyan troops then moved into the Strip and established an airbase, a civil administration, and extended Libyan citizenship to the inhabitants of the area. From that moment, Libyan maps represented the area as part of Libya.

Following a year of inconclusive talks, Chad and Libya submitted the dispute to the ICJ in September 1990. There, Libya failed to exhibit the signed original copy of the 'agreement' of 1972 by which Chad is said to have ceded the Strip to Libya (Ricciardi, 1992, 17: 301). If indeed Chad ceded the strip to Libya, then it means sovereignty belonged to Chad because Chad could not have ceded what it did not have. The onus was thus on Libya to show that there was indeed a cession of the Strip in 1972. Libya failed to do so. In its ruling delivered on 3 February 1994, the ICJ held that the Aouzou Strip belongs to Chad.[3] The Court declared that once agreed, the boundary stands, for any other approach would vitiate the fundamental principle of the stability of boundaries. The formal and final transfer of the Strip from Libya to Chad took place four months later, on 30 May 1994.

After he seized power, Déby at first tried to create a more stable state structure. He instituted multi-party elections but which he always won by fraud. New rebel groups emerged between 1991 and 1994 but failed to unseat Déby, thanks to French support. Unfazed, several groups resumed, from 1997 to 2002, their fight against Déby but again failed to unseat him, thanks once more to French support. Although several groups gave up their rebellions following the signing of a peace agreement, the civil war resumed in 2005, this time with clear links to the armed conflict in neighbouring Sudan's Darfur region. Chad has always had a propensity for getting involved in civil wars in other countries, providing secondary warring support to this or that side involved in the conflict. For example, in 1998 and 1999 Chad backed the government of the Democratic Republic of Congo in that country's civil war against domestic rebel groups and intervening neighbouring states. Further, Chad gave secondary warring support to the government of Sudan in 2003 against the JEM, to the government of Algeria in 2004 against the FIS, to the Biya regime in Cameroun in 2018 against the Ambazonia war of national liberation, and to the Mali government against the Azawad insurgency.

Sudan-South Sudan

South Sudan has a 2,135-kilometre-long border with Sudan. Its independence from Sudan had major economic, political and social implications (Yousif & Rothbart, 2012; Brosché & Rothbart, 2013). Relations between the two countries were hostile. Each accused the other of supporting insurgents seeking to overthrow its government and therefore threatening its internal security. These accusations and counter-accusations in fact masked the deep dispute between both countries over a vital natural resource, oil. Each country sought to have access to and control the critical economic asset. Violence erupted in North Kordofan, the Blue Nile, Abyei and the Heglig Oilfield, Abyei being the richest oilfield with an area of 10,460 square kilometre

(Yousif & Rothbart, 2012). War started when South Sudan invaded and briefly occupied the small border town of Heglig before being pushed back by the Sudanese army. Small-scale clashes continued until an agreement on borders and natural resources was signed on 26 September 2012, resolving most aspects of the conflict. The war, also known as the Heglig Crisis, was a brief one that lasted six months, from 26 March to 26 September 2012.

The brief war was fought over oil-rich regions between South Sudan's Unity and Sudan's south Kordofan states, that is, along the entire Sudan-South Sudan border, although the main fighting took place at Heglig in the Abyei region. It nevertheless resulted in hundreds of fatalities, massive displacement of civilians, and gross human rights violations committed by both sides. South Sudan put its casualty numbers at 31 killed while Sudan claims it is 1,200 killed; South Sudan puts the Sudanese casualty numbers at 256 killed but Sudan claims its casualties were only 100 wounded.

CLAIM TO ETHNIC PEOPLE AND THE TERRITORY WITHIN ANOTHER STATE

Principally because of the artificiality of African political boundaries, the continent is no stranger to boundary disputes, to calls for boundary adjustments and to territorial claims largely based on ethnicity and/or historical title. The two classic cases in point are the claims of Somalia to ethnic Somalis in Ethiopia and Kenya, and the claims of Morocco to the Western Sahara and Mauritania based on the historic title. Each of these two states pursued a policy of territorial aggrandizement, the one to establish so-called 'Greater Somalia' and the other to establish so-called 'Greater Morocco'.

Somalia-Ethiopia

The Somalia/Ethiopia war was fought over claim by Somalia to ethnic Somalis of the Ogaden and Haud regions in Ethiopia and to the territories they inhabit. The Ogaden has a population of 15.65 million inhabitants and an area of 327,068 square kilometre. Somalia also claimed the Northern Frontier District (now known as the North Eastern Province) of Kenya along with the Somalis who inhabit it but did not go to war with Kenya over that claim. Nevertheless, the Somali jihadist insurgency known as Al-Shabab has regularly made murderous terrorist attacks not only in the North Frontier District but also deep inside Kenya as far as Nairobi and Mombasa. The North Eastern Province has a population of 3.5 million inhabitants and an area of 127 358 square kilometre. Djibouti is another territory inhabited by Somalis and which was claimed by Somalia before the territory's independence in

1977. It is a small country of 900,000 inhabitants and an area of 23,200 square kilometre.

It is the case that the boundaries of many African states sometimes cut across ethnic communities. But there has been no interstate war in Africa fought just to reclaim ethnic communities within the borders of another state. Any such claim would necessarily involve a claim to the territory inhabited by the ethnic communities concerned. Somalia went to war against Ethiopia, ostensibly simply to claim ethnic Somali communities in Ethiopia. The war lasted eight months, from 13 July 1977 to 15 March 1978, with Ethiopia emerging victorious. The Somali war against Ethiopia was in reality an expansionist war to reclaim not just Somali-speaking people but Somali-inhabited territories as well. Somali-speaking people could not be reclaimed without also seizing the territories they inhabit and thus changing the boundary alignment between Somalia and Ethiopia in those areas. Somalia lost in war, in law and in international relations and had to give up its claims. Had the Somali dream of unification of all Somali people in 'Greater Somalia' prevailed, the Ogaden and Haud regions in Ethiopia, the North Eastern Province of Kenya and the Republic of Djibouti would today all form part of 'Greater Somalia'. That would have added at least a population of some 20 million to Somalia and increased its size by a massive 477,626 square kilometre.

Morocco and Adjacent Countries

Morocco made extensive irredentist sovereignty claims to parts of southwest Algeria, to the whole of Mauritania (De la Serre, 1966) and to the Western Sahara (Wild, 1966). In 1956, France declared Mauritania a French overseas territory. The territory proclaimed itself in 1958 as the Islamic 'Republic' of Mauritania enjoying internal autonomy as a Member State of the French Community. France's grant of independence to Mauritania in 1960 was opposed by Morocco which argued that Mauritania was a Moroccan province that had been temporarily separated from the Moroccan 'empire' by the French colonizer. King Mohamed V of Morocco championed the concept of 'Greater Morocco'. He claimed that the historic and natural boundaries of the Moroccan 'empire' extended to Senegal and Niger, covering not only the Colomb-Béchar and Tindouf regions and Mauritania but also all of Spain's Saharan possessions (De la Serre, 1966).

Morocco fought unsuccessful expansionist wars against each of those countries in a bid to establish 'Greater Morocco'. It later abandoned its first two claims but not the last claim (Spain's Saharan possessions). Regarding the Western Sahara, the ICJ in its advisory opinion in 1975 rejected Morocco's sovereignty claim to the Western Sahara based on such purely political expression as history or purely moral expression as personal allegiance.⁴ This ruling notwithstanding, Morocco continues to occupy the territory to this day, the political organs of the UN apparently deadlocked on the issue. In early 2021, the Western Sahara matter was further complicated when American president Trump recognized Morocco's sovereignty claim to the Western Sahara in disregard of international law.

APPETITE FOR REGIME CHANGE IN THE STATE NEXT DOOR

The war between Libya and Egypt and that between Tanzania and Uganda were not fought over border alignment or claim to a piece of territory. Both wars seem to have been provoked by the antagonistic postures and clash of personalities of the leaders of those countries, Muammar Gaddafi vis-à-vis Anwar Sadat and Idi Amin vis-à-vis Julius Nyerere. Each found the other irksome and sought to overthrow or at least humiliate him. It is an unedifying situation where two countries are dragged into war as a result of personal antagonism between their leaders. A third case is that of Idriss Déby of Chad and Omar al-Bachir of Sudan where each supported the insurgency in the other's country in a bid to overthrow the other.

Uganda and Tanzania

The objective of Tanzania's armed action against Uganda was to procure regime change in Uganda, whose president was considered erratic and annoying by Tanzania. Milton Obote, the independent president of Uganda was a friend of Julius Nyerere, himself the independent president of his country, Tanzania. Relations between the two countries were excellent. In 1971, Idi Amin overthrew Obote by coup d'état. Tanzania offered Obote sanctuary. Relations between Uganda and Tanzania became frosty and quickly deteriorated. Obote was soon joined by 20,000 refugees fleeing Amin's iron-fisted rule and his efforts to wipe out any opposition to his rule. In 1972, a group of exiles based in Tanzania attempted without success to invade Uganda and remove Amin. Amin accused Nyerere of backing and arming his enemies. Internal rebellion against Amin's murderous rule intensified as various attempts were made to remove him from power. By October 1978, Tanzania-based anti-Amin exiles had joined the insurgency against Amin. Uganda declared a state of war against Tanzania and invaded the Kagera region of Tanzania in an attempt to annex it, claiming that the region belonged to Uganda. That invasion marked the beginning of the five-and-a-half month Uganda-Tanzania war which started on 30 October 1978 and ended on 11 April 1979 (Mambo & Schofield, 2007). Ugandans prefer to call it the Liberation War.

The Tanzania army, the TPDF, met the invasion head-on using rocket launchers to hit targets in Uganda (Acheson-Brown, 2001). It was determined to remove Idi Amin from power and make way for a new and friendly regime in Kampala. Tanzanian forces were joined by several anti-Amin insurgency groups and exiles united as the UNLA. Libya dispatched an expeditionary force that included some Palestinian Liberation Organization fighters to help Uganda (Ronen, 1992). The Tanzanian army and its UNLA ally advanced towards Kampala and halted at the vast deep-water swamp north of Lukaya where a decisive three-day battle was fought, ending in victory for them. Pressing their advantage, the TPDF and UNLA forces quickly advanced, capturing Entebbe Airport and then taking Kampala on 10 April 1979. The Libyan forces retreated to the northern town of Jinja from where they were repatriated through Kenya and Ethiopia. The war was over. Amin fled, first to Libya and later to Saudi Arabia where he died many years later.

The Tanzanian army remained in Uganda to maintain peace while the UNLF, the political wing of the UNLA, organized elections to return the country to civilian rule. The Ugandan and Libyan military casualties in the war were 1,600, and both Tanzania and UNLA 520. In addition, 1,500 Tanzanian civilians and 500 Ugandan civilians were killed in the war. Tanzania had to foot the costly bill of the war and the subsequent peace-keeping role it assumed in Uganda. However, the war debt of over 120 billion Shillings (about US$ 51,771,612) was eventually repaid by Uganda in 2007. Apart from the Libyan intervention on the side of Uganda, there was no other external intervention. Surprisingly, there was no third-party peace mediation attempt; not even by the OAU which in fact considered Tanzania the aggressor, influenced perhaps by the fact that Tanzania had been the backer of the 1977 coup in the Seychelles which brought France-Albert René to power from 1977 to 2004 (died on 27 February 2019).

Libya/Egypt

Libya has a long and rich history going back to ancient times (Oyeniyi, 2019). This history would be incomplete without space to mention that in the 1970s Muammar Gaddafi made the promotion of Arab unity the centrepiece of Libya's foreign policy. He consulted Egyptian and Syrian leaders on this matter, and they were very receptive to the policy, especially President Abdel Gamal Nasser who was a leading proponent of Arab nationalism. Nasser died in September 1970 and his successor Anwar Sadat subscribed to the idea of Arab unity. Negotiations between Libya, Egypt and Syria culminated in the creation of the Federation of Arab Republics (FAR) in

1972, consisting of those three countries. However, only symbolic gestures of unity were ever adopted, such as a common national flag. As Gaddafi aggressively campaigned for immediate unity with Egypt, Sadat's interest in unity steadily declined. Part of the reason for Sadat's loss of interest was that he took a personal dislike to Gaddafi. He considered him an annoying and unfit leader.

When Egypt and Syria launched a coordinated attack on Israel in October 1973, initiating the Yum Kippur War, they did not bother to consult Libya. Libya was miffed. In that war, the Israeli counter-attack rolled back the territorial gains Egypt had made in the early stages of the war, demonstrating doubtful military effectiveness in yet another Arab war (Pollack, 2004). Sadat then decided to negotiate with Israel the return of the Sinai Peninsula to Egypt in return for a guarantee to not engage in further attacks on Israel. Gaddafi could not comprehend Egypt's limited war objectives and the ceasefire. He was so angry that he accused Sadat of cowardice, of undermining the FAR and of betraying the Arab cause. Sadat responded by revealing he had intervened earlier that year to prevent Libya from sinking a civilian passenger ship carrying Jewish tourists in the Mediterranean Sea. Thereafter, Egyptian-Libyan relations soured and were marked by frequent accusations against each country's leaders. Further discussions regarding the pursuit of unity were abandoned.

In the 1970s, differences between Sadat and Gaddafi concerning Israel led to a further deterioration of relations between Egypt and Libya. Unnerved by Sadat's peace policy, Gaddafi sought to increase Libya's role in Middle Eastern affairs. Bolstered by strong oil revenues, he began acquiring a significant stock of weapons from the Soviet Union. He also sponsored Egyptian dissidents such as the Muslim Brotherhood, armed Egyptian insurgents and made plans to assassinate Sadat. The Egyptian president responded by supporting subversion in Libya, backing anti-Libyan groups taking refuge in neighbouring Chad, and encouraging plots to assassinate Gaddafi. As Libya began sponsoring dissidents and assassination plots to undermine Sadat, Egypt responded in kind to weaken Gaddafi. Both presidents traded insults (Schanche, 1977).

Relations between the two presidents and the two countries deteriorated very fast and became so bad that war broke out between both states in mid-1977. It was a short Arab vs. Arab four-day border war fought from 21 to 24 July 1977 and which ended abruptly in a ceasefire (Benjamin, 1977). In early July 1977, Gaddafi dispatched troops to the Egyptian frontier where they began clashing with border guards (Chaplin, 1977). Sadat responded by moving many troops to the area, while the Egyptian General Staff drew up plans for an invasion to depose Gaddafi. Sadat boasted that he intended to occupy Tripoli and depose Gaddafi.

Clashes along the border intensified in July 1976. On 21 July, a Libyan tank battalion raided the town of Sallum after Egyptian border guards stopped a large crowd of Libyans organized to march to Cairo to denounce Sadat. The Egyptian forces ambushed the Libyan tank battalion and subsequently launched a large counter-attack. They conducted airstrikes against Libya's Gamal Nasser airbase and sent a mechanized force 24 kilometre deep into Libyan territory before withdrawing. Over the next two days, heavy artillery fire was exchanged across the border, while Egyptian jets and commandos raided Libyan locales. On 24 July, the Egyptians launched a large raid against the Nasser Airbase and struck Libyan supply depots. The United States, President Houari Boumediene of Algeria and PLO leader Yasser Arafat all weighed in, urging an end to attacks and a mediated solution. Sadat then suddenly declared a ceasefire. But sporadic fighting occurred over the next few days as Egyptian troops withdrew across the border. Relations between the two countries remained tense. No formal agreement was ever reached. Nevertheless, both countries upheld a truce and gradually withdrew their forces from the border. Gaddafi softened his rhetoric against Egypt in the following years but actively rallied other Arab states to isolate the country (Howe, 1977).

Sudan-Chad

The major divide in Chad is along religious lines – Arab-Muslims of the north and Christians of the south. This division drives Chadian politics and fuels the enduring civil wars in that country. During French colonial rule, only the southern part of the country was effectively governed and developed to any greater extent. This gave the southerners a political edge which saw a southerner becoming Chad's president at independence. But the north/south divide was so entrenched that when one side was in power, the other side usually started a revolutionary war to counter it. As a result, Chad's presidency has oscillated between Christian southerners and Muslim northerners, not through the ballot box but through insurgencies and coup d'états which quickly morphed into civil wars involving France and Libya at various times. By the mid-1990s, Chad's endless episodes of civil wars had somewhat stabilized. In 1996 Idriss Itno Déby, a northerner, became president. But two years later, in 1998 an armed rebellion began in the north, led by Déby's former defence chief Youssouf Togoimi. A Libyan peace deal in 2002 failed to put an end to the fighting.

In 2003, conflict in the neighbouring Darfur region in Sudan spilled across the border into Chad. Refugee camps in eastern Chad became filled with refugees fleeing from Darfur and refugees escaping from Chadian rebel violence. Chad's rebels received weapons and assistance from the government of Al-Bashir in Sudan. At the same time, Sudan's rebels in Darfur got help from Déby's government in Chad. The Sudanese government tried to overthrow Déby, using Chadian rebels as proxy. In December 2005, the rebels attacked Ndjamena but failed to capture it, thanks to French intervention. Déby responded by providing support to Sudan's rebels operating in Darfur, especially the Justice and Equality Movement (JEM), which was then on the offensive in Darfur. In February 2008, three rebel groups joined forces and launched another attack on Chad's capital. The attack was repulsed by French troops sent to shore up Déby's government. Many of the rebels were former allies of Idriss Déby. They accused him of corruption towards members of his own tribe. They turned against him after he changed the constitution to run for re-election in 2006 and gave himself power to change the constitution whenever he thought it necessary to do so. The three groups involved in the attack in 2008 were armed by Sudanese security forces intent on cutting off the support that Déby was giving to Sudanese rebels in Darfur.

The Chad-Sudan war through their respective proxies appeared to be a continuation of the internal armed conflicts in Chad and in Sudan (Darfur region). These conflicts included competition for power and land. The populations of eastern Chad and western Sudan established social and religious ties long before nation's independence, and these remained strong in spite of disputes between the governments of both countries. Over the years, relations became strained due to the conflict in Darfur and a civil war in Chad, which both governments accuse the other of supporting. The internal Chadian conflict resurfaced when Déby reverted to a one-man military rule. He relied heavily on a close-knit group of kinsmen, used government finances for his own agenda and distributed aid in return for civilian loyalty. The strategy adopted by Khartoum for managing security within its border included treating the weak surrounding states as merely extensions of its internal limits. It is in this context that Sudanese security helped in bringing Déby to power in 1990. It is in this same vein that Sudan engaged militarily in Eritrea, Ethiopian, Uganda, DRC and CAR in the 1990s.

Khartoum used a combination of extortion and retribution to control its provincial elites in Darfur. It also used the same tools to influence its transborder limits. The immense area of central Africa (Chad, CAR, northern DRC and areas of Libya and Sudan) has rarely been governed by state authority. Across this isolated area, Khartoum, Kinshasa, Kigali, Kampala and even Asmara are always competing for influence. In Chad, the implementation of the reforms promised by Déby in an August 2007 agreement with opposition parties was slow and uneven. Throughout the country, government forces continued to arbitrarily arrest and detain civilians and suspected rebels, often on the basis of ethnicity. Those arrested were subjected to cruel and unusual punishment. Chad's prison conditions are among the harshest on the African continent. Weak institutions of justice contributed to a culture of exemption and impunity. The government does not investigate or prosecuted serious abuses against civilians, such as killings and rapes by government security forces and rebels following clashes in May 2009. More than 250,000 Sudanese refugees and 168,000 Chadian displaced people live in camps and elsewhere in eastern Chad. In April 2010, approximately 5,000 new Sudanese refugees arrived from West Darfur, following renewed fighting there between the Sudanese rebel group JEM and Sudanese government forces. In January 2010, Déby and Al-Bashir patched up their differences. Déby paid a visit to Khartoum, and Bashir paid a return visit to Ndjamena.

AGGRESSION BY STATES FROM OUTSIDE AFRICA

Some of Africa's armed conflicts have involved a direct clash with power outside Africa. Egypt fought against Britain, France and Israel from 29 October to 7 November 1956 in connection with the Suez Canal crisis. It also fought against Israel from 5 June 1967 to 10 June 1967 in the Six-Day war, and from 6 October 1973 to 25 October 1973 in the Yom Kippur war. Ugandan and Israeli soldiers engaged in a ninety-minute battle at Entebbe Airport when Israel raided Entebbe to rescue Israeli hostages held by Palestinian hijackers. Somali forces fought American forces during America's Operation Restore Hope in the Horn of Africa. In Libya, Muammar Gaddafi's army battled the Euro-American aerial war against Libya to bring about regime change in that country.

Egypt-Israel

The Suez Canal Crisis

Egypt's 120-mile-long Suez Canal was constructed over a period of ten years from 1859 to 1869, under the supervision of a French diplomat, Ferdinand de Lesseps. This man-made waterway, opened in 1869, connects the Mediterranean Sea to the Indian Ocean by way of the Red Sea. It allows goods to be shipped from Europe to Asia and back more directly, making it most valuable to international trade. Under the 1936 Anglo-Egyptian Treaty, Egypt allowed British military presence in the Canal Zone. In 1954, however, the Egyptian military began to pressurize the British to end its military presence. The British stayed put. In July 1956, Egyptian leader Gamal Abdel Nasser nationalized the Canal, making British military presence redundant. The United States had earlier promised to provide funds to Egypt for the construction of the Aswan Dam on the Nile river. When the United States reneged on this promise, Nasser was furious. He argued that nationalization of the Canal would ensure that tolls from the ships passing through the Canal would pay for the construction of the Aswan Dam. It was the Soviet Union that provided Nasser with the much-needed money and also arms.

Angered by Nasser's nationalization of the Canal, the British decided on an armed attack to retake it. To this end, the British got into an alliance with the French and the Israelis. The French eagerly agreed to join the British, believing that Nasser was supporting rebels in the French colony of Algeria. The plan was for the British, French and Israeli forces to attack Egypt simultaneously. But when the Israelis attacked Egypt on 29 October 1956, the British and French did not and only joined the fighting two days later. Egypt found itself fighting against Britain, France and Israel in a war that would last ten days, from 29 October to 7 November 1956. Israeli armed forces pushed into Egypt towards the Suez Canal. They were soon joined by British and French forces, a development that nearly brought the Soviet Union into the conflict and almost damaged US-Soviet relations.

The Soviet Union threatened to rain down nuclear missiles on Western Europe if the Israeli-British-French forces did not withdraw. The event was a pivotal one among Cold War superpowers. The United States condemned the Soviet threat of a nuclear conflict, but at the same time, it issued stern warnings to the British, French and Israelis to give up their campaign and withdraw from Egyptian soil, threatening all three nations with economic sanctions if they persisted in their attack. The British and French forces withdrew by December 1956. Israel finally bowed to US pressure in March 1957, relinquishing control over the Canal to Egypt which thereby emerged victoriously. The Suez Canal crisis marked the first use of a UN peace-keeping force, UNEF, an armed contingent dispatched by the UN to Egypt to supervise the end of hostilities and the withdrawal of the three occupying forces.

The Six-Day War

Egypt and Israel were at war for six days, from 5 to 10 June 1967. Egypt was supported by a coalition of Arab countries, namely, Jordan, Syria, Iraq, Algeria, Kuwait, Libya, Morocco, Pakistan, Sudan and Tunisia, as well as the PLO. The background to this war can be traced to the 1948 Arab-Israeli War which ushered in an era of tense relations between Israel and its Arab neighbours. Since then, the armed forces of the two sides remained on the *qui vive*. In June 1967, tensions became dangerously high when Egypt mobilized its forces along the Israeli border in the Sinai Peninsula. Fearing an imminent attack, Israel launched a series of pre-emptive air strikes against Egyptian airfields destroying all of Egypt's warplanes on the ground. Israel then launched a simultaneous ground offensive into the Gaza Strip. This forced the Egyptian leader Gamal Abdel Nasser to order the evacuation of the Sinai, which the Israelis then occupied.

Syria and Jordan launched ground attacks against Israel. Israel counter-attacked, seizing East Jerusalem and the West Bank from Jordan, and the Golan Heights from Syria. The war was over in six days. A ceasefire was signed on the 11th of June. The casualties and displacements were high for a brief Six-Day war. About 1,000 Israelis and some 20,000 Arabs were killed. In addition, 300,000 Palestinians fled the West Bank, and 100,000 Syrians left the Golan Heights, to become refugees. Israel's stunning victory left the Jewish nation in control of territory four times its previous size. Egypt lost the 23,500-square-mile Sinai Peninsula and the Gaza Strip. Jordan lost the West Bank and East Jerusalem. Syria lost the strategic Golan Heights. When Sadat became president of Egypt after Nasser, he wanted to recover the Sinai Peninsula. He conceived of a daring plan to attack Israel again, which, even if unsuccessful, might convince the Israelis that peace with Egypt was necessary. He formed a new alliance with Syria, and a concerted attack on Israel was planned. The attack took place in October 1973 in what became known as the Yom Kippur War.

The Yom Kippur War

This was a twenty-day war fought from 6 to 25 October 1973. On 6 October 1973, hoping to win back territory lost to Israel during the third Arab-Israeli war in 1967, Egyptian and Syrian forces launched a coordinated attack against Israel on Yom Kippur (Day of Atonement), the holiest day in the Jewish calendar. The attack took the Israeli Defence Forces by surprise. Egyptian troops made impressive advances with their up-to-date Soviet weaponry. They swept deep into the Sinai Peninsula. Syria succeeded in forcing the occupying Israeli troops out of the occupied Golan Heights. With the help of America which airlifted arms to it, Israel counter-attacked and recaptured the Golan Heights. A ceasefire negotiated by the UN went into effect on 25 October 1973. This unexpected Egyptian-Israeli ceasefire exposed Syria to military defeat. Israel seized even more territory in the Golan Heights. In 1974, there was signed the first of two Egyptian-Israeli disengagement agreements provided for the return of portions of the Sinai to Egypt. In 1979, President Sadat and Prime Minister Menachem Begin of Israel signed the Camp David Accords, the first peace agreement between Israel and one of its Arab neighbours. In that year, Syria voted with other Arab states to expel Egypt from the Arab League. In 1982, Israel fulfilled the 1979 peace treaty by returning the last segment of the Sinai Peninsula to Egypt.

Uganda-Israel

On 27 June 1976, an Air France flight from Tel Aviv bound for Paris was hijacked to Entebbe in Uganda by two members of a dissident wing of the Popular Front for the Liberation of Palestine. The hijackers demanded freedom for imprisoned Palestinians in Israel. The flight hostages were released two days afterwards, except for some ninety-four main Israeli passengers and the crew of the plane. These were threatened with death if their demands were not met. President Sadat of Egypt and Yasser Arafat of the PLO tried to negotiate with the hijackers and the Ugandan government but were rebuffed by the hijackers. On 4 July 1976, 100 commandos of the Israeli Defence Force carried out 'Operation Thunderbolt', a counter-terrorist hostage-rescue mission at Entebbe Airport. The raid on Entebbe lasted just ninety minutes during which there was fighting between the commandos and Ugandan troops at the airport. At 102 hostages were rescued. But the commander of the Israeli commando, three hostages, three hijackers and forty-five Ugandan soldiers were killed. The toll of fifty-two deaths was a heavy one for fighting that lasted a mere ninety minutes. Following the raid, Amin is said to have ordered the killing of hundreds of Kenyans living in Uganda in retaliation for Kenya's assistance to Israel in the raid. The OAU Chairman (Seewoosagur Ramgoolam of Mauritius) complained of Israeli act of aggression and requested the UN Security Council to convene. At the meeting of the Council on the 9th July 1976, the UN secretary-general Kurt Waldheim told the Council that the raid was a serious violation of the sovereignty of a Member State of the UN. But otherwise, nothing substantial came out of the Security Council meeting.

Somalia-United States of America

In January 1991, Somali rebels drove President Barre from Mogadishu. No central government emerged to take the place of the overthrown government. The US closed its embassy in Mogadishu that same year though the two countries never broke off diplomatic relations. The country descended into chaos and a humanitarian crisis of staggering proportions began to unfold (Fitzgerald, 2002). In April 1992, the UN adopted resolution 751 creating a UN operation in Somalia (UNOSOM) to provide humanitarian assistance. Four months later, in August 1992, the United States began sending food aid under Operation Provide Comfort. Intense fighting between the Somali warlords impeded the delivery of aid to those who needed it most. The UN then contemplated stronger action. It set up UNITAF under the authority of Chapter VII of the UN Charter. Chapter VII allows for the use of force to maintain peace and does not require the consent of the states involved. In

March 1993, UNITAF metamorphosed into UNOSOM II which saw its efforts to protect aid deliveries being directly challenged by warlord Muhammad Farah Aideed. Aideed's attack on UN troops in 1992 caused him to be named a 'wanted man' by UNITAF. In December 1992, the United States had begun Operation Restore Hope under which US troops were dispatched to Somalia to assist with famine relief as part of the larger UN effort.

The most significant of the challenges by warlord Aideed came on 3 October 1993. Aideed's forces shot down two Black Hawk helicopters in a battle which led to the death of eighteen US soldiers and hundreds of Somalis. The downing of the Black Hawk came when Delta Force arrested twenty Somalis. During the assault, the helicopter was shot down and the rescuers were ambushed, killing eighteen Americans. The deaths turned the tide of public opinion in the United States, prompting President Bill Clinton to pull US troops out of combat four days later. All US troops left the country in March 1994. President Clinton ordered the National Security bureaucracy to consider how and when the United States should become involved in peace-keeping operations, thus marking a turning point in the relationship between the United States and the UN in matters of peace-keeping operations (Rutherford, 2008). The resulting document was Presidential Decision Directive 25, Issued on 3 May 1994. The Directive outlined a series of factors that the National Security bureaucracy must consider before involving the United States in peace-keeping: eight factors that must be weighed before deciding in favour of peace-keeping in the UN and nine additional factors before becoming involved in a Chapter VII action. In 1995, the UN also withdrew from Somalia. Fighting continued in the country.

Libya-Euro/American Coalition

In Libya, Muammar Gaddafi's army battled the Euro-American aerial war against Libya to bring about regime change in that country. On 19 March 2011, a nineteen-state NATO-led coalition began a military campaign in Libya, ostensibly to impartially implement UNSC Resolution 1973, in response to events during the first Libyan civil war (Betts, 1994). The ten votes in favour of the resolution included those of the five permanent members plus those of three African non-permanent members (Gabon, Nigeria and South Africa). Five states abstained. Apparently, the intention of the UNSC was to have an immediate ceasefire in Libya, including an end to attacks against civilians. According to the resolution, the attacks on civilians constituted crimes against humanity, suggesting that the mandated action against Libya under Chapter VII of the UN Charter fell within the framework of 'the Responsibility to Protect' (Chesterman, 2011). The resolution imposed a ban on all flights in Libya's airspace – a no-fly zone. It tightened sanctions on Gaddafi's government and its supporters. The military campaign lasted seven months and two weeks, from 19 March 2011 to 31 October 2011. It ended in the killing of Gaddafi and the overthrow of the Great Socialist People's Libyan Arab Jamahiriya. Led essentially by Britain and France, nineteen states took part in the military campaign: Belgium, Bulgaria, Canada, Denmark, France, Greece, Italy, Ireland, Netherlands, Norway, Romania, Spain, Turkey, UK, US, Jordan, Qatar, Sweden and United Arab Emirates. An armada of 21 war ships and an air fleet of 260 fighter planes took part in the attack. American and British naval forces fired over 110 Tomahawk cruise missiles. The French Air Force made sorties across Libya and its jets launched air strikes against Libyan Army tanks and vehicles. Coalition forces undertook a naval blockade of Libya. The attack did not employ foreign ground troops. Libya claimed that over 2000 civilians were killed and over 700 wounded. NATO of course denied these civilian casualty figures but gave no figures, although Human Rights Watch estimated that about 120 civilians were killed. The war cost the coalition billions of dollars.

WARS OF NATIONAL LIBERATION

There are still cases of decolonization struggles in Africa. These hardly get media headlines for two main reasons. First, until recently, these struggles began and were pursued through non-violent means. Second, the continental intergovernmental organization has remained fixated on white colonialism. It quickly and prematurely proclaimed the end of colonialism in the continent, ignoring the emerging trend of black-on-black or African-on-African colonialism in the continent. Contrary to the broad view that the decolonization project in Africa is over, the fact of the matter is that Africa has not yet completely eradicated colonialism in the continent. Africa's anti-colonial project has never been and could never have been confined to white colonialism. The continental organization, the AOU and its successor the AU reject colonialism in all its forms and manifestation. Similarly, the UN Declaration on the Granting of Independence to Colonial Countries and Peoples recognizes the ardent desire of the UN to end 'colonialism in all its manifestations' and proclaims 'the necessity of bringing to a speedy and unconditional end colonialism in all its forms and manifestations'. A vivid reminder of the reality that colonialism has not been completely eradicated in Africa is Cameroun's colonial war in Ambazonia and Morocco's colonial war in the Western Sahara. The people of either territory are fighting a war of national liberation against an occupying latter-day colonizer. If the threat of black imperialism and territorial expansionism is not checked, perceived small nations will become prey to annexationist-minded adjacent states. This scenario is not far-fetched. There are examples, between 1960 and 1980, of efforts by some countries to annex their neighbours. These efforts failed, but they teach us that imperialism has no colour. One notes how Imperial Ethiopia tried to occupy and annex Eritrea, how apartheid South Africa wanted to annex Namibia as one of the provinces of South Africa, how Morocco claimed Mauritania as part of its territory and how Somalia claimed territories within adjacent states and even Djibouti.

South West Africa (Namibia)

Apartheid South Africa held on to Namibia, determined to annex it as a province of South Africa, an ambition it had since the mandate period. Eventually, however, it was compelled to give up that ambition, first because of the ICJ advisory opinion in *Legal Consequences for States*, second because of the twenty-five-year SWAPO guerrilla War of Independence against South Africa launched in 1966 and third because of sustained pressure from the UN. These actions paved the way for Namibian independence on 21 March 1990.

But even so, part of Namibian territory, Walvis Bay (both the town and the bay on which it lies) and the off-shore islands known as Penguin Islands, remained under South African control. Walvis Bay is the principal deep-water port in Namibia. In 1920, the League of Nations gave South Africa a mandate over southwest Africa, and in 1922 the Bay was also turned over to the South African administration. The conflict between Namibia and South Africa arose from the latter's continued occupation of Walvis Bay despite Namibian decolonization. Eventually, the conflict was resolved in 1994 when South Africa pulled out of the Bay and Islands on 28 February 1994 and sovereignty over them reverted to Namibia as of 1 March the same year.

Eritrea

Imperial Ethiopia annexed Eritrea but was forced to pull out of the territory after a thirty-year War of Independence waged by Eritrea. The Eritrean War of Independence was fought from September 1961 to May 1991. Eritrea was an Italian colony from 1882 to 1941 and a British protectorate from 1941 to 1951 after Italy was defeated by the allies. On the question of the future of Eritrea after the British left, the UN British delegation proposed a division of Eritrea along religious lines – the Christian part to Ethiopia and the Muslim part to Sudan. However, the UNGA decided to federate Eritrea to Ethiopia, hoping to reconcile Ethiopian claims of sovereignty and Eritrean legitimate aspirations for independence. The UN framed a federal constitution for Eritrea and Ethiopia which took effect in 1952. Commissioner Anzio Mattienzo was tasked by the UNGA to supervise the process of federating.

Eritrea became a constituent state of the Federation of Ethiopia and Eritrea. The federation was supposed to last for ten years, after which Eritrea could claim sovereign statehood. During that period Eritrea was to enjoy the status of a mini sovereign federated state with autonomy. It had a parliament and was responsible for a number of subject matters. But Ethiopia began to gnaw into Eritrea's autonomy so much so that within a matter of a few years that autonomy existed only in name, especially with the abolition of the Eritrean parliament. Eritrea's declining autonomy coupled with growing discontent with Ethiopian rule and hegemony in Eritrea gave birth to an independent movement, the ELF. The ELF was created on 1 September 1961, led by Hamid Adris Awate, in the mountain of Adal in southwestern Eritrea. In 1962, Ethiopian Emperor Haile Selassie unilaterally dissolved the federation and annexed Eritrea. This action triggered a thirty-year armed struggle by Eritrea against Ethiopia.

The independence struggle was clearly a resistance to the annexation of Eritrea by Ethiopia long after the Italians left the territory. The initial zonal commands of the ELF were predominantly Muslim areas. In the beginning, few Christians joined the liberation movement. But later there was a growing influx of Christians joining the liberation struggle. These were mainly university-educated volunteers. Internal struggles within the ELF command coupled with sectarian violence among the various zonal groups splintered the organization. In 1970, members of the ELF fell out and several groups broke away from it. Later, what was left of the ELF joined with some other new groups to form the EPLF. In 1974, Emperor Haile Selassie was ousted from power in a coup and the monarchy ended. The new government that came to power, known as the Dergue, took three to four years to get complete control of both Ethiopia, Eritrea and parts of Somalia. At this time, many of the ELF splinter groups joined the EPLF which became, under the leadership of Ramadan Mohammed Nour and Isaias Afwerki, the dominant armed Eritrean group fighting against the Ethiopian government. Much of the equipment used to combat Ethiopia was captured from the Ethiopian Army. By 1977, the EPLF was poised to drive the Ethiopians completely out of Eritrea. It used a simultaneous military invasion from the east by Somalia in the Ogaden to siphon off Ethiopian military resources. At that point, Ethiopia received massive arms and troop support from the Soviet Union and Cuba. Between 1978 and 1986, the Derg launched eight major offensives against the independent movements, but all failed to crush the guerrillas. In 1988, at the Battle of Afabet, the EPLF captured the headquarters of the Ethiopian Army in northeastern Eritrea, prompting the Ethiopian Army to withdraw from its garrisons in Eritrea's western lowlands. Throughout the conflict, Ethiopia used anti-personnel gas, napalm and other incendiary devices.

At the end of the 1980s, the Soviet Union informed Mengistu that it would not renew its defence and cooperation agreement with Ethiopia. With the cessation of Soviet supplies and support, the morale of the Ethiopian Army plummeted. The EPLF along with Ethiopian rebel forces began to advance on Ethiopian positions. The Ethiopian rebel forces were primarily ethnic liberation movements such as the OLF and the TPLF. The former US president, Jimmy Carter, with the help of some US government officials and UN officials, attempted to mediate in peace talks with EPLF, hosted by the Carter Presidential Center in Atlanta, Georgia, in September 1989. Ashagre Yigletu, deputy prime minister of the Ethiopian government, helped negotiate and signed a November 1989 peace deal with the EPLF in Nairobi, along with Jimmy Carter and Al-Amin Mohammed Seid. However, hostilities resumed soon after the deal was signed. Yigletu also led the Ethiopian government delegation in peace talks with TPLF leader Meles Zenawi in November 1989 and March 1990 in Rome. In the months leading up to the May 1991 fall of the Mengistu regime, the United States played a facilitative role in peace talks in Washington, DC. In mi-May 1991, Mengistu resigned, left a caretaker government in Addis Ababa and fled the country. A high-level US delegation was present in Addis for the 1–5 July 1991 conference that established a transitional government in Ethiopia. Having defeated the Ethiopian forces in Eritrea, the EPLF attended as an observer and held talks with the new transitional government regarding Eritrea's relationship with Ethiopia. The outcome of those talks was an agreement in which Ethiopians recognized the right of Eritreans to hold a referendum on independence. The referendum was held in April 1993 and the Eritrean people voted almost unanimously (99.83%) in favour of independence. The integrity of the referendum was verified by the UN through UNOVER. On 28 May 1993, the UN formally admitted Eritrea to kits membership.

Western Sahara, Ifni, Mauritania and Morocco

In 1884, Spain claimed a protectorate over the coast from Cape Bojador to Cape Blanc. Later, the Spanish extended their area of control. In 1958, Spain joined the previously separate districts of Saguia el-Hamra (in the north) and Rio de Oro (in the south) to form the single province of Spanish Sahara. Raids and rebellions by the indigenous Saharan population kept the Spanish forces out of much of the territory for a long time. The territory was eventually subdued by joint Spanish and French forces in 1934. Another uprising from 1956 to 1958 was also subdued by Spain aided again by France. In 1971, a group of young Sahrawi students began organizing what came to be known as The Embryonic Movement for the Liberation of Saguia el-Hamra and Rio de Oro. The movement tried without success to gain backing from several Arab governments, including Algeria and Morocco. It drew only faint notices of support from Libya and Mauritania. Disappointed, the movement eventually relocated to Spanish-controlled Western Sahara to start an armed rebellion. The POLISARIO was formally constituted on 10 May 1973 in the Mauritanian city of Zouirate. Its declared intention was to militarily put an end to Spanish colonization in Western Sahara. Its manpower grew when its action against the *Tropas Nomadas*, Nomad Troops (Spain's Saharawi-staffed auxiliary forces) forced them to desert to POLISARIO in large numbers, bringing weapons and training with them. A UN Visiting Mission headed by Simeon Ake in June 1975 concluded that the Sahrawi supported independence as opposed to Spanish rule or integration with a neighbouring country. The mission concluded that this amounted to an 'overwhelming consensus' and that the POLISARIO Front was by far the most powerful political force in the country. Sahrawi fighters would later fight in the anti-colonial war to wrestle Ifni from Spain and in the expulsion of Mauritania from the Western Sahara. They are still locked in a protracted war to push Morocco out of the Western Sahara and take control of their territory.

Ifni

This piece of territory is a little enclave on the southwest coast of Morocco. It was incorporated into the Spanish Empire in 1860, and this obtained international recognition at the Berlin conference of 1884. In 1946, the region's various coastal and inland colonies were consolidated as Spanish West Africa. When Morocco regained independence from France and Spain in 1956, it expressed keen interest in all of Spain's remaining colonial possessions in Morocco, claiming that they were historically and geographically part of Moroccan territory. Sultan Mohammed V encouraged efforts to re-capture those territories from Spain and personally funded anti-Spanish conspirators, Moroccan insurgents and indigenous Sahrawi rebels to claim Ifni back for Morocco. The Ifni War, sometimes called the Forgotten War in Spain (*la Guerra Olvidada*), was a series of armed incursions by Moroccan insurgents into Spanish West Africa, beginning in October 1957 and culminating in the abortive siege of Sidi Ifni. The war, conducted primarily by elements of the Moroccan Army of Liberation, was considered a part of the general movement for the decolonization of Africa. Morocco committed a significant portion of its resources and manpower to the capture of Spanish possessions.

The war lasted eight months and one week, ending on 30 June 1958 in victory for the Spanish and French military. Between them, France and Spain deployed a joint air fleet of 150 planes. The Spaniards were 9,000 strong and the French 5,000. Morocco lost 1,000 people dead in the Ifni War. On the side of Spain and France 300 people died, 80 were missing and 574 were wounded. However, the conflict also ended in Moroccan political victory: a reduction in the size of Spain's enclave of Sidi Ifni and the end of Spanish protectorate in Morocco. The treaty of Angra de Cintra sanctioned territorial changes. Cape Juby Strip was ceded to Morocco by Spain. Most of Ifni was annexed by Morocco. Spain retained possession of Ifni until 1969, when the UNGA resolved in Resolution 2072 (XX) of 16 December 1965 that it be returned to Morocco. Spain kept control of Spanish Sahara until the 1975 Moroccan Green March prompted it to sign the Madrid Accords with Morocco and Mauritania.

Spain withdrew from the Spanish Sahara in 1976 after partitioning it between Morocco and Mauritania. Following Spain's withdrawal in accordance with the 1976 Madrid Accords signed under the pressure of Morocco's Green March into the Western Sahara, the Sahrawi conflict erupted. Under that treaty, Spain transferred administrative control of the Western Sahara to Morocco and Mauritania, but not sovereignty. The UN did not recognize the accord, considering Spain as the administrative power of the territory. The POLISARIO Front proclaimed the SADR on 27 February 1976. The ICJ had issued its verdict on the former Spanish colony just weeks before, which each party interpreted as confirming its rights on the disputed territory.

Mauritania

The War pitted the POLISARIO against Morocco from 1975 to 1991 and Mauritania from 1975 to 1979. It was the most significant phase of the Western Sahara conflict. Mauritania, under the regime of Ould Daddah, had a weakened army of 3,000 men, which was unable to fend off attacks. After repeated strikes at the country's principal source of income, the iron mines of Zouerate, the government was nearly incapacitated by the lack of funds and the ensuing internal disorder. Ethnic unrest in the Mauritanian Armed Forces also strongly contributed to the ineffectiveness of the army. Forcibly conscripted black Africans from the south of the country resisted getting involved in what they viewed as a northern intra-Arab dispute. The tribes of northern Mauritania often sympathized with POLISARIO, fearing possible Moroccan regional ambitions and resenting the perceived increasing dependence of the Daddah regime on Moroccan support.

In 1977, a group of French technicians was taken prisoners by POLISARIO during a raid on Zouerate iron mines. France intervened, code-naming its involvement 'Operation Lamantin'. The French Air Force deployed jets to Mauritania in 1978 under the orders of President Valery Giscard d'Estaing. The warplanes fitted with napalm repeatedly bombed POLISARIO columns heading for Mauritania. The POLISARIO Front launched a raid on the capital

Nouackchott, with no let-up in the pace of attacks. Under continued pressure, the Daddah regime finally fell in 1978 to a coup d'état led by war-weary military officers who immediately agreed to a ceasefire with POLISARIO. A comprehensive peace treaty was signed on 5 August 1979, in which the new Mauritanian government recognized Saharawi rights to the Western Sahara and relinquished its claims to any part of the Western Sahara. Mauritania withdrew all its forces and would later proceed to formally recognize the SADR, causing a massive rupture in relations with Morocco. Morocco immediately annexed in August 1979 the Mauritanian evacuated Titis al-Gharbiya region, roughly the southern half of Rio de Oro.

Morocco

The POLISARIO, the liberation movement of the Western Sahara, fought against Morocco in 1970 and from 30 October 1975 to 6 September 1991. In late 1975, the Moroccan government organized the Green March of some 350,000 Moroccan citizens, escorted by around 20,000 troops, who entered the Western Sahara, trying to establish a Moroccan presence. At first it was met with little resistance by the POLISARIO. But Morocco later engaged in a long period of guerrilla warfare with the Saharawi nationalists. During the late 1970s, the POLISARIO Front, desiring to establish an independent state in the territory, attempted to fight both Mauritania and Morocco. Both sides of the conflict benefit from external support. POLISARIO was supported by Algeria in 1976, by North Korea from 1978 and by Libya until 1984. Morocco was supported by France from 1977 to 1978 under Operation Lamantin but has since limited its support by providing aid. Morocco is also supported by Saudi Arabia and the United States.

In 1979, Mauritania withdrew from the conflict and renounced its territorial claims after signing a peace treaty with the POLISARIO. In that same year, the UNGA adopted Resolution 34/37 of 21 November 1979 titled 'Question of Western Sahara'. In that resolution, the UN deplored Moroccan continued occupation of the Western Sahara, urged Morocco to terminate it and join the peace process and reaffirmed

> the inalienable right of the people of Western Sahara to self-determination and independence, in accordance with the Charter of the United Nations, the Charter of the Organization of African Unity and the objectives of the UNGA Resolution 1514, and the legitimacy of their struggle to secure the enjoyment of that right.

That resolution notwithstanding, the war continued, though in low intensity, throughout the 1980s. Morocco made several attempts to take the upper hand from 1989 to 1991.

Moroccan war strategy consisted largely of keeping POLISARIO troops off by building a huge sand wall known as the Moroccan wall. The Moroccan army stationed a number of troops roughly the same size as the entire Saharawi population to defend the wall, enclosing the Southern Provinces, the economically useful part of the Western Sahara – Bou Craa, El-Aaiun and Smara. This stalemated the war. No side has been able to achieve decisive gains. However, artillery strikes by Morocco and sniper attacks by the guerrillas have continued. Morocco is economically and politically strained by the war. It faces heavy burdens due to the economic costs of its massive troop deployments along the wall. Saudi Arabia, France and the United States provide military aid to Morocco to relieve the situation. But matters have gradually become unsustainable for all parties involved. On 7 October 1989, POLISARIO launched a massive attack against Moroccan troops in the Centre of the Western Sahara. But it sustained heavy casualties and withdrew. In September 1991, Tifariti offensive by Morocco was the last military operation and successful manoeuvre in the Western Sahara War against the Sahrawi guerrilla fighters. A ceasefire agreement was finally reached between both sides in September 1991. Some sources put the final death toll between 10,000 and 20,000 people. Today, Morocco controls about 75% of the territory, while the POLISARIO Front controls 25%. A peace process attempting to resolve the conflict has not yet produced any permanent solution to Saharawi refugees and territorial agreement between Morocco and the Saharawi Republic.

Ambazonia

This former Trust Territory of the British Southern Cameroons was first a British sphere of influence from 1833 to1887. From 1887 to 1914 it was part of the German protectorate of *Kamerun* (1884–1916). Under Article 119 of the Versailles Peace Treaties, Germany renounced 'in favour of the Principal Allied and Associated Powers all her rights and titles over her overseas possession'. The territories concerned included *Kamerun* which Britain and France divided into two, one becoming the British Cameroons and the other the French Cameroun. In 1922, each power placed its area under the Mandates System of the League of Nations and undertook to administer the same as a mandated territory of the League and under its supervision. The British Cameroons and French Cameroun were each a Class B Mandated Territory.

In June 1923, Britain enacted the Cameroons under British Administration Order-in-Council No. 1621. The instrument divided the British Cameroons into two parts, a northern part and a southern part, to be administered as though they formed an integral part of the Protectorate of Nigeria. Article 3 of the Order-in-Council provided that the northern part of the British

Cameroons and the southern part were to be administered as if they formed part of Northern and Southern Nigeria, respectively. After the creation of the UN, the British Cameroons were placed under the international trusteeship system by trusteeship agreements approved by the General Assembly on 13 December 1946. Following constitutional developments in Nigeria, the Southern Cameroons (Ambazonia) were granted the status of a separate province within Nigeria and administered as such.

The contiguous territory under the French administration, known as French Cameroun, attained independence on 1 January 1960 within the boundaries of the French Cameroun Trust Territory, under the name and style of *République du Cameroun* ('Cameroun', often translated into English as 'Cameroon'). It became a member of the UN on 20 September 1960. In the case of the British Cameroons, the UNGA recommended that Britain organizes plebiscites, under UN supervision, in order to ascertain the wishes of the inhabitants. Bizarrely, the choice they were given was limited to deciding whether 'to achieve independence by joining' (i.e., federate with) either Nigeria or Cameroun. The choice of sovereign statehood which should have been included as one of the options, as required by international law, was inexplicably excluded. In the circumstances, the Trust Territory opted to federate with Cameroun. It was a free association arrangement. Ambazonia and Cameroun were the two constituent federated states of the federation. On 21 April 1961, the UNGA adopted resolution 1608 (XV) in which it endorsed the decision to achieve independence by federating with Cameroun to form an aggregative federation of two federated states, equal in status. It decided that the Trusteeship Agreement concerning the Cameroons under UK administration be terminated on 1 October 1961 upon the Southern Cameroons federating with Cameroun on that same date. A significant twist in the adoption of Resolution 1608 was that Cameroun voted against it and thereby rejected the free association and also thereby maintained its international boundary with the Southern Cameroons as unchanged in alignment and character. The plebiscite result for the British Northern Cameroons showed its option for integration with Nigeria on 1 June 1961. Consequently, an Anglo-Nigeria agreement of 29 May 1961 confirmed that 'the Northern Cameroons shall be admitted to the Federation of Nigeria and incorporated in Northern Nigeria' on 1 June 1961.

After seven years of self-government (1954–1961) as a British-administered Trust Territory, Ambazonia was poised for independence but was instead manoeuvred into a free association with Cameroun, effective 1 October 1961. A month before that appointed date, on 1 September 1961, Cameroun unilaterally enacted a law amending its March 1960 constitution. The amendment law was passed off as 'the federal constitution' and promulgated by Ahidjo who at the time was president only of Cameroun. That document asserted a veiled annexationist claim to Ambazonia. On 1 October 1961, Cameroun discreetly assumed a controlling administration of Ambazonia as if it were its colonial dependency. This was the first of a number of studied attempts by Cameroun to undo and frustrate Ambazonia's autonomy, independence, and territorial integrity. Strangely, neither the British nor the UN reacted to this colonial takeover of Ambazonia by Cameroun, a development that is patently against international law.

Cameroun's emotional slogans such as 'unification', 'reunification' and 'integration' are euphemisms it uses to take over the unfortunate adjacent territory of Ambazonia, to conceal colonization and to disguise colonial expansion. Somalia, Morocco, Cameroun and Libya resorted to such sloganeering in their respective expansionist attempt. International law rejects sovereignty claims based purely on such political expression as history or purely moral expression as 'reunification'. Furthermore, Imperial Ethiopia and Cameroun each used 'federalism' as a bait and switch strategy, a pis-aller strategy, a mere temporary expedient to mask black-on-black colonialism. As it turned out, on 1 October 1961, Cameroun had merely suffered to come into being, temporarily, a form of 'federation' between the two countries, as did Ethiopia vis-à-vis Eritrea. Ten years later, in 1972, Cameroun, again like Ethiopia, ended such autonomy as Ambazonia still had left, dissolved the federation, abolished the federated state of Ambazonia, sacked and destroyed its state structures (government, parliament and judiciary), and other state institutions. Since then, Ambazonia has forcibly been fragmented into two parts and formally annexed as provinces of Cameroun. Ambazonia finds itself an imprisoned territory fraudulently represented as part of the territory of Cameroun. It sees and experiences Cameroun as a colonial state in every aspect, in fact, far worse than European colonization. It experiences that country's administration of Ambazonia in French and along French tradition as a colonial administration. It experiences that country's French-monolingual 'police' and military forces encamped, billeted and garrisoned in Ambazonia as an army of occupation. Cameroun's colonial project is in complete violation of commitments made and assurances given by it to the UN to the effect that Cameroun is not an expansionist state and would not annex Ambazonia. Inexplicably, neither the AU nor the UN has reacted to this new colonialism and violation of the well-established international law principle of *uti possidetis* and the AU principle of intangibility of frontiers inherited from colonization as of the date of achievement of independence.

There are thus two remaining decolonization projects in the continent, the ongoing legitimate self-determination struggle, or war of national liberation, of the people of Ambazonia against annexation and colonial occupation by the adjacent French-speaking state of Cameroun and the equally legitimate self-determination struggle of Western Sahara against Moroccan occupation.

These two cases are struggles for decolonization, for freedom and statehood, in circumstances of colonization by an adjacent country.

NOTES

1. *Case Concerning the Frontier Dispute (Burkina Faso v Mali)*, Judgement of 22 December 1986, 1986 ICJ Rep.
2. Tombalbaye was murdered in 1975 at the age of fifty-six in in a military coup. Power passed to another southern Christian, Felix Malloum. But he was forced out of office in 1979 by an insurgency led by Goukouni Oueddei, a northern Muslim. He fled the country.
3. *Case Concermning the Territorial Dispute (Libya v Chad)*, 1994, ICJ Rep 6.
4. *Western Sahara*, Advisory Opinion, 16 October 1975, 1975 ICJ Rep.

Part Three

A NEW DIMENSION OF CONFLICTS IN AFRICA

DOMESTIC AND TRANSBORDER TERRORISM

Armed conflicts have not yet been eliminated in Africa, but they have diminished since around 2010. Even military coups have somewhat been dampened, although there now seems to be a renewed appetite for coups, especially in West Africa, the home of coups d'état in Africa. Between May 2021 and January 2022, the military seized power in five countries: Chad (2 May 2021), Mali (24 May 2021), Guinea (5 September 2021), Sudan (25 October 2021) and Burkina Faso (24 January 2022). However, the current security challenge in the continent is not this resurgence of the coup phenomenon but new types of armed conflicts that have emerged in the form of domestic and transborder jihadist terrorism. Jihadist terrorism seeks a new territorial configuration in spaces where jihadists operate. It seeks to establish an Islamic state carved out of Muslim areas that they seek and claim to occupy, such as Muslim northern parts of the following three countries: Nigeria, Cameroun (one time a province of the Sokoto Caliphate) and Chad. Terrorist threats by jihadist terrorist groups defy national and sub-regional boundaries. Combating them is different from combating local terrorist groups which, in some cases, are in fact more of insurgency groups seeking to overthrow a dictatorship and accede to power. Transborder terrorist threats require greater synergies between AU Member States and the various regional forces of the African Standby Force.

The Boko Haram Islamic insurgency was founded in 2002 in Maiduguri, Nigeria. It gained widespread exposure in 2009 and spread across the Nigerian border into the northern part of Cameroun and Chad. However, in May 2021 the Boko Haram leader, Abubakar Shekau, was killed by ISWAP, a rival jihadist insurgency operating in West Africa. It would therefore appear that Boko Haram then became integrated into ISWAP. ISIS-affiliated Al-Qaeda in the Islamic Maghreb (AQIM) was founded in Algeria in 2007 to overthrow the Algerian government. It has a foothold in Libya, Mali and Niger. Al-Shabab ('the Youth') is another Islamic group affiliated to the Islamic State of Iraq and the Levant. It is a Muslim fundamentalist group founded in Somalia in 2006 as part of Al-Qaeda. It has dug in its heels in that country, occasionally carrying out deadly bombings in Mogadishu and making deadly incursions into Kenya. Another affiliated Islamist militant group linked to Al-Shabab in Somalia has been trying since 2017 to establish a bridgehead in the Cabo Delgado province of Mozambique. The appellation Mozambique was given by the Portuguese. It derives from the Mozambique island called Mussa Bin Bique, the name of an Arab trader who first visited the island and lived there about the fifteenth century. The Islamic militant group in Cabo Delgado attempts to establish an Islamic province in the region. The main insurgent faction there is Ansar al-Sunna, a native extremist faction with tenuous international connections. Observers believe that from mid-2018 ISIL became active in that Mozambican province and claimed its first attack against Mozambican security forces in June 2019. The insurgency intensified in 2020 and as of early 2021 had claimed at least 4,000 lives and 400,000 internally displaced persons. South Africa, Rwanda, Zambia and Tanzania are fighting alongside Mozambique, supported by Russia, Uganda, the United States, Portugal and Britain, after Mozambique at first ruled out foreign forces coming in to join in the fight against the Islamic militants. By September 2021, the Islamic militants had been routed but not defeated.

On 11 September 2001, a series of coordinated Al-Qaeda terrorist suicide attacks were carried out in New York (the Twin Towers of the World Trade Centre) and Washington, DC (the Pentagon), using four hijacked commercial airplanes. About 3,000 people were killed and hundreds injured in those attacks. Since then, the global security architecture has taken on a completely different shape. Nations have gone back on their rhetorical pledge to uphold human rights. They invoke national security concerns as the reason for the change of mind. In America and Europe, immigration laws have been reformed and made ridiculously strict. A new wave of racialist nationalistic spirit has gripped America and countries in Europe. The world economy has shifted in its character. World trade now focuses to a large extent on resources that are crucial to the production of weapons and communication technology. In particular, the so-called 'War on Terror' has exposed the weak structure that exists in the UN. American President Bush's declaration of an 'Axis of Evil' kicked off a twenty-first-century nuclear arms race with North Korea and Iran signalling their ambition to join the club of eight states with nuclear capability (United States, United Kingdom, France, Russia, China, India, Pakistan and Israel). Some other potential nuclear states are in the process of emerging. Others are likely to follow suit. There is no compelling reason why some states should have nuclear weapons, which they use to terrorize or blackmail other countries, while other countries are prevented from having the same weapon. If having nuclear capability is dangerous for humanity, then it must be so in respect of any country that has it. De-nuclearization would be good for the world. It is simply frightening to imagine the state of terror in which the world would be were terrorist organizations to acquire or have access to nuclear capability.

Chapter 7

An Overview

Terrorism in its lexical meaning is the systematic use of violence and terror to achieve political ends. Throughout history, terror has been used to spread fear for a variety of purposes. In the past half century or so, the phenomenon of terrorism has become widespread and has reached a new intensity. Terrorism impacts individual safety and security. It also impacts state security and stability. It causes grave human rights violations, especially the right to physical integrity, to life, to freedom from fear and to freedom and security in general. It creates animosity, xenophobia and distrust among people. It destabilizes communities and states, impeding their social and economic development.

States therefore have a vested interest in fighting terrorism. Also, asymmetric threats like violent extremism have led to the establishment of ad hoc regional mechanisms to fight terrorism. One such mechanism is the G5 Sahel Joint Force fighting terrorism in the Sahel. Another one is the MNJTF fighting in the Lake Chad area against Boko Haram seemingly now absorbed by ISWAP which is a more formidable jihadist group. Both the G5 Sahel and the MNJTF were authorized jointly by the UNSC and the AU PSC. Moving forward, the two forces would have to streamline their day-to-day command and control, reporting and accountability. Further, the many actors involved in the security sector need to be better organized so as to avoid duplication and competition.

MEANING OF 'TERRORISM', 'TERRORIST ACT' AND 'TERRORIST'

No definite legal meaning is as yet attached to terrorism, not even in relevant UN instruments.[1] International law leaves the term undefined. In this regard, it is more concerned with occluding the sources of terrorism than getting bogged down with the problem of definition (Brownlie, 2003). This pragmatic approach focuses on identifying particular manifestations of terrorism and imposing on states an international obligation to criminalize them (Shaw, 1998).

At the domestic level, municipal legal systems use different definitions of 'terrorism' or 'terrorist act' when prosecuting 'terrorist' offences. Anti-terrorism laws in Africa criminalize a wide range of activities as 'terrorist acts'. But these laws assign no clear legal meaning to the term 'terrorism' or 'terrorist act'. In states that still retain capital punishment, an act of 'terrorism' invariably attracts the death sentence even though the act may be ill-defined or defined in a way that is overly broad.[2] This creates a terminological morass. The problem of course is that governments in Africa select a particular definition of terrorism to frame their arguments and political positions. The several African governments then typically reach different conclusions based on the same set of facts. The various definitions serve as political or moral backdrops. But they shed little clarity in framing a single problem, that of terrorism.

Terrorism, as now generally understood, is a comparatively recent phenomenon in Africa.[3] During the anti-colonial struggle, every colonial power demonized those fighting for national liberation as terrorists carrying out acts of terrorism (Efrat, 1976; Roach, 2005). Even today, despotic regimes and expansionist states characterize democracy fighters and peoples fighting for self-determination as 'terrorists', hoping thereby to elicit foreign support for their bloody oppression, repression and their annexation agenda. Such political instrumentalization of the crime of terrorism was and continues to be rejected by the AU and in fact the international community as a whole. The OAU 1999 Convention on the Prevention and Combating of Terrorism explicitly reaffirms 'the legitimate right of peoples for self-determination and independence pursuant to the principles of international law and the provisions of the Charters of the OAU and the UN as well as the African Charter on Human and Peoples' Rights'. Article 3 (1) of that treaty is emphatic that 'the struggles waged by peoples in accordance with the principles of international law for their liberation or self-determination, including armed struggle against colonialism, occupation, aggression and domination by foreign forces shall not be considered as terrorist acts'.

The terms 'terrorism' and 'terrorist' continue to be widely and abusively used. This is partly because those words are not defined under international law. African states often prescribe the death sentence for their ill-defined terrorism-related offences, thereby undesirably introducing elements of arbitrariness and discrimination in the use of that penalty. It is not certain that all terrorism-related offences are the 'most serious' for which therefore the death penalty *may* legitimately be prescribed and applied after the most rigorous international standards have been met. In both law and practice, the world is moving away from using the death penalty as a sentence, even for the most serious crimes. The ICC, for example, prosecutes the most heinous international crimes, which may involve acts of terrorism. But the death penalty is not an available sentence to the court under the Rome Statute.

Lack of a commonly accepted definition for terrorism has prompted some countries to simply adopt externally initiated or externally influenced anti-terrorism measures. Lack of an agreed definition has also increased the temptation for the political establishment to exploit the definitional loophole in the anti-terrorism campaign. The loophole gives leeway to suppress and oppress political opponents and journalists in the name of fighting terrorism. In some countries, it is an offence to wear or use items associated with terrorists, which could be just about anything. It is generally impossible to identify terrorists merely through their physical appearance and what they wear. Likewise, it is difficult to know in advance who the real terrorists are and therefore the target of the war against terror. African countries often give the military and police leeway to organize random sweeps (cordon and search operations) as part of anti-terrorism measures. They give the security forces such draconian powers under the broad goal of fighting terrorism. But this terror-for-terror method is a hopeless effort because terrorism cannot effectively be fought with terrorism. Such measures run the risk of becoming a threat to national stability because they create fear, terror and disaffection among a large section of the population. Fear and disaffection in turn create volatile security situations which too often escalate into political and religious violence, polarizing an already weak and fragile state (Bamidele, 2014). What this means is that ill-conceived and foolishly implemented anti-terrorism measures may undermine the cohesion of the state and accentuate ethnic, religious, regional and political fault lines thus providing the basis for instability and insecurity.

TERRORIST MOVEMENTS IN AFRICA

Terrorist organizations in Africa that are known to international security agencies include Al-Shabab which has a long connection with Al-Qaeda, Boko Haram, AQIM and AIAI, the Islamic Union. These movements identify with the Muslim faith and have ties with a terrorist organization based in the Middle East. The nature of political Islamic ideology and its unforeseen repercussions transcends national borders and requires multilateral interventions. These terrorist movements in Africa operate within a narrow geographical area in the country where they have their base and from time to time carry out attacks in a targeted adjacent country. Al-Shabab is based in the interior of tormented Somalia but from time to time carries out attacks deep inside Kenya. Al-Ittihad Al-Islamiya was also based in Somalia but was succeeded in 2006 by the Islamic Courts Union. Boko Haram has its base in northeast Nigeria but has been able to expand and entrench itself in the predominantly Muslim north of Cameroun. Al-Qaeda in the Islamic Maghreb is based in northern Mali. It takes part in the Azawad insurgency seeking to procure the secession or autonomy of that part of Mali and, occasionally, makes incursions into Niger. Of these movements, Boko Haram appears to be the only African 'homegrown' terrorist organization although it affects allegiance to ISIS.[4] The other terrorist organizations appear to be localized tentacles of Al-Qaeda. A number of obscure terrorist groups exist in Egypt. But they would seem to be nondescript, at least to an outsider, and often tend to operate in the context of Egypt's volatile political and religious contestation.

The number of terrorist organizations in Africa may be small. But that does not mean things will continue to stay that way or that the reach of these groups will continue to be localized. For example, since the second half of 2020, an Al-Qaeda-affiliated group has moved to Cabo Delgado in Mozambique and is fighting government forces to establish a foothold in that part of Mozambique. It also does not follow that attacks that are carried out by the various terrorist groups mentioned above are small in scale or less destructive. The AU acknowledges that the continent is vulnerable to terrorism.

> The great vulnerability or exposure of the continent to terrorism is in part attributed to the vast expanses of unoccupied territory found in most African states; coupled with the porousness, length, isolation, and lack of surveillance of their borders, which promote, or at least permit, crime and illegal migration; and, above all, due to the mismanagement and corruption of security services, combined with the circulation of illegal small arms and light weapons throughout most of the continent. (AU, 2010)

The Uganda-based LRA periodically commits atrocities in Uganda and in Central African Republic, Democratic Republic of Congo and Sudan. But it would probably not be reckoned as a terrorist organization. Brigadier Dominic Ongwen, a commander of the LRA, was arrested and tried in the ICC. He was charged not with terrorism but with war crimes and crimes against humanity. The particulars of the offence against him did not recite perpetration of acts of terrorism. The LRA may be viewed as an insurgency group. It has been seeking for years to overthrow the Ugandan regime of Yoweri Museveni. Its goal appears to be to institute in Uganda a brand of political governance based, so it seems, on some Biblical teachings. The armed group occasionally spreads terror among a section of northern

Uganda. Perpetrating acts that spread terror among the population seems to be a tactical use of violence. Insurgency groups, and government forces fighting an insurgency, do spread terror among the civilian population. That does not make insurgency groups per se terrorist organizations. No one ever argued that rebels involved in intrastate wars or conflicts in Africa are terrorists. Such a controversial contention would mean all freedom fighters or insurgents seeking the overthrow of a despotic or oppressive regime or militaries that overthrow such a regime are terrorists. There is a big difference between terrorism and armed conflict and between terrorism and legitimate political activism.

Terrorist groups have become sophisticated. They know and realize that terror attacks promote their agenda through politicization and media publicity. They have demonstrated the ability to develop the mutually reinforcing symbiotic overlap of terrorist activities with criminalities. Such criminalities include domestic and transboundary human trafficking and kidnapping for ransom. They also include religious radical militias and illicit trafficking in small arms and light weapons, money laundering and terrorist financing. They further include illegal siphoning of crude oil by international smuggling syndicates, and sea piracy especially off the coast of Somalia and in the Gulf of Guinea. Terrorist groups have also taken advantage of vulnerabilities, found in almost every African state, to use as safe havens and recruiting grounds. Vulnerabilities include poverty, economic distress, ethnic and religious fault lines, fragile governance, weak state institutions and rampant human rights abuses (Bamidele, 2015).

STATE TERRORISM AND ACCOUNTABILITY FOR ACTS OF TERRORISM

Contemporary discourse on terror and terrorism tends to focus on the international dimensions or manifestations of terrorism. But terror at the state level is quite common in Africa. And yet this fact continues to elude mainstream literature on the subject. During the anti-colonial struggle, freedom fighters were demonized as terrorists and national liberation movements as terrorist organizations. Strangely, colonial terror unleashed on the colonized people and the atrocities committed by the colonial forces were not reckoned as terrorism, and neither their sponsors nor their perpetrators nor those who aided and abetted those crimes were ever held accountable (Hübschle, 2006). Today, a distinct form of state terrorism is that of 'post-colonial' terrorism in countries chafing under despotic rule. Furthermore, colonial terrorism lingers on in Africa and is experienced in territories under occupation and oppression by an adjacent expansionist state – Ambazonia annexed and under the colonial rule and oppression of Cameroun and the Western Sahara occupied by Morocco. Manifestations of colonial terrorism cannot be ignored in the fight against terrorism. The state apparatus that unleashes terror is a more organized and more lethal set-up than any terrorist group can possibly be.

Also, in many parts of the continent, transboundary or international terrorism is on the increase and has become widespread (Cilliers, 2004; Makinda, 2006). In Africa's civil wars, both insurgency groups and governments adopt practices that rely heavily on the use of fear and terror. Those practices terrify civilians. They cause more death and destruction than international terrorism. Insurgency groups and governments engage in or sponsor terrorism. A favourite state terror technique consists in using the label of 'state security' or of 'combating terrorism' as cover for violent acts and the spread of terror among the population. By so doing, a government puts itself and the terrorist on an equal footing. Unhappily, insufficient attention has been paid to state terrorism or state sponsorship of terrorism. The focus on the rhetoric of 'security' has created a context in which the state's illegitimate use of violence often goes unquestioned and unpunished.[5]

There are institutions mandated to investigate and prosecute perpetrators of international crimes whether by state or non-state actors. These institutions consist of regional human rights bodies and the ICC.[6] The ECHR has compulsory jurisdiction over applications by state parties, and by individuals after local remedies have been exhausted. The IACtHR grants access to states parties to the AConHR, and to individuals either through a state party or the IAComHR. The AfCtHPR hears applications from states parties to the protocol establishing the court and also hears and determines cases referred to it by the AfCom HPR. The ICC, a permanent court, has universal jurisdiction with respect to war crimes, crimes against humanity, genocide and aggression, committed by nationals of states parties to the Rome Statute in the territory of a party or a non-party. The court also has jurisdiction over crimes committed by non-state parties upon referral to the court by the state itself or by the UNSC.

The prohibition of terrorism or the spreading of terror is not mentioned *expressis verbis* in the Rome Statute.[7] However, the ICC will exercise jurisdiction over a terrorist-related offence if the particulars of the offence fall within the definition of any of the existing international crimes over which the court has jurisdiction, namely, war crime, crime against humanity or genocide. Acts or threats of violence intended to spread terror among the civilian population would constitute terrorism and may be charged and prosecuted as a war crime. Similarly, the violation of the laws and customs of war such as murder, cruel treatment and wanton destruction of cities, towns or villages not justified by military necessity can properly be charged and prosecuted as war crime. Acts perpetrated during the war may involve attacks directed against the civilian population. They may be carried out as a matter of state policy or the policy of an organization. An attack may be widespread or systematic in nature. Any such conduct would constitute an act of terrorism and may be charged as a crime against humanity. A terrorist act would amount to the crime of genocide if it involves the killing of one or more persons belonging to a particular national, ethnical, racial or religious group. Additionally, the killer must have intended to destroy, in whole or in part, a national, ethnical, racial, or religious group, as such. Finally, the killing must have taken place in the context of a manifest pattern of similar conduct directed against that group or a conduct that could itself effect such destruction.

Under the African human rights system, the victim of state violence or terror can file a complaint with the African Commission on Human and Peoples' Rights against the state. But he cannot file a case against a state directly before the African Court on Human and Peoples' Rights. The court has jurisdiction over applications by any of the current thirty state parties (as of 2021) to the protocol establishing the court.[8] It also has jurisdiction over cases that are referred to it by the commission. Direct access to the court by an individual or a nongovernmental organization is possible only where a state party has made a declaration under Article 34 (6) of the protocol accepting the competence of the court to receive cases from individuals and relevant nongovernmental organizations with observer status before the AfCom HPR. As of 2021, only nine state parties have made the declaration under Article 34 (6).[9] Of these nine states, at least four (Rwanda, Tanzania in 2019, Benin in 2020 and Côte d'Ivoire in 2020) decided to withdraw their respective declarations that give individuals and nongovernmental organizations the right to directly bring cases of human rights violations against those states, before the court. The states in question are unhappy with particular rulings of the court against them. The relevance and potential effectiveness of the African Court in the context of state terrorism cases are yet to be tested.

NOTES

1. In international humanitarian law, the term 'terrorism' refers to attack against the civilian population intended to spread terror. The OAU 1999 Convention on the Prevention and Combating of Terrorism does not define 'terrorism'. It defines 'terrorist act'. The definition is long, involved and too broad.

2. The UN Special Rapporteur on Human Rights while Countering Terrorism has highlighted the fact that some of the definitions used by states are vague, overly broad and may give rise to adverse consequences for human rights. See Report of the Special Rapporteur on the Promotion and Protection of Human Rights and Fundamental Freedoms while Countering Terrorism, 28 December 2005, E/CN.4/2006/98, para 27.

3. This is not to suggest that the continent has not been affected by the phenomenon of terrorism in terms of the number of victims of terrorist attacks and in terms of the activities of groups considered to belong to known terrorist movements. Algeria, Egypt, Kenya, Libya, Mali, Mauritania, Morocco, Niger, Nigeria, Somalia, Tanzania and Tunisia, for example, are well known as sanctuaries for terrorist movements, and also for having been the theatre of terrorist attacks and hostage taking. Africa has therefore not been spared from the wave of terrorist attacks occurring from time to time in Asian, the Middle East, Europe, America and Canada. South Africa's old terrorism laws, abused during the apartheid era, were repealed between 1992 and 1996. Its current law on terrorism is the Terrorism Act 33 of 2004. Terrorism as defined in section 1 of that statute applies to acts committed in and outside South Africa.

4. ISIS is also known as Daesh, abbreviation for al-Dawla al-Islamiya fi al-Iraq wa al-Sham.

5. For some studies on state terror, see Bettina Koch, Priya Dixit, Dina Rashed, Peter R Moody and Yelena Biberman (see references below).

6. International courts and tribunals include ad hoc ones with jurisdiction limited in time, space and subject matter: the now defunct International Criminal Tribunal for the former Yugoslavia, and the International Criminal Tribunal for Rwanda; and 'hybrid' courts and tribunals such as the Special Court for Sierra Leone, the Extraordinary Chamber in the Courts of Cambodia and the Special Tribunal for Lebanon.

7. By contrast, Art 4 (d) of the Statute of the International Criminal Tribunal for Rwanda, and Art 3 (d) of the Statute of the Special Court for Sierra Leone, incorporate 'acts of terror' as a stand-alone war crimes offence in the context of non-international armed conflict. This identical provision in both statutes reflects Article 4 (2)(d) of Additional Protocol II to the 1949 Geneva Conventions which lists 'acts of terrorism' as one of a number of acts that 'are and shall remain prohibited at any time and in any place whatsoever'. Art 8 of the Law on the Establishment of the Extraordinary Chambers in the Courts of Cambodia provides for jurisdiction over one terrorism related offence, namely attacks against internationally protected persons.

8. Algeria, Benin, Burkina Faso, Burundi, Cameroun, Chad, Côte d'Ivoire, Comoros, Congo, Gabon, Gambia, Ghana, Kenya, Libya, Lesotho, Mali, Malawi, Mauritania, Mauritius, Mozambique, Niger, Nigeria, Rwanda, Sahrawi Arab Democratic Republic, Senegal, South Africa, Tanzania, Togo, Tunisia and Uganda.

9. Benin, Burkina Faso, Côte d'Ivoire, Ghana, Mali, Malawi, Tanzania and Tunisia.

Chapter 8

Combating Terrorism through Law

The 'war on terror' requires that individuals should collectively defeat that common invisible enemy by sacrificing their own freedom on the altar of security measures of surveillance or espionage. Terrorism is defined differently in the world and therefore has global and local dimensions. The elusive war on terror exposes the structural weakness of democracy, exposes the weak underbelly of globalization and betrays the ideology of liberty. A good number of African states are experiencing this asymmetric 'new' terror war waged by terrorist networks, religious extremists, heavily armed ethnic or clan militias, bandits and criminal gangs operating within and across national borders (Ogenga, 2015; Bamidele, 2015). These asymmetric wars are now the nastiest and most potent security threat to African states. They are waged by unconventional forces of faceless enemies rather than conventional armies of nations. Consequently, the involvement of militaries in combating these threats has stirred controversy. When such wars are waged, civilians are caught up as casualties and end up living in a military-like state (Ogenga, 2015). Many therefore question the wisdom of fighting terror with terror.

What has further complicated global security has been the emergence of global asymmetric wars. These wars are characterized by the quest for global power with non-state actors, terrorist groups and individuals fighting for recognition. Terrorist groups waging a war tend to be successful because they are driven by strong beliefs attached to nationalism or religion. It is more difficult to fight such groups using conventional methods. But then, there is no method open to states other than conventional means. States must work within the morality of international law and respect the rules of engagement they can employ. Most states would feel reluctant to employ the same strategy used by terrorist organizations because using terror strategies would inflict heavy losses in terms of infrastructural damage, civilian casualties and economic down-spiral. But then, rather than formulate working strategies for defeating terrorist organizations, states are always working hard to fight the tactics employed by such groups and therefore easily become victims (Ogenga, 2015; Bamidele, 2014). It is difficult to fight an ideology through military incursions, martial operations and media propaganda. It makes sense therefore to combat terrorism through law, which is not to suggest that resorting to law alone can root out terrorism in Africa or anywhere else. Rooting out terrorism is clearly a task that is 'mission impossible'. It is doubtful that any country has set for itself such a very ambitious agenda.

INTERNATIONAL LEGAL FRAMEWORK

Since 1963, the UN has adopted a number of 'terrorism-related' conventions and protocols obliging states to criminalize certain acts considered to be related to terrorism.[1] These instruments constitute the worldwide legal framework in the international fight against terrorism whether by the lone-wolf terrorist such as Timothy McVeigh, the American domestic terrorist who carried out the 1995 Oklahoma City bombing that killed 168 people or self-confessed international terrorist organizations or localized terrorist groups. Besides this framework, it seems that in international law states may adopt forceful measures in response to terrorist activities. For example, in certain situations actions against states sponsoring terrorism may be justifiable in the context of self-defence, including pre-emptive or anticipatory self-defence. The justification for this is that states generally are under an obligation not to sponsor terrorist activity or assist it in any way.

The 11 September 2001 terrorist attack in America spurred the UNSC to pass Resolution 1373 of 28 September 2001 adopted under Chapter VII of the UN Charter. The resolution was adopted to stimulate action in what was to become 'the global fight against terrorism'. It mandates states to adopt legislation combating terrorism.[2] It requires UN Member States to criminalize terrorism as a serious crime in national and regional legislation along with terrorist funding and other ancillary offences. However, many African countries were tardy in enacting anti-terrorism legislation. They took the view that transborder terrorism was not a clear and present threat to their environment. In some countries with a large Muslim population such as Nigeria (identified by Osama Bin Laden in 2004 as a fertile ground for jihadist action), it was even argued that anti-Muslim sentiment was the motivation for such proposed legislation (Bamidele, 2015). However, this attitude of benign neglect of possible terrorist attacks changed when Al-Shabab emerged in Somalia and Boko Haram in Nigeria. Both are big countries with a substantial Muslim population. Al-Shabab began carrying out terrorist attacks not only in Somalia but also deep in Kenya (Ogenda, 2015). Boko Haram carried out attacks not only in Nigeria but also in the northern part of Cameroun. These groups signalled their presence not only by carrying out deadly terrorist attacks but also by kidnapping for ransom and taking hostages.

Resolution 1373 however makes little reference to human rights, except in connection with the exchange of information, extradition and abuse of the right to asylum. Under the OAU 1999 Convention on the Prevention and Combating of Terrorism, States Parties 'undertake to establish criminal offences for terrorist acts'. By 2003, when the convention entered into force, UN Member States were already under obligation, flowing from UNSC Resolution 1373, to engage in the global fight against terrorism by adopting legal and administrative counter-terrorism measures.

AFRICAN LEGAL FRAMEWORK

Africa has adopted two terrorism-related instruments. These are the OAU 1999 Convention on the Prevention and Combating of Terrorism and the AU 2004 Protocol to the OAU Convention on the Prevention and Combating of Terrorism.[3] Both instruments, together with the 2002 Protocol Relating to the Establishment of the PSC of the African Union, constitute Africa's legal framework for combating terrorism. Under the 1999 Convention, States Parties undertake, among other things, 'to review their national laws and establish criminal offences for terrorist acts . . . and make such acts punishable by appropriate penalties that take into account the grave nature of such offences'.[4] The convention spells out areas of cooperation, the jurisdiction of a State Party, request for extra-territorial investigations (*commission rogatoire*) and mutual legal assistance, and the commitment of States Parties 'to extradite any person charged with or convicted of any terrorist act carried out on the territory of another State Party and whose extradition is requested by one of the States Parties'.

The AU 2004 Protocol states in Article 2 that the treaty is a supplement to the 1999 Convention. Its main purpose is to enhance the effective implementation of the convention and to give effect to Article 3(d) of the 2002 Peace and Security Council Protocol. The said Article 3(d) mandates the Peace and Security Council to 'co-ordinate and harmonise continental efforts in the prevention and combating of *international* terrorism in all its aspects'.[5] Combating international terrorism could be problematic for many African states. First, there are practical limits on the ability of most African states to prosecute terrorist offences committed elsewhere. Second, if a terrorist act is committed in a foreign country or jurisdiction against a third state, it is not evident that every African state has sufficient legislation to assume jurisdiction to prosecute the terrorist suspect who has been arrested locally.

The 2004 Protocol to the OAU Convention on Combating Terrorism sets out the commitments by States Parties under the protocol. It declares that the Peace and Security Council 'shall be responsible for harmonising and coordinating continental efforts in the prevention and combating of terrorism'.[6] The commitment of States Parties includes taking all necessary measures to protect the human rights of their populations against all acts of terrorism. It further includes establishing national focal points in order to facilitate exchanges and rapid sharing of information on terrorist groups and activities at regional, continental and international levels. It furthermore includes submitting to the PSC annual reports on the implementation of the 1999 Convention. The protocol elaborates and clarifies the role of the AU Commission and that of regional mechanisms in preventing and combating terrorism (Ewi, 2006; Boukrif, 1999).

The obligations assumed by African states under the OAU instrument are additional to the general obligations imposed by UNSC Resolution 1373. Anti-terrorism legislation would probably have been unnecessary if all African countries already had sufficient security laws that could be used to deal with terrorism crimes.[7] The practice of most African states in this regard consists in prosecuting terrorism-related offences under their amended criminal/penal codes. States lacking an adequate legal framework to try domestic or international terrorism have had to enact appropriate legislation consistent with their commitment under the OAU 1999 Convention. Disappointingly, most of Africa's anti-terrorism laws do not reflect the human rights obligations of the state. Counter-terrorism legislation often restricts the enjoyment of human rights. It often grants wide discretionary and investigative powers to executive authorities. Such great latitude given to the executive branch of government is constitutionally problematic because courts in most African countries are constitutionally not invested with power to control executive actions in the context of the 'war on terrorism'.

GRAVE HUMAN RIGHTS ABUSES IN IMPLEMENTING COUNTER-TERRORISM MEASURES

Many states still find it difficult to implement anti-terrorism measures while at the same time refraining from human rights abuses. Human rights abuses in the course of implementing anti-terrorism measures diverge from the overarching security concerns and undermine national cohesion and democratic principles. Effective implementation, within the law, of strategies for anti-terrorism initiatives and associated threats helps to eliminate group activities by terrorists. It also helps combat other forms of criminality and security threats. Such strategies could include border surveillance and control, and the prevention of the falsification of travel documents such as ID cards and passports. ECOWAS has a Counter-terrorism Strategy and Implementation Plan and the AU has a Protocol and Plan of Action on the Prevention and Combating of Terrorism (Bamidele, 2014). The AU and ECOWAS concede by these initiatives that terrorism has no borders, religion, gender, race, ethnicity or nationality, and that the threat of terrorism to one state is a threat to all states in the region and the continent. The AU and ECOWAS initiatives aim, among other things, at denying terrorist groups safe havens, eradicating sources of financing, reducing state vulnerability and enhancing emergency preparedness and response capabilities with the ultimate goal of preserving states' territorial integrity and sovereignty, and ensuring the safety of citizens. But these programmes need to be made operationally effective (Bamidele, 2014).

In 2001, the International Commission of Jurists commissioned an eminent panel composed of eight distinguished jurists from different parts of the world to conduct a study on counter-terrorism and human rights (International Commission of Jurists, 2009). The survey was conducted over a period of eight years, from 2001 to 2009. Its outcome was a very comprehensive 213-page published report on counter-terrorism and human rights. The report found extensive evidence of grave human rights abuses in the context of counter-terrorism measures. Abuses committed often include abducting persons and holding them in secret places of detention where they are tortured or otherwise ill-treated. Suspects in these secret detention centres are placed beyond the basic protections afforded by human rights standards, international humanitarian law and all domestic constitutional guarantees. Abuses also include holding 'terrorist' suspects *incommunicado* for extended periods before being charged. The report found that individuals charged with terrorism are often tried before special or military courts. The charges are always broadly framed under anti-terrorism legislation that encroaches upon freedoms of speech, opinion and assembly. The report further found that many counter-terrorism measures lack basic safeguards such as due process and adequate oversight mechanisms. It found an entrenched pervasive culture of secrecy in carrying out counter-terrorism measures. The secrecy demanded by the work of the intelligence and security bodies frequently amounts to impunity for wrongdoing. Innocent victims of human rights violations find themselves with no avenue for redress (Schönteich, 2000).

Overall, the study frowns on pursuing counter-terrorism with a war paradigm. This way of responding to terrorism has drawn the following comment from 'Justice', a UK nongovernmental organization.

Terrorism sows terror and many states have fallen into a trap set by terrorists. Ignoring lessons from the past, they have allowed themselves to be rushed into hasty responses, introducing an array of responses which undermine cherished values as well as international legal framework carefully developed since the Second World War. These measures have resulted in human rights violations, including torture, enforced disappearances, secret and arbitrary detentions, and unfair trials. There has been little accountability for these abuses or justice for their victims. (https://justice.org.uk)[8]

The reality of terrorist threat cannot be underestimated or downplayed. However, another reality is that anti-terrorism measures adopted by African states often have a potential negative impact on human rights. More often than not, African states resort to the most violent methods in the fight against terrorism. In some countries, persons accused of involvement in acts of 'terrorism' have been disappeared, tortured or extra-judicially killed by state security agents. 'Terrorist' suspects are abducted, held incommunicado without charge for extended periods in secret locations under life-threatening conditions and subjected to torture and cruel, inhuman and degrading treatment (Schönteich, 2000). In Algeria, for instance, a 'terrorist' suspect may be held in police custody *incommunicado* for twelve days with the possibility of extension by the investigating magistrate for up to twenty months.[9] In Egypt, the state of emergency law authorizes detention of any suspect without charge for a period of at least thirty days, renewable indefinitely if the judge deems it necessary for the purpose of the investigation (Cilliers & Sturman, 2002). In Cameroun, suspects are often arbitrarily held *incommunicado* in secret locations for months on end, if not years.

Extreme measures such as these offend against human rights norms that protect the right to life and the right to personal integrity and security. They also offend against judicial guarantees and protections in the context of the fight against terrorism. To begin with, international law prohibits torture even in such very difficult circumstances as combating terrorism, whether organized or not. A state of course often faces difficult choices on how to respond to national security imperatives. But the law cannot be silent even in the face of national imperatives. In admittedly difficult circumstances of terrorism, it is still critical for the state to uphold human dignity and human rights. The law does not suffer extreme measures to be used as a weapon in fighting terrorism. If it did, that would nonsensically be like fighting fire with fire or fighting homicide with homicide. Such a strategy is bound to be and has always been counterproductive.

The wisdom of international human rights law is that it is eminently essential to uphold the core values and principles of democracy and the rule of law against those who seek to destroy them through acts of terrorism.

International human rights law therefore ordains that counter-terrorism measures adopted by states to meet national security challenges must rest upon the foundation of full respect for human rights and the rule of law. The measures adopted must not violate obligations in international human rights instruments, including those articulated by the AfComHPR. General principles and standards of law apply equally to non-terrorism and terrorism-related cases.

Terrorist suspects do not lose their humanity and human rights just because they stand accused of terrorism and are labelled 'terrorists'. Measures taken by states to fight terrorism must be subject to appropriate supervision. They must not be arbitrary, discriminatory or restrictive of procedural rights. The necessity for these safeguards is even greater in the context of suspects from communities that are already marginalized, persecuted or oppressed on account of their ethnicity, culture, separate identity or minority status. Neglect of these basic safeguards only goes to increase the threat of terrorist acts and serves instead as a 'recruiting sergeant' for radicals (Martin, 2016).

Initial emotion-driven widespread support for far-reaching counter-terrorism measures has diminished markedly in many countries, especially in the face of grave human rights violations by states in the name of combating terrorism. Scandalized by widespread serious abuse of human rights by governments, the general public in Africa is increasingly pressing governments to respect human rights while combating terrorism. These are hopeful developments that portend future respect for human rights even in the context of combating terrorism. There is no necessary incompatibility between fighting terrorism and upholding international human rights standards.

NOTES

1. 1963 Convention on Offences and Certain Acts Committed on Board Aircraft; 1970 Convention for the Suppression of Unlawful Seizure of Aircraft; 1971 Convention for the Suppression of Unlawful Acts Against the Safety of Civil Aviation; 1973 Convention on the Prevention and Punishment of Crimes against Internationally Protected Persons, including Diplomatic Agents; 1979 International Convention against the Taking of Hostages; 1980 Convention on the Physical Protection of Nuclear Material; 1988 Protocol for the Suppression of Unlawful Acts of Violence at Airports Serving International Civil Aviation; 1988 Convention for the Suppression of Unlawful Acts Against the Safety of Maritime Navigation; 1988 Protocol for the Suppression of Unlawful Acts Against the Safety of Fixed Platforms Located on the Continental Shelf; 1991 Convention on the Making of Plastic Explosives for the Purpose of Identification; 1997 International Convention for the Suppression of Terrorist Bombings; 1999 International Convention for the Suppression of the Financing of Terrorism; 2005 International Convention for the

Suppression of Acts of Nuclear Terrorism. See, United Nations Office on Drugs and Crime, *Legislative Guide to the Universal Legal Regime Against Terrorism*, 2008.

2. UNSC Res 1373 of 28 Sept 2001, UN Doc S/RES/1373.
3. The former instrument entered into force in 2003 but the latter is yet to.
4. Article 2(a) Article 2(a).
5. Emphasis added.
6. Articles 3 and 4.
7. On the need for a South African terrorism law, one commentator argued that an anti-terrorism law was not needed because the country already had sufficient security laws for use for that purpose. See, Schönteich M., 'South Africa's Arsenal of Terrorism Legislation', *9 Afr. Sec. Rev. 2* (2000).
8. https://justice.org.uk accessed on 1 July 2018.
9. Art 25 (2) Algerian Criminal Procedure Code; Art 51 (3) Criminal Procedure Code of Algeria; Law No. 01-08 of 26 June 2001 amending and supplementing Ordinance No. 66-155 of 8 June 1966 on the Algerian Code of Criminal Procedure.

Chapter 9

Punishing Acts of Terrorism

Acts of terrorism must be punished. But the procedure leading up to punishment must be consistent with the dictates and standards of international law. The process of arrest, trial, conviction, the prescribed penalty and sentencing of the 'terrorist' suspect must be transparent and consistent with international law and standards.

INTERNATIONAL STANDARDS: JUDICIAL SAFEGUARDS

In 2002, the former UN high commissioner for human rights, Sergio Vieira de Mello, asserted that in combating terrorism the winning strategy is respect for human rights and upholding the primacy of the rule of law. In his view, 'The best – the only – strategy to isolate and defeat terrorism is by respecting human rights, fostering social justice, enhancing democracy and upholding the primacy of the rule of law.'

Respecting human rights of course includes respecting the right to life. States cannot in one and the same breath condemn murder and then prescribe the death penalty as a legitimate sentencing option for the crime. Such a position is morally indefensible. Murder is murder, whether perpetrated by a non-state actor or the state itself. A key international human rights protection against the use of the death penalty for counter-terrorism is Article 6(2) of the 1966 ICCPR. There, it is provided that 'in countries which have not abolished the death penalty, sentence of death may be imposed only for the *most serious crimes*'. This provision tolerates the death penalty in retentionist states only when the sentence is imposed for the 'most serious crimes' and, then, only in cases where it can be shown that there was an intentional killing.¹ The idea of 'most serious crime' is not a subjective concept. It is a concept requiring a 'systematic and normatively persuasive response'.² A state cannot simply decide that a particular conduct answers the description of 'most serious crime' and then proceed to prescribe the death penalty for it. Conduct does not become a 'most serious crime' just because a state chose to label it as a 'terrorist act'. Nor does an act constitute a 'most serious crime' just because it relates to or is captured under the rubric of 'national security'. The conduct or act must involve intentional killing to meet the threshold of 'most serious' under international law. If therefore a terrorism-related killing is intentional, the crime is a serious one even if the motive for the terrorist attack is considered a laudable one.

The global community is moving away from the use of the death penalty. The number of countries that have abolished the death penalty in law or practice for all crimes stood at 16 in 1977, 96 in 2010, and 142 in 2017, among them 38 African states, 144 in 2020 and as of 2021, 108 for all crimes and 144 in law or practice. Today, more than two-thirds of the countries in the world have abolished the death penalty in law or practice. It can be asserted with some confidence that there is an evolving standard according to which states and judiciaries now consider the death penalty to be a violation per se of the prohibition of torture or other cruel, inhuman or degrading treatment. Arguably, a customary norm prohibiting the death penalty under all circumstances is probably in the process of formation.³

There is an evolving customary norm of non-applicability of the death penalty even in the case of very serious crimes. This is reflected by the non-prescription of the death penalty for terrorist-related offences created by the UN. In fact, the UN legal infrastructure does not require the imposition of the death penalty. None of the UN instruments on terrorism requires or even mentions the imposition of the death penalty as a punishment for a terrorism-related offence. The death penalty is absent as one of the sentences available to international tribunals. The ICC has jurisdiction over some of the most serious offences that can be committed such as genocide, war crimes and crimes against humanity. Yet the international community has not prescribed the death penalty for any of these crimes. The statute for other international criminal tribunals such as those for Lebanon, Rwanda, Sierra Leone and the former Yugoslavia exclude the death penalty as a punishment.

The UNODC has emphasized that counter-terrorism measures be based on human rights standards. Where an international convention creates an offence without a penalty clause, the penalty for any such offence cannot be the death sentence. The penalty gap has to be filled by reference to a penalty consistent with International Human Rights Law (Gallahue et al., 2012). The international human rights system frowns at legislative measures increasing the number of capital offences or reinstating the death sentence. Creating new capital offences or broadly defining capitally punishable terrorism-related offences is inconsistent with international law.[4]

A year after the adoption of Resolution 1373, the OHCHR made the important clarification that 'measures to combat terrorism . . . are only legitimate if they respect the fundamental principles and universally recognized standards of international law, in particular, international human rights law and international humanitarian law' (OHCHR, 2002). Even so, and in spite of a clear legal framework for the promotion and protection of human rights in Africa, 'African human rights protection mechanisms have not achieved any notable progress in terms of effectively protecting human rights in the context of the fight against terrorism undertaken by many African states' (Kane, 2015).

Even where the death penalty is tolerated as an available sentence, international minimum fair trial standards must be respected.[5] Non-observance of fair trial standards in the context of the death penalty constitutes a breach of due process of law.[6] The resulting imposition of the death penalty constitutes a violation of the right not to be arbitrarily deprived of one's life. That right is guaranteed under Article 6 of the ICCPR and under Article 4 of the ACHPR. It is contrary to International Human Rights Law for a state to arbitrarily deprive a person of their right to life or to reduce the protections afforded to those facing the death penalty (Inter-American Commission on Human Rights, 2018). The use of the death penalty while countering terrorism is incompatible with International Human Rights Law. Reintroducing the death penalty for crimes of terrorism would be contrary to the spirit of the ICCPR. It would also be contrary to repeated calls by the UNGA and the AfComHPR regarding the use of the death penalty. Calls have been made to states that still retain capital punishment to progressively restrict the use of that penalty, to reduce the number of offences for which it might be imposed and to establish a moratorium on executions with a view to abolishing the death penalty. Calls have also been made to abolitionist states not to reintroduce the death penalty (CTITF, 2015).

The right to a fair trial is guaranteed in Article 7 of the ACHPR and in a number of international instruments.[7] The right underpins non-derogable rights, such as the right to life.[8] It cannot therefore be diminished where this would circumvent the protection of the right to life.[9] Full adherence to fair trial rights is particularly necessary where the potential punishment is death. This is because it is important to avoid the risk of a mistaken execution of an innocent person. Where the state's criminal justice system is not capable of reliably respecting fair trial standards, the right thing to do is for the state to impose a moratorium on the application of the death penalty for all offences.[10] This precautionary measure is dictated by the reality that even fair trials can produce wrong outcomes. The only sure way to prevent an innocent person from being mistakenly put to death is to remove the death penalty as a sentencing option.

African trials in terrorism-related cases often fall well below standards of due process.[11] Fair trial rights are guaranteed under Articles 14 and 15 of the ICCPR and under Article 7 of the ACHPR. These guarantees must be fully observed when the death penalty is being used for terrorist crimes. They apply during the trial and for all stages preceding and succeeding the trial.[12] The practice where the executive is vested with broad discretion in referring terrorist suspects to military or special tribunals is frowned upon by international human rights monitoring bodies. In many such cases, the executive holds the ultimate power to review the decisions of those courts. Moreover, these tribunals are characterized by lower fair trial guarantees. They limit access to counsel. They intrude into the attorney-client confidentiality. They impose strict limitations on the right to bail and to appeal. They use extra-legal practices to obtain evidence. The AfComHPR, the UN Working Group on Arbitrary Detention and the Special Rapporteur on the Promotion and Protection of Human Rights and Fundamental Freedoms while Countering Terrorism have all concluded that the military justice system should be prohibited from imposing the death penalty under all circumstances.[13]

In states that still retain the death penalty, the imposition of the death penalty for terrorism must result from judicial proceedings that meet international fair trial standards. These standards include the following minimum guaranteed rights: the right to a fair and public hearing by an independent and impartial court of competent jurisdiction, the right to freedom from torture, the right to be presumed innocent until proved guilty, the right to be informed promptly of the details of the charge and in a language which the arrestee understands, the right to legal defence and to be tried without delay, the right not to be convicted of any offence on account of any act or omission which did not constitute a crime under national or international law at the time when it was committed and the right to have one's sentence reviewed.[14] There have been cases where a death sentence is carried out before the offender has had time to appeal or to seek pardon or commutation of the sentence. For example, this happened in Chad in August 2015 when three Boko Haram suspected 'terrorists' were executed within three days of their death sentence. Such swift execution amounts to a denial of the right of appeal or the right to seek pardon or commutation of sentence. It is tantamount to arbitrary deprivation of life and thus a violation of International Human Rights Law.

African states treat terrorist cases as a special category of criminal cases. They oust the jurisdiction of the ordinary criminal courts in respect of those cases. They confer jurisdiction over such cases to 'special' criminal courts or to military tribunals. It is a mystery why it is thought that the ordinary criminal courts though staffed with competent judicial officers are incompetent to try or are disqualified from trying such cases. It is not unusual for anti-terrorism laws to grant full freedom to executive authorities to decree expeditious, summary or some other 'special' procedures that pay scant regard to the rights of the accused person. One such procedure consists in conducting the 'trial' of a 'terrorist' suspect in camera and in the absence of his counsel, and denial of the right against self-incrimination (Cilliers & Sturman, 2002).

In Sudan, for instance, the anti-terrorism law gives the president of the Supreme Court power to create one or more anti-terrorism courts whose rules of procedure are determined after consultation with the minister of justice.[15] Proceedings and investigations before the anti-terrorism courts are conducted by the minister of justice via the 'terrorism combating bureau'[16] and sentences can only be carried out with the express approval of the president of the Republic.[17] In Egypt, in terms of a 1981 law on states of emergency, trials for acts of terrorism are conducted in military courts whose members are military force members appointed by the minister of defence. These courts may try civilians, and appeals against their decisions are reviewed by military courts of appeal whose decisions need to be confirmed by the president of the Republic. The situation is the same in Cameroun Republic. There too, terrorism cases are tried by the military tribunal. The magistrate and prosecutor are soldiers accountable to the minister of defence.

Africa's preference for military tribunals or 'special courts' could well be because those 'courts' are under the direct orders and control of the executive. Generally, they pronounce a pre-determined verdict and sentence, irrespective of the evidence adduced. These 'courts' are in fact political tools. They are handy tools for repression and for spreading terror under the thin disguise of fighting terrorism. In many African countries 'terrorism' is just about any conduct or activity that challenges those in power or the political system in place. The basic problem with these expedients relates to proper court procedures and to their competence, independence and impartiality to hear and determine cases of alleged terrorism. Using these expedients violates the guarantees relating to fair trial and judicial independence captured in Article 14 of the ICCPR and Articles 7 and 26 of the ACHPR, as well as a body of AfComHPR case-law on the subject.[18]

The AfComHPR has spoken loudly and clearly on this issue. It has explicitly stated that 'the only purpose of military courts shall be to determine offences of a purely military nature committed by military personnel'. It has clarified that military courts 'should not in any circumstances whatsoever have jurisdiction over civilians'.[19] It has gone further to declare that 'in the determination of any criminal charge against a person, or of a person's rights and obligations, everyone shall be entitled to a fair and public hearing by a legally constituted competent, independent and impartial judicial body'.

The commission has cautioned that military tribunals must 'not be created to displace the jurisdiction belonging to ordinary judicial bodies', and that even such courts are 'required to respect fair trial standards enunciated in the African Charter'.[20] The Human Rights Committee has forthrightly stated that even in times of war or states of emergency 'only a court of law may try and convict a person for a criminal offence'[21] and that 'the right to be tried by an independent and impartial tribunal is an absolute right that may suffer no exception'.[22]

The vague and imprecise definition of the offence of terrorism found in the terrorism legislation of African states has the nugatory effect of severely limiting freedom of expression and information.[23] The right to freedom of expression and information may of course be subject to certain restrictions. But the restrictions must be legitimate. They must fall within the framework of the general principles of legality and the primacy of law. The UN has strongly recommended 'the inclusion of precise definitions in [anti-terrorism] instruments' and the 'avoidance of any unwarranted linkages between asylum-seekers and terrorists'.[24] When definitions are too broad and vague, there is a risk that the *terrorist* label might be abused for political ends, for example, to criminalize legitimate activities of political opponents in a manner amounting to persecution.

African states tend to treat a political offence as a terrorist crime. Africa's Refugee Convention applies to 'political offences'.[25] Under the convention, a person can seek and be granted asylum in an African country owing to well-founded fear of being persecuted in his home country for reasons of political opinion. Many countries have simply excised the term 'political offences' from their criminal legislation and converted the content of offences of that category into crimes of terrorism.

A state has the right to take necessary measures to safeguard its security and integrity. It may do so by criminalizing conduct that endangers its security and integrity. But the state does not have a free hand in this matter to do as it pleases. The state is subject to international law. It is bound to comply with principles of International Human Rights Law, international law and criminal law. Labelling as 'terrorist acts' behaviour which has no relation to terrorism is a violation of the principle of legality of offences. A state sometimes has recourse to that expedient in order to deny a 'terrorist' suspect the right of *non-refoulement*. The argument for denying the suspect that right appears to be that the accusation against him does not amount to a political offence (to which the principle of *non-refoulement* applies) but to an ordinary crime, a terrorist act. This argument leads to the conclusion that the state is thus at liberty to deport or *refoule*. In that way, the state in question avoids extradition procedures. Those procedures are generally perceived in the continent as long, burdensome and ineffective. State legislative practice designed to defeat the application of the principle of *non-refoulement* is inconsistent with international law and with the jurisprudence of UN human rights bodies.

Article 3 of the ICCPR requires that the state party should, before expelling or deporting an alien, provide him with sufficient safeguards and an effective remedy. The UN Committee against Torture recognizes the need for close cooperation between states in the fight against crime. It also recognizes the need for effective measures to be agreed upon by states for that purpose. It has nevertheless stated that such measures must fully respect the rights and fundamental freedoms of the individuals concerned.[26] To respect the principle of *non-refoulement* does not mean affording terrorists impunity. Sometimes states extradite suspected terrorists in violation of basic rules of human rights protection.[27] Conventions on terrorism do not establish an absolute obligation to extradite terrorist suspects.[28] But they do include the principle of *aut dedere aut judicare* (an offender may be tried by the state on whose territory he is found). Thus, a terrorist suspect who is in the territory of a third state and who faces the risk of serious human rights violations in the requesting state if extradited thereto may be tried by the courts of the third state rather than extradited to the requesting state.[29]

AFRICA AND THE DEATH PENALTY FOR 'TERRORIST' OFFENCES

In African states that still retain capital punishment, the death penalty is a sentencing option for terrorism-related offences. The notion of 'terrorist act' or 'act of terrorism' in such offences embraces a wide gamut of activities. Casting the definitional net so wide raises legitimate fears of a high risk of extending the death penalty to acts that do not constitute serious crimes. It also raises fears that in Africa, combating terrorism involves the arbitrary, discriminatory and unlawful use of the death penalty in violation of international human rights standards. International standards posit that in states that still retain the death penalty, its use must be confined to crimes that constitute the 'most serious' in international law. Moreover, the capital offender must have the right to guarantee due process. African states appear to be dismissive of these minimum standards. They appear to favour a repressive approach. They do not seek a balance between protecting the public interest and upholding the human rights of persons under their jurisdiction. Unlike the European and the Inter-American human rights systems, the African system is by comparison timid when it comes to promoting human rights within the framework of the fight against terrorism (OHCHR, 2002).

The law is never silent even in the context of combating terrorism. States do not have a free hand to resort to any measures they please. 'War on terrorism' cannot be a blank cheque for the president and his military when it comes to human rights of citizens and their right to human dignity. Counter-terrorism measures taken by states must comply with 'the general principles of international law, as well as the African Charter on Human and Peoples' Rights'.[30] Member States of the UN have a legal obligation to ensure that all measures taken to combat terrorism are 'in accordance with international law, in particular International Human Rights Law, refugee law, and international humanitarian law'.[31]

The anti-terrorism legislation of a few African countries suffices to illustrate the point that in Africa 'terrorist act' means just about any conduct. Cameroun's anti-terrorism law is a localized version of that of France. Chad copied that law from Cameroun and used it to prosecute and sentence to death ten Boko Haram suspects who were then executed in 2015. Chad has now repealed that law. Also, in 2015, Cameroun's military tribunal sentenced to death eighty-nine presumed members of Boko Haram for crimes related to 'terrorism' punishable under that country's Law on the Repression of Terrorism passed in 2014. The death penalty in Cameroun's anti-terrorism law is available even for acts that do not involve intentional killing or even killing at all. Paradoxically, under that country's anti-terrorism law the death penalty may be imposed for non-violent activities such as advocating for a federal form of state or calling for judicial or educational reforms. These activities are treated as constituting crimes of so-called 'national security', the definition of which is extremely broad. No distinction is made between violent 'terrorist' acts which cause intentional death and the peaceful exercise of the rights to freedom of opinion, expression, movement and assembly. The criminalization of, and the prescription of the death penalty for, non-violent activities are in clear breach of the rule of law and the availability of that penalty only for the most serious crimes. Even if the non-violent activities were criminal, they clearly do not meet the threshold of 'most serious crimes'. Criminalizing them as terrorism-related offences raises very serious concerns on the use of the death penalty as a counter-terrorism measure.[32]

Cameroun authorities use the anti-terrorism law even against journalists.[33] They use that law as a tool of terror. The provisions of the anti-terrorism law are overly broad with easy potential for abuse of political opponents and the right to freedom of expression and information. They allow authorities to detain indefinitely those accused of terrorism.[34] The anti-terrorism law of Cameroun provides for prosecution in the military tribunal which, ironically, is vested with jurisdiction to try even civilians and to pass the death sentence. Civilians tried by a military tribunal are often denied their rights to a fair trial and to the appeals process. Much of this contravenes International Human

Rights Law. The AfComHPR has repeatedly stated that military courts 'should not in any circumstances whatsoever have jurisdiction over civilians' and that the only purpose of these courts is 'to determine offences of a purely military nature committed by military personnel'.[35]

In Egypt, a wide range of violent, non-violent and inchoate actions 'aimed at undermining Egypt's independence, unity or territorial integrity' are considered terrorist acts and are punishable by death.[36] On 7 May 2015, Egypt executed six members of the jihadist group Ansar Beit al-Maqdis, with ties to Daesh.[37] In Equatorial Guinea, terrorism is punishable by death under the country's received Spanish Penal Code of 1963. In 2010, four persons were convicted of treason and terrorism, sentenced to death and executed in connection with what was said to be an attack against the Presidential Palace. In Somalia, the Penal Code of 1962 prescribes the death sentence for terrorism. Since 2013 a number of people have been accused of and executed for 'a vast range of crimes provided for within the framework of the anti-terrorist laws'.[38] In 2012, Ethiopia used its 2009 Anti-Terrorism Proclamation to convict journalists and members of opposition political parties for 'criticizing the government, demanding reforms and discussing demonstrations and arrests' and at least one journalist was given eighteen years for offences related to terrorism. In 2015, Algeria passed sixty-two death sentences for acts of terrorism and crimes related to terrorism under Algeria's 1966 Penal Code as amended in 2009. The death penalty is commonly provided for in the criminal legislation of African countries in respect of acts of terrorism.[39]

In Benin, Cameroun, Chad, Egypt, Gambia, Libya, Morocco, Sudan and Uganda, a person can be sentenced to death for committing vaguely defined terrorist acts in general. Examples of conduct that may be death eligible as 'acts of terrorism' or 'terrorism-related offences' include 'vandalizing, looting, or killing people' (Libya); 'participation in criminal gangs and terrorist groups' (Congo, Egypt, Mali, Mauritania and Sudan); 'terror, ecological disaster or other social disruption, gang attacks on the people, armed resistance to authorities' (Egypt); 'forming or attempting to form a criminal organization, to stage attacks that may jeopardize life or property or tranquillity' (Sudan); 'treason and activities aimed at overthrowing the regime' (Eritrea and Guinea); 'harm to buildings' (Guinea), 'sabotage of transport, communication facilities, public service or special equipment' (Central African Republic, Congo and Ethiopia); 'taking of hostages and kidnapping' (Chad, Ethiopia and Morocco); possession and/or use of chemical, biological and nuclear weapons' (Cameroun, Chad, Ethiopia, Mauritania and Niger); 'intention to kill without actual loss of life or causing serious injury to a person' (Chad, Ethiopia and Mauritania); 'arson and possession and/or use of explosives and firearms and other arms' (Central

African Republic, Congo, Guinea, Mauritania and Morocco); 'hijacking of and endangering aircrafts, ships or fixed platforms' (Ethiopia, Mauritania and Sudan). Much of this legislation makes a complete ass of the fight against terrorism through law.

WOULD KILLING TERRORISTS DETER TERRORISM?

This question recalls the basic debate whether the death penalty deters crime. It is a trite observation that the death penalty has cultural, religious and political dimensions and that it is practiced for crime prevention and not for revenge. Evidence from around the world shows that the death penalty has no unique deterrent effect on crime even historically.[40] Some would concede the general validity of that statement. But they would marshal the following line of argument in support of the view that the death penalty is appropriate for terrorist-related activities. Terrorism is a crime of a particular kind and nature. Terrorists attack by bomb explosions or by indiscriminate shooting. Such conduct causes massive loss of lives. Terrorist acts are therefore completely different in nature, in objective and in motivation. No particular individual as such is targeted. But the objective of such attacks, which in some instances is state-sponsored, is to destabilize society and to affect the integrity and security of the state.[41] Terrorism thus involves mass casualties and affects the international community. It causes widespread fear among the masses and disrupts daily life. The crime of terrorism can therefore be deterred only by confronting terror with terror, killing the killers, life for life, smashing terrorist organizations and their cells and thereby systematically eliminating terrorists. If these measures are taken, it is contended in conclusion, then over time there will be no more terrorists spreading terror, devastation and death through terrorist attacks.

People often identify the phenomenon of terrorism with the rise of the suicide jihadist in the 1990s. But terrorism existed long before then. From the 1960s to the 1980s, numerous Marxist-based groups carried out terrorist attacks, especially in Europe. Some of the best known of these groups are the Red Army Brigade, the Red Army Faction (*Baader-Meinhof* Gang), *Action Directe*, Weather Underground, and the Symbionese Liberation Army. Much of the attacks by these groups did comparatively small-scale killings. They tended to be focused more on hostage-taking for ransom, especially of persons of some importance and stature. It is however the suicide jihadist who started the phenomenon of perpetrating attacks causing large-scale killings. Africa has experienced mass killings carried out in Somalia and Kenya by Al-Shabab, in Nigeria by Boko Haram, in Mali by Al-Qaeda in the Maghreb and in Algeria and Egypt by little-known terrorist groups. But by and large the scale, magnitude and frequency and intensity of terrorist acts in Africa do not compare with those that occur in countries like Australia, Canada, Denmark, France, Germany, India, Pakistan, Russia, Turkey, the United States and the United Kingdom.

Yet, African states are unlikely to refrain from prescribing the death penalty for 'terrorist' offences. The incarceration by some Western countries of convicted terrorists and the 'easy' life in prison by the convicts are not likely to impress most African heads of state. The concern of African rulers is not so much about the possibility of mass killings of their citizens. Rather, it is more about the somewhat amorphous concepts (in the African context) of 'national security' and 'territorial integrity'. In Africa, there is a general lack of interest in improving prison conditions and facilities, much of which has not changed significantly since colonial times. African rulers believe prison conditions must be Spartan, particularly harsh, rather than be like prison conditions in the West which they see as equivalent to conditions in a four-star hotel.

As an illustration of what African leaders would consider to be conditions of a four-star-hotel prison, take the following cases. In Norway, a terrorist, Anders Breivik murdered seventy-seven fellow Norwegians. He was not executed but jailed for twenty-one years, a very lenient punishment by African sentencing standards. In 2017, he sued the Norwegian government claiming a denial of his human rights. The alleged denial of human rights included the following 'indignities': denial of an upgrade of his PlayStation device which he uses to while away time, denial of the use of metal cutlery obliging him to manage with the inferior alternative of plastic eating utensils and denial of access to private communication with his supporters outside of the prison. An African government would wonder at the impudence and temerity of the prisoner in suing the government and would consider such claimed 'deprivation' the ultimate affront. In Australia, another terrorist mass murderer, seventy-three-year-old Ivan Milat, was sent to jail for the rest of his life. But calculations showed that ending his days in prison will cost the taxpayer a tidy sum of $320,000 per annum to keep him behind bars (Letford, 2017). And yet, in abolitionist states the only punishment option for even a terrorist crime is imprisonment for an extended period, the cost of incarceration to the taxpayer notwithstanding.

The traditional terrorist attack is usually premeditated. It is done on a large scale so as to grab media and world attention. It often results in a massive amount of property damage and the deaths of hundreds or even thousands of people.[42] A nagging question is why Muslim terrorists commit mass murder, often taking their own lives along with the lives of their victims. A number of explanations have been advanced. It is said the operatives desire to be martyred and to be remembered as such in history. Many religious communities believe in reward after death and endless enjoyment in heaven. Thus, male suicide jihadists are socialized to believe that

> should they die as a result of killing infidels, they are guaranteed a place in paradise where they can spend eternity deflowering 72 virgins who are blessed with white skin, no body hair and large breasts (female martyrs get one male partner who, we are assured, will satisfy them). (Letford, 2017)

In the case of non-Muslim terrorists, it would seem all they seek is publicity for 'heroism' or simply media attention and 'fame', even if for the crime. In some other cases, they seek to avenge some grievance they nurse, especially against the state.

The goal of a terrorist attack is to invoke and spread fear, using violence as a method of getting across a political, religious, racial or other point. Many terrorist attackers are on suicide missions that claim their own lives along with those of innocent victims. At one time it was fashionable for terrorists to blow up airplanes in mid-air, killing innocent victims and themselves. Tight airport security aided by advanced technology has made this option almost impossible. In the current *méthode du jour* the terrorist blows up buildings or other structures with a human presence inside so as to cause mass murder and inflict maximum damage to property. Alternatively, the terrorist drives into a crowd in a car or truck, killing as many people as possible. Again, the terrorist could detonate planted bombs in crowded places, killing as many people as possible. These standard or traditional terrorist methods of mass murder and destruction are rare in Africa, the only notable such cases being the 2011 Boko Haram terrorist attack on the UN building in Abuja, Nigeria; the 1998 Al-Qaeda and Egyptian Islamic Jihad attack on the US Embassies in Nairobi and Dar es Salam; and the Al-Shabab episodic but resilient attacks in Somalia and Kenya since 2013.

In some abolitionist countries such as the UK and Australia, for example, voices have been heard calling for the reintroduction of the death penalty for terrorist mass murderers. In Australia, a Morgan poll conducted in 2014 found that 52.5% of Australians supported the return of the death penalty for terrorists (Letford, 2017). Support for hanging convicted terrorists is based on the following practical arguments. Jailing terrorist offenders merely creates a focus of radicalization. It costs the taxpayer so much money to keep a convicted terrorist in jail where he enjoys relative comfort whereas that money could be channelled towards social sectors like education and health. Executing a convicted terrorist ensures that he is denied a voice and is forever forgotten. Moreover, executing the terrorist ensures that relatives of victims of the terrorist attack and survivors of the attack do not endure daily reminders in the media of what they experienced (Letford, 2017).

However, there is increasing support for the view that the death penalty for terrorists is ineffectual, counterproductive and does little to reduce terror and crime.[43] The threat of execution is an ineffective strategy for preventing terrorism. Despite popular claims and often-repeated statements by politicians, capital punishment fails to prove that it is the best and most efficient deterrent. People willing to commit large-scale acts of violence aimed at inflicting terror upon a society do so knowing that they could come to serious physical harm. They therefore show little or no regard for their own safety. It is naive to think terrorism can be controlled or eliminated by using the death penalty or threat of its application. Executing terrorists, especially jihadists who aspire to martyrdom, is hardly an effective way to deal with the scourge of terrorism. It does not necessarily make the targeted state safe. There is no evidence that the death penalty improves public security or that it addresses violent crime, including terrorist-related acts. Executing 'terrorists' does not project an image of strength on the part of a government but an image of panic and hopeless desperation. 'Gaining popular support by using demagogic rhetoric might be easy and politically expedient, but on the long run it does little to produce deterrence and safety' (Kuttab, 2017). The death penalty does not deter determined terrorists. 'It is hard to deter people who are willing to die, and therefore the death penalty for those who have decided to die and commit suicide is not a deterrent'.[44]

Executing especially minor terrorist operatives has the effect of turning criminals into martyrs. It invites retaliatory strikes or kidnappings or hostage-taking from admirers who are then induced into espousing a similar cause. Dead terrorists do not talk. Killing terrorists therefore deprives the state of a good intelligence asset. Imprisoning terrorists would seem a better counter-terrorism option in the long run. In the 1973 debate in the UK on whether to repeal the death penalty in Northern Ireland, the House of Commons decided that executing terrorists, whose goal is often to martyr themselves, only increased violence and put security officers at risk. The House reasoned that executing persons convicted of terrorist-related acts increases the incidence of terrorism. For the House, terrorism's greatest weapon is popular support. 'Our most powerful weapon against terrorism', commented one observer, 'is our commitment to the rule of law. We must use the courts to make clear that terrorism is a criminal act, not jihad, not heroism, not holy war. And then we must not make martyrs out of murderers' (Stern, 2001).

A question connected with the debate on the use of the death penalty against 'terrorists' is whether torture should be used against terrorists. Most people would agree that torture is never to be used in any circumstance whatsoever. But, the radical fringe of those in favour of capital punishment would argue that in certain cases it is not easy to draw the line between torture and legal methods of coercion. They and rightists would argue that if strategies can be utilized to force the 'terrorist' to divulge information that is essential to the safety of the nation or the regime in place, then government has the responsibility to do everything possible to force the 'terrorist' to provide that information. They would argue further that when it comes to terrorism, national security concerns should trump all else. This somewhat fascist view would probably find favour with not a few African regimes.

CONCLUSION

UN human rights bodies are unanimous in their disapproval of the use of the death penalty for 'terrorist' offences. Critical analysis shows that the label 'terrorist' provides no analytical assistance on whether a crime is 'most serious'. Terrorist suspects are rarely afforded fair trial rights demanded by international standards. Death sentences passed on convicted 'terrorist' offenders are probably arbitrary and discriminatory. The use of the death penalty even for terrorism-related offences therefore breaches many international human rights standards that governments are under obligation to uphold even in the face of the global fight against terrorism. The death penalty would seem to be neither an appropriate nor a legitimate response to terrorist threats and actions.

Close monitoring of the actions of states by continental mechanisms for the protection of human rights would contribute towards ensuring full respect for human rights even while the state engages in combating terrorism. The AfComHPR has creatively established a number of special mechanisms modelled after those of the UN.[45] The work of these mechanisms is additional to the commission's activities carried out under its protective, promotional and interpretative mandates. From time to time the commission issues authoritative statements on the provisions of the charter, by way of 'principles and guidelines' and 'comments'.[46] Furthermore, in the discharge of its protective mandate, the commission has laid down a rich and impressive jurisprudence. It has dealt extensively with the subject of terrorism in its *Principles and Guidelines on Human and Peoples' Rights while Countering Terrorism in Africa.*[47] In 2005, it acknowledged that 'the acts, methods and practices of terrorism in all its forms and manifestations [are] aimed at the destruction of human rights, fundamental liberties and democracy'. But it noted with disapproval the 'legislation, measures and practices of states parties that may be inconsistent with the provisions of the ACHPR'.[48] It cautioned that in the long run, the measures could prove to be counterproductive in the fight against terrorism. It called on African states to ensure that the measures taken to fight terrorism fully comply with their obligations under the African Charter on Human and Peoples' Rights and other international human rights treaties, including the right to life, the prohibition of arbitrary arrest and detention, the right to a fair hearing, the prohibition of torture and other cruel, inhuman and degrading penalties and treatment, and the right to seek asylum.[49]

Special procedures and mechanisms of the commission have focused on promoting human rights within the framework of measures aimed at preventing and combating terrorism. Important human rights issues identified by the commission as requiring its special attention in the fight against terrorism include the right to life, the prohibition of arbitrary arrest and detention, the right to a fair hearing, the prohibition of torture and other cruel, inhuman and degrading penalties and treatment, and the right to seek asylum.[50] Strengthening the counter-terrorism measures of the African Commission is important. Equally important is widening the scope of the mandate of relevant special mechanisms[51] so that they are able to deal with a number of the more practical aspects of the fight against terrorism, tasks currently being undertaken by state parties. For example, relevant special mechanisms could be vested with a review mandate. The mandate would enable them to review domestic legislation on the fight against terrorism to ensure its conformity with provisions of the ACHPR as interpreted by the commission. The review process should include necessary suggestions on ways of harmonizing legislation that is at variance with relevant principles and guidelines set out by the commission (OHCHR, 2002).

The principle of complementarity is enshrined in the protocol establishing the African Court on Human and Peoples' Rights. The complementarity between the commission and the court should come in handy, enabling the commission to refer to the court cases it receives. On the basis of this principle, the commission may refer a communication to the court for review. The cross-transfer of cases between the two bodies fosters cooperation with respect to the interpretation to be given to the relevant provisions of the charter in the context of the fight against terrorism. This is a strategy available to the commission to ensure that a binding decision is made on the appropriate reparation to a victim of human rights violations.

Rule 118(3) of the Commission's Rules of Procedure allows the commission to submit a communication before the court against a state party. This provision has been used before.[52] It ought to be used more often by the commission to refer to the court cases of serious human rights violations such as those that frequently take place in states in the aftermath of a violent conflict, revolt or uprising. A more technical approach to the question of human rights protection in the context of the fight against terrorism could profitably involve constructive dialogue. Such a dialogue could be built around the PSC. Parties to the dialogue would include the political organs of the AU, the Regional Economic Commissions and African civil society.[53] The aim would be to improve cooperation on information exchange in the fight against terrorism.[54] Another aim would be to harmonize national anti-terrorism legislation with human rights instruments.

NOTES

1. UN Human Rights Council, 24th Session, Question of the Death Penalty: Report of the Secretary-General, 1 July 2013, A/HRC/24/18.

2. UN Human Rights Council, 5th Session, Civil and political Rights, including the Question of Disappearances and Summary Executions: Report of the Special Rapporteur on Extrajudicial, Summary or Arbitrary Executions, 29 January 2007, A/HRC/4/20.

3. Interim Report of the Special Rapporteur on Torture and Other Cruel, Inhuman or Degrading Treatment or Punishment, 9 August 2012, A/67/279.

4. UN Economic and Social Council, Substantive Session of 2010, *Capital Punishment and Implementation of the Safeguards Guaranteeing Protection the Rights of those Facing the Death Penalty*, 18 December 2009, E/2010/10, para. 54. Article 4(2) of the American Convention on Human Rights, for example, provides that the application of capital punishment 'shall not be extended to crimes to which it does not presently apply'. The Inter-American Court of Human Rights asserted in a 1983 Advisory Opinion that Art. 4(2) establishes 'a cut off as far as the penalty is concerned and doing so by means of a progressive and irreversible process applicable to states which have not decided to abolish the death penalty altogether as well as to those states which have done so'. (I/A Court H.R., Advisory Opinion OC-3/38 of 8 September 1983, *Restrictions to the Death Penalty (Article 4(2) and 4(4) of the American Convention on Human Rights)*, (Ser. A) No. 3 (1983, paras. 56, 59).

5. ICCPR, Article 6 and Safeguards Guaranteeing the Protection of the Rights of those facing the death penalty, approved by the UN Economic and Social Council Resolution 1984/50 of 25 May 1984.

6. UNGA, 67th Session, Report of the Special Rapporteur on Extrajudicial, Summary or Arbitrary Executions, 9 August 2012, A/67/275, para. 25: 'It is arbitrary to impose the death penalty where the proceedings do not adhere to the highest standards of fair trial'.

7. See also, ICCPR, art 14; European Convention on Human Rights, Art 6; Inter-American Convention on Human Rights, Art 8; the revised Arab Charter on Human Rights, Art 13; the Rome Statute; and Common Art 3(1)(d) of the 1949 Geneva Conventions. Certain aspects of the right to a fair trial have the status of customary international law.

8. The Office of the High Commissioner for Human Rights has stressed that under international and regional human rights law, 'the protection against arbitrary deprivation of life is non-derogable even in a state of emergency threatening the life of the nations' and thus even in the context of countering terrorism. See OHCHR,

Human Rights, Terrorism and Counter-Terrorism Factsheet, Factsheet No. 32; World Coalition, note 37 above.

9. Human Rights Committee, 72nd Session, General Comment No. 29: Article 4: Derogations during a State of Emergency, 31 August 2001, CCPR/C/21/ Rev.1/ Add. 11.

10. Human Rights Council, 14th session, Report of the Special Rapporteur on Extrajudicial, Summary and Arbitrary Executions, 20 May 2010, A/HRC/14/24, para. 51(a).

11. Cf. United Nations Counter-Terrorism Implementation Task Force, 'Right to a Fair Trial': http://www.un.org/en/terrorism/ctitf. accessed 9 Feb 2018.

12. UNGA, 63rd Session, Report of the Special Rapporteur on the Promotion and Protection of Human Rights and Fundamental Freedoms while Countering Terrorism, 6 August, 2008, A/63/223.

13. See, for example, Commission on Human Rights, 55th Session, Report of the Working Group on Arbitrary Detention, 18 December 1998, E/CN.4/1999/63, para. 80.

14. ICCPR, Articles 7, 10, 14 and 15; ACHPR, Article 5, 6, 7; ACHPR, *Principles and Guidelines on Human and Peoples' Rights while Countering Terrorism*, 2015, Parts 3 & 4.

15. Art 13(1) (2), Terrorism (Combating) Act 2000 of Sudan. For a discussion of the use of military courts outside the African continent, see also, C Martin, 'The Role of Military Courts in a Counter-Terrorism Framework: Trends in International Human Rights Jurisprudence and Practice' in Ana Maria Salinas et al (eds), *Counter-Terrorism: International Law and Practice*, Oxford, OUP, 2016, chap 26, p. 713.

16. Art 15(i) (2), Terrorism (Combating) Act 2000.

17. Art 17, Terrorism (Combating) Act 2000.

18. Civil Liberties organization et al v Nigeria, Communication No. 218/98, decision of 7 May 2001; *Forum of Conscience v. Sierra Leone*, Communication No. 223/98, Decision of 6 November 2000; *International Pen et al v. Nigeria*, Communication No. 137/94, 154/96 and 161/97, Decision of 31 October 1998; *Annette Pagnoule (on behalf of Abdoulaye Mazou) v Cameroun*, Communication No. 39/90, Decision of April 1997; *Civil Liberties Organization v Nigeria*, Communication 151/96, Decision of 15 November 1997; *Centre for Free Speech v Nigeria*, Communication No 206/97, Decision of 15 November 1999.

19. ACHPR, *Fair Trial Principles and Guidelines*, Section I (a) (c) 17.

20. ACHPR, Fair Trial Principles and Guidelines, s. A (1)3; ACHPR, *Principles and Guidelines on Human and Peoples' Rights while Countering Terrorism in Africa*, part 4, B, p. 24, 2015.

21. UNHRC, General Comment 29, para 16.

22. UNHRC, *Gonzalez del Rio v Peru*, Communication No. 263/1987, 28 October 1992, UN Doc CCPR/C/46/D/263/1987.

23. The OAU 1999 Convention on Preventing and Combating Terrorism does not define 'terrorism'. But it provides a long and undesirably very broad definition of 'terrorist act'. In terms of Article 1 (3), 'terrorist act' means: '(a) any act which is a violation of the criminal laws of a State Party and which may endanger the life,

physical integrity or freedom of, or cause serious injury or death to, any person, any number or group of persons or causes or may cause damage to public or private property, natural resources, environmental or cultural heritage and is calculated or intended to: (i) intimidate, put in fear, force, coerce or induce any government, body, institution, the general public or any segment thereof, to do or abstain from doing any act, or to adopt or abandon a particular standpoint, or to act according to certain principles; or (ii) disrupt any public service, the delivery of any essential service to the public or to create a public emergence; or (iii) create general insurrection in a State; (b) any promotion, sponsoring, contribution to, command, aid, incitement, encouragement, attempt, threat, conspiracy, organisation, or procurement of any person, with the intent to commit any referred to in paragraph (a)(i) to (iii)'.

24. UN General Assembly, *Note on International Protection*, para 39, 11 September 2002, UN Doc A/AC.96/965.

25. For the purposes of that convention, the term refugee means 'every person who, owing to well-founded fear of being persecuted for reasons of race, religion, nationality, membership of a particular social group or political opinion, is outside the country of his nationality and is unable or, owing to such fear, is unwilling to avail himself of the protection of that country, or not having a nationality, and being outside the country of his former habitual residence as a result of such events is unable or, owing to such fear, is unwilling to return to it'. The term refugee also applies 'to every person who, owing to external aggression, occupation, foreign domination, or events seriously disturbing public order in either part or the whole of his country of origin or nationality, is compelled to leave his place of habitual residence in order to seek refuge in another place outside his country of origin or nationality'. See Art I (1) and (2), OAU Convention Governing the Specific Aspects of Refugee Problems in Africa 1969, OAU Doc CM/267/Rev.1.

26. See, for example, UNCAT, *Josu Arkauz Arana v France*, Communication No. 63/1997, 5 June 2000, UN Doc CAT/C/23/D/63/1997 para 11.5 regarding the deportation of a suspected ETA terrorist from France to Spain.

27. South Africa, Tanzania, The Gambia, Kenya, and Nigeria.

28. Cf. Art. 8 (2) of the OAU 1999 Terrorism Convention.

29. Judicial opinions in *Case Concerning the Arrest Warrant of 11 April 2000 (Democratic Republic of the Congo v Belgium)* ICJ Rep. 2002, p. 3, recognize that 'subsidiary universal jurisdiction' has been provided as an obligation in a number of treaties on international crimes, including various kinds of terrorist activities. In a case of terrorist acts, for example, a state in whose territory a terrorist suspect is present must either extradite him to a state that has a link with the offence or prosecute the alleged offender itself: *aut dedere aut prosequi*.

30. OAU Convention on the Prevention and Combating of Terrorism 1999; 2004 Protocol to the OAU Convention on the Prevention and Combating of Terrorism; 2002 Protocol Relating to the Establishment of the Peace and Security Council of the African Union.

31. UNSC Res 1456 of 20 Jan 2003 (UN Doc S/RES/1456 para 6).

32. UN Human Rights Council, 24th Session, Question of the Death Penalty: Report of the Secretary-General (Secretary-General's Report), 1 July 2013, A/HRC/24/18.

33. Journalists arrested and imprisoned are accused of acting against government policy by reporting on widespread indiscriminate killing of civilians and systematic burning down of villages and towns by government forces in English-speaking Cameroons.

34. As of September 2017, an impressive number journalists from Ambazonia had already faced charges under Cameroun's 2014 anti-terrorism law. They were held in custody awaiting, under harsh conditions, for long periods often exceeding six months. In some cases, the detainees were held incommunicado for up to three months and invariably subjected to torture, cruel, inhuman or degrading treatment such as repeated physical assault, being stripped naked, hands handcuffed and feet shackled. They faced trial before the military court charged with terrorism or inciting terrorism. Government has repeatedly warned Ambazonians to stop discussing or writing articles on 'secession' or federalism or calling for educational and judicial reforms in Ambazonia, threatening to charge anyone who does so with 'propagating false information' under the anti-terrorism law. Angela, 'In Cameroon, anti-terror law is used to silence critics, suppress dissent' 20 September 2017 https://www.timeslive .co.za/ideas/2017-09-20-cameroon accessed 27/4/2018.

35. ACHPR, Comm. 54/91-61/91-96/93-98/93-164/97-196/97-210/98, *Malawi African Association, Amnesty International, Ms Sarr Diop, Union Internafricaine des Droits de l'Homme and RADDHO, Collectif des Veuves et Ayants-Droits, Association Mauritanienne des Droits de l'Homme v Mauritanie* (2000), paras. 93-100; ACHPR, *Principles and Guidelines on the Right to a Fair Trial and Legal Assistance in Africa* (section L: right of civilians not to be tried by military courts); *Principles and Guidelines on Human and Peoples' Rights while Countering Terrorism in Africa*, 2015, p.24.

36. Art 83 (A), Penal Code of 1937 as amended in 2010.

37. World Coalition Against the Death Penalty, *The Death Penalty for Terrorism – Detailed Fact Sheet*, July 2016.

38. UNGA, Issue of the Death Penalty: Secretary General's Report, No. A/HRC/24/18, 1 July 2013.

39. The death penalty for terrorism was also passed in Mali in 2011 under its 2001 Penal Code, in Mauritania under its 2010 Anti-Terrorism Law, in Morocco under its 1962 Penal Code as amended in 2007, in Sudan under its 2001 Law on Terrorism and in Tunisia under its 2015 Counter-Terrorism and Money-Laundering Law. Other countries that prescribe the death penalty for terrorism and terrorism-related offences include: Burkina Faso (1996 Penal Code), Central African Republic (2010 Penal Code), Eritrea (1957 Penal Code as amended in 1991), Gambia (2003 Anti-Terrorism Law as amended in 2008), Guinea (1998 Penal Code), Liberia (1976 Penal Code as amended in 2008), Libya (2014 Anti-Terrorism Law), Niger (2008 Law amending the Penal Code), Nigeria (2011 Anti-Terrorism (Prevention) Law), South Sudan (2008 Penal Code), Uganda (2002 Anti-Terrorism Law) and Zimbabwe (2002 Criminal Law).

40. For example, the death penalty was practiced in France from the Middle Age until 1977. In eighteenth-century France, the act of execution by guillotine was prevalent during the Revolution/Reign of Terror. But it failed to prevent crime.

41. Western powers often accuse some Middle East countries of sponsoring terrorism.

42. For example, Yakub Memon on 12 March 1993 exploded 12 bombs in Mumbai within 2 hours killing 257 people and seriously wounding 713. Timothy McVeigh in 1995 detonated explosives in Oklahoma City killing 168 people. Al-Qaeda operatives in 1998 bombed American Embassies in Kenya and Tanzania killing 224 people and wounding thousands. Al-Qaeda operatives on 11 September 2001 crashed two hijacked aeroplanes into the Twin Towers of the World Trade Centre in New York killing 2,996 victims and destroying both iconic towers. Four terrorists on 7 July 2005 bombed the London Tube killing 52 people. On 26 August 2011, Boko Haram detonated a car bomb explosion in the UN building in Abuja killing at least 21 people and wounding 60. On 21 September 2013, Al-Shabab attacked the Westgate shopping mall in Nairobi leaving 67 people dead and 175 wounded. On 2 April 2015, Al-Shabab stormed the Garissa University College in Kenya leaving 152 persons dead and at least 79 wounded. The Mogadishu truck bomb by Al-Shabab in October 2017 left 300 people dead and hundreds wounded.

43. Several delegates to the 30th session of the Human Rights Council made the observation that the death sentence does not serve any deterrent purpose in combating terrorism. They deplored the expansion of the use of the death penalty for terrorism-related crimes. They emphasized that counter-terrorism measures must be consistent with the common values of justice and human rights. They pointed out that a vague definition of terrorism contravened human rights. See A/HRC/30/21; World Coalition Against the Death Penalty, *The Death Penalty for Terrorism – Detailed Fact Sheet*, July 2016.

44. htps://www.israelnationalnews.com/News/News.aspx/238387 accessed 9 Feb 2018.

45. Such as special rapporteurs, working groups and focal points.

46. For example, the commission's comment on the right to life guaranteed under Article 4 of the African Charter.

47. The document was adopted in 2015 and published in 2016.

48. African Commission on Human and Peoples' Rights, *Resolution on the Protection of Human Rights and the Rule of Law in the Fight against Terrorism*, adopted at the 37th Ordinary Session, 21 November to 5 December 2005, para 11 of the Preamble.

49. African Commission on Human and Peoples' Rights, *Resolution on The Protection of the Human Rights and the Rule of Law in the Fight against Terrorism*, para 2. This resolution omits to mention freedom of expression as a consideration warranting particular attention in the framework of the fight against terrorism.

50. Cf. *Fair Trial Principles and Guidelines*; the *Robben Island Guidelines for the Prohibition and Prevention of Torture* (17-23 Oct 2002, ACHPR/Res. 61 (XXXII) 02); the *Protection of Human Rights Defenders in Africa* (21 Nov to 5 December 2005, ACHPR/Res. 83 (XXXVIII) 05); *Resolution on the Observance of a Moratorium on Capital Punishment* (1–15 Nov 1999, ACHPR/Res. 42 (XXVI) 99); *Declaration of Principles and Freedom of Expression in Africa* (1-15 Nov 1999, ACHPR/Res. 62 (XXXII) 99.

51. For example, the Special Rapporteurs on Freedom of Expression and Access to Information in Africa, on the Situation of Human Rights Defenders in Africa and on the Situation of Refugees, Asylum Seekers, Migrants and IDPs; the Working Group on the Death Penalty, Extrajudicial, Summary or Arbitrary Killings; and the Committee on the Implementation of the Robben Island Guidelines.

52. In March 2011, the commission referred to the court a complaint against Libya. The complaint alleged the bombing of Benghazi city by the Libyan air force and the arrest and detention of peaceful demonstrators following the popular uprising in that city against the government: *ACHPR v Great Socialist People's Libyan Arab Jamahiriya* (Application No. 004/2011, Order for Provision Measures of 25 March 2011).

53. For further discussion on this, see Ewi M.A. & Anton du Plessis, 'Criminal Justice Responses to Terrorism in Africa: The Role of the African Union and Sub-Regional Organizations', in Ana Maria Salinas et al (eds), *Counter-Terrorism: International Law and Practice*, Oxford, OUP, 2016, chap 36, p. 990.

54. Art 5, OAU Convention adopted in Algiers; Art 3 (h), (i), and (l), Protocol to the OAU Convention; Art 16 of the Peace and Security Council Protocol.

Part Four

AFRICAN APPROACHES TO CONFLICT RESOLUTION

Conflict resolution is the process of settling conflicts. In this endeavour, 'modern' and traditional tribunals, reconciliation, peace negotiations, peacekeeping, sanctions and so on are variously pressed into service.

Chapter 10

Some Indigenous Mechanisms for Settling Conflicts

The uncritical wholesale adoption of 'modern' methods of conflict prevention, management and resolution both at regional and continental levels in Africa suggests that these are considered the most suitable methods of resolving Africa's endemic conflicts. The rationale for doing so appears to be that 'modern' conflicts are deep, widespread, complex and capable of being addressed only by 'modern' strategies. However, more than half a century of efforts at conflict management and resolution through conventional peacekeeping and even mediation and negotiation have not achieved the expected spectacular results. In fact, in some cases, such as in Rwanda, Somalia, Angola, Darfur (Sudan) and the Congo Democratic Republic, those methods have been dismal failures. For some time now, therefore, African conflict scholars have been arguing that in spite of some of their shortcomings, African indigenous systems of conflict management and resolution are relevant even in the context of 'modern' conflicts and ought to be incorporated into mainstream conflict management strategies in Africa (Osaghae, 2000; Tuso, 2000; Mazrui, 1995; Menkhaus, 2000; Malan, 1997). This is a welcome attitudinal change although some have reservations about this shift in attitude in the context of intergenerational roles and conflict resolution, that is to say, the role of youths in the traditional approaches of conflict resolution (Babo, 2018).

Human societies ultimately deal with conflict by negotiating peace or imposing one. However, although 'peace' may be imposed by force, genuine peace does not come from the barrel of the gun but from truth-dialog and reconciliation using a variety of formal or informal processes. These processes may include direct and indirect talks, third-party mediation and spiritual intercession. In some cultures, recourse is sometimes had to marriage, sport, art, music or cultural exchanges, as tools of peace diplomacy. Traditional Africa apprehends conflict containment, management and resolution as based on concepts such as goodwill, togetherness, open and frank dialog, understanding, harmonious relationship, peace, the common good and community well-being. Africans believe that without awareness of societal good and harmony there can be no goodwill, without goodwill there can be no peace and without peace there can be no community well-being. Conflicts arise when any of these values is not respected. It then becomes the duty of the community to resolve the conflicts through age-old tested community processes.

In traditional Africa, long-established mechanisms exist for resolving conflicts and achieving reconciliation and peaceful co-existence within the community and between communities. Such mechanisms include the *palaver*, the *inkandla*, the *indaba*, the *kgotla*, the *gada* and the *mato oput*[1] and a host of others. These are prototypes of peace and reconciliation mechanisms in African traditional society. Community shared values constitute the philosophical underpinnings of these mechanisms and processes and account for their effectiveness in settling conflicts and achieving peace and reconciliation (Bah, 1994). The fundamental principles and practices that inform African traditional conflict resolution mechanisms are sometimes criticized as backward, underdeveloped, too flexible and uncertain. They are dismissed as ill-suited to deal with the changing nature and complexity of many contemporary conflicts experienced even by traditional communities. Examples given of such complex conflicts include mass killings, mass destruction of property, territorial disputes and competition over resources such as farmland, grazing land and water. This is a valid observation. But adaptability is one of the hallmarks of indigenous law and custom.

THE PALAVER IN WEST AFRICA

The *palaver*, or its other forms in the continent, is a traditional mechanism involving elders of the community summoned by the chief to meet at the chief's palace or some other designated place to resolve intra-community conflicts or problems. Being a long-established people-driven mechanism, it does not suffer from mistrust and lack of credibility. Its outcome is accepted and sustained by the people. The time for holding the palaver is usually determined by the community's seer or astrologer. The seer looks for an auspicious period and then informs the chief who then calls the meeting on a date within that period. It is believed that by calling the meeting within that time even the ancestors and the cosmic world play their respective parts in ensuring that peace and reconciliation are achieved.

At the behest of the chief, the village crier would sound the sacred gong or beat the sacred drum. This is a coded call to the elders, seasoned problem-solvers and peacemakers, to proceed at once to and forgather at the place where meetings of the kind are usually held. That place is normally under the shade of a sacred tree or under the roof of a specially sanctified house in the chief's palace. There, the sitting arrangement is either casual, ordered, semi-circle-like or horseshoe-like. The two sides to the dispute are also summoned to appear. As many community members are interested in the case also turn up since, in the words of an African aphorism, 'a case forbids no one'. Sometimes, before a matter is opened for discussions one of the elders, usually a spiritual officeholder, performs certain rituals intended to emphasize the awe and solemnity of the occasion. An elder who holds the spiritual office is a person who is well versed not only in customary law and procedures but also in esoteric practices. He would produce an object revered by the community and pour water or a liquid concoction on it, or sprinkle the object with the blood of a chicken killed on the spot for the occasion. When performing this ritual, he utters some such imprecation as: 'Whoever sees the truth or knows the truth in this matter and does not say it, may the gods visit him with condign punishment'.

A meeting of this nature is taken very seriously. The conversation could be and often is heated and even acrimonious. With deep listening, great patience, demonstrated honesty and humility, the elders approach the issues before them with flexibility and fairness, and speak with authority. Not infrequently they express their views in riddles, parables and aphorisms. The use of proverbs is not accidental. Elders, by virtue of the wealth of experience accumulated over the years, know the importance of proverbs in speeches. When they gather to discuss matters of the community, they use relevant proverbs as props to oratory (Sone, 2012: 112). Since proverbs constitute the soul of verbal art, an elder who has no command of proverbs is 'linguistically impotent' (Tala, 1999: 138). Proverbs used in peace and reconciliation processes are actually so many historical references, warnings and recommendations intended to ensure that compromise prevails.

Common sayings of the wise include: 'He who elects not to speak has accepted what is said'. 'When the cock crows continuously in the afternoon it means there is something wrong'. 'An irresponsible person does not rule over responsible people'. 'The stubborn fly follows the corpse to its grave'. 'When an elderly person eats without asking questions, he dies without knowing what killed him'. 'A child standing up or even on a tree, cannot see what an elderly person sees sitting down'. 'The mouth of an elder is without teeth but never without words of wisdom'. 'An elderly person listens, and then talks'. 'He who gives never lacks'. 'Youthfulness is like a stream, if not directed to its course it meanders'. 'A person without a link to family is like a tree without roots'. 'It is ignorance that made the rat to challenge the cat to a fight'. 'The venom of a viper does nothing to the shell of a tortoise'. 'The fact that the viper has left its environment does not mean it has lost its venom'. 'You can put a knife in a man and draw it out, but it does not matter how many times you say 'sorry', the wound is still there'. 'A man who lives by the bank of a river does not use spittle to wash his hands'. 'The protection of the young chick lies under the wings of its mother'. 'If the right hand washes the left hand, the left hand equally washes the right hand'. 'Foolish people have nothing to say in a discussion'. 'A verbal wound is as bad as a physical wound'. 'Words spoken in anger are words spoken in foolery'.

African elders are noted and appreciated for their dexterity and deep knowledge in traditional matters and practices, particularly as regards conflict management and resolution. This positive role is rightly extolled as the basis of the strength of traditional conflict resolution mechanisms. However, it appears from a case study of the Kroumen and the Lobi-Daraga in Côte d'Ivoire that youths in those communities doubt the effectiveness of traditional conflict resolution practices and challenge the traditional Bodior ritual of conflict resolution and peacemaking (Bado, 2018). The youths' reservation stems from one incident. In 2006, the traditional Bodior ritual of conflict resolution and peacemaking was performed to resolve the 1999 deadly conflict between Kroumen and Lobi-Daraga communities. Notwithstanding the performance of the ritual, more than ten years afterwards lingering mistrust persists and reconciliation and social cohesion remain elusive (Bado, 2018). Of course, this single study proves nothing. It is not generalizable even in the context of the attitude of African youths towards traditional conflict resolution mechanisms.

A conflict resolution meeting is a form of public hearing involving greater exposure and shaming. Problems are resolved in a spirit of humanity, without bitterness. In this way, peace is restored in the community and also between victim and offender. For, the process is designed to foster peace and promote reconciliation. It is not designed merely to punish the wrongdoer because human experience shows that retribution only excites bitterness and provokes a cycle of vengeance. The main thrust of the entire process is the desire to settle problems amicably. This is what underpins the African character. The legendary hospitality of the African and his accommodating spirit are the driving force behind his enduring quest for peace and reconciliation whenever community harmony is disrupted by conflict. The culture of elders sitting under a tree and talking until they achieve consensus is a tradition rooted in philosophy – the philosophy that agreement can be arrived at only when popular and broad-based discussions have been carried out exhaustively. For example, clan elders in northern Somalia play a critical role in reconciling warring factions. Elders in other parts of the continent also play a similar role. In Liberia, for instance, at several points in the civil war in that country, traditional rulers were involved in the search for peace along the lines of the famous 'palaver hut' reconciliatory meetings. Although this effort had limited success, the intervention of traditional leaders, with all the mythical powers they are assumed to have, made negotiations among the Liberian warlords possible (Osaghae, 2000).

In traditional Africa, whenever something goes wrong in society there is no censure without the community elders first searching for the right solutions through conversation or dialog. The peace and reconciliation process often goes on for hours on end or even for days. A critical aspect of the process is that there is always a break for an arranged common meal taken on the spot by everyone present. This eating and drinking together are intended to emphasize brotherhood and to promote reconciliation. Although talking may last long, it is open, frank, free, full and truthful. Africans, it has often been remarked, talk too much apparently unmindful of the fact that time is money. Indeed, when watching an African traditional dispute-settlement process, one is struck by what the lawyer would describe as the tedious prolixity and apparent irrelevance of witness testimony. Ordinarily, the African witness seems to relish a taste for oratorical display. African elders give the parties and their witnesses free rein to say at length what they want to say. Odd as it may seem, this wordiness, this loquacity conduces to reconciliation. This is because the parties are allowed to express themselves freely and fully, thereby experiencing a kind of catharsis. By speaking their minds fully, the parties feel an emotional release and feel relieved at having spoken their minds fully on the matter at hand.

The final phase in the process is the formal reconciliation of the parties. This takes the form of swearing reciprocal oaths. The act of oath-swearing is a kind of ritualizing remorse and forgiveness, a ritualizing of reconciliation. In swearing the oath, the 'offender' acknowledges wrongdoing, apologizes to the victim and promises to refrain from antisocial conduct. In swearing the oath, the victim accepts the apology and indicates that he has forgiven and 'forgotten'. This act of reconciliation is cemented by warm embraces (rather than the cold bear hugs and plastic smiles often seen in modern settings) and the sharing of drinks and a meal in a spirit of brotherhood. What started as a contentious matter then ends up as something of a feast! The common meal taken at the end signifies that the conflict has been resolved to the mutual satisfaction of both sides and that reconciliation of hearts and minds has been achieved. The purpose of the procedures employed in the *palaver* is not to establish the rights and wrongs of the case but to restore unity and harmony in order to effect a reconciliation of hearts and minds. The *palaver* thus always ends with a meal taken together (Bah, 1994, 1999).

The party found wanting is required to make a token 'fine', which is usually in the form of some livestock, the common 'currency' in traditional Africa. Since the process emphasizes reparation rather than retribution, the 'fine' is not considered or treated as punishment. It is not retribution. It is a symbolized but significant expression of admission of wrongdoing and an indication of acceptance to abide by the norms of the community. Where the facts of the matter warrant it, the party at fault is required to compensate the victim or his family by making a payment fixed by the elders or by mutual agreement between the parties. In some communities, a higher payment may be required following a killing.[2] In traditional Somalia, for example, when a person of one family murders a person of another family, he may be required to make amends to the family of the deceased (Menkhaus, 2000) which may take the form of giving the victim's family or clan as many as 120 camels, a deterrent payment. Payment of compensation to the victim or his family is meant to assuage injured feelings or physical impairment or loss of a blood relation. This is not a price for the lost life since human life is priceless. It is a material way of making amends, of apologizing, of saying 'I am sorry', to the aggrieved family. In contemporary peace and reconciliation discourse, this is known as 'restorative justice'. Restorative justice methods include victim-offender mediation of crimes, peacemaking process and family-group 'conversation' (Anyangwe, 2018).

Mediating disputes in African tradition involves the victim, the offender and the community. All three parties are involved in dealing with the question of restitution to the victim and the restoration of peace and harmony between offender and victim as well as between offender and the community at large. During the *palaver* process the elders get information from both sides of the conflict and figure out the things that connect, and those that divide, the parties. The elders look for causes and for core issues. They investigate the relationship between the parties. They recall previous cases as guide to their decision and adjust their analysis if no previous case on the subject is available. The process is underpinned by such values as respect for elders and traditions, respect for the wisdom of elders, community harmony, the interdependence of members of the community, patience and honesty, emotional healing and the moral duty of elders to settle disputes in the community. Strategies pursued in conflict resolution include the admonition to 'forgive and forget', holding the *palaver* at a divinely auspicious moment, making timely interventions so that the dispute does not get out of hand, ensuring that the discussion during the *palaver* is open and exhaustive and resorting to peace-building expedients such as compensation, intermarriage and rituals in the form of symbols and imprecations. The goals of the reconciliation process are to put an end to the conflict, to bring about a positive change in the relationship of the parties involved and in their relationship with the community, and to secure peace and stability in the short and long term through distributive, restorative and transformative justice.

Where the problem threatening the peace, tranquillity and stability of the community is considered to be of supernatural origin, the chief-in-council consults the village oracle for a prophecy. The oracle would find out from the ancestors the causes of the evil that has befallen the community. He or she would also ascertain the corrective measures that should be taken in order to restore peace in the land. The oracle, priest, soothsayer, seer, the messenger of the gods, or wise-one, as that person is variously called, is in many cases a woman. Women tend to be more psychic than men. The oracle acts as a medium between the visible world of the living and the invisible world of the departed ancestors. She is a medium between those worlds as the African conception of the cosmic world consists of three interconnected spheres of existence – that of the departed, that of the living and that of the unborn. The world so apprehended imposes an intergenerational responsibility on the living, a duty owed to both those who have gone and those who are still to come.

Often times, one hears broad and unqualified statements about the claimed underclass status of the woman in traditional African society. But many traditional African communities have a long history of women rulers, decision-makers, combatants, spiritual leaders and strong mothers and wives.

> The world's first civilizations arose from the spiritual, economic and social efforts of African women and African women, in turn, went on to lead those Matriarchal societies. . . . The rituals and culture of African matriarchy . . . promoted fecundity, exchange and redistribution. . . . Early man was unaware of the link between sexual intercourse and birth; they thought only women created life. Consequently, women were the first Gods, which formed the basis of gender equality in Africa. . . . African women are responsible for the greatest invention for the well-being of humankind, namely, food security. It is the practice of organized agriculture that made population expansion, food surpluses and civilization possible. . . . In the years just before colonization, African women were largely equal to men. (Chengu, 2015)

In the religious sphere, women in many African societies fulfil the role of a medium and so contribute to social solidarity and community cohesion. In some indigenous cultures, women became soldier-priestesses, leading men into battles. The Amazons of ancient Dahomey [since renamed Benin] were redoubtable women warriors. 'They left the care of the household chores to their effeminate husbands whilst they waged their formidable wars of conquest against tribal enemies' (Elias, 1956: 100). In the late 1980s, Museveni's government in Uganda had to contend with the rebellion led by a woman, Alice Lakwena, who had convinced tough Acholi warriors that she had religious powers that would protect them from bullets and these warriors followed her into battle. Similarly, in the 1960s, Alice Lenshina in Zambia was a leader priestess in defiance of the government of President Kenneth Kaunda. Each of these women was briefly the Joan of Arc of the communities they led into war. Although each was militarily defeated, as Joan of Arc and Boadicea were, it was sociologically significant that a woman could convince members of an ethnic community to follow her into war (Mazrui, 1995).

Generally, the African mother possesses a moral force as the homemaker and as guardian of community traditions. She wields considerable influence over the fate of members of the community. She mediates in local disputes. She is the backbone of peace and reconciliation processes. In some communities, the mother of twins is believed to have mystical powers and is often sent as a peace mediator to end conflicts. As a peace envoy, the African woman goes forth to mediate peace brandishing the leaves of the tree which, all over Africa, symbolizes peace.

> Universally, women have an important part in advancing the cause for Peace. As child-bearers, they seek the sort of conditions that enable people to live in peace. Through their tenderness, women present themselves as counsellors and custodians of human values. . . . The woman is the pivot of the family; she is the mother hen who is interested in gathering all her chickens at the sight of any hawk. . . . She is the moderate voice which closes all ranks; the trouble shooter who quells impending social upheavals. Even if the woman is presented in the Bible as the source of sin to the world through Eve, in the Garden of Eden, she is also presented as the source of salvation to the world through Mary in the birth of Jesus Christ. She is therefore a mother who cannot ignore her children dying in the streets for want of food, for want of shelter, for want of genuine democratic structures. Her pains of childbirth and pangs of motherhood urge her to create order where chaos is imminent. (Ngwane, 1996: 74)

In traditional African societies elderly women commonly organize themselves into 'secret' sisterhood associations to safeguard the interests of womanhood and of traditional morality by ritualistically dealing with anyone who breaches such interest or morality. Examples of traditional *soror* societies in the former British Southern Cameroons Trust Territory (Ambazonia) are the *anlu* in Kom, the *takumbeng* in Bamenda (Jua, 1993; Tanga, 2006; Fonchingong, 2007; Kah, 2011) and the *liengu* ('yengo' or 'jengu') among the Bakweri (Ardener, 2002). The *anlu* strategy for dealing with culprits is a ritualized form of permissible harassment through shaming and ridiculing.

> On a set day the women, dressed in leafy vines . . . paraded to the culprit's compound around five o' clock in the morning. There they danced, sang mocking and usually obscene songs composed for the occasion, and defiled the compound by defecation or urinating in the water storage vessels. If the culprit was seen, he could be pelted with stones or a type of wild fruit called 'garden eggs'. . . . They would prohibit the offender from visiting other compounds and instruct the people that no one should visit him. Sometimes the culprit fled to another compound or even another village, but *anlu* was continued. At the next weekly market, the women voluntarily attended, dressed in their vines, and publicly ridiculed the culprit by dancing and singing mocking songs. When his endurance was at an end, he put the *anlu* vines around his neck as a sign of capitulation and went to the women to plead for pardon. If his pleas and indemnity goods were accepted, they took him naked to the stream and bathed him . . . a ritualistic [cleansing] act which removed the guilt. (Ritzenthaler, 1960)

The *takumbeng*, a 'secret' association of elderly women, takes necessary action whenever the transgression committed by the culprit(s) is so grave that it is felt necessary to place a curse on him/them. The elderly women would parade stark naked in public and in front of the person, exhibiting their genitalia as a ritualistic curse inviting evil or even death to befall the hapless man or men. They pressurize the person by talking and singing: shaming and ridiculing. This curse operates on the mind of the culprit(s) and is usually effective. It is therefore a dreaded curse. Men run away or cover their faces whenever *takumbeng* women came out, for fear of seeing their nakedness and bringing a terrible curse upon themselves and their family.

Among the Bakweri, women are said to have more power on account of the very important society called *liengu* (or *yengo*) and in which only women are allowed to be members.

> *Yengo* is one of the highest holy spirits who is said to live only on the mountains and who is presumed to be a remnant from the time when the Boobees and Batekkas lived on the mountains. There was a young girl in Mapanja who was a member of *yengo*, by the way, a cousin of Mbua Mosekao. She had to stay in the yengu house for a year and a half, to become fully instructed in the mysteries of the *yengo* society. The yengo girls are not allowed to leave the yengo house. . . . No people were allowed, with the exception of medicine man who was their teacher, to enter the yengo house. (Ardener, 2002: 111)

Sisterhood organizations give added weight to the moral authority that the woman commands and the mystical powers she is deemed to possess. Partly for these reasons, the action of women for a specific objective, such as for peace and reconciliation, is never ignored. In today's conflict-torn countries of Africa, women are often vanguards for peace and reconciliation. They boldly march in the streets calling for peace, order and national reconciliation. They appeal to the enduring African values of tolerance, humaneness and harmony. In war-torn countries, women always form peace associations and march in the streets calling for peace. For example, the 'Women of Liberia Mass Action for Peace' led by Leymah Gbowee and the Mozambique 'Culture for Peace' led by Graça Machel made a significant contribution in ending the conflict in their respective countries.

THE MATO OPUT AMONG THE ACHOLI IN UGANDA

Ritualized forms of reconciliation exist in many East African communities. The best known is probably the *mato oput* in Uganda (Allen, 2008). Mato Oput is both a process and a ritual ceremony. Its aim is to restore relationships between clans that would have been affected by either an intentional murder or accidental killing. It helps to bring together the two conflicting parties with the aim of promoting forgiveness and restoration, rather than revenge (Tom, 2006). The mechanism is thus ostensibly not punitive. It does not aim at establishing whether an individual is guilty or not, rather it seeks to restore marred social harmony in the affected community. The offending party is simply required to publicly acknowledge wrongdoing. Once the party has accepted responsibility for their deviant behaviour they are then welcomed back into the community.

> *Mato Oput* involves the drinking of a concoction of the blood of a sheep and a bitter root. This is shared between former adversaries only after elaborate negotiation and when compensation has been agreed as an expression of remorse and indication that the conflict has been resolved. The sharing is done by representatives of both sides of the conflict. *Mato Oput* occurred only rarely and historically after murder within a moral community rather than after a local war. (Allen, 2008)

The Mato Oput ceremony is conducted because it is believed that after the ceremony the hearts of the offender and the offended will be free from holding any grudge between them. Although it has various forms across different clans, its common characteristics include the slaughtering of a sheep provided by the offender and a goat provided by the victim's relatives. The two animals are cut into halves and then exchanged by the two clans who then drink the bitter herb known as 'oput'. The bitter herb is drunk to symbolically wash away bitterness. Drinking of the bitter herb is a symbolic act that the two conflicting parties accept the bitterness of the past and promise never to taste such bitterness again (Tom, 2006; IRIN, 2005; Lacey, 2005). The payment of compensation follows the ceremony. The victim or his or her family is compensated for the harm done, for example, in the form of cows or cash. It is believed that *mato oput* brings true healing in a way that formal justice system cannot (IRIN, 2005; Lacey, 2005).

The acknowledged relevance and importance to post-conflict community peace and healing commended the *mato oput* for integration into the 2006–2008 Juba Comprehensive Peace Agreement between the Ugandan government and the enduring but elusive Ugandan insurgent group known as the Lord's Resistance Army. The Accountability and Reconciliation part of that agreement describes *mato oput* as the traditional rituals performed by the people of the Acholi tribe to reconcile parties formerly in conflict, after full accountability. The parties to the agreement committed themselves to promote appropriate reconciliation measures to address issues arising from within or outside Uganda with respect to the conflict. Under the agreement also, the government recognized the centrality of the traditional justice and reconciliation framework and committed itself to promote truth-telling and to support traditional reconciliation interlocutors. The mechanism was considered as supplementary rather than complementary to the peace process.

The government of Uganda's recognition of the *mato oput* mechanism does not come as a surprise. Generally, African states acknowledge and implicitly or explicitly support traditional conflict resolution mechanisms. In Kenya, for example, the Wajir District has a mechanism for dealing with conflicts in governance and traditional competition for resources. In 1994 civil society groups in that district formalized the mechanism by establishing what became known as the Wajir Peace and Development Committee. The committee has since received consistent support from the state (AHSI, 2004, 5: 4). This was a welcome initiative by civil society groups in the area because it signified their commitment to providing the basic necessities of rural development and filling the yearning gap of conflict prevention and resolution in the district in question. This may be contrasted with most African NGOs that are urban-focused and have rarely ventured into the area of community development and conflict prevention and resolution.

THE GADA SYSTEM AMONG THE OROMO IN ETHIOPIA

The *gada* system is a traditional process of conflict management among the Oromo ethnic people of Ethiopia. The system goes through thirteen identifiable steps described by one author taking the example of a potential inter-family conflict triggered by the murder of an individual (Tuso, 2000). When violence causes the death of an Oromo person the kin both of the offender and of the deceased become anxious to avoid escalation of the conflict into a cycle of violence. Community members immediately approach the leadership of the community for immediate intervention. They demand that the offender's kin conform to the Oromo traditional law of collective responsibility where a kinsman causes the death of another person. This demand is based on the fact that under Oromo traditional law, every kinsman of a killer is deemed a party to the killing and therefore liable for revenge by the victim's kin. Community members however act to avoid spilling more blood. The Oromo believe that spilling Oromo blood would poison the total environment, risking the health of all community members.

> Thus, it becomes important to recruit *jarsa biya* (elders) of the killer's kin groups to assure the kin of the dead person that they are working on the case in compliance with the law (*sera*) and custom (*adda*), that they will soon begin criminal procedures (gumma), and that they are eager to work earnestly on reconciliation (*arara*). (Tuso, 2000)

At the eighth step of the *gada* system, the elders would have heard the case, in open session and then in camera with the conflicting parties, and would have recessed to deliberate among themselves. At step eight, the elders pronounce the verdict. They do so in a manner that seeks to bring the expected peace and reconciliation outcome between the parties and restoration of peace and harmony among the spirits of the people, the deity and the ecosystem. If murder was committed, the blood payment price would be determined.

> Usually in such a case, the family members of the dead person, with assistance of the kin and clan wise men, will put forward the demands for the price. However, the guilty party may petition for lenience, and the elders usually support moderation in such matters and may lean towards recommending more symbolic gestures in paying the price rather than profit making. All these things are sorted out ahead of time. (Tuso, 2000)

The guilty part is then implored by the spokesperson of the elders to accept wrongdoing. The guilty party readily accepts his guilt. His relatives and the wise from his community would have urged him to do. Thereafter, the elders turn their attention to the aggrieved party and implore him to accept the truth, to forgive and to be reconciled. Since it is in everyone's interest to move towards reconciliation, the aggrieved party usually readily accepts. The Oromos believe that receiving continued blessings from above is dependent upon their forgiving, forgetting and totally reconciling, making sure that family and clan members will not inherit bitterness and animosity as a result of the conflict. The parties at loggerhead and members of their respective communities then gather for the ceremony of reconciliation. Drink is prepared for the occasion. The participants share the drink as the elders conduct the ceremony. The last step in the long process is bonding.

> The activities the conflicting parties undertake during the post-reconciliation ceremony are also very critical. For example, if the conflict has involved the loss of human life, family members usually will take further steps to overcome the memory of bitterness and animosity resulting from the conflict. Such actions may involve marriage arrangements or child adoption between the family members. Another type of activity involves providing lifelong services to a family member whose livelihood has been affected seriously as the consequence of the death of a person in the conflict. For example, if a mother has lost her son, depriving her of the natural help she would normally receive from him, the person and the family responsible for the death will provide lifelong assistance on the farm and other areas of her need. (Tuso, 2000)

SHARED AFRICAN VALUES

In traditional Africa, rituals are also performed to prevent the escalation of inter-community tension and to effect reconciliation. Emissaries are sent to an adversary to show willingness to engage in peace dialog and reconciliation. They take with them objects like kola nuts, cowries, palm wine, African beer in kegs or calabashes and other items or paraphernalia. On arrival, the lead emissary performs ritual ceremonies after which he presents to the adversary the various objects the emissaries have brought along with them. These small items are in fact symbolic 'olive branches' inviting the other side to the dialog table. Even when hostilities appear inevitable, there is no rush to take up arms.

> The actual declaration of war was often postponed for several moons. The enemy was offered a choice in the shape of objects symbolizing war or peace, such as a quiver of arrows or two sheaves of millet or maize. The use of weapons, which was controlled, was both gradual and selective. Before the start of hostilities, a prisoner of war was released, who could, if the opportunity arose, act as a go-between, trying to restore normal relations between the parties to the conflict. An effort was also made to prevent positions from hardening and becoming non-negotiable. (Bah, 1994, 62: 14)

Border areas between communities or tribes are frequently sources of conflict over land. The usual way of preventing encroachment on land by a contiguous community is by sacrificing an animal on a spot in the contested border area. The animal is sacrificed in the presence of the two communities concerned. Alternatively, a sacred tree is planted on the particular spot as a symbol of peace. Sometimes cairns are planted for the same purpose. Today, in cities all over Africa, demonstrators march carrying branches or leaves of these trees as symbol of peace, indicating they march and sing for peace.

The peace and reconciliation processes in traditional Africa have been criticized as 'feudal', localized and limited, and therefore not replicable in the management and resolution of 'modern' conflicts.

> [T]here seem to be serious and even insurmountable obstacles to the application of traditional strategies to modern conflicts. These limits derive for the most part from the characteristics of conflict management in traditional societies. . . . The first of these is that management strategies were localised and particularistic, and that in spite of the similarities and common assumptions they involved, few, if any, strategies were generalised beyond local boundaries. The absence of a generalised model of conflict management may indeed be regarded as one of the weaknesses of traditional systems . . . In the postcolonial period, traditional conflict management strategies remain localised, although the exigencies of colonial rule necessitated the generalisation of practices among enlarged ethnic groups. . . . The relevance and applicability of traditional strategies have been greatly disenabled by the politicisation, corruption, and abuse of traditional structures, especially traditional rulership, which have steadily delegitimised conflict management built around them in the eyes of many, and reduced confidence in their efficacy. . . . The limit placed on localisation is reinforced by the fact that modern states in Africa, with the diverse groups which compose them, do not have the common moral and customary order on which conflict management is hinged in the traditional society. . . . This in turn points to another area where traditional conflict management systems had shortcomings, since contests for power were often only resolved through splitting the polity and vanquishing the rivals. Finally, the expansive nature of modern conflicts also limits the extent to which traditional strategies can be applied. (Osaghae, 2000)

This is a robust critique. But traditional strategies are effective in managing and resolving intra- and inter-community conflicts within the modern state. There is no reason to believe that if traditional strategies are properly harnessed and adapted, they will not continue to be effective even at the wider national level. Tradition strategies are underpinned by values shared by the community. First, the peace and reconciliation processes are largely based on the tested principles and practices of customary law. This is a living law, the nature of which is organic, flexible and adaptable. In customary law, the concept of individualization of punishment is diluted in instances where the offender and his extended family (or clan) are held accountable for a crime (e.g., stealing stock, poultry or farm produce) on the sufficient reasoning that the family benefits or stands to benefit from the crime or its proceeds. The family takes the benefit and must also take the burden. Family solidarity means solidarity even in times of adversity when a family member is in trouble. For example, the family or kin group of a murderer is very much involved in the *gada* cultural institution practised by the Oromo people of Ethiopia.

> The gada system of conflict management moves through thirteen identifiable steps on its way to managing and resolving conflict and arriving at arara (reconciliation) so that harmonious relations cane be restored among conflicting parties, God the Creator, the community, and surrounding world. (Tuso, 2000)

In modern law one would say the accountability of the family is based on the theory of complicity, that is, accomplice before or after the fact. In customary law jurisprudence, however, this is not just a question of visiting the family with the iniquities of the individual, nor is it an application of a form of collective punishment. It is not vicarious liability either, since it is not the family alone but both the individual and the family who are held accountable.

Second, contrary to early anthropological scholarship on African society and the views of some of Africa's 'leaders', democracy is not alien to governance in traditional Africa. For instance, Kikuyu society and Xhosa society, described respectively by Jomo Kenyatta in his *Facing Mount Kenya* (1936) and by Nelson Mandela in his *Long Walk to Freedom* (1994), fittingly illustrate the democratic nature of African society. The democratic process in traditional African society emphasizes public and collegial decision-making and a strong organized community where group interest is always put above individual interest, while at the same time individual rights are protected by community ethics. 'The perception of belonging to a group is almost always paramount over a sense of individuality. One acts as a member of a group and is responsible to that group' (Solanke, 1982).

The end purpose of reconciliation is thus to demonstrate that the group interest is above the interest of the individual. African communitarianism emphasizes African values, consensus, family, community cohesiveness and kinship ties rather than individualism. Living in Africa, it has been said, means giving up an individualist, competitive, egotistic, aggressive and dominant way of life so as to live alongside other men in peace and harmony with the living and the dead, with the natural environment and with the spirits which people that environment or which endow it with life (Khushalani, 1983). African social and traditional religious beliefs rest on the enduring concept of the individual as part of a corporate group. Indigenous culture encourages *ubuntu*, that is, fellowship and sharing; it encourages *harambe* or *njangi*, meaning, coming or pooling together. There are always kinship obligations and clan responsibilities. That is why the whole idea of economic individualism finds it difficult to thrive in African society. This value system has drawn from the human rights activist the criticism that the role of the individual in African society is largely insignificant, that it is within the group that individuals find security and that African society upholds and promotes group rights at the expense of individual rights. This is of course hyperbole. Just because traditional African society conceives of an individual as part of a corporate group or considers group interest as above individual interest does not mean the individual is considered insignificant. In any event, this African value system conduces to the achievement of peace and reconciliation because it is predicated on human interdependence.

Third, communitarianism as an indigenous shared value emphasizes social justice, social management, the popular participation of all members in community activities, the individual's reaction and relationship with other individuals in the community, and the community as the source of morality and social values. This has produced a fundamental cultural ethic of mutual assistance and cooperation in the means of production. This is what underscores the concept of community solidarity. Community solidarity means community brother/sisterhood or what is now commonly referred to as African brotherhood. Such a value system conduces to reconciliation because although siblings might quarrel, they nevertheless remain siblings and are bound to get on together in a spirit of forgiveness and siblinghood. This spirit of forgiveness is what Mazrui calls 'Africa's short memory of hate' (Mazrui, 1995). He submits that perhaps the most important of Africa's cultural resources or traditional mores which may be tapped to help contain or resolve conflict is Africa's short memory of hate. Africans, he points out, have frequently displayed a remarkable capacity to 'let bygones be bygones'. He gives some high-profile examples to illustrate his point.

> Jomo Kenyatta was imprisoned for years by the British and denounced by a British Governor as a 'leader unto darkness and death'. However, when he was finally released from detention to lead a newly emerging independent Kenya, Kenyatta became one of the country's leading Anglophiles. He . . . crowned his metamorphosis with the publication of a book entitled Suffering without Bitterness. Nelson Mandela lost nearly three decades of the best years of his life imprisoned under the white man's laws. But he came out of prison in 1990 ready to forgive and forget provided apartheid was ended. . . . Ian Smith in old Rhodesia unleashed the horrors of a Unilateral Declaration of Independence (UDI) upon his people, and was therefore instrumental in initiating a war in which thousands of Africans were killed. When . . . Zimbabwe became independent in 1980, this architect of the blood-letting UDI was not tried . . .

but became a member of parliament of the new Zimbabwe and . . . a beneficiary of the African's short memory of hate. As the Nigerian civil war was coming to an end, many people expected 'rivers of blood' in the former Biafra resulting from vengeance perpetrated by the victorious Federal side. . . . There was no free-for-all orgy of revenge. There were no Nuremburg trials. . . . Interestingly, . . . Africa's rapid moments of forgiveness are not a matter for headlines. From the point of view of global journalism, to kill is news, to forgive is not. A shot is a story, an embrace seldom worth recounting. Africa's short memory of hate is therefore not celebrated internationally. Nevertheless, this limited memory of animosity is an important cultural resource, a valuable traditional more, for future conflict resolution. (Mazrui, 1955)

Equality within the community has always been central to the traditional African way of living. African traditional culture is not attuned to individual competition, but to cooperation within the community. That is why in all rural African societies one finds cooperative self-help associations for clearing, farming and harvesting farmlands; for building homes and other shelters; for saving money (thrift associations); and even for pooling resources to educate a child (educational grant). Like the saying goes, it takes a village to educate a child. Again, such an ethos conduces to the achievement of peace and reconciliation.

Other African attributes that conduce to peace and reconciliation are religious and racial tolerance, dialog, political accountability and the principle of economic sharing. Before the introduction of Christianity and Islam in Africa, the continent experienced no religious wars. Even today, it seems religion is divisive mainly when it reinforces other fault lines or differentiations such as ethnicity or party-political allegiance. In some states in West, Central and East Africa, for example, Christianity and Islam simply reinforce the ethnic or geographical divide between north and south. In Nigeria, Christianity tends to reinforce Igbo identity since almost all Igbo are Christians, while Islam tends to reinforce Hausa-Fulani identity given that almost all Hausa-Fulani are Muslims. In pre-2010 Sudan, Islam and Christianity reinforced the ethno-cultural differences between the north and the south. But otherwise, in Africa, religious consideration is generally not a factor that is seriously taken into account in electing or appointing to public office. Senegal is 80% Muslim but it had a Roman Catholic president (Leopold Sedar Senghor). Muslims had no problem with that. Even when Senegal had a Muslim president (Diouf and also Wade) each had a wife who was not only white but a Christian. Again, Muslims had no problem with that. Côte d'Ivoire, half Muslim and half Christian, now has a Muslim president, Ouattara, but his wife is white and a Christian. In Tanzania the Muslim half of the population has a better record of accepting the leadership of Julius Nyerere (a Roman Catholic) than the Christian half had of accepting the leadership of Ali Hassan Mwinyi (a Muslim). Added to this Muslim-Christian dichotomy in sub-Sahara Africa is another religious component that consists of partial or full allegiance to African traditional religion. This is ecumenicalism at work in Africa (Mazrui, 1995). However, the ethnicity factor often comes into play, and the reason for this is the question of identity.

African culture promotes love, reconciliation and racial tolerance. Africans are probably the only people who have never aspired to conquer and dominate other peoples and who practically embrace other peoples. African societies are thus perhaps the least guilty of racial conduct against other races. In fact, Africans in history have been victims of racism, slave trade and colonial oppression.

> Battered and bastardized through slavery, divided and denigrated through colonialism, de-personalized and dehumanized through Apartheid; and continuously exploited and robbed through neo-colonialism, the African in his short-term hate memory, has forgiven these humiliations to accommodate a universal culture and a universal family in our global village. Most of our African leaders graduated from the confines of prisons, into which they had been thrown by colonial masters but from which they came with gentle words of forgiveness. (Ngwane, 1996: 162)

CONCLUSION

The number and intensity of conflicts in the world continue to escalate, challenging peace practitioners to find the most appropriate approach that would end them and ensure reconciliation, good neighbourliness and enduring peaceful co-existence. The subject of mechanisms for conflict resolution, peace and reconciliation continues to be of interest in transitional justice scholarship in Africa because of the seemingly endless violent conflicts in the continent. The paradox is that although credible, effective and time-tested mechanisms exist in rural Africa for securing peace and reconciliation, the state in Africa has failed to tap into those mechanisms in the management of conflicts.

Conflict resolution mechanisms in rural Africa are considered by the state as complementary to, and not a substitute for, conventional criminal justice processes. However, it is well to bear in mind that for people living in a close-knit community such as one finds in rural Africa, public expression and acknowledgement of wrongdoing may in itself be as significant as a judicial criminal process because it reflects negatively not only on the wrongdoer but also on his family, kindred or clan. Also, the person responsible for the physical act of killing may be more psychologically relevant from the point of view of accountability than the more remote person who ordered the killing. Furthermore, in communities where formal policing and the conventional court system are non-existent or have collapsed or are geographically remote, as in most of rural Africa, victims of crime turn to their local chiefs as representing a means of redress that is more accessible and more trustworthy than appealing to an unreliable and corrupt system of criminal justice. In many communities, traditional justice mechanisms have therefore assumed an enhanced significance in resolving conflicts as well as in building and safeguarding peace and stability. African traditional peace and reconciliation practices are significant not only at personal level but also in healing the community and in pre-empting the dangers of escalatory revenge. These practices are an acknowledgement of the fact that reconciliation looks and speaks to the future, whereas accountability is preoccupied with the past. The past is yesterday but the future is tomorrow which must be safeguarded for long-term social stability.

NOTES

1. The *palaver* in West Africa; the *inkandla*, *Indaba* and *kgotla* in Southern African among the Zulu, Xhosa and Twana peoples, respectively; and the *mato oput* in East Africa. Etymologically, *palaver* comes from the Spanish word *palabre*, which means 'talk'. *Indaba* is the Zulu/Xhosa word for 'talk', lengthy discussion or meeting. It has the same meaning and serves the same purpose as *palaver*.

2. In some communities, an offer of payment for murder is considered 'blood money' and is never accepted by family members of the deceased.

Chapter 11

Indigenous System and Transitional Justice
Rwanda's Gacaca

INTRODUCTION

Transitional justice seeks to address challenges that confront society within a period of political change. It is characterized by various responses that seek to confront the wrongdoings of repressive predecessor regimes. Such responses include truth commissions, prosecutions, amnesty and traditional applications of justice. In post-conflict transitional justice practice, the desiderata of restorative justice[1] as well as truth and reconciliation are considered the foundations of lasting peace in a society fractured by serious conflict. The goals of a transitional justice system could be several. One of them is setting the historical record straight from the accounts of events given by victims and perpetrators. Others are ensuring accountability for misdeeds, deterring potential perpetrators from future criminality, reconciling perpetrator and victim in order to put final closure on the turbulent past, helping rebuild and heal broken individual and community relations and achieving restorative justice which is not an end in itself but a means to ends such as peace and reconciliation. These goals are considered critical in satisfying the retributive demands of society, deterring future criminality, eradicating the culture of impunity, assuaging bruised feelings and helping to rebuild dislocated relations at individual and community levels.

In this quest, states emerging from conflict often have to consider two seemingly opposing exigencies – the exigency of accountability with its emphasis on retribution and the exigency of peace and national reconciliation with its emphasis on amnesty or immunity. This ambivalence is reflected in the types of transitional justice mechanisms established by those African states that have recently experienced violent conflicts resulting in a deeply fractured and divided society. Examples are the situations experienced in

Burundi, Central African Republic, Ivory Coast, Kenya, Liberia, Libya, Sierra Leone, South Africa, South Sudan, Rwanda and Uganda. In some of these countries, a transitional justice mechanism was set up as an ad hoc judicial or quasi-judicial body. The body was mandated to promote reconciliation by granting amnesty to perpetrators of minor offences who confessed their wrongdoing. Additionally, the body was mandated to satisfy society's demand for retribution by holding perpetrators of the more serious offences accountable for their crimes, especially if the perpetrators showed no remorse. In some other countries, such as Ivory Coast, for example, the ad hoc mechanism was in the nature of a commission of public inquiry. Its mandate was to ascertain the truth of past criminality to grant amnesty to perpetrators who confessed and pleaded for forgiveness, to recommend for prosecution perpetrators who showed no remorse for their misdeeds, and, overall, to achieve the objective of national peace and reconciliation.

In its ongoing fight against the elusive rebel Lord's Resistance Army (LRA), the Uganda government adopted a carrot-and-stick approach. In 2000, it passed an Amnesty Act to facilitate the grant of amnesties to LRA soldiers. This reconciliatory approach was a bait meant to lure LRA rebels from the bush and end the insurgency. The strategy went hand in hand with certain accountability measures such as military action against the rebels, referral of the LRA case to the ICC in 2003 and the establishment in 2011 of an international crimes' division in the High Court of Uganda to try rebels for the most serious crimes perpetrated by them. The mandate of similar commissions established elsewhere was not dissimilar. The Liberia Truth and Reconciliation Commission was established in 2006 to promote national peace, security, unity and reconciliation. The Sierra Leone Truth and Reconciliation Commission, established at the end of the civil war in January 2002, was mandated to facilitate national healing by enabling victims and perpetrators of atrocities during the civil war to tell their stories. As in the case of Liberia, the Commission granted conditional amnesties to minor perpetrators of crimes during the civil war. A special court for Sierra Leone, established in 2002 with the assistance of the UN, was vested with jurisdiction to try persons with the greatest responsibility for the commission of crimes against humanity, war crimes and serious violations of international humanitarian law, as well as crimes under relevant Sierra Leonean law committed within the territory of Sierra Leone since 30 November 1996. Kenya's Truth, Justice and Reconciliation Commission (2008–2013) sought to promote peace, justice, national unity, healing and reconciliation. Innovatively and principally, it also investigated economic injustices as it was believed that the root cause of the 2008 post-election violence lay in economic crimes, particularly the misappropriation of land (Lanegran, 2015, 6(4): 63). However, Kenya's Truth Commission had no power to grant amnesty. Its recommendatory power was confined to recommending amnesty for some perpetrators under limited conditions and prosecution of some other perpetrators.

The Rwanda *gacaca* mechanism, like the South African Truth and Reconciliation Commission that preceded it, has received scholarly attention. While the *gacaca* mechanism stressed accountability, it also sought to achieve national peace and reconciliation. It was not a truth and reconciliation commission *stricto sensus*. It did not hold public hearings to determine who merited amnesty and who needed to be prosecuted. Rather, it sought to achieve national reconciliation by prosecuting suspected perpetrators of heinous crimes, thereby signalling non-tolerance of impunity. However, trials took place not in the conventional criminal courts but in revamped customary criminal tribunals directed to emphasize both accountability and national reconciliation. Rwanda's post-conflict peace and reconciliation mechanism insisted on accountability but at the same time encouraged confession as a trade-off for a significant reduction of punishment.

The genocide in Rwanda in 1994 claimed about 800,000 lives in just a matter of weeks, sending shock waves around the world. The new government that had just come to power decided to take appropriate measures to deal with the perpetrators of the genocide. It insisted on accountability, strongly arguing that eradicating the culture of impunity was a condition *sine qua non* for ending once and for all the vicious cycle of violence that had plagued Rwanda for a long time. The *génocidaires* and their accomplices had to be prosecuted and punished. The government was not persuaded that the South African truth and reconciliation model under which individual amnesties could be granted to offenders commended itself to Rwanda for adoption. The government rejected that model on the reasoning that only after the guilty had been punished would it then be possible for the victim and the innocent to create a joint future together (Uvin, 2003: 116). A major problem that stood in the way of criminal accountability was that the criminal justice system in the country had practically collapsed and heavy funding had to be sourced to capacitate judges, prosecutors, lawyers, crime investigators and police officers. Much funding was also needed to reform the justice system, construct courthouses and prisons, and provide logistical support and judicial salaries. Government therefore embarked on a fast-tracking criminal justice reform programme. This took about two years to complete. The prosecution of suspects began by the end of 1996 and by mid-2001 about 3,500 persons had been tried (Uvin, 2003: 116). The international community lent support by establishing the ICTR to try those most criminally responsible for the genocide. Later, the ICC was created with jurisdiction to try genocide, war crimes, crimes against humanity and aggression. At the UN, there was adumbrated a new doctrine known as the Responsibility to Protect (R2P)

(Clark & Kaufman, 2009). For its part, the Rwandan government figured out how to deal with thousands of genocide cases not referable to the ICTR.

GACACA TRIBUNALS

Practical necessity more than anything else impelled the Rwandan government to use the *gacaca* mechanism as a tool for the prosecution of genocide suspects. The Arusha Peace Agreements, signed in 1993 between the then Rwandan government and the Rwanda insurgency, made provision for the establishment of a National Unity and Reconciliation Commission (NURC). The commission was duly established in 1999 by a law of 12 March which mandated it to promote lasting unity and reconciliation through public dialog. This mandate was consistent with the new government's declared policy of national unity and reconciliation. The policy was adopted as a national program of action designed to bring about post-genocide social reintegration and peaceful co-existence among Rwandans. Truth-telling was considered a high value in national healing. The conviction was that truth creates confidence among people and progressively allows them to live in harmony (National Unity & Reconciliation Commission, 2000). At one of the early public meetings of the NURC, it was realized that detainees on suspicion of genocide and other murders were so many that the cases could not possibly be disposed of for decades in the conventional criminal justice system. At the time of the genocide in 1994, there were only 244 judges and 12 prosecutors in the whole country. It was practically impossible for this small number of judicial personnel to try the approximately 130,000 persons detained on suspicion of genocide. As a palliative, a special law was passed to enable cases to be disposed of with dispatch. That law guaranteed a reduced sentence for offenders who pleaded guilty, thereby encouraging guilty pleas. Further, a crash training program was rolled out, enabling an additional 841 judges and 210 prosecutors to be quickly trained.

In spite of this significant increase in the number of judicial and prosecuting personnel, the courts were only able to dispose of 600 cases per annum. As of the year 2000, there were more than 129,400 cases still pending. At the rate of processing 600 cases every year it was going to take over 200 years to dispose of all the pending cases! Besides, more detainees were dying in prison each year than were judged, and the heavy burden of feeding the thousands of detainees continued to fall on their relatives. This was socially, economically and politically costly for the government and society (National Unity & Reconciliation Commission, 2000). Faced with this hard reality, the government seriously considered any available feasible alternative option that would enable it to overcome these difficulties and at the same time achieve its stated accountability and sentencing goals in this matter. These goals included the eradication of the culture of impunity through an appropriate sentence for perpetrators, the restoration of national unity and harmony fractured by the genocide and the imposition of a form of sentence that would not only be punitive but also reparative in the sense that it would assist the country's economy. That form of sentence is communal labour or service, *les travaux d'intérêt général*, which in Rwanda involved working in the fields and plantations as well as assisting in the construction of rural roads and public buildings. Community work is a common activity in traditional African society, but it is undertaken as a civic duty rather than as a form of punishment. It was against this backdrop that the government decided to adopt, adapt and modernize the traditional community-based conflict resolution mechanism known as *gacaca*, a system in which members of the community played a significant role (National Unity & Reconciliation Commission, 2000).

In traditional Rwanda, the *gacaca* mechanism was used to mediate inter-family squabbles, minor conflicts and petty offences involving a few people. The primary goal of the process was reconciliation and community harmony, not punishment. The traditional g*acaca* did not deal with cases involving serious crimes, let alone killings of genocidal proportions. In the aftermath of the genocide, however, the *gacaca* mechanism was transformed and pressed into service as a criminal tribunal to try perpetrators of genocide and other killings. The revamped new-look *gacaca* was vested with jurisdiction to deal with grave crimes, offences far different in complexion from the petty offences that traditional *gacaca* were accustomed to handling. It was vested with power to punish those found guilty of genocide, to effect reconciliation between perpetrator and victim, and to uphold elements of traditional accountability in the form of payment of reparation to the victim by the perpetrator (Bornkamm, 2012). But it had no power to grant amnesty.

Quite apart from the demands of expediency, there is another plausible reason why the resort may have been had to the *gacaca* mechanism. A truth commission could well have been established along the lines of the South African Truth and Reconciliation Commission, the Argentinian or Chilean National Truth Commission, Guatemala's Historical Clarification Commission or El Salvador's United Nations Truth Commission. But the government of Rwanda was not impressed with the amnesty aspect of these truth commissions. Moreover, a truth commission set up by or at the behest of those in power and were involved in the Rwanda civil war would not in all probability have enjoyed broad national legitimacy and support for its composition, integrity, findings and recommendations. Furthermore, as a small country of 12.6 million inhabitants and 26,338 square kilometrein area, Rwanda remained polarized along ethnic and political lines. It was therefore difficult to find nationals acceptable countrywide as impartial. A truth commission composed of foreign nationals, even if 'impartial', was not an attractive proposition either. Those members would lack an understanding of the historical, political and social context of the genocide. In the end, the government had recourse to the *gacaca* mechanism for two main reasons. It did so out of the practical need for a credible system of speedy trials. It also did so out of the conviction that the *gacaca* participatory system of justice would be welcome by the public and its sentences accepted as just and fair by both victims and convicted offenders.

A law formally creating *gacaca* tribunals in each Rwandan local community was passed in October 2000. A year later, about 255,000 *gacaca* judges were elected and given training from April to May 2002. A total number of 12,101 *gacaca* tribunals were established by July 2004. The distribution was 8,260 at village level and 3,090 at district level. Public awareness campaigns were conducted to explain the importance, processes and role of the revamped *gacaca* tribunals. Explanations were provided on the role of the remodelled *gacaca* as a transitional justice mechanism with the mandate to hold perpetrators of genocide and other killings accountable while also seeking to ascertain truth, to ensure justice and to achieve reconciliation (Clark & Kaufman, 2009; Hinton & O'Neil, 2009; Quinn, 2009; Huyse & Satter, 2008). The tribunals only became operational after the competence and credibility of its judges were acknowledged, its procedural rules clearly understood by the entire community and the population felt that their safety from possible attacks by remnants of perpetrators of genocide would be assured during the trial process. This was important because it made the revamped *gacaca* tribunals culturally suited, understood and appreciated, and their decisions readily accepted.

Each *gacaca* tribunal consisted of a panel of nine judges, '*Inyangamugayo*' or persons of integrity, elected by the inhabitants of the venue of the tribunal from among members of the community. A *gacaca* tribunal had jurisdiction to try homicide and other serious crimes, including actual genocidal killing. But it had no jurisdiction to try cases involving planning, instigating or overseeing the commission of acts of genocide, presumably because of the complex nature of the evidence required in such cases. Each tribunal held public hearings in the presence of at least hundred members of the community where the accused is alleged to have committed a crime. Operating in a fractured community setting, the tribunal heard evidence and arguments from both victims and accused persons.

> Each prisoner ... [was] brought before the tribunal in the community where he or she [was] alleged to have committed a crime. The entire community [would] be present and act[ed] as a 'general assembly', discussing the alleged act or acts,

providing testimony and counter-testimony, argument and counter-argument. The community . . . elect[ed] among those present 9 people to constitute the bench. These people [had to] be of high moral standing, non-partisan and not related to those accused. (Uvin, 2003: 117)

An accused person who pleaded guilty by confessing at the start of the trial got away with a reduced sentence. The confession procedure was in fact one of the innovative elements of the law setting up *gacaca* tribunals.

Prisoners who confess[ed] and ask[ed] for forgiveness . . . receive[d] dramatic reductions in penalties. Reductions [were] greatest for those who confess[ed] before the proceedings against them start[ed], either while in prison or at the very beginning of the *gacaca* proceedings, when they [were] explicitly asked if they want[ed] to confess. Reductions [were] smaller for those who confess[ed] only during the *gacaca* procedure, while penalties [were] unchanged for those who [did] not confess at all but [were] found guilty. (Uvin, 2003: 117)

The maximum sentence the tribunal was empowered to pass was life imprisonment since at that time capital punishment had foresightedly been abolished in Rwanda. Had that penalty not been abolished, death sentences would have been passed and executions would have run the gauntlet of being perceived and experienced as revenge genocide or pogrom against the vanquished Hutu carried out by the Tutsi victors in power. Community service was a sentencing option opened to the judges. A person sentenced to pay damages or a fine but who could not pay in money or property worth could, in lieu, pay the monetary equivalent in manual labour. The law instituting *gacaca* tribunals made provision for appeal against conviction and/or sentence. But this provision was little used (Third National Summit Report on Unity & Reconciliation, 2004) because most convicted persons resigned themselves to their fate.

HYBRID JUSTICE MECHANISM

The *gacaca* mechanism emphasized truth-telling, forgiveness and reconciliation. Sentences were imposed bearing in mind the desiderata of national reconciliation and rehabilitation. Truth-telling was stressed because it was considered a key element in eliminating groundless suspicions among the people. On the whole, sentences passed elicited public trust in the mechanism. National reconciliation was built on that foundation of trust. The mechanism did not only focus on the issue of justice. It was also concerned with truth-seeking for purposes of national healing as well as for historical accuracy and psychological understanding of the genocide. In fact, part of the tribunal's mandate was to ascertain and record details of the genocide as actually experienced in the villages, to collect data and statistics on the genocide and the modus operandi of the perpetrators. This was an important aspect of the tribunal's functions because in obtaining such information it had the leeway to explore the motivations behind the genocide. Another important aspect of the work of the tribunal was that it pursued not only the goal of retribution but that of restorative justice as well in the form of reparation for survivors of genocide.

> Part of the *gacaca* proceedings consist[ed] of a detailed listing of all the damages suffered by each survivor – destruction of property, physical harm or loss of relatives and providers. When the procedure [was] completed the claimants receive[d] a statement of their losses and . . . use[d] this to receive reparations from a public fund set up for that purpose. (Uvin, 2003: 117–118)

The *gacaca* tribunals showed that it is feasible to create hybrid processes that combine rituals with formal mechanisms (Clark, 2008). However, the mechanism faced enormous challenges. This was particularly the case at the beginning when the system 'compromised on principles of justice as defined in internationally-agreed human rights and criminal law' as there was then 'no separation between prosecutor and judge, no legal counsel, no legally-reasoned verdict, great encouragement of self-incrimination, and a potential for major divergences in the punishments awarded' (Uvin, 2003: 118). Another challenge was the sheer numbers, size and scope of *gacaca* tribunals, each requiring supervision.

A 2003 initial study of the *gacaca* tribunals, conducted almost ten years after the genocide and after one year of operation, came out with some interesting findings (National Unity and Reconciliation Commission, 2003). It was found that only about a quarter of the population actively participated in the mechanism and that generally many educated and well-off people shunned it, so that in the early days only poor rural people, for the most part, appeared before the tribunals. It was also found that the quest for truth and apology remained in some ways elusive and that although many accused persons testified, they refused to tell the truth and to confess. One explanation for this studied attitude by accused persons could be the fact that Rwanda is predominantly a Catholic country. The Catholic tradition is attuned to private confession to the priest rather than the public confession of wrongdoing promoted by Protestant tradition and which benefited the truth and reconciliation process in a largely Protestant South Africa.

The Rwandese themselves have a tradition of secrecy or secretiveness known as *ibanga*. People nurtured in a culture that requires them to keep secrets, to act secretively and not to divulge secret information, and people inculcated with a belief system requiring confession of wrongdoing to be made only to persons called to holy orders, are unlikely to open up to a group of lay state officials even if chosen from their own local communities. The 2003 study further found that many of the early witnesses who appeared before the tribunals were threatened with death or bodily harm by unknown persons. In the absence of a system of witness protection, many witnesses declined to talk for fear of adverse consequences and this sometimes frustrated or impeded the work of the tribunals. In fact, even at the level of providing general information relating to the genocide only a few people were willing to talk openly about what happened, again perhaps because of the Rwandese *ibanga* culture. The study did however show that the mechanism was more efficient and effective than the conventional criminal courts and that it had the capacity to facilitate reconciliation.

Most people, the study concluded, were convinced that confessions and team community work facilitated reconciliation between offenders, victims and the community. An overwhelming majority of genocide survivors were willing to forgive those who not only confessed but also asked for forgiveness. *Gacaca* judges were on the average around forty years of age and were very familiar with their environment. Their educational level was much higher than that of the general population of the venue of the tribunal. The judges were convinced of the need for much-reduced punishment as a trade-off for confessions, although they denied that this aspect of the *gacaca* mechanism was a form of camouflaged amnesty. The fact that at the beginning judges were sometimes intimidated and feared for their personal security probably impacted on the effectiveness of their work, on their decisions and on the appropriateness of the sentences they passed.

Nevertheless, the judges were generally considered as men and women of integrity fully committed to the search for truth and justice even though surprisingly, they initially received no remuneration for their work. However, some of the judges were not above suspicion. Moreover, the *gacaca* mechanism appeared to rest on a presumption that detained accused persons were guilty until proved guilty. The mechanism seemed obsessed with seeking confession as the ultimate form of evidence, the genuineness of which the judges did not seem bothered about. In fact, a confession was regarded as the best evidence, and conviction and sentence were readily based on it alone (Third National Summit Report, 2004).

> The *gacaca* law contains a politically astutely designed set of incentives to encourage popular participation and acceptance. The confessions procedure, which is requirement for complete confession, including the names of all other people involved in the crime, is already setting in motion an avalanche of confessions, including the implication of other people, which is likely to lead

to significant debates as people seek to explain themselves, implicate others, contextualize events, and so on. Hence the *gacaca* procedure could produce more truth than the formal justice system has so far managed to do. In addition, the confessions procedure and the community service commutation option bring significant reduction in length of prison sentences, even for those found guilty. (Uvin, 2003: 118)

A later study carried out in 2008 (Nzabandora et al., 2008) found that a much greater number of people than previously participated in the *gacaca* mechanism, an indication of greater public confidence in the process and the high level of its success. More offenders confessed and asked for forgiveness, and more victims readily forgave. Offenders readily paid compensation ordered to be paid and embraced unity and reconciliation. However, it appeared there were more people willing to forgive than those willing to confess and apologize and that a significant number of offenders were not willing to dialog. A 2011 survey conducted in one commune after the *gacaca* mechanism wound down showed that the majority of survey participants, in response to general questions, expressed support for the mechanism, but in response to more specific questions such as those regarding security and the credibility of confessions, expressed dissatisfaction with it (Pozen et al., 2014).

On balance, after some initial hesitation and dissatisfaction with its operation, the *gacaca* mechanism was positively received and supported by the general public. Support for the mechanism was partly due to the limitations of the Arusha-based International Criminal Tribunal for Rwanda. That Tribunal, which came to the end of its mandate and wound down around 2014, focused on retribution and did not involve the victims or the community to any significant extent. Apology received little attention in its sentencing practice as in the case of the International Criminal Tribunals for the former Yugoslavia. That is because, in the conventional criminal justice system, contrition when expressed by the perpetrator is taken into account merely as a factor for mitigation of sentence at the discretion of the trial judge.

It is uncertain how much the Rwandan government invested materially and financially in its transitional justice system. But it evidently did not lack funding support from the international community to have justice done. *Gacaca* tribunals seem to have been just as generously funded as was the South African TRC considered to have been

'one of the best-conceived, best-funded, and well-staffed mechanisms of its kind' (Shea, 2000: 5), with 'a staff of up to 350, a budget of some USD 18 million each year for two-and-a-half years (plus an additional, smaller budget of another three years), and four large offices around the country, [dwarfing] previous truth commissions in its size and reach'. (Freeman & Hayner, 2003: 140).

CONCLUSION

The use of *gacaca* tribunals in Rwanda was dictated by realism and the circumstances prevailing in the country at the material time. Rwandese criminal law, like that of many states, had no genocide-specific provision at the time. The perpetrators of genocide could have been tried for aggravated murder. But prosecution for that crime would not have adequately reflected the nature and gravity of the crime of genocide. Besides, even if there had been a law specifically dealing with the crime of genocide, the number of those arrested and detained for suspected involvement in that crime was over 130,000, so many that trying them in the conventional criminal courts would have taken 200 years, according to optimistic estimates. The *gacaca* traditional justice mechanism, suitably adapted to meet the special circumstances at hand, was therefore cleverly resorted to out of expediency.

NOTE

1. This is a process that encourages all those involved in a particular conflict to collectively determine how to deal with the aftermath of the conflict, and the injustices incurred, and its implications for the future.

Chapter 12

The African Union and Conflict Resolution Arrangements

Preventing, managing and resolving conflicts in Africa are a big challenge. The challenge is compounded not only by the huge size and population of the continent but also by the fact that the continent has a large number of sovereign states and three disputed territories. There are also two enclaves on the continent and a number of dependent island territories close to the continent all under the sovereignty of former colonial powers. Africa has a land area of 30.2 million square kilometre and a population of about 1.5 billion people. Of Africa's current fifty-four states, forty-eight are in the mainland and six are island nations – Cape Verdes, Comoros, Madagascar, Mauritius, Sao Tome & Principe and Seychelles. In addition to the current fifty-four sovereign countries, there are three disputed territories regarding which the AU is silent, namely, Somaliland, which declared itself independent of Somalia and is de facto a state although it is not yet recognized de jure as a sovereign nation by any other country; the Western Sahara which proclaimed its independence as the SADR and is recognized by the AU and a number of African and other states; and the former UN Trust Territory of the British Southern Cameroons (Ambazonia) which by an act of self-determination reasserted its independence in 2017 and is fighting a decolonization war against République du Cameroun colonial occupation and oppression. There are also several dependent territories still controlled by former colonial powers. These are the Tromelin Island and Mayotte, controlled by France; Ascension Island and Saint Helena administered by the United Kingdom; the Canary Islands off the coast of Morocco as well as Ceuta and Melilla which are enclaves on the northern coast of Morocco, all held by Spain; and Madeira Islands off the coast of Morocco, held by Portugal.

UN PEACE AND SECURITY FRAMEWORK

The UN was established in 1945 by 'the peoples' of the nations of the world. In doing so, 'the peoples' of the world took care to declare their determination 'to save succeeding generations from the scourge of war, which . . . has brought untold sorrow to mankind'.[1] One of the declared purposes of the UN is to maintain international peace and security. To that end, the organization is mandated 'to take effective collective measures for the prevention and removal of threats to the peace' and 'to bring about by peaceful means, and in conformity with the principles of justice and international law, adjustment or settlement of international disputes or situations which might lead to a breach of the peace'.[2] The UNGA is one of the principal organs of the organization. It has the power to 'consider the general principles of cooperation in the maintenance of international peace and security'[3] and 'may discuss any questions relating to the maintenance of international peace and security brought before it'.[4]

However, 'primary responsibility for the maintenance of international peace and security' is vested in the Security Council.[5] This does not preclude 'the existence of regional arrangements or agencies for dealing with such matters relating to the maintenance of international peace and security as are appropriate for regional action'.[6] The UN Charter directs the Security Council, where appropriate, to utilize such regional arrangements or agencies for enforcement action under its authority.[7] It requires the council at all times to be kept fully informed of activities undertaken or in contemplation under regional arrangements for the maintenance of international peace and security.[8] The system of collective security under the UN thus acknowledges the existence of regional arrangements for regional security.

> As a consequence of the predominantly regionalist approach of the states which took part [at the founding of the UN], provision was expressly made to ensure that the new arrangements for collective security in the Charter, operating under the Security Council, should not stultify the arrangements already in being on a regional basis. (Sands & Klein, 2001: 149)

Regional arrangements remain relatively subordinate to the Security Council. In the matter of pacific settlement of disputes, Article 33 of the Charter includes resort to regional arrangements as a method which the parties must use 'first of all', before having recourse to the Security Council. Article 52 (2) imposes upon the parties the obligation to utilize regional procedures for settlement. However, Article 52 (4) specifically states that 'this Article in no way impairs the application of Articles 34 and 35', so that the council's own right to investigate a dispute or situation and the Member State's right to appeal to the council is preserved (Sands & Klein, 2002: 150).

The frequency, intensity and level of intrastate conflicts plaguing Africa would suggest that security governance in the continent is either inadequate or insufficient. The necessity of cooperation between regional organizations and the UN in matters of peace and security is evident and is based on the idea that such cooperation represents the best hope for conflict prevention, management and resolution. Within that cooperation framework, regional organizations have assumed more responsibility in matters of peace and security. They have become the chief support in global security governance, taking initiatives in conflict management (Tavares, 2010). This allows the UN to play a larger role in preventive diplomacy and in becoming the instrument of last resort in conflict resolution (Rivlin, 1992).

In the context of conflict management, economic and political realities dictate African cooperation with the UNSC, the EU and major states such as America, Britain, France, Germany and Russia. The UNSC is the global institution with the primary responsibility for peace and security in the world. Its political authority is critical in communicating to conflicting parties the importance and urgency of reaching a settlement. At the African level, diplomacy concentrates more on identifying and elaborating the political substance of the initiative to resolve a given conflict. Diplomacy at the level of the other cooperating partners emphasizes the role the international community seeks to play in order to ensure that the world is behind Africa's initiative. Cooperating partners also emphasize the fact that they are ready to help in technical and material terms to provide concrete solutions to crises. This cooperation arrangement has cynically been simplified in some quarters as meaning that the UN issues the order, the Europeans pay and the Africans do the fighting. The simplism does however contain a grain of truth. Cooperating partners in the peace and security process share various responsibilities to some degree or another. The African side invests its people in large numbers in conflict resolution, while the rest pay and monitor whereas they should not just do so. They ought not to deal with the peace process by remote control. Peacekeeping in Africa ought not to be the sole responsibility of Africans. Others need to join in, although not to the same extent in human terms. In Sierra Leone, for example, non-African combatants played a decisive role in assuring peace. Clichés like 'Africa for Africans', 'African solutions for African problems' and 'African problems to be resolved by Africans' are misplaced and unhelpful in the context of conflict management and resolution in Africa. It is not only Africans alone who can devise political solutions to conflict problems. The US and the EU in cooperation with the AU played an important role in ending the border conflict between Ethiopia and Eritrea.

Efforts at conflict resolution demand both workability and inclusiveness – local, regional, continental and international cooperation. There is no necessary contradiction between inclusiveness and practicality. In fact, inclusiveness has been seen in practice to be the best way forward. However, in pursuing external diplomacy with regard to conflict management and resolution in Africa, the continental organization may want to bear in mind that North African Mediterranean countries appear to look more and more to Europe rather than to the rest of Africa. The EU-Mediterranean Partnership and separate EU negotiations with North African countries have the effect of wooing most North African Mediterranean states away from Africa both politically and economically. Also, the role of the Arab League and the Islamic Conference Organization in Africa is such that some of the African members of those bodies have used their concurrent membership in African organizations to solicit support for purely Arab/Middle Eastern causes. The Arab League could possibly also become an instrument that promotes the interests of its Member States in Africa against African countries that are not its members. It speaks volumes that in June 2021, Egypt and Sudan referred their Nile-related dispute with Ethiopia to the Arab League rather than to the AU which they both considered ineffective.

THE OAU PEACE AND SECURITY ARRANGEMENT

The OAU was founded on 25 May 1963. On that date, the Charter of the Organization was adopted by a conference of Heads of States and Governments in Addis Ababa. The thirty-two states that signed the charter included all African states at the time, with the exception of countries not then independent (Gambia, Malawi and Zambia), apartheid South Africa, and Spanish and Portuguese colonial possessions in the continent categorized by the UN as non-self-governing (Brownlie, 1971: 1). At that time, anti-colonial agitations and struggles were gaining momentum in Spanish and Portuguese colonies and in countries under white minority regimes in the continent. At its founding, the OAU was confronted with two major types of political challenges – the total liberation of the continent from colonialism and interstate conflicts involving some African states. In order to meet the challenge of decolonization of the rest of the continent, the OAU Charter propounded the doctrine of 'eradication of all forms of colonialism from Africa'.[9] This liberation agenda was vigorously pursued by the organization. The problem of interstate armed conflicts was highlighted by armed clashes between some foreign powers and an African state and also armed clashes between one African state against another. The interstate armed conflicts in the continent as of 1963 were: the 1956 Suez Canal conflict in which an African state, Egypt, faced an invasion by Britain, France and Israel to seize control of the Suez Canal; the 1960 Congo conflict in which America, Belgium and France were deeply involved; and the border war between Morocco and Algeria in October 1963.

Given this background, the OAU Charter envisaged continental conflict management and resolution only in the context of interstate conflicts. Intrastate conflicts or civil wars escaped consideration. The reason for this benign neglect of civil wars appears to be the broad charter-proclaimed principle of 'non-interference in the internal affairs of States' and 'respect for the sovereignty and territorial integrity of each State and for its inalienable right to independent existence'.[10] Relatively young states emerging from colonial rule notoriously tend to reiterate as paramount norms the preservation of state sovereignty and non-interference in the internal affairs of states. In Africa, these two norms were declared in the charter of the OAU and are reiterated in the formal constitutional text of the African Union, the Constitutive Act of the Continental Organization.

Member States of the OAU committed themselves by way of a pledge under Article XIX of the Charter 'to settle all disputes among themselves by peaceful means'. And to that end, they decided 'to establish a Commission of Mediation, Conciliation and Arbitration'. Significantly, their commitment was to settle by any of those means only disputes that were '*among* themselves' and not those *within* themselves as well. The OAU provision may have been influenced by the UN Charter provision on pacific settlement of disputes (chapter VI) which similarly envisages only interstate disputes. Article 33 of the UN Charter provides:

> The *parties to any dispute*, the continuance of which is likely to endanger the maintenance of international peace and security, shall, first of all seek a solution by negotiation, enquiry, mediation, conciliation, arbitration, judicial settlement, resort to regional agencies or arrangements, or other peaceful means of their own choice.

The OAU Charter postponed the definition of the composition and the conditions of operation of the Commission of Mediation to a separate protocol to be approved by the Assembly of Heads of State and Government. One year later, on 21 July 1964, the 'Protocol of the Commission of Mediation, Conciliation and Arbitration' was signed by thirty-three states. But the commission did not have its first meeting until 11 December 1967. In between those two dates, the work of the commission was carried out by the Council of Ministers and other OAU bodies. The protocol provided the background to the early constructive work of the OAU in conflict resolution between Member States. The test case in that endeavour was the successful resolution of the Sand War between Morocco and Algeria. Article XII of the Protocol vested in the Commission 'jurisdiction over disputes between States only'. The reason for so severely limiting the jurisdiction of the commission can be found in the OAU's unwarranted broadly interpreted principle of non-interference in the internal affairs of Member States. Internal conflicts, however intense, widespread and genocidal, were unfortunately considered internal matters of the state concerned to be dealt with as that state saw fit. The commission's jurisdiction was confined to interstate conflicts which, fortunately, were less frequent and less deadly than were initially thought. It is civil wars that quickly became Africa's nightmare, with their frequency and deadliness. The OAU had no conflict resolution mechanism for civil wars and other violent internal conflicts. Interstate conflicts occurred less frequently and whenever they occurred, they were brief. There was little or no work for the commission. It soon became redundant and fell into desuetude. It became obvious that a new body was needed to deal with the phenomenon of endless civil wars in the continent.

Until recently, therefore, the OAU was constrained by its charter from intervening in internal African conflicts, no matter the barbarity of the conflict and the loss of lives it occasioned, as in the Nigerian civil war from July 1967 to January 1970 and the Ethiopian civil war from September 1974 to May 1991. The continental organization carved for itself only a very limited role in conflict management. The situation changed in the 1990s. The 1990 Addis and the 1993 Cairo summits of African Heads of State and Government directed the OAU to get involved in resolving internal conflicts in Member States. This mandate needed to be strengthened. Working within the UN framework, the OAU expanded its role by taking primary responsibility for identifying the causes of conflict and providing early warning of conflict in Africa. The organization assumed responsibility for mobilizing support and assistance for post-conflict reconstruction. In 1993, the OAU Assembly of Heads of State and Government adopted a declaration on the establishment of a new body within the OAU, known as *Mechanism for Conflict Prevention, Management and Resolution,* to concern itself with conflicts in Africa in the manner indicated by its name.[11]

In a statement establishing the mechanism, the OAU Assembly made a self-critique acknowledging that no single internal factor has contributed more to the present socio-economic problem in the continent than the scourge of conflicts in and among African countries.

> They have brought about death and human suffering, engendered hate and divided nations and families. Conflicts have force millions of our people into a

drifting life as refugees and displaced persons, deprived of their means of livelihood, human dignity and hope. Conflicts have gobble-up scarce resources, and undermined the ability of our countries to address the many compelling needs of our people. . . . In June [1992] . . . we decided in principle to establish within the OAU, and in keeping with the principles and objectives of the Charter of the Organization, a Mechanism for Conflict Prevention, Management and Resolution. We took that decision against the background of the history of many prolonged and destructive conflicts in our continent and of our limited success of finding solutions to them, notwithstanding the many efforts we and our predecessors expended. In so going we were also guided by our determination to ensure that Africa through the Organization of African Unity plays a central role in bringing about peace and stability in the continent. We saw in the establishment of such a mechanism the opportunity to bring to the processes of dealing with conflicts in our continent a new institutional dynamism, enabling speedy action to prevent or manage and ultimately resolve conflicts when and where they occur. (Declaration by the Assembly of Heads of State and Government on the Establishment within the OAU of a Mechanism for Conflict Prevention, Management and Resolution, 1993, paragraphs 9 to 12)

The Assembly then went on to give a brief 'job description' of the newly created body.

The Mechanism will be guided by the objectives and principles of the OAU Charter; in particular, the sovereign equality of Member States, non-interference in the internal affairs of States, the respect of the sovereignty and territorial integrity of Member States, their inalienable right to independent existence, the peaceful settlement of disputes as well as the inviolability of borders inherited from colonialism. It will also function on the basis of the consent and the cooperation of the parties to the conflict. The Mechanism will have as a primary objective, the anticipation and prevention of conflicts. In circumstances where conflicts have occurred, it will be its responsibility to undertake peace-making and peacebuilding functions in order to facilitate the resolution of these conflicts. In this respect, civilian and military missions of observation and monitoring of limited scope and duration may be mounted and deployed. (Declaration, paragraphs 14-15)

In setting these objectives, the Assembly let it be known that African leaders were convinced that prompt and decisive action in these spheres will, in the first instance, prevent the emergence of conflicts, and where they do inevitably occur, stop them from degenerating into intense or generalized conflicts.

Emphasis on anticipatory and preventive measures, and concerted action in peace-making and peacebuilding will obviate the need to resort to the complex and resource-demanding peacekeeping operations, which African countries will find difficult to finance. However, in the event that conflicts degenerate to the extent of requiring collective international intervention and policing, the assistance or where appropriate the services of the United Nations will be sought under the general terms of its Charter. In this instance, our respective countries will examine ways and modalities through which they can make practical contribution to such a United Nations undertaking and participate effectively in the peacekeeping operations in Africa. (Declaration, paragraphs 15-16)

The Assembly declared the readiness of the OAU to cooperate and work closely with the UN not only with regard to issues relating to peace-making but, and especially, also those relating to peacekeeping. Where necessary, recourse would be had to the UN to provide the necessary financial, logistical and military support for the OAU's activities in Conflict Prevention, Management and Resolution. This would be in keeping with the provisions of Chapter VII of the UN Charter on the role of regional organizations in the maintenance of international peace and security.

The setting up of the *Mechanism* reflected a continental commitment and a framework for resolving intra- and interstate conflicts in Africa. Remarkably for an organization that hitherto avoided involvement in internal conflicts of its Member States, the mechanism assumed a clear mandate to concern itself with such conflicts. What was lacking were expertise and resources for peace enforcement. The OAU became involved in and oversaw major and sophisticated mediation and negotiation in North Africa (Morocco-Algerian war) and in the Horn of Africa (Ethiopia-Eritrea war; Eritrea-Djibouti war). Its lack of capacity to enforce peace and to ensure the implementation of agreements painstakingly negotiated was resolved by having recourse to the UN in this regard. Recourse to the UN, where necessary, is understandable. The UN has undoubted expert and financial capacity and can mobilize military power for successful intervention in conflict zones. Such capacity has been demonstrated several times outside Africa, in conflict places such as Iraq, Bosnia, Yugoslavia and East Timor. Unfortunately, that capacity has not been utilized positively and effectively in Africa. This fact has given rise to the common perception and feeling in Africa that there is a double standard operating when it comes to issues of peace=keeping and conflict prevention in Africa. This unpalatable international reality has been impressed on Africans by the history of failed UN interventions in Africa in countries such as Burundi, Central African Republic, Congo Kinshasa, Côte d'Ivoire, Ethiopia, Rwanda, Sierra Leone, Somalia and Sudan.

THE AU PEACE AND SECURITY ARRANGEMENT

During the thirty-six years of its existence, the OAU distinguished itself in its uncompromising fight for the liberation of the entire continent from white colonialism. At the same time, however, the organization came under heavy criticism for being weak in addressing other continental challenges. It also came under heavy criticism for maintaining a conspiratorial silence over the dismal human rights records of African regimes and for its inability to shed off the perception that it is simply a club of African rulers – a club where the continent's authoritarian leaders (many of them military officers who had come to power by overthrowing elected civilian leaders) launder their bad image especially when dignified by being 'elected' Chairman of the OAU. After thirty-six years, it was felt that a new and better-suited organization needed to be created to take up the new political challenges of the continent. The challenges are many: elusive quest for continental union, interminable conflicts represented by civil wars, routinized revolutionary overthrow of governments by the military, territorial aggrandizement ambitions of some African states, high levels of poverty and disease, bad governance and a generalized climate of fear and insecurity.

On 9 September 1999, African leaders meeting in Sirte, Libya, announced the creation of a new organization for the continent to be known as the African Union. The AU was officially launched in Durban, South Africa, on 9 July 2002, as a successor organization to the OAU. The Organization of African Unity (1963–1999) was strong in its anti-colonial fight but otherwise was weak and incapable of exerting any influence within and outside Africa. On a visit to the United States, the Shah of Iran made an assessment of the OAU to President Jimmy Carter. He said he believed that the organization is an impotent body. This sums up the perception of the OAU by the international community. African peoples themselves came to see the OAU as a mere club of African leaders where they meet and plot to be each other's keeper. The AU signalled its intention to make a paradigm shift through its conception as a union of African countries and peoples. Its Constitutive Act declares in Article 3 the objectives of the organization to be, inter alia, to achieve greater unity and solidarity between the African countries and the peoples of Africa; to defend the sovereignty, territorial integrity and independence of Member States; to accelerate the political and socio-economic integration of the continent; to promote and defend African common positions on issues of interest to the continent and its peoples; to encourage international cooperation; to promote peace, security and stability on the continent; to promote democratic principles and institutions; to promote and protect human rights; and to advance the development of the continent.

In contrast to the OAU which came to be seen as a union of African leaders, the AU was conceived as a union of African peoples and is therefore expected to focus on peoples of the continent, addressing their multiple problems including conflict prevention, management and resolution. The objectives of the AU stated in Article 3 of its Constitutive Act include the promotion of peace, security and stability on the continent. The organization's peace and security architecture mirrors, by and large, the UN collective security system.[12] The matter of anticipating and preventing conflicts in the continent is a subject related to promoting peace, security and stability in Africa. For this purpose, the AU established a PSC.[13] The council was established as an operational structure for the effective implementation of the decisions taken in the areas of conflict prevention, peace-making, peace support operations and intervention, as well as peace-building and post-conflict reconstruction. In the preamble to the protocol establishing the PSC, African leaders lament the continued prevalence of armed conflicts in Africa. They express concern that no single internal factor has contributed more to socio-economic decline on the continent and the suffering of the civilian population than the scourge of conflicts within and between states. Conflicts in Africa have forced millions of people, including women and children, into a drifting life as refugees and internally displaced persons, deprived of their means of livelihood, human dignity and hope. Given these facts, the prevention of conflicts and the promotion of collective security, durable peace and stability become essential. Also essential is the development of strong democratic institutions and culture, the observance of human rights and the rule of law and the implementation of post-conflict recovery programmes and sustainable development policies.

The objectives of the PSC include the following: to promote peace, security and stability, to anticipate and prevent conflicts (including undertaking peace-making and peace-building functions for the resolution of these conflicts), to promote and implement peace-building and post-conflict reconstruction activities to consolidate peace and prevent the resurgence of violence, and to coordinate and harmonize continental efforts in the prevention and combating of international terrorism in all its aspects.[14] In carrying out these stated objectives, the PSC is directed to be guided by a number of principles, including peaceful settlement of disputes and conflicts, early responses to contain crisis situations so as to prevent them from developing into full-blown conflicts.[15] The guiding principles of the council include peaceful settlement of disputes and conflicts, and early responses to contain crisis situations.[16]

The functions of the Council include promotion of peace, security and stability in Africa; early warning and preventive diplomacy; peace-making, including the use of good offices, mediation, conciliation and enquiry; peace support operations and intervention; peace-building and post-conflict reconstruction; and humanitarian action and disaster management. The council has power to anticipate and prevent disputes and conflicts, as well as policies that may lead to genocide and crimes against humanity; to undertake peace-making and peace-building functions to resolve conflicts where they have occurred; and to authorize the mounting and deployment of peace support missions.[17] Institutional capacity for peace-building at the end of hostilities involves, inter alia, consolidation of the peace agreements that have been negotiated; and implementation of disarmament, demobilization and reintegration programmes. The Peace and Security Council was effectively established in 2006 to boost the AU's peace initiatives but it does not seem anything concrete has come out of any peace initiative it might have undertaken.

A key element of the AU Constitutive Act is Member States' commitment to the principle of 'peaceful settlement of disputes by negotiation, mediation, conciliation or arbitration'. African states maintain that conditions of peace and security constitute the cornerstone on which African solidarity and cooperation can be built. The creation of the Commission of Mediation, Conciliation, and Arbitration was to underscore regional and organizational commitment to peaceful settlement of regional conflicts. On the ground, the AU has made some attempts to face the peace and security challenges in the continent. In 2002, the AU did send a peacekeeping mission to Burundi. A UN mission eventually took over. IGAD worked to help reconcile the various sides in Somalia. In 2004, ECOWAS authorized the creation of a standby peacekeeping unit of 6,500 trained soldiers for rapid deployment to any country that might be faced with a crisis. Eight industrialized countries agreed to provide financial support and training for the AU's plans to set up a similar standby force at the continental level. The EU pledged 250 million euros for the AU's peace fund.

The AU attempted to end conflicts in Darfur. It negotiated two ceasefires in 2004, but these did not work out. Part of the reason for the failure was that the AU sent peacekeeping troops to monitor the ceasefire but without the mandate to use force to protect civilians or themselves. In May 2005, the AU negotiated with the Sudanese government and two rebel groups to sign a peace agreement to end the violence. Two Arab rebel groups rejected the agreement and the violence continued, increasing in intensity. A contingent of 7,000 soldiers sent by AU to monitor the ceasefire proved ineffective because it was too small for the vast area it was assigned to cover. The UN, lacking both funding and the military support of the wealthy countries, left the AU to deploy what was in effect a token force and without a mandate to protect civilians. In August 2006, the UNSC approved the sending of 20,000 peacekeeping troops to Darfur. But Sudan opposed the resolution arguing that the action would be an infringement of its sovereignty.

Two AU bodies remain little known – NEPAD and CENSAD. NEPAD is advertised as the development programme for Africa and as the framework for progress through which African countries and the AU itself are measured. But there is potential for it to expand its role to embrace aspects of conflict resolution. Through its good governance principles and its peer review mechanism, it can play an important role in the prevention of internal conflict in African states. CENSAD is one of Africa's regional economic organizations but shies from making itself known. It used to be a community of Sahelian states but has long gone beyond that. Under the strong influence of Libya, it looks like a 'fast track AU'. Its members have adopted ambitious plans, including entering into obligations of a political, security and military nature. It is well-positioned to play a role in dealing with conflicts among its members.

Perhaps it is a shortcoming of the AU that it appears to be more concerned with preventing, managing and resolving conflicts than trying to ascertain and understand their root causes. Being an intergovernmental organization, the AU treads very carefully when it comes to causes of conflicts in Africa. Different Member States have different views of these causes. States have strong views on the causes of conflicts in which they are involved. As far as it is known, there is no official AU position on the causes of political conflicts in African countries. The organization appears to have adopted the somewhat curious policy of 'see nothing, pretend to hear nothing, and say nothing'.

Even though the organization appears well-positioned to engage in efforts at conflict resolution in the continent, it is the case that it is plagued by severe financial problems, lack of leadership and lack of serious commitment to conflict resolution. Moreover, the organization has no general right to interfere in the internal conflicts of Member States. Its principles of respect for state sovereignty and territorial integrity, and of non-interference in domestic affairs of Member States weaken the position of the AU in conflict resolution. The AU has no powers to act in respect of internal conflicts, except, theoretically, in cases of genocide, war crimes and crimes against humanity, as stated in Article 4 h of the AU Constitutive Act. But even in those cases, the AU has not betrayed any inclination to act. Part of the problem is that those concepts are not defined in any AU instrument, and the AU itself has not vested jurisdiction in any of its organs to make an authoritative determination in regard to them.

In this connection, the AU suffers from a trust deficit. This explains why non-state actors involved in an armed conflict with a state hardly appeal for AU intervention. They are aware that such intervention is unlikely to be forthcoming. The history of the organization shows that whenever it has had to act it tends to side with the government in power. It has always been a defender of the status quo, so to speak. Uncritical support for the regime in power has limited the organization's peacekeeping effectiveness. The AU is supposed to be objective and neutral in any conflict. The only situation where the AU probably has a carte blanche to act is in respect of interstate conflicts to prevent escalation of a conflict or to prohibit designs and actions by its members that would undermine regional peace and security. But then, the AU has no record of achieving peace in any situation of conflict. It has never brought about an effective ceasefire. AU members have always remained divided in the face of any armed conflict. The difficulty of achieving a consensus in the AU continues to plague its conflict resolution efforts.

THE AFRICAN ECONOMIC COMMUNITIES AND PEACE AND SECURITY FUNCTIONS

In order to fulfil the objective of promoting peace, security and stability on the continent, the AU developed a two-tier peace and security arrangement, at the continental level and at regional level.[18] The Assembly of Heads of State and Government, the Executive Council, the Permanent Representative Council (PRC), and the Peace and Security Council handle at continental level threats to peace and security. At the regional level, the regional economic communities have taken on the added responsibility of dealing with peace and security matters. This is an expanded key responsibility quite apart from their core responsibility which is economic. The current regional economic communities of the African Union are AMU, CENSAD, COMESA, EAC, ECCAS, ECOWAS, IGAD and SADC.[19] The primary responsibility of these eight bodies is forging regional economic partnerships. However, they have also embraced peace and security mandates as an added key responsibility and have, to that end, developed mechanisms for conflict prevention, management and resolution within their respective regions.

Mechanisms that have since been developed form part of the overall security architecture of the African Union. The structures at the continental level work in synergy with the regional mechanisms. As an example, the regional mechanisms within the economic communities adapt continental visions and policies to their respective regions and provide guidelines for the implementation of various activities by national governments. Take another example. The African Standby Force (ASF) is constituted by regional standby brigades collectively. These brigades are mobilized and coordinated by regional economic communities. They are required to engage in African peacekeeping support operations. At the continental level, the AU provides headquarters-based strategic planning capacity for the management, direction and coordination of the activities of the ASF. Peace support operations by the ASF are guided by two technical conceptual base documents: the

Policy Framework for the Establishment of the African Standby Force and the Military Staff Committee (Part 1) (2003),[20] and the Roadmap for the Operationalization of the African Standby Force (2005).[21]

The regional organizations have political and economic objectives, as well as a peace and stability mandate. The AU security arrangement acknowledges the existence of regional mechanisms for conflict prevention, management and resolution. The complexity and interrelated nature of conflict resolution and peace-building call for solutions through a strong regional foundation with decisive international support. The protocol on the African Peace and Security Council 'appropriates' regional mechanisms as part of the overall security architecture of the African Union, giving them primary responsibility for promoting peace, security and stability in Africa. Africa's regional economic communities thus constitute the building blocks of Africa's peace and security framework. They have become 'first respondents' in preventing, managing and resolving conflicts occurring within their respective regions. Some of these bodies, like ECOWAS, SADC and CENSAD have undertaken peacekeeping missions.

Others like IGAD and EAC are cautious and have tended to embrace peace facilitation, mediation or negotiation activities. Still others like COMESA, AMU and ECCAS shy away from peace and security matters and stay within their economic mandate. This would seem a reflection of lack of hegemonic leadership in those regions to stimulate regional cooperation or to lead the peace and security agenda of the region. The peace and security role of regional economic communities has gained prominence over the years, particularly so because they are well-positioned to assume peace and security functions. They are well-positioned to do so first because they have the ability to intervene in situations where the UN or even the AU is politically constrained from taking initial action; second because they are closer to the scene of events and therefore respond timeously and with speed; third because they can be flexible and even improvise to meet any unforeseen contingency; and fourth because they have the added advantage of familiarity with the environment on the ground.

Some of the regional organizations have thus demonstrated that regional bodies can play an important and, in some cases, a central role in dealing with conflicts. Their success is due to a number of reasons (Brown, 2015). Regional organizations have the advantage of regional proximity and the sense of balance that allows them to politically define the nature of any conflict within their respective regions. This political and geographical proximity enables them to experience the effects and the repercussions of a given conflict, prompting them to seek support from extra-regional sources, if necessary, in order to bring the conflict to an end. Credibility is what regional organizations bring to conflict resolution. Generally, they are seen to be fair, even-handed and knowledgeable. They can therefore sponsor and spearhead peace efforts. Their initiatives tend to receive the backing of extra-regional organizations, both continental and non-African, due to the trust placed upon them. The downside, however, is that regional organizations are made up of individual countries, some of which are large and influential within the sub-region. Each region in Africa has countries that are strong economically or militarily, allowing their governments to influence the initiatives that the regional organization promotes. In many cases, the leader of an influential state takes the initiative and secures the support of other Member States of the region in order to launch a peace effort in the name of a given regional organization.

ECOWAS, SADC and IGAD have quickly become the main bodies engaged in conflict prevention, management and resolution. Additionally, they are also involved in preventing the proliferation of small arms and light weapons in their respective regions. Conflict resolution and peace-building are by nature complex and interrelated. Solutions are sought through a strong regional foundation with decisive international support. These bodies play a critical role in regional peacekeeping either in their own right or through mandated operations under Chapter VII of the UN Charter. Their role has kindled considerable international and African interest. That notwithstanding, the role, or potential role, of the AU in conflict prevention, management and resolution deserves acknowledgement, revitalization and encouragement. The AU itself needs to project leadership and a stronger image. Its stamp of approval for the activities of regional organizations is likely to be needed more and more in the future. There is no reason to believe that only Member States of regional organizations make the best mediators or are the ideal sources of peacekeeping troops in their respective regions. The use of troops from countries within a region in which there is a conflict could, in some cases, be unwise. Utilizing, for example, an official from one region of the continent to mediate a conflict in another region, and using in one region troops mainly from another region, could be more appropriate. Responsibility for such deployment would best be taken by the African Union.

In the fulfilment of its peace and security mandate, the PSC works in consultation with regional mechanisms, keeping each other fully and continuously informed of its activities. The council is also required to cooperate and work closely with the UN Security Council as well as with other relevant UN agencies in the promotion of peace, security and stability in Africa. Where necessary, the PSC appeals to the UN to provide necessary financial, logistical and military support for the African Union's activities in the promotion and maintenance of peace, security and stability in the continent, in keeping with the provisions of Chapter VIII of the UN Charter on the role of Regional Organizations in the maintenance of international peace and security. In this way, the African Union has sought to rationalize the competing jurisdictional claims of the regional and universal systems and to avoid a conflict between the respective security systems of the UN and the AU.

Hoping to strengthen its early warning capacity, the AU established a Conflict Management Centre.[22] But the centre remains relatively weak due to underfunding and political and bureaucratic difficulties. These two problems have rendered the centre almost irrelevant. Most Member States simply want to confine the role of the AU to early warning, preventive diplomacy and monitoring peace processes. They are not enthusiastic about the AU engaging in regional peacekeeping or establishing mutual security arrangements between states. They see these as tasks to be undertaken by regional bodies. This attitude has contributed to the AU's non-effective peacekeeping efforts.

Norms and identity are particularly important in the African context. They explain successful conflict intervention missions by African regional economic communities. These communities take on the role of 'my neighbour's keeper'. This role is said to be informed by African philosophical thinking expressed in the form of wise sayings. Some of the wise sayings are actually instructions or directives on what to do in a conflict situation: 'Assist a neighbour whose hut is on fire to prevent it from engulfing one's own property'; 'First put out the fire, and then sit down to ask who started the fire'; 'If you buy a house, you also "buy" the neighbours of the house'; 'Better a close neighbour than a distant brother'; 'Huts close together will be destroyed by fire'. These aphorisms capture norms of African humanitarianism and neighbourly solidarity. They posit that conflict requires a response from neighbours because they pose an immediate risk of spreading to adjacent countries. They reflect African humanitarian attitudes on the subject of intervening in conflicts. They however appear to diverge from Western diplomatic and legal norms of state sovereignty and non-intervention (Aning, 1999; Brown, 2015: 13).

The immediate vulnerability of states in a region to both the spread of violence and the negative economic and social consequences of it provides strong incentives for regional leaders to take on the challenge of resolution. Security threats necessitate and legitimate extraordinary political measures and actions like the use of force. A regional economic community is therefore often moved to take conventional security tasks because of the belief that its original goals of economic cooperation, integration and growth cannot be attained in a conflict-ridden environment. Legitimate reasons for taking on that added responsibility include regional identity and familiarity with the regional environment. By taking on conventional security activities, a regional economic community does not thereby signal a security community in the making because the communities often lack military assets and often have to turn to the continental organization and even the UN.

NOTES

1. Preamble to the UN Charter.
2. Art 1, UN Charter.
3. Art 11 (1), UN Charter.
4. Art 11 (2), UN Charter.
5. Art 24 (1), UN Charter.
6. Art 52 (1), UN Charter.
7. Art 53 (1), UN Charter.
8. Art 54, UN Charter.
9. Art III (1)(d), OAU Charter.
10. Art III (2)(3), OAU Charter.
11. AHG/Decl.3/XXIX of 30 June 1993.
12. Declaration of the Assembly of Heads of State and Government on the Establishment within the OAU of a Mechanism for Conflict Prevention, Management and Resolution (1993). This declaration was adopted by the 29th Ordinary Session of the Assembly of Heads of State and Government held in Cairo, Egypt, from 28 to 30 June 1993 (AHG/Decl.3/XXIX).
13. Protocol Relating to the Establishment of the Peace and Security Council of the African Union (2002). This protocol was adopted by the AU Assembly in Durban, South Africa, in July 2002, in terms of Article 5(2) of the AU Constitutive Act, and entered into force in December 2003.
14. Protocol Relating to the Establishment of the Peace and Security Council of the African Union (2002). This protocol was adopted by the AU Assembly in Durban, South Africa, in July 2002, in terms of Article 5(2) of the AU Constitutive Act, and entered into force in December 2003.
15. Article 3, Protocol on the Peace and Security Council.
16. Article 4, Protocol on the Peace and Security Council.
17. Article 4, Protocol on the Peace and Security Council.
18. Article 7, Protocol on the Peace and Security Council.
19. The UN divides the world for various purposes into regions, Africa being one of them. Confusingly, however, Africa also divides the continent into regions even though it is itself a region, a region of the UN.
20. These acronyms stand for African Maghreb Union (AMU), Sahel-Saharan States (CEN-SAD), the Common Market for Eastern and Southern Africa (COMESA), East African Community (EAC), the Economic Community of Central African States (ECCAS), the Economic Community of West African States (ECOWAS), Inter-Governmental Authority on Development (IGAD) and Southern African Development Community (SADC). CEN-SAD, the little known of these regional organizations, is made up of West, North, Sahelian and some Horn of Africa States with a strong Muslim community. Founded on 2 February 1998 with headquarters in

Tripoli, Libya, it has twenty-nine members. In addition to being a regional economic community, which the treaty establishing it describes as a 'comprehensive economic union', CEN-SAD also emphasizes two areas of 'deepened cooperation', namely regional security and sustainable development.

21. Adopted by the African Chiefs of Defence Staff at their 3rd meeting on 14 May 2003 in Addis Ababa, Ethiopia (Exp/ASF-MSC/2 (1)), and revised at their 4th meeting in January 2004 in Addis Ababa, Ethiopia. Part 2 is the appendices to Part 1.

22. Produced at an Experts Meeting on the relationship between the AU and the Regional Mechanisms for Conflict Prevention, Management and Resolution held in Addis Ababa from 22 to 23 March 2005.

Bibliography

Abbott, Pamela. 7 October 2019. "Ben Ali: The Tunisian Autocrat Who Laid the Foundations for His Demise." *The Conversation*.
Abdullah Ibrahim. 2004. *Between Democracy and Terror: The Sierra Leone Civil War*. Dakar: Council for the Development of Social Science Research in Africa.
Acheson-Brown, Daniel. 2001. "The Tanzanian Invasion of Uganda: A Just War?" *International Third World Studies Journal and Review* 12: 1–11.
ACHPR. 2015. *Principles and Guidelines on Human and Peoples' Rights While Countering Terrorism*. Banjul: Createch Printers.
Adebayo, Adekeye. 2002. *Liberia's Civil War: Nigeria, ECOMOG, and Regional Security in West Africa*. Boulder, CO: Lynne Rienner Publishers.
Adedeji, Adebayo (ed.). 1999. *Comprehending and Managing African Conflicts*. London: Zed Books.
Adeeb, Yousif, and Daniel Rothbart. 2012. "Sudan and South Sudan: Post-Separation Challenges." School of Conflict Analysis and Resolution (S-CAR), George Mason University. beyondintractability.org (accessed 6 May 2021).
Afako, Barney. 2002. "Reconciliation and Justice: 'Mato Oput' and the Amnesty Act." *Accord: An International Review of Peace Initiatives* 11: 67.
African Human Security Initiative. 2004. "African Commitments to Conflict Prevention and Peacekeeping: A Review of Eight NEPAD Countries." *AHSI Paper* 5 (August): 4.
Akol, Lam, and Storris McCall. 2020. *The Genesis and Struggle: Of the Anya-Nya in South Sudan*. Osborne Park: Africa World Books.
Allcock, John B. (ed.). 1992. *Border and Territorial Disputes*. Harlow: Longman.
Allen, Tim. 2008. "Ritual (Ab)use? Problems With Traditional Justice in Northern Uganda." In *Courting Conflict? Justice, Peace and the ICC in Africa*, edited by Nicholas Weddell and Phil Clark, p. 47. London: Royal African Society.
Allie, Joe. 2005. "The Kamajor Militia in Sierra Leone: Liberators or Nihilists?" In *Civil Militia: Africa's Intractable Security Menace*, edited by D. J. Francis, p. 59. Burlington: Ashgate.

Anand, Patel R. 1966. "Attitude of the Asian-African States Towards Certain Problems of International Law." *International and Comparative Law Quarterly* 15(1): 55–75.
Aning, Emmanuel Kwesi. 1999. *Security in the West African Subregion: An Analysis of ECOWAS' Policies in Liberia*, p. 17. Copenhagen: University of Copenhagen.
Annan, Kofi. 1998. *The Causes of Conflict and the Promotion of Durable Peace and Sustainable Development in Africa*. Report of the United Nations Secretary General to the Security Council, Doc A/52/871-s/1998/318, New York.
Annan, Kofi. 2004. *Progress Report of the UN Secretary General: Causes of Conflict and the Promotion of Durable Peace and Sustainable Development*, UN Doc A/59/285 (2004).
Anyangwe, Carlson. 2000. *Question of the Chagos Archipelago Sovereignty Dispute: Mauritius v. UK*. Lusaka: Afronet.
Anyangwe, Carlson. 2003. "African Border Disputes and Their Settlement by International Judicial Process." *South African Yearbook of International Law* 29: 29.
Anyangwe, Carlson. 2004. "Mutations in the Political Boundaries and Status of Pre-Independence Swaziland: Some Legal Remarks." *Zambia Law Journal* 36: 21.
Anyangwe, Carlson. 2006. "The Constitutive Act of the African Union." *Zambia Law Journal* 38: 43.
Anyangwe, Carlson. 2012. *Revolutionary Overthrow of Constitutional Orders in Africa*. Bamenda: Langaa Research and Publishing.
Anyangwe, Carlson. 2018. "Transitional Justice in Africa: The South African Model." *Journal of International Studies and Development* 7: 1.
Aquarone, Marie-Christine. 1995. "The 1985 Guinea/Guinea-Bissau Maritime Boundary Case and its Implication." *Ocean Development and International Law* 26(4): 413.
Ardener, Shirley (ed.). 2002. *Swedish Ventures in Cameroon 1883–1933. Trade and Travel, People and Politics – The Memoir of Knut Knutson*. Oxford: Berghahn Books.
AU. 2010. *Report of the AU Commission Chairperson on Measures to Strengthen Cooperation in the Prevention and Combating of Terrorism in Africa*, 249th Meeting of the Peace and Security Council, 22 November 2010, PSC/PR/2 (CCXLIX) 2.
Babo, Alfred. 2018. "Traditional Mechanisms of Conflict Resolution in Modern Africa: The Bodior Ritual and the Enduring Kroumen Versus Lobi-Dagara Conflict in Southern Cote d'Ivoire." *African Study Monograph* 39(2): 83–95.
Bah, M. Thiemo. 1994. "Traditional Peacemaker." In *Sources*, Vol. 62, p. 14. Paris: UNESCO.
Bah, M. Thiemo. 1999. "Les Mécanismes Traditionnels de Prévention et de Résolution des Conflicts en Afrique Noire." In *Les Fondements Endogènes d'une Culture de la Paix en Afrique: Mécanismes Traditionnels de Prevention et de Resolution des Conflits*, pp. 1–26. Paris: UNESCO.
Bamidele, Oluwaseun. 2014. "Transnational Terrorism, Armed Conflict and Fragility in African States." *The Davies Papers: Africa Series* 6: 1–16.
Bamidele, Oluwaseun. 2015. "Combating Terrorism: Anti-Terrorism Law, Boko Haram and Insecurity in Nigeria." *African Journal of Democracy and Governance* 2(3&4): 133–148.

Beah, Ishmael. 2007. *A Long Way Gone: Memoirs of a Boy Soldier*. New York: Farrar, Straus and Giroux.
Beck, Robert E. 1967. "The Wandering Missouri River: A Study in Accretion Law." *North Dakota Law Review* 43: 429.
Benjamin, Milton, and Schmidt William. 1 August 1977. "Arab vs. Arab." *Newsweek*, p. 29.
Bensted, Roland. 2011. "A Critique of Paul Collier's 'Greed and Grievance' Thesis of Civil War." *African Security Review* 20(3): 84–90.
Bergner, Daniel. 2003. *In the Land of Magic Soldiers: A Story of White and Black in Africa*. New York: Farrar, Straus and Giroux.
Betts, Richard. 1994. "The Delusion of Impartial Intervention." *Foreign Affairs* 73(6): 20–33.
Biberman, Yelena. 2016. "Violence by Proxy: State-Sponsored Rebels and Criminals in Chechnya." In *State Terror, State Violence: Global Perspectives*, edited by Bettina Koch, p. 135. New York: Springer.
Bodea, Christina, and Ibrahim Elbadawi. 2007. *Riots, Coups and Civil Wars: Revisiting the Greed and Grievance Debate*. The World Bank Policy Research Working Paper 4397.
Bornkamm, Paul Christopher. 2012. *Rwanda's Gacaca Courts: Between Retribution and Reparation*. Oxford: Oxford University Press.
Boukhars, Anouar, and Jacques Roussellier. 2013. *Perspectives on Western Sahara: Myths, Nationalism, and Geopolitics*. Lanham, MD: Rowman & Littlefield.
Boukrif, Hamid. 1999. "Quelques commentaires et observations sur la Convention de l'Organisation de l'Unité africaine sur la Prévention et la Lutte Contre le Terrorisme." *Revue Africaine de Droit International et Comparé* 1999: 764.
Boutros-Ghali, Boutros, and El-Asfahany Nabia. 1972. *Les Conflits des frontières en Afrique*. Paris: Ed. Techniques et Economiques.
Bowd, Richard (ed.). 2010. *Understanding Africa's Contemporary Conflicts: Origins, Challenges and Peacebuilding*. African Human Security Initiative, Monograph 173. Pretoria, Institute for Security Studies.
Brian, Ferguson R. 2002. *State, Identity and Violence: Political Disintegration in the Post-Cold War World*. London: Routledge.
Brosché, Johan, and Daniel Rothbart. 2013. *Violent Conflict and Peacebuilding: The Continuing Crisis in Darfur*. London: Routledge.
Brown, Leann. 2015. "Why Regional Economic Organizations Take on Conventional Security Tasks." *Air and Space Power Journal-Africa and Francophonie* 6(4): 5–20.
Brownlie, Ian (ed.). 1971. *Basic Document on African Affairs*. Oxford: Clarendon Press.
Brownlie, Ian. 1979a. *African Boundaries*. London: Hurst.
Brownlie, Ian. 1979b. "Lesotho-South Africa." In *African Boundaries: A Legal and Diplomatic Encyclopedia*, edited by Ian Brownlie, p. 1109. London: C. Hurst & Co.
Brownlie, Ian. 2003. *Principles of Public International Law*. Oxford: Oxford University Press.
Castagno, Alphonso A. 1964. "The Somali-Kenyan Controversy." *Journal of Modern African Studies* 2(2): 165–188.

Chaplin, Denis. 1977. "Libya Military Spearhead Against Sadat." *Military Review* LIX(11): 42–50.
Chengu, Garikai. 2015. "The Origins of the Oppression of African Women." *The Herald* [Zimbabwe], 28 August.
Chesterman, Simon. 2011. "Leading From Behind: The Responsibility to Protect, the Obama Doctrine, and Humanitarian Intervention After Libya." *Ethics & International Affairs* 25(3): 279+.
Chorley, Richard J. 1984. *Geomorphology*. New York: Methuen.
Cilliers, Jakkie. 2004. "Human Security in Africa. A Conceptual Framework for Review." A Monograph for the African Human Security Initiative. www.africanreview.org.
Cilliers, Jakkie, and Kathryn Sturman (eds). 2002. *Africa and Terrorism: Joining the Global Campaign*, Monograph Series No. 74. ISS, Pretoria: ISS.
Clark, Phil. 2007. "Hybridity, Holism and 'Traditional' Justice: The Case of Gacaca Courts in Post-Genocide Rwanda." *George Washington International Law Review* 39: 765–837.
Clark, Phil, and Zachary Kaufman (eds). 2009. *After Genocide: Transitional Justice, Post-Conflict Reconstruction, and Reconciliation in Rwanda and Beyond*. New York: Columbia University Press.
Collier, Paul, and Hoeffler Anke. 2002. *Greed and Grievance in Civil War*. The World Bank Policy Research Working Paper 2355.
Colson, David A., and Robert W. Smith (eds). 2005. *International Maritime Boundaries*, Vol. 4. Leiden/Boston: Martinus Nijhoff.
Connell, Dan, and Tom Killion. 2011. *Historical Dictionary of Eritrea*. Lanham: Scarecrow Press.
Coser, Lewis A. 1956. *The Functions of Social Conflict*. London: Macmillan.
Counter-Terrorism Implementation Task Force. 2015. *Basic Human Rights Reference Guide: Conformity of National Counter-Terrorism Legislation with International Human Rights Law*. OHCHR.
Crocker, Chester, Fen Osler Hampson, and Pamela Aall. 2005. *Grasping the Nettle: Analyzing Cases of Intractable Conflict*. Washington, DC: USIP Press.
Dahrendorf, Ralf. 1965. *Class and Class Conflict in Industrial Society*. Stanford, CA: Stanford University Press (Classic Reprint by Forgotten Books, 2018).
Dauré-Serfaty, Christine. 1993. *La Mauritanie*. Paris: L'Harmattan.
De la Serre, Françoise. 1966. "Les Revendications Marocaines sur la Mauritanie." *Revue Française de Sciences Politique* 16(2): 320–331.
Deltombe, Thomas, Manuel Domergue, and Jacob Tatsitsa. 2011. *Kamerun! Une Guerre Cachée aux Origines de la Françafrique 1948–1971*. Paris: La Découverte.
Denov, Myriam S. 2010. *Child Soldiers: Sierra Leone's Revolutionary United Front*. New York: Cambridge University Press.
DFID. 2001. *The Causes of Conflict in Africa*. London: Department for International Development.
Dixit, Priya. 2016. "Securitization and Terrorization: Analyzing States' Usage of the Rhetoric of Terrorism." In *State Terror, State Violence: Global Perspectives*, edited by Bettina Koch, p. 31. New York: Springer.

Dorman, Andrew. 2009. *Blair's Successful War: British Military Intervention in Sierra Leone*. Burlington, VT: Ashgate.
Drysdale, John. 1964. *The Somali Dispute*. London: Pall Mall Press.
Dzurek, Daniel J., and Clive Schofield. 2001. "Parting the Red Sea: Boundaries, Offshore Resources and Transit." *Maritime Briefing* 3(2): 5–43.
Efrat, E. S. 1976. "Terrorism in South Africa." In *International Terrorism: National, Regional and Global Perspectives*, edited by Yonah Alexander, p. 194. New York: Praeger.
Elbadawi, Ibrahim, and Sambanis Nicholas. 2000. *Why Are There So Many Civil Wars in Africa? Understanding and Preventing Violent Conflict*. World Bank Report.
Elias, Olawale T. 1956. *The Nature of African Customary Law*. Manchester: Manchester University Press.
Ellis, Stephen. 1998. "Liberia's Warlords Insurgency." In *African Guerrillas*, edited by Christopher Clapham, pp. 155–171. Oxford: James Currey.
Ellis, Stephen. 2007 [1999]. *The Mask of Anarchy: The Destruction of Liberia and the Religious Dimension of African Civil War*. London: Hurst & Co.
Emmanuel, Nikolas. 2016. "Third-Party Incentive Strategies and Conflict Management in Africa." *Air and Space Power Journal* 7(1): 14.
Eppel, Shari. 2008. *Matabeleland: Its Struggle for National Legitimacy, and the Relevance of This in the 2008 Election*. Berlin: Heinrich Boll Foundation.
Ewi, Martin, and Kwesi Aning. 2006. "Assessing the Role of the African Union in Preventing and Combating Terrorism in Africa." *African Security Review* 15(3): 32–46.
Fearon, James, and David Laitin. 2003. "Ethnicity, Insurgency, and Civil War." *America Political Science Review* 97(1): 75.
Fitzgerald, Nina J. 2002. *Somalia: Issues, History, and Bibliography*. New York: Nova Publishers.
Fonchingong, Charles. 2007. "Crossing Urban-Rural Spaces: The Takumbeng and Activism in Cameroon's Democratic Crusade." *Cahiers d'Etudes Africaines* 47(185): 117–143.
Freeman, Mark, and B. Priscilla Hayner. 2003. "The Truth Commissions of South Africa and Guatemala." In *Reconciliation After Violent Conflict: A Handbook*, edited by D. Bloomfield, p. 140. Stockholm: International Institute for Democracy and Electoral Assistance.
Gallahue, Patrick, and Rick Lines. 2012. *The Death Penalty for Drug Offences: Global Overview 2012: Tipping the Scales for Abolition*. London: Harm Reduction International.
Galtung, Johan. 1969. "Violence, Peace and Peace Research." *Journal of Peace Research* 6: 167.
Gberie, Lansana. 2005. *A Dirty War in West Africa: The RUF and the Destruction of Sierra Leone*. Bloomington: Indiana University Press.
Gerdes, Felix. 2013. *Civil War and State Formation: The Political Economy of War and Peace in Liberia*. Frankfurt/New York: Campus Verlag & University of Chicago Press.
Global Witness. 2002. *Logs of War: The Timber Trade and Armed Conflict*. Fafo Report 379. London: Fafo Institute for Applied Social Science.
Gluckman, Max. 1963. *Custom and Conflict in Africa*. Oxford: Basil Blackwell.

Goredema, Charles, and Anneli Botha. 2005. *African Commitment to Combating Organised Crime and Terrorism: A Review of Eight NEPAD Countries*, p. 64. Pretoria: Institute for Security Studies.

Haile-Selassie, Teferra. 1997. *The Ethiopian Revolution, 1974–1991: From a Monarchical Autocracy to a Military Oligarchy*. London: Kegan Paul.

Hartung, William, and Moix Bridget. 2000. *Deadly Legacy: US Arms to Africa and the Congo War*. New York: World Policy Institute.

Hefny, Mohamed. 1995. "International Water Issues and Conflict Resolution: Some Reflections." *RADC* 7: 360–361.

Heggoy, Andrew Alf. 1970. "Colonial Origins of the Algerian-Moroccan Border Conflict of October 1963." *African Studies Review* 13(1): 17–22.

Heimer, Franz-Wilhelm. 1979. *The Decolonization Conflict in Angola, 1974–76: An Essay in Political Sociology*. Geneva: Institut Universitaire de Hautes Études Internationales.

Hill, Geof. 2005. *The Battle for Zimbabwe: The Final Countdown*. Johannesburg: Struik Publishers.

Hinton, Alexander Laban, and Kevin Lewis O'Neil (eds). 2009. *Genocide, Truth, Memory and Representation*. Durham: Duke University Press.

Hirsch, John. 2000. *Sierra Leone: Diamonds and the Struggle for Democracy*. Boulder: Lynne Rienner Publishers.

History.com Editors. 2009. "Suez Crisis." https://www.history.com/topics/cold.war/suez-crisis (accessed 8 May 2021).

Hoffman, Danny. 2007. "The City as Barracks: Freetown, Monrovia, and the Organization of Violence in Postcolonial African Cities." *Cultural Anthropology* 22(3): 400–428.

Howe, Marvine. 7 August 1977. "The Battle with Egypt May Have Won Him New Sympathy Among Arabs." *The New York Times*, p. E5.

Huband, Mark. 1998. *The Liberian Civil War*. London: Frank Cass.

Hübschle, Annette. 2006. "The T-word: Conceptualizing Terrorism." *African Security Review* 15(3): 2.

Huggins, Chris. 2002. *The Human Cost of Conflict in Sudan*. Oxford: Oxfam.

Human Rights Watch. 2004. *Human Rights Watch World Report 2004: Human Rights and Armed Conflict*. New York: Human Rights Watch.

Hutchful, Eboe, and Abdoulaye Bathily (eds). 1998. *The Military and Militarism in Africa*. Dakar: Codesria.

Huyse, Luc, and Mark Salter (eds). 2008. *Traditional Justice and Reconciliation After Violent Conflict: Learning From African Examples*. Stockholm: International IDEA.

Inter-American Commission on Human Rights. 2018. "Norms and Principle of International Human Rights and Humanitarian Law Applicable in Terrorist Situations." https://www.cidh.oas.org/Terrorism/Eng/part.c.htm (accessed 8 February 2018).

International Commission of Jurists. 2009. *Assessing Damage, Urging Action: Report of Eminent Jurists Panel on Terrorism, Counter-terrorism and Human Rights*. Geneva: ICJ.

IRIN. 2005. "Uganda: Traditional Ritual Heals Communities Torn Apart by War." *IRIN News*, 9 June.

Italiaander, Rolf. 1961. *The New Leaders of Africa*. London. Prentice-Hall.

Iyob, Ruth. 1997. *The Eritrean Struggle for Independence: Domination, Resistance, Nationalism, 1941–1993*. Cambridge: Cambridge University Press.
Jackson, Robert, and Carl Rosberg. 1986. "Sovereignty and Underdevelopment: Juridical Statehood in the African Crisis." *Journal of Modern African Studies* 24(1): 1–31.
Jalloh, Balimo. 2001. "Conflicts, Resources and Social Instability in Sub-Sahara Africa – The Sierra Leone Case." *Internationales Afrika-Forum* 37(2): 166–180.
James, Martin W., III. 2011. *A Political History of the Civil War in Angola 1974–1990*. Piscataway, NJ: Transaction Publishers.
Jiuyong, Shi. 2010. "Maritime Delimitation in the Jurisprudence of the International Court of Justice." *Chinese Journal of International Law* 9(2): 271.
Jones, Stephen. 1945. *Boundary-Making*, p. 7. New York: Columbia University Press.
Jua, Rosalyn. 1993. "Women's Role in Democratic Change in Cameroon." In *Anglophone Cameroon Writing*, edited by N. Lyonga, E. Breitinger, and Bole Butake. University of Bayreuth Press, 180–183.
Kah, Henry. 2011. "Women's Resistance in Cameroon's Western Grassfields: The Power of Symbols, Organization, and Leadership, 1957–1961." *African Studies Quarterly* 12(3): 1–25.
Kane, Ibrahim. 2015. "Reconciling the Protection of Human Rights and the Fight Against Terrorism in Africa." In *Counter-Terrorism: International Law and Practice*, edited by Ana Maria Salinas de Frias, p. 839. Oxford: Oxford University Press.
Keen, David. 2000. "Incentives and Disincentives for Violence." In *Greed and Grievance: Economic Agendas in Civil Wars*, edited by Mats Berdal and David Malone, pp. 19–43. Boulder, CO: Lynne Rienner.
Keen, David. 2005. *Conflict & Collusion in Sierra Leone*. Oxford: James Currey.
Kendie, Daniel. 2005. *The Five Dimensions of the Eritrean Conflict 1941–2004: Deciphering the Geopolitical Puzzle*. Gaithersburg: Signature Book Printing.
Khushalani, Yougindra. 1983. "Human Rights in Asia and Africa." *Human Rights International Journal* 4: 403.
Kinne, Lance. 2001. "The Benefits of Exile: The Case of FLAM." *The Journal of Modern African Studies* 39(4): 597–621.
Koch, Bettina. 2016. "Terror, Violence, Coercion: States and the Use of (Il)legitimate Force." In *State Terror, State Violence: Global Perspectives*, edited by Bettina Koch, p. 1. Switzerland: Springer.
Kornprobst, Marcus. 2002. "The Management of Border Disputes in African Regional Sub-Systems: Comparing West Africa and the Horn of Africa." *Journal of Modern African Studies* 40(3): 369–393.
Koroma, Abdul Karim. 2004. *Crisis and Intervention in Sierra Leone 1997–2003*. Freetown and London: Andromeda Publications.
Krain, Matthew. 2005. "International Intervention and the Severity of Genocides and Politicides." *International Studies Quarterly* 49(3): 363–388.
Kuttab, D. 2017. "Death Penalty Does Little to Reduce Terror and Crime." https://www.byline.com/column/5/article1525 (accessed 9 February 2018).
Lacey, Marc. 2005. "Atrocity Victims in Uganda Choose to Forgive." *New York Times*, 18 April.

Lanegran, Kimberly. 2015. "Justice for Economic Crimes? Kenya's Truth Commission." *Air and Space Power Journal – Africa and Francophonie* 6(4): 63.
Lauterpacht, Hersch (ed.). 1955. *Oppenheim's International Law: A Treatise – Vol. I. Peace*. London: Longman.
Le Billon, Philippe. 2003. "Getting It Done: Instruments of Enforcement." In *Natural Resources and Violent Conflict: Options and Actions*, edited by Ian Bannon and Paul Collier, pp. 215–286. Washington, DC: The World Bank.
Legg, Paul. 15 January 2011. "Ben Ali's Smooth Rise to Power in Tunisia Contrasts With Sudden Decline." *The Guardian*.
Letford, Tony. 2017. "Death Penalty for Wannabe Martyrs." *The Spectator*, June.
Lewis, Ioan Myrddin. 1960. "The Somali Conquest of the Horn of Africa." *Journal of African History* 1(2): 213–230.
Lewis, Ioan Myrddin. 1963a. "Pan Africanism and Pan Somalism." *Journal of Modern African Studies* 1(2): 147–161.
Lewis, Ioan Myrddin. 1963b. "The Problem of the Northern Frontier District." *Race and Class* 5(1): 48–60.
Lodge, Tom. 1999. *Towards an Understanding of Contemporary Armed Conflict in Africa*. Whither Peacekeeping in Africa, Monograph No. 36.
Lujala, Paivi. 2005. "A Diamond Curse? Civil War and a Lootable Resource." *Journal of Conflict Resolution* 49(4): 538–562.
Madiebo, Alexander. 1980. *The Nigerian Revolution and the Biafran War*. Enugu: Fourth Dimensions Publishers.
Makinda, Samuel. 2006. "Terrorism, Counter-Terrorism and Norms in Africa." *African Security Review* 15(3): 20.
Malan, Jannie. 1997. *Conflict Resolution Wisdom From Africa*. Denver: Accord.
Mambo, Andrew, and Schofield Julian. 2007. "Military Diversion in the 1978 Uganda-Tanzania War." *Journal of Political and Military Sociology* 35(2): 299.
Marchesin, Philippe. 2010 (Reprint of 1992 Edition). *Tribus, Ethnies et Pouvoir en Mauritanie*. Paris: Karthala Editions.
Martin, Claudia. 2016. "Chapter 26: The Role of Military Courts in a Counter-Terrorism Framework: Trends in International Human Rights Jurisprudence and Practice." In *Counter-Terrorism: International Law and Practice*, edited by Ana Maria Salinas, p. 757. Oxford: Oxford University Press.
Martinez, Luis. 2000. *The Algeria Civil War, 1990–1998*. New York: Columbia University Press.
Mays, Terry M. 2002. *Africa's First Peacekeeping Operation: The OAU in Chad*. Greenwood.
Mazrui, Ali. 1995. "Towards Containing Conflict in Africa: Methods, Mechanisms and Values." *East African Journal of Peace and Human Rights* 2: 81.
McEwen, Alec C. 1991. "The Establishment of the Nigeria/Benin Boundary, 1889–1989." *The Geographical Journal* 157(1): 62–70.
McGregor, Andrew. 2007. "The Leading Factions Behind the Somali Insurgency." *Terrorism Monitor* V(8), 26 April.
McLlarky, K. A. 1987. "Guinea/Guinea-Bissau: Dispute Concerning Delimitation of the Maritime Boundary." *Maryland Journal of International Law* 11(1): Article 7, 93.

McNeely, Jeffrey. 2002. "Overview: Biodiversity, Conflict and Tropical Forests." In *Conserving the Peace: Resources, Livelihoods, and Security*, edited by R. Matthew, pp. 31–55. Winnipeg: International Institute for Sustainable Development/IUCN – The World Conservation Union.

Menkhaus, Ken. 2000. "Traditional Conflict Management in Contemporary Somalia." In *Traditional Cures for Modern Conflicts: African Conflict 'Medicine'*, edited by William I. Zartman, p. 183. Boulder: Lynne Rienner Publishers.

Mesfin, Wolde Mariam. 1964. "The Ethio-Somalian Boundary Dispute." *Journal of Modern African Studies* 2(2): 189–219.

Messmer, Pierre. 1998. *Le Blancs s'en Vont: Récit de Décolonisation*. Paris: Albin Michel.

Moody, Peter R. 2016. "Killing the Chicken to Scare the Monkey: Some Notes on State Terror in the People's Republic of China." In *State Terror, State Violence: Global Perspectives*, edited by Bettina Koch, p. 115. New York: Springer.

Moore, Christopher. 2014. *The Mediation Process: Practical Strategies for Resolving Conflict*. New Jersey: Wiley and Sons.

Moran, Mary H. 2008. *Liberia: The Violence of Democracy*. Philadelphia: University of Pennsylvania Press.

Murithi, Timothy. 2006. "Towards a Symbiotic Partnership: The UN Peacebuilding Commission and the Evolving AU/NEPAD Post-conflict Reconstruction Framework." In *Dialogue of the Death – Essays on African and the United Nations*, edited by Adekeye Adebajo and Scanlon Helen, p. 243. Johannesburg: Fanele Publications.

Mutwol, Julius. 2009. *Peace Agreements and Civil Wars in Africa: Insurgent Motivations, State Responses, and Third-Party Peacemaking in Liberia, Rwanda, and Sierra Leone*. New York: Cambria Press.

Mwanasali, Musifiki. 2006. "Africa's Responsibility to Protect." In *Dialogue of the Deaf – Essays on African and the United Nations*, edited by Adekeye Adebajo and Helen Scanlon, p. 89. Johannesburg: Fanele Publications.

National Unity and Reconciliation Commission. 2000. *Report on the National Summit on Unity and Reconciliation*. Kigali: National Unity and Reconciliation Commission.

National Unity and Reconciliation Commission. 2003. *Opinion Survey on Participation in Gacaca and National Reconciliation*. Kigali: National Unity and Reconciliation Commission.

National Unity and Reconciliation Commission. 2004. *Third National Summit Report on Unity & Reconciliation*. Kigali: National Unity and Reconciliation Commission.

Ngwane, George. 1996. *Settling Disputes in Africa*. Yaoundé: Buma Kor.

Nicolini, Beatrice (ed.). 2006. *Studies in Witchcraft, Magic, War and Peace in Africa: Nineteenth and Twentieth Centuries*. New York: Edwin Mellen Press.

Njoku, Harry M. 1987. *A Tragedy Without Heroes: The Nigerian - Biafran War*. Enugu: Fourth Dimensions Publishers.

Nyarota, Geoffrey. 2006. *Against the Grain*. Cape Town: Struik Publishers.

Nzabandora, Joseph. 2008. *The Causes of Violence After the 1994 Genocide in Rwanda*. Kigali: Premier Consulting Group.

Obasanjo, Olusegun. 1980. *My Command: An Account of the Nigerian Civil War 1967–70.* Ibadan: Heinemann Publications.
Oberschall, Anthony. 1978. "Theories of Social Conflict." *Annual Review of Sociology* 4: 291.
Oduntan, Gbenga. 2015. *International Boundary Disputes in Africa.* London: Routledge.
Ogenga, Fredrick. 2015. "From Al-Qaida to Al-Shabaab: The Global and Local Implications of Terror in Kenya and East Africa." *African Journal of Democracy and Governance* 2(3&4): 149–170.
OHCHR. 2002. *Statement on Racial Discrimination and Measures to Combat Terrorism.* 1 November. UN Doc A/57/18 Chapter XI (C) para 3.
Okpara Uche. 2014. "Conflicts About Water in Lake Chad: are Environmental, Vulnerability and Security Issues Linked?" University of Leeds. SRI Paper No. 67.
Okumu, Wafula, and Anneli Botha (eds). 2008. *Understanding Terrorism in Africa: Building Bridges and Overcoming the Gaps*, p. 33. Pretoria: Institute for Security Studies.
Olukoshi, Adebayo, and Liisa Laakso (eds). 1996. *Challenges to the Nation-State in Africa.* Helsinki: Nordiska Afrikaainstitutet.
Omoniyi, Adewoye. 1984–1985. "The Idea of Benin Union." *Journal of the Historical Society of Nigeria* XII(3&4): 171–180.
Osaghae, Eghosa E. 2000. "Applying Traditional Methods to Modern Conflict: Possibilities and Limits." In *Traditional Cures for Modern Conflicts: African Conflict 'Medicine'*, edited by Zartman I. William, p. 201. Boulder: Lynne Rienner Publishers.
Ottaway, David. February 2020. *Hosni Mubarak's Dramatic Rise and Fall From Power.* Washington, DC: The Wilson Center. wilsoncenter.org (accessed 8 May 2021).
Oyeniyi, Bukola A. 2019. *The History of Libya.* Santa Barbara, Ca: ABC-CLIO.
Oyeniyi, Bukola. 2011. "Conflict and Violence in Africa: Causes, Sources and Types." *Transcend Media Service.*
Özerdem, Alpaslan. 2008. *Post-War Recovery: Disarmament, Demobilization and Reintegration.* New York: Palgrave Macmillan.
Pazzanita, Anthony G. 1991. "The Conflict Resolution Process in Angola." *The Journal of Modern African Studies* 29(1): 83–114.
Pelissier, Rene. 1965. "Spain's Discreet Decolonization." *Foreign Affairs* 43(3): 523.
Pollack, Kenneth Michael. 2004. *Arabs at War: Military Effectiveness, 1948–1991.* Lincoln, Nebraska: University of Nebraska Press.
Pouzen, Joanna, Neugebauer Richard, and Joseph Ntaganira. 2014. "Assessing the Rwanda Experiment: Popular Perceptions of Gacaca in its Final Phase." *International Journal of Transitional Justice* 8(1): 31–52.
Price, F. 2005. "The Bakassi Peninsula: The Border Dispute between Nigeria and Cameroon." In *Inventory of Conflict Environment Case Studies*, No. 163.
Prunier, Gérard. 2003. *Darfur: The Ambiguous Genocide.* Cornell: Cornell University Press.
Quandt, William. 1998. *Between Ballots and Bullets: Algeria's Transition From Authoritarianism.* Washington, DC: Brookings Institution Press.

Quinn, R. Joanne (ed.). 2009. *Reconciliation(s): Transitional Justice in Post-Conflict Societies*. Montreal and Kingston: McGill-Queen University Press.

Rashed, Dina. 2016. "Violence From Above, Violence From Below: The State and Policing Citizens in Mubarak's Egypt." In *State Terror, State Violence: Global Perspectives*, edited by Bettina Koch, p. 93. New York: Springer.

Ratsimbaharison, Adrien. 2011. "Greed and Civil war in Post-Cold War Africa: Revisiting the Greed Theory of Civil War." *African Security Study*, Online 29 November.

Rex, John. 1981. *Social Conflict: A Conceptual and Theoretical Analysis (Aspects of Modern Sociology)*, p. 1. London: Longman.

Reyner, Anthony S. 1963. "Morocco's International Boundaries: A Factual Background." *Journal of Modern African Studies* 1(3): 313–326.

Reynolds, Andrew, and Alan Kuperman (eds). 2015. *Constitutions and Conflict Management in Africa: Preventing Civil War Through Institutional Design*. Philadelphia: University of Pennsylvania Press.

Ricciardi, Matthew M. 1992. "Title to the Aouzou Strip: A Legal and Historical Analysis." *Yale Journal of International Law* 17: 301.

Ritzenthaler, Pat. 1960. "Anlu – A Women's Uprising in the British Cameroons." *African Studies* 19(3): 482.

Rivli, Benjamin. 1992. "Regional Arrangements and the UN System for Collective Security and Conflict Resolution: A New Road Ahead." *International Relations* 11: 95–110.

Roach, Kent. 2005. "A Comparison of South African and Canadian Anti-Terrorism Legislation." *South African Journal of Criminal Justice* 18: 127.

Ronen, Yehudit. 1992. "Libya's Intervention in Amin's Uganda – A Broken Spearhead." *Asian and African Studies* 26(2): 173–183.

Rothchild, Donald S. 1997. *Managing Ethnic Conflict in Africa: Pressures and Incentives for Cooperation*. Washington, DC: Brooklyn Institution Press.

Rothchild, Donald S. 1999. *Managing Ethnic Conflicts*. Washington, DC: Brookings Institute.

Rutherford, Kenneth. 2008. *Humanitarianism Under Fire: The US and UN Intervention in Somalia*. Boulder: Kumarian Press.

Sands, Philippe, and Pierre Klein. 2001. *Bowett's Law of International Institutions*. London: Sweet & Maxwell.

Schanche, Don. 27 July 1977. "Egypt, Libya Trade Insults; Sadat Calls Khadafy a Child." *The Los Angeles Times*, p. 13.

Scherrer, Christian P. 2002. *Genocide and Crisis in Central Africa: Conflict Roots, Mass Violence, and Regional War*. Westport: Greenwood Press.

Schönteich, Martin. 2000. "South Africa's Arsenal of Terrorism Legislation." *African Security Review* 9: 2.

Schwarzenberger, Georg. 1976. *A Manual of International Law*. London: Professional Books.

Shaw, Malcolm. 1997. *International Law*. Cambridge: Cambridge University Press.

Shea, Dorothy. 2000. *The South African Truth Commission: The Politics of Reconciliation*. Washington: USIP.

Shearer, A. Ivan. 1994. *Starke's International Law*. London: Butterworth.
Shyaka, Anastase. 2004. *The Rwandan Conflict: Origin, Development, Exit Strategies*. Kigali: Palotti Press.
Singer, David, and Melvin Small. 1982. *Resort to Arms: International and Civil Wars, 1816–1980*. Beverly Hills: Sage Publications.
Slackman, Michael. February 2020. "Hosni Mubarak, Egyptian Leader Ousted in Arab Spring, Dies at 91." *The New York Times*.
Smock, David, and Gregorian Hrach (eds). 1993. *Making War and Waging Peace: Foreign Intervention in Africa*. Washington: US Institute of Peace.
Snyder, Frederick, and Sathirathai S. Surakiart (eds). 1987. *Third World Attitude Towards International Law: An Introduction*. Dordrecht: Martinus Nijhoff.
Solanke, Jolayemi. 1982. "Traditional, Social and Political Institutions." In *African History and Culture*, edited by Olaniyan Richard, p. 33. Lagos: Longman.
Sone, Enongene Mirabeau. 2012. "The Role of Elders in Moulding Youth in Contemporary Cameroon: A Study of Selected Proverbs." *Commonwealth Youth and Development* 10(2): 112.
Sorour, Ayman. 2006. "Explosive Remnants of War in North Africa." *Journal of Conventional Weapons Destruction* 10(2): 44–47.
Souaidia, Habib. 2001. *La Sale Guerre*. Paris: Folio Actuel.
Stern, Jessica. 2001. "Execute Terrorists at Our Own Risk." *New York Times*, 28 February.
Stiff, Peter. 2000. *Cry Zimbabwe: Independence – Twenty Years On*. Johannesburg: Galago Publishing.
Stohl, Rachel. 1999. "Albright Speech and Report Link Arms and Conflict in Africa." *Weekly Defense Monitor* 3(28): 6.
Tala, Kashim. 1999. *Orature in Africa*. Saskatschewan: Saskatschewan University Press.
Tanga, Pius. 2006. "The Role of Women's Secret Societies in Cameroon's Contemporary Politics: The Case of Takumbeng." *African Journal of Cross-Cultural Psychology and Sports Facilitation* 18: 44–58. https://journals.co.za/doi/pdf/10.10520/AJA18183816_7.
Tareke, Gebru. 2009. *The Ethiopian Revolution: War in the Horn of Africa*. New Haven: Yale University Press.
Tatah Mentan. 2004. *Dilemmas of Weak States: African and Transnational Terrorism in the Twenty-First Century*. Aldershot: Ashgate.
Tavares, Rodrigo. 2010. *Regional Security: The Capacity of International Organisations*. New York: Routledge.
Tempest, Rone. 3 June 1989. "In Senegal and Mauritania, Ethnic Conflict Rages Amid Talk of War." *Los Angeles Times*. latimes.com (accessed 10 May 2021).
Thomas, Charles, and Toyin Falola. 2020. "The Anomaly of Eritrean Secession, 1961–1993." In *Secession and Separatist Conflicts in Postcolonial Africa*. Calgary: University of Calgary Press.
Thomson, Jamie, and Ramzy Kanaan. 2003. *Conflict Timber: Dimensions of the Problem in Asia and Africa. 1: Synthesis Report*. Washington, DC: United States Agency for International Development.

Tom, Patrick. 2006. "The Acholi Traditional Approach to Justice and the War in Northern Uganda." In *Beyond Intractability*, edited by Guy Burgess and Heidi Burgess Heidi. Conflict Research Consortium. Boulder: University of Colorado.

Torres-García, Ana. 1963. "US Diplomacy and the North African 'War of the Sands'." *The Journal of North African Studies* 18(2): 324–348.

Touval, Saadia. 1963. *Somali Nationalism*. Cambridge, MA: Harvard University Press.

Touval, Saadia. 1967. "The OAU and African Borders." *International Organisations* 21(1): 102.

Tuso, Hamdesa. 2000. "Indigenous Processes of Conflict Resolution in Oromo Society." In *Traditional Cures for Modern Conflicts: African Conflict 'Medicine'*, edited by William I. Zartman, p. 79. Boulder: Lynne Rienner Publishers.

UNEP Programme. 2001. "Environmental and Socioeconomic Impacts of Armed Conflict in Africa." In *Africa Environment Outlook 2*, UNEP, 2006.

US State Department. 1974. *Lesotho-South Africa Boundary* (Report). International Boundary Study No. 143.

Uvin, Peter. 2003. "The *Gacaca* Tribunals in Rwanda." In *Reconciliation After Violent Conflict: A Handbook*, edited by D. Bloomfield, p. 116. Stockholm: International Institute for Democracy and Electoral Assistance.

Vasu, Gounden, and Solomon Hussein. 2001. "Conflict Resolution in Africa: A Comparative Analysis of Angola and South Africa." ACCORD, ResearchGate.

Verbelen, Filip. 2002. *Role of the African Timber Trade in the Creation of Conflict and Poverty – A Call for Action*. Greenpeace.

Vinci, Anthony. 2006. "Greed and Grievance Reconsidered: The Role of Power and Survival in the Motivation of Armed Groups." *Civil Wars* 8(1): 25–45.

Wallensteen, Peter (ed.). 1988. *Peace Research Achievements and Challenges*. Boulder and London: Westview.

Wehr, Paul. 2020. *Conflict Regulation*. New York: Routledge.

Wild, Patricia. 1966. "The OAU and the Algeria-Morocco Border Conflict: A Study of New Machinery for Peacekeeping and for the Peaceful Settlement of Disputes Among African States." *International Organization* 20: 78.

Wild, Patricia B. 1966. "The Organization of African Unity and the Algerian-Moroccan Border Conflict: A Study of New Machinery for Peacekeeping and for the Peaceful Settlement of Disputes Among African States." *International Organizations* 20(1): 18–36.

Willis, Michael. 1996. *The Islamic Challenge in Algeria: A Political History*. New York: New York University Press.

Woods, Larry, and Timothy Reese. 2008. *Military Interventions in Sierra Leone: Lessons From a Failed State*. Fort Leavenworth, Kansas: Combat Studies Institute Press.

World Coalition Against the Death Penalty, Factsheet 2016.

Zartmam, Ira William. 1965. "The Politics of Boundaries in North and West Africa." *Journal of Modern African Studies* 3(2): 155–173.

Zartman, Ira William. 1985. *Ripe for Resolution: Conflict and Intervention in Africa*. New York and Oxford: Oxford University Press.

Zartman, Ira William (ed.). 2000. *Traditional Cures for Modern Conflicts: African Conflict 'Medicine'*. Boulder: Lynne Rienner Publishers.

Index

Accretion, 66
Africa and the death penalty for terrorist acts, 247–50
African economic communities and peace and security functions, 309 et seq.
African human rights system, 231
African Standby Force, 97, 172, 310
African terrorism-related instruments, 235–36
African Union, 297
African wise sayings, 267
Africa's recurrent conflicts, 7–18
Africa's short memory of hate, 280
Agenda for Peace, 174
Aggression from outside Africa, 204–9
Aldeamento, 140
Algeria, 31, 113, 115, 191–93
Al-Qaeda, 8, 162, 221 et seq., 228
Al-Shabaab attacks in Kenya, 35
Amalgamation for administrative convenience, 163
Ambazonia, 36, 63, 190, 209, 216–19, 272, 297
Angola, 110–13
Angolan peace accords, 112–13
Anlu, 272–73
Aouzou Strip, 28, 34, 36, 37, 117, 188, 191, 195

Arabization, 116, 125
Arab Spring, 153
Armed conflict (international and non-international), 3, 4
AU peace and security arrangement, 305
Avulsion, 66

Bakassi, 68, 70–73
Bangladesh v Myanmar, 84
Benin, 29, 47
Biafra, 165
Black Scorpion, 165, 181
Blood diamonds, 183
Boko Haram, 8, 49, 221, 225, 234, 235, 252
Botswana, 52–56
Botswana v Namibia, 52
Boundary, 1, 2, 23–25, 45, 47, 61, 89
British overseas possessions, 38
Burkina Faso, 47, 52, 56, 193–94
Burkina Faso v Mali, 56
Burundi, 126–28

Cameroon v Nigeria, 56, 67–73
Cameroun, 31–34, 36, 52, 56–57, 59, 63, 67, 69–73, 106, 128–30
Casamance, 121
Ceausescu moment, 154

Central African Republic, 117–19
Chad, 28, 34, 37, 49, 116, 195
Chagos, 39–42
Child soldiers, 180–81
Civil war, 103
Coastal geography (impact), 93 et seq.
Cobra militia, 132
Colonization, 190, 209
Combating terrorism through law, 233
Communitarianism, 280
Compromis d' arbitrage, 97
Confessions, 293, 294
Conflict, 3, 27 et seq.
Conflict management, 171
Conflict mediation, 174–77
Conflict mitigation and resolution, 18–28
Conflict scholarship, 5
Conflict theory, 5–7
Conflict timber, 183
Conflict types, 170
Congo-Brazzaville, 131–33
Congo-Kinshasa, 157–58
Convention for the Settlement of Investment Disputes, 3
Convention on the Law of the Sea, 2, 62, 63, 75, 88–90, 94
Convention on the Prevention and Combating of Terrorism (OAU), 235
Côte d' Ivoire, 47, 79–85, 119–20, 286
Counter-terrorism and human rights, 236–39
Coup d'état, 12

Declaration on Friendly Relations, 44
Declaration on the Granting of Independence, 44
Decolonization, 44, 103, 106
Defeated opponents, 172
Dereliction, 66
Dergue, 158 et seq.
Dispute, 3, 61 et seq.
Diversionary theory, 105
Djibouti, 28, 34, 48, 76–78, 97, 106, 133, 188

DRC v Burundi, Rwanda and Uganda, 24

Early warning system, 19
East Timor-Portugal v Australia, 44
Economic impact of conflicts, 104
Egypt, 34, 99, 100, 153–54, 200–202
Elders in African society, 267, 268
Equatorial Guinea, 63, 67, 72, 74
Equidistance method, 64
Eritrea, 28, 35, 36, 48, 76–78, 97, 106, 191, 210–12
Ethiopia, 15, 28, 34–36, 80, 106, 160, 197–98
Ethnicity, 126, 177–79
Ethnicization of power, 106, 177–79
Ethnic state capture, 177 et seq
Expansionist, 4, 27, 28, 169

Foreign military bases in Djibouti, 189
Franco-Portuguese Agreement, 85, 88
French overseas territories, 43
Frontier, 4, 46

Gabon, 74
Gacaca tribunals, 287 et seq.
Gada, 275
Génocidaires, 287
Geology, 54, 94
Ghana, 30, 47, 79
Greed and grievance theory, 15–16, 105
Guerra Civil Angolana, 112
Guerra Olvidada, 213
Guinea Bissau, 85
Guinea Bissau v Senegal, 87–88
Guinea-Conakry, 85
Guinea v Guinea Bissau, 86, 87
Gukurahundi, 114
Gulf of Maine case, 94

Harambe, 279
Historical discontent, 156–57

Ibanga, 292
Ifni, 213
Impact of civil war, 184–86

Imprecision of the border line, 23
Incommunicado, 237, 238
Indigenous systems of conflict resolution, 265 et seq.
Insurgencies, 151–52
Intangibility of frontiers, 190
Intercession, 171
International humanitarian law, 4, 103
Interstate wars, 107, 187–90
Intervention, 179–80
Intrastate armed conflict, 103, 106
Islamic jihadism, 142
Islamic State West Africa, 8

Judicial settlement preference, 96

Kamerun, 57, 128, 216
Kenya, 35, 73, 89–93, 134–35
Killing perpetrators of terrorist acts, 250

Land boundary conflicts, 45–58
Laval-Mussolini Agreement, 76
Law of the Sea Convention, 62, 63
Law of the Sea Tribunal, 80–82
League of Arab States, 78
Legal Consequences for States, 210
Lesotho, 49, 50
Liberia, 135–39
Libya, 28, 34, 36, 37, 59, 64, 154–55, 195, 200–202, 208–9
Libya v Chad, 37
Libya v Malta, 95
Liengu, 272–73
Long wars, 4

Mali, 160–63, 193–94
Maritime zone claims, 2, 79–85
Marquisards, 182
Mato oput, 274
Mau Mau, 134
Mauritania, 31, 47–49, 198, 214
Mauritius, 40, 41
Mauritius v UK, 39
Mavrommatis Palestine Concession (Jurisdiction), 3

Median line, 61
Military coups, 109, 151
Minimum fair trial standards, 243
Morocco, 27–28, 30–31, 191–93, 197, 198, 212, 215
Mozambique, 143–45
Mozambique peace proposals, 141
Mysticism and war, 138, 181–83

Namibia, 52–56
Newly formed islands, 66
Nicaragua v Honduras, 94
Niger, 163
Nigeria, 29, 32, 33, 47, 49, 52, 56, 57, 59, 69, 70, 106, 163–66
Ninja militia, 132, 133
Njangi, 279
Non-refoulement, 246, 247
Northern Cameroons, 31–33
Northern Cameroons case, 31–34
North Sea Continental Shelf case, 94

Oath-swearing, 269
OAU peace and security arrangement, 300
Ogaden, 34, 197
Oklahoma City bombing, 234
Opération Epervier, 117
Operation Jack Scott, 134
Opération Panther
Operation pay yourself, 166
Operation Restore Hope, 208
Opération Sangari, 119
Opération Turquoise
Opinio juris, 44

Palaver, 266
Pastoralists, 10
Peace and Security Council of the AU, 97
Peacekeeping, 21, 58
Personalized forms of government, 149
Personal rule and overstay in power, 152
Politics of ethnicity, 177–79

Power-sharing government, 177
Preventive deployment, 174
Punishing acts of terrorism, 241 et seq.

Raid on Entebbe, 207
Red Terror, 158
Regional peace and security arrangements, 298
Relevant circumstances, 94, 97
Reliction, 66
Religion and occultism, 115, 181–83
Religion as cause of civil war, 115 et seq.
Resolution, 1373 of, 28 September, 2001 (UNSC), 234
Resolution, 1608 (XV) of, 21 April, 1961 (UNGA), 32, 33, 217
Resource conflicts, 24
Ripeness of conflict for mediation, 176
Rwanda, 285 et seq.

Saint Egidio, 116, 142
Sand War, 191, 192
Scramble for Africa, 23, 28, 30
Sedimentation, 66
Seer, 266, 271
Self-determination, 41, 44
Senegal, 47, 48, 86, 121
Sex slavery, 17
Shared African values, 277
Shelf claims, 63
Sierra Leone, 166
Six Day War, 188, 192
Somalia, 28, 34, 35, 76, 89–93, 106, 122–24, 197–98
Somalia v Kenya, 97
South Africa, 49, 50
Southern Cameroons, 33, 36
South Sudan, 37, 38, 99, 145–46, 196–97
South West Africa, 210
Spanish and Portuguese overseas possessions, 45
Special circumstances, 94, 95

Special Court for Sierra Leone, 138, 167
State terrorism, 229–31
Sudan, 37, 49, 99, 100, 124–26, 196–97
Suez Canal Crisis, 204
Swaziland, 49–51

Tadic case, 4
Takumbeng, 272
Tanzania, 199–200
Territorial aggrandizement, 4, 27, 169
Territory, 5, 65
Terrorism, 221 et seq.
Terrorist movements, 227–29
Thalweg, 61
Togo, 30
Transitional justice, 285
Travaux préparatoires, 92
Truth and reconciliation commissions, 286, 294
Tunisia, 64, 155–56
Tunisia v Libya, 64, 65, 95

Ubuntu, 279
Uganda, 73, 199–200
UN peace and security framework, 298
Uti possidetis, 2, 35, 51, 56, 190, 194, 218

Vienna Convention on the Law of Treaties, 191–92

War and peace theory, 105
Wars of independence, 7
Wars of national liberation, 209–19
Wealth sharing, 99
Western Sahara, 27–28, 30–31, 36, 198, 199, 212
Western Sahara case, 27, 28, 31
White Terror, 158

Yom Kippur War, 206

Zimbabwe, 114–15

About the Author

Carlson Anyangwe is professor of laws, holds the LLM and PhD from the University of London and until his recent retirement was an academic of many years' standing teaching international law, human rights law and criminal law and procedure in a number of African universities. He was associate and acting dean of the School of Law, University of Zambia. He also held successive management positions at the Walter Sisulu University in South Africa as director of the Law School, executive dean of the Faculty of Management Sciences and Law, and rector of the Butterworth Campus of that University. He served for ten years as member of the African Human Rights Commission's Working Group of Experts on the Death Penalty in Africa. He is a rated researcher of the National Research Foundation (NRF) of South Africa and is currently linked to the Nelson Mandela School of Law, University of Fort Hare, East London, South Africa. He has authored many books, book chapters, consultancy reports and conference papers, as well as numerous articles in scholarly journals.

www.ingramcontent.com/pod-product-compliance
Lightning Source LLC
Chambersburg PA
CBHW021341300426
44114CB00012B/1034